WHY GLOBAL POVERTY?

A Companion Guide
to the Film **The End of Poverty?**

by **Clifford W. Cobb and Philippe Diaz**

with contributions
by **Beth Portello and Richard Castro**

published jointly
by **Robert Schalkenbach Foundation
and Cinema Libre Studio**

Clifford W. Cobb & Philippe Diaz

Why Global Poverty?
  A Companion Guide to the Film *The End of Poverty?*

ISBN 978-0-911312-94-2

Library of Congress control number: 2009939129

  Cover design by Vajramati
  Book design by Lindy Davies

Robert Schalkenbach Foundation
90 John Street, Suite 501
New York NY 10038

Tel: 212-683-6424 Toll-free: 800-269-9555
Fax: 212-683-6454
Email: books@schalkenbach.org
www.schalkenbach.org

Cinema Libre Studio
8328 De Soto Avenue
Canoga Park, CA 91304

Tel: 818-349-8822
www.cinemalibrestudio.com

FIRST PRINTING, 2009

Contents

Introduction by Clifford Cobb   VII

Director's Narrative by Philippe Diaz   1

Complete transcript of the film *The End of Poverty?*   35

Interviews

The following are interviews that were conducted in the process of making the film The End of Poverty? *An asterisk appears by the name of each person who appears in the film.*

Charles Abugre, Head of Policy, Christian Aid, Ghana   69

*Jaime de Amorim, National Coordinator, Landless Workers Movement, Brazil   75

*Nimrod Arackha, Tanzanian Mine Workers Development Organization   78

*John Ayila, Local Leader at Yala Swamp, Kenya   81

William Batt, Government Analyst (retired)   85

Richard Biddle, Teacher   87

William Blum, Historian, Author   90

Chesa Boudin, Author and Activist, Caracas, Venezuela   92

*Miriam Campos, National Coordinator for the Empowerment of Indigenous People   95

*Nora Castañeda ,President, Bank for the Development of Women, Caracas, Venezuela   98

Shivani Chaudhry, Housing and Land Rights Network   102

*John Christensen, Director, Tax Justice Network   106

*Cliff Cobb, Historian, Author   113

George Collins, Teacher   122

Jose Eli da Veiga, Economics Professor, University of Sao Paulo   125

Shelton Davis, Anthropologist   129

Roland Denis, Author   134

Maria de Oliveira, Regional Director, INCRA (National Institute for Agrarian Reform), Recife, Brazil   136

Patrus Ananias de Sousa, Minister of Social Development and Combating Hunger, Brazil   139

Edward Dodson, Manager, Fannie Mae (retired)   142

*William Easterly, Economist, Author   145

*David Ellerman, Former World Bank Official   151

*Joshua Farley, Ecological Economist, International Consultant 157

Luis Carlos Fazvoli Agronomic Institute of Campinas, Southern
    Brazil   164

*Pablo Fernandes Huaratsi, Neighborhood Leader, Bolivia   165

*Four Women in Recife, Brazil   168

Mason Gaffney, Economist, Author   170

*Alvaro Garcia Linera, Vice President of Bolivia (as of 2006)   175

*Susan George, Author, Activist   180

Eva Golinger , Author   189

Lucas Junior Gonzales, Community Activist, Coehlos Favela, Recife,
    Brazil   193

Quisia Gonzalez, Medical Doctor   194

*Rosa Angela Graterol and son, Felix La Vega Barrio, Caracas,
    Venezuela   198

Damon Gross, Program Director, Robert Schalkenbach Foundation 199

*Jerome Guillet, Investment Banker, Editor, European Tribune   202

Ted Gwartney, Assessor   208

Matt Harris, Business Consultant   211

Fred Harrison, Author, Journalist   213

Gilbert Herman, Software Engineer (retired)   218

*Chalmers Johnson, Political Scientist, Author   220

Gitu-wa-Kahengeri, Freedom Fighter *(Mau Mau)*   227

*Kipruto Arap Kirwa, Minister of Agriculture, Kenya   228

*Miloon Kothari, UN Rapporteur on Housing   233

*Edgardo Lander, Professor, Social Sciences, Venezuelan Central
    University, Caracas   239

*Serge Latouche, Author   245

Odenda Lumumba, Director, Kenya Land Alliance   253

*Abel Mamani, Water Minister, Bolivia   257

John McArthur, Deputy Director, UN Millennium Project, Earth
    Institute, Columbia Univerity   260

Almeri Mello, Anti-poverty Activist, Brazil   269

*Maria Luisa Mendonça, Director, *Rede Social,* Sao Paulo   271

*Eric Mgendi, Communications Coordinator, Action Aid, Kenya   276

*Pedro Montes Coria, Miner, Potosí, Bolivia   281

*Mashengu Wa Mwachofi, Member of Kenyan Parliament, 1979-1988   283

*Godfrey Ngao, Mine Operator, Tanzania   289

Bruce Oatman, Social Worker   291

*Joseph Odhiambo and Family, Kibera (Nairobi), Kenya   294

*Dr. H.W.O. Okoth-Ogendo, Author, Law Professor   295

*Marcela Olivera, Activist, Coalition for the Defense of Water and Life, Bolivia   300

*Oscar Olivera, Leader, *La Coordinadora de la Defense del Agua*, Bolivia   304

Juan Patricio Quispe, Leader, Association of Families for The Defense of Gas, 2003 (La Paz, Bolivia)   309

*John Perkins, Author, *Confessions of an Economic Hitman*   311

Heather Remoff, Anthropologist, Author   323

*Raquel Rolnik Secretary of Urban Programs, Ministry of Cities, Brazil   327

*Amartya Sen, Nobel Laureate Economist, Author   332

*Jim Shultz, Executive Director, Democracy Center   338

*Joao Pedro Stedile, National Coordinator, Landless Workers' Movement, Brazil   344

Squatters, Northern Brazil   347

*Joseph Stiglitz, Former Chief Economist, World Bank   349

*Taquiro, Farmer, Venezuela   358

*Eric Toussaint, Author, Activist   361

*Luciana Vanderlei and Husband, Recife, Brazil   367

Adriana Veiga Aranha, Special Adviser on *Fome Zero,* Brazil's Official "End Hunger" Program   369

*Antonio Vinidcativo and Edinaldo, Sugarcane Harvesters, Pernambuco State, Brazil   372

*Grace Wambi, Tea Plucker, Kenya   376

*Michael J. Watts, Director, Institute of International Studies, Professor of Geography, University of California, Berkeley   377

*Eduardo Yssa, Bolivia, Aymaran   384

Afterword

Where Do We Go from Here?   388

Index   398

Acknowledgments

This book was the product of far more people than can be acknowledged here, including everyone involved in the production of *The End of Poverty?* all of the people interviewed, and all who helped arrange for those interviews.

Luci Alcantara
Pat Aller
Bill Batt
Cristian Bettler
Cassandra Brewer
Dr. Ernesto O. Calderón
Genaro Carpio
Richard Castro
Alexandre Elaiuy
Andrea Farley
Jean Friedman-Rudovsky
Batya Gilbert
Toni Gwartney
Fabien Hameline
Gil Herman
Julia Horvath
Ivy Kim
Claudia Lopez

Jean Makunga
Tracey Morris
Njoki Karaga
Ramiro Pare
Boris Rios
Sonny Rivera
Craig Rixford
Kindra Ruocco
Lindsey Salls
Nick Santillan
Robbie Sherre
Laura Lee Smith
Matt Stillman
Mark Sullivan
Brian Waldbillig
Vajramati
Tom Von Doom

Introduction

This book is a continuation and elaboration of the film *The End of Poverty?* It tells the story of what has caused the persistence of poverty despite substantial growth of the global economy over the past century. It contains an introduction by the director of the film, a complete transcript, and over seventy interviews conducted in making the film.

The themes of the film and the book can summarized as follows:

1. Poverty is not a natural phenomenon, at least not in the modern world. It arises because of institutions that enrich a small number of people and deny opportunities to billions of others.

2. The institutions that generate poverty today have a history. Approaching the problem of poverty without historical understanding creates a skewed understanding of why people are poor and leads some people to "blame the victims." In the same way that wealth inequality in the United States is related to a history of racial oppression that restricted property ownership among racial minorities until quite recently, the enduring consequences of colonial history still afflict the citizens of many countries.

3. Relief efforts that attempt to overcome poverty are doomed to failure unless they address the causes of poverty. Some external factors causing the poverty of entire nations are international debt, unfair trade practices, externally imposed privatization programs, resource wars financed by dominant global interests, the power of multinational corporations to avoid taxes and regulations, intellectual property regimes enforced by international institutions, and inherited patterns of trade and marketing that enable former colonial powers to reap most of the profits of commerce.

4. Factors within nations that cause poverty and extreme inequality include centuries of concentration of land ownership that ignore traditional norms of reciprocity, the dominance of national economies by monoculture and the export of a few raw materials, corporate and state-owned monopolies, limited availability of credit to small-scale businesses, the breakdown of laws and practices that have sustained the commons, and traditions that ignore the productivity of women.

5. All of the factors that cause poverty on a large scale are systemic problems. Efforts to improve the lives of a few individuals will not change

those patterns. The problems that give rise to poverty are not localized. They are connected to a centuries-old geopolitical order that enables elites to become rich from the work of others. That global order will change only if the poor become organized to resist domination and if some elites actively work to overturn the systems that give them privileges.

6. To achieve systemic economic reform, what is most needed is political change. However, when nations have attempted to gain control of their own resources and their own economies, the leaders who have done so have been accused of being communist and have been assassinated, often by agencies of the US government. In extreme cases, the US (or European powers) have sent in troops to regain control of foreign nations. These actions have been extensively documented (see interviews with Perkins, Blum, and Golinger in this volume), but this film and book are unusual in making a direct connection between the violence perpetrated by the US and the poverty of billions of people. Essentially, the problem is that governments can either be loyal to their own people or loyal to the corporate interests protected by the US government. The most important step US citizens could take to end global poverty would be to change the overall direction of American foreign policy so that other nations can direct their own economic affairs.

7. A topic emphasized in only a few interviews (Latouche, Lander, Guillet, and Garcia Linera), but which plays an important part in the film, is the question of how resources can be shared on a global basis. Leaders have always been faced with the difficult question of how to distribute income and wealth within a single nation—according to merit or need or productivity. Now, however, the question is being asked on a global basis. How should the remaining oil, water, and other scarce resources be shared among nations? How should rights to add greenhouse gases be distributed? The film ends with the hope that we can find a way to resolve those questions by sharing the gifts of nature equitably.

The ultimate purpose of *The End of Poverty?* is contained in the tagline "Think again." If viewers take seriously the challenge posed by this film, that is exactly what they will do.

We realize that the film raises far more questions than it answers. Some solutions are provided in the film regarding specific polices. But debt relief, tax reform, land reform, and policies to restore the commons are only a beginning. We need to change the direction of American foreign policy and reframe the economic ideology that underlies current policies. Those are giant tasks. That is where you as viewer and reader come in. We invite you to consider the following actions:

A. Visit the main website connected with the film: **www.theendofpoverty.com**, particularly the section on "Take Action." Follow the links there to specific campaigns to cancel debts, increase transparency, reduce reckless economic growth, and others. Also, join the blog at **http://endpoverty.ning.com** and share your wisdom with others.

B. Visit an additional website associated with the film: **www.povertythinkagain.com**. Learn there about Henry George's ideas about sharing the earth, ideas that inspired production of this film.

C. If you are student, talk to your teachers, professors, and fellow students about projects you might do based on what you have learned from the movie and this book. If this movie inspires even a few students to orient their studies toward solving problems related to globalization, poverty, and resource conflicts, it will have been a success. Of course, we are hoping that thousands will be influenced to think about how to become engaged as activists or scholars to make a difference.

D. If you belong to a church, synagogue, fraternity, sorority, labor union, service club, or any other organization, we urge you to organize a showing of *The End of Poverty?* and prepare a list of discussion questions. Study guides will be available at **www.theendofpoverty/book** or **www.whyglobalpoverty.com**.

E. If you are not actively involved in any groups, we encourage you to create a group in your area devoted to both study and action. You can easily set one up online through Meetup.com where there are already dozens of groups on that site under the rubric "end poverty," which are mostly oriented toward development assistance. Join an existing group or start a new one around the rubric "poverty think again" or a similar phrase that challenges conventional wisdom.

Above all, recognize that you are not alone. Millions of others feel disempowered by the current economic and political system. Join with others to make your voice heard. You can make a difference.

— *Clifford Cobb*

Director's Narrative: How this Film Came into Being

Part I: Introduction

The End of Poverty? is a feature-length documentary that explores some of the root causes of global poverty today. This is the story of how and why it was made and of some challenges we faced making it.

Initially, I explain the origins of this project, how I came to be involved in it, and a little bit about how it was made. In the following sections of this chapter, I describe our experiences and some of the lessons we learned in the developing countries where we filmed: Venezuela, Brazil, Bolivia, Kenya and Tanzania.

My Background

I have lived in the US many years, arriving from France where I was a relatively successful movie producer specializing in what we call *le cinéma d'auteurs*. I started making movies at the age of thirteen. When I later studied philosophy of art and political philosophy at *La Sorbonne,* I came to believe that movies could make a difference in the world. Most of the films that I had produced in France tackled world issues in one way or another. Once I moved to the United States, I created a company named Cinema Libre Studio, meaning "liberation films," which specializes in producing and distributing socio-political documentaries and independent features.

In France, I began my career as a director. Later, I produced many feature films, as well as several documentaries. In 1999, I had a chance to return to my work as a director, by making a film in war-torn Sierra Leone. I had contacted Action Against Hunger, an international nonprofit organization, about making a film to explain that famine and hunger are not natural phenomena, as many people believe, but political. Sierra Leone had been torn by civil war for nine years because of the involvement of European and North American countries in the conflict.

This became the feature-length documentary *Nouvel Ordre Mondial (Quelque Part en Afrique)*—"The Empire in Africa." It ended up being one of

1

the most difficult experiences of my life, but one which certainly prepared me for the future challenge of making a film on poverty around the world. The success and impact of the film, which premiered during Critics' Week at the Cannes Film Festival in 2000, and the awards we received around the world, encouraged me to use documentaries as tools to make a difference.

Origins of this Project

One day my wife, Beth Portello (who co-founded Cinema Libre Studio), received a phone call from Matthew Stillman, asking us if we would

be interested in producing a movie on the true causes of poverty. He was on the board of the Robert Schalkenbach Foundation of New York, which seeks to promote the ideas of Henry George, a self-taught American economist and contemporary of Karl Marx. In his classic tome, *Progress and Poverty,* George proposed that progress does not alleviate poverty, but rather creates it.

We immediately researched Henry George and understood that his basic concept was as follows: Originally a commu-

Philippe Diaz

nity owns and controls its natural resources, such as timber, water, and so on, but with land being the most significant. Once progress arrives, it shifts the control and ownership of these resources into the hands of a very few individuals or corporations. This "progress" pushes away, in a literal and not so literal sense, the people of this community, who are forced out from the economic center by increased rents and are marginalized from any future economic development. Now they have to pay for these resources, which were once shared.

We soon met with Stillman who flew in from New York and the then-president of the foundation, Cliff Cobb. Although I was indeed very impressed by Henry George's analysis of his time, I was by no means ready to do a biopic or Georgist monograph. After months of research, discussions and several proposals, the Foundation allowed me to expand the scope of the film beyond a narrowly Georgist perspective, in order to explain the true historical and political causes of poverty in the world. They agreed to finance the majority of the budget for the film with the balance brought in by our company through reduced salaries, production resources, equipment, and post-production services. These reduced salaries for writing/directing and producing were, in fact, used to keep our company going while we were in production and we ended up making the film for no salaries at all, which was always the idea.

The budget was barely adequate for a feature-length documentary that would eventually entail over one hundred hours of interviews filmed in eight countries on four continents: South America (Venezuela, Brazil, Bolivia), Africa (Kenya and Tanzania), Europe (France and England) and North America. When we combined the financial realities with the complexities of the issue of poverty, we realized that we would have to limit our investigation to a few specific topics.

Cinematic Choices

We also decided to make the film with a small crew since we would be going into slums and the homes of poor people which we knew to be small and crowded. Our itinerary was punishing and we planned to move fast and visit multiple cities in several countries, which required mobility. To cut expenses and keep the crew mobile, I decided to operate the camera myself, and Beth, who was producing the film, would do the sound. All of the equipment would have to be contained in four, large-wheeled suitcases filled with production gear: lighting equipment, tripod, tapes, camera accessories, and sound equipment. I hand-carried the camera in a bag that was larger than aviation regulations and which, therefore, required an elaborate explanation at every airport x-ray machine. Beth always carried the tapes on board to ensure

Beth Portello

that they did not get lost in the luggage, which would have been disastrous.

The content of the film, which we hoped would change people's perception of the true causes of poverty, was our highest concern. However, the form of the documentary was also very important to me. I have seen many documentaries ruined either by too little or too much investment in the form of the film. I knew also that I could not turn the subject of poverty into "cinema"—in which the craft of filmmaking would overshadow the content. I would, therefore, have to refrain from using zooms and any other

3

kinds of effects unless they were absolutely necessary to the context of the scene. The camera would be mostly fixed on a tripod or handheld when the subject necessitated such. I had decided from day one that I wanted to distinguish visually between the experts who would be interviewed in nice settings and the poor who would be interviewed in their normal surroundings. It is one thing to fight poverty from a comfortable office in a university or an international organization—which does not diminish the importance of those who do—but it is another to live it on a day-to-day basis. To wake up hungry every day, without knowing where one can find enough money to feed one's family, is simply not the same thing.

I decided very early on that the light would be my ally in this complex cinematic question. I would install my experts in a comfortable setting and light them with three to four lamps, ultimately using diffusion and colored gels. When filming those living in poverty we would use natural light which very often was almost none. I also decided to film our impoverished subjects with a handheld camera in their neighborhoods and in their homes, unless the subject was sitting facing the camera. The experts were invariably shot with a fixed and immobile camera.

Audio was a struggle throughout the shoot. I was never a fan of the wireless microphones that most television or documentary crews use, because it obliges the interviewee to strip in order to pass the wire under his or her clothing. Not only does this create an awkward beginning for everyone, but most of the time, you can see the mics in the shot. On top of that, those mics cut off all the ambient sound around the interviewee making it less natural. I decided to use a shotgun microphone instead, either affixed to a tripod or handheld by Beth in case of any on-the-fly interviews. Our goal was to create a natural environment for the interviews; I know from experience that a very comfortable interviewee will share a lot more than one made uncomfortable by the setting.

In each country we visited, the crew would be completed with a "fixer" to organize the local shoots and some additional local helpers to facilitate our production schedule in order to avoid wasting time. Cliff joined us for the majority of our travels and was an indispensible part of the process. He was always self-reliant and flexible, but also remained aware of our agreement, giving me total freedom. At the same time, his deep knowledge of this subject matter coupled with the fact that he has spent his life working to understand the issues at the deepest level made him the best critic of my work. Throughout the process, when I would get tired and ready to accept a simplistic explanation of a complex problem, he would always be there to challenge me and bring me back to the uncompromising track.

Originally I wanted to show both sides of the poverty debate. We even filmed some experts who were proponents of the mindset that "progress and technology will solve everything"—that mosquito nets and bags of fertilizer could solve the poverty conundrum. This is the theory that Bono's economic sidekick, Jeffrey Sachs, has touted in his best-selling book, *The End of Poverty*, as have the opponents of Latin America's new progressive leaders. But the first cut of the film was more than three hours long, so these interviews were left on the hard drive of the editing system.

Additionally, with a limited travel budget, we chose countries with two criteria: first, countries with governments that were open to acknowledging and talking about the poverty challenges they faced; and second, countries that represented a specific issue in the thesis we were trying to develop, such as land rights in Kenya. As absurd as it sounds, many governments that face dire poverty still deny their condition despite the fact that one can see evidence of it on every street. (One could easily say the same of the United States.)

We discussed possible titles for the film all the way through development, production and well into post-production. We determined that "The End of Poverty?" would be the best title because it challenges the concept that we can end poverty within the current economic system. For me, it is also a direct challenge to Jeffrey Sachs and his book, *The End of Poverty*, no question mark. Sachs has become "Mr. Poverty" in the United States and has convinced millions of people that mosquito nets and bags of fertilizer are the solution. In his book, Sachs reflects on the role that he played in Bolivia in 1985 when he was an economic advisor to the government that was struggling with hyperinflation. Some credit him with turning the Bolivian economy around through "shock therapy" and liberalizing the markets. Others believe he destroyed the Bolivian economy for generations to come. Sachs devotes a chapter to reflect upon his Bolivian experience and opines that, with distance, he has discovered the true reason for which Bolivia is the poorest country in South America: because it is too high in altitude! (Does this absurd idea really merit a response?)

The biggest challenge of all was distilling the 100 hours of footage. To make the film appealing to a large audience, we decided to cut out over an hour. Moreover, we had to leave out many fascinating experts and equally fascinating poor people who spoke candidly about the reasons for their situations. This is why we decided to spend the time and energy to recount this adventure and include those voices in this book. We had to give back a little bit of what they had given us. It should be noted that the ideas and comments included in this presentation are specifically those of the author; not of the experts or people who have collaborated on this book.

Part II: Venezuela

We landed in Caracas late at night on December 1, 2006, two days before the historic re-election of Venezuelan President, Hugo Chávez, which would definitely be the first shock of our trip. Caracas is a hodge-podge of an almost-modern city in the developed world coupled with the chaos of a Third World city that developed too fast. Throughout the day, every day, traffic jams clog the streets, since there is only one major artery going through the entire city. Honking horns provide the background music.

In most of the world's cities, the poor are hidden as far away as possible from the city center, provided that the distance is not so great as to prevent them from going to work by bus or bike or on foot. Today more than one billion people live in the slums of the global South and their conditions have deteriorated in the last fifty years.

Caracas has one unusual characteristic: the most populated barrios are not located in the outskirts of the city. They are, instead, located very close to the city center along the hillsides. Because Caracas was settled in the narrow valley of the *Cordillera de la Costa*, the barrios were built into these steep ravines. Where else would the poor get access to free land but on unstable hillsides, which could potentially slide with the next heavy rain? In Caracas the flat, stable lands are reserved for the rich. The presence of many steep ravines encircling the city center explains why so many barrios have survived that would otherwise have been considered unacceptable to the development of tourism.

As it turns out, this situation would literally save Chávez on several occasions. The Miraflores Palace—the White House of Caracas—is located within walking distance of one of the largest barrios, 23 de Enero. During the coup in 2002, when Chávez was illegally detained by a coalition supported by right-wing television stations and the U.S. government, more than one million people poured down from the barrios demanding the return of their president. His safety was actually ensured by his loyal guard during that crisis, but those million people surrounding Miraflores and paralyzing the city for days showed popular support for the deposed president and reinforced such support within the military.

The election took place on the second day of our arrival and the streets were alive with political banners and pro-Chávez supporters, or *Chávistas* whose slogan was *Diez Millones de Votos*. Their goal was to secure ten million favorable votes. All over the city, red-shirted Chávez supporters flashed ten fingers to show their support.

On the day of the election, lines started to form by 3:00 a.m. in front of each barrio's polling station with people who wanted to vote before they went to work. By noon, the line would wind all the way up that hill as far as we could see; probably a mile long. When we raised the question of transparency and accountability, we were shown the Venezuelan system. The voters would first register at a table, then go inside the polling booth where a touch-screen, direct-response electronic (DRE) voting machine was installed. The computers were protected by cardboard walls to guarantee privacy. After they voted, paper ballots were generated, inspected by the voters, and then deposited into a ballot box for possible recount. The voters would check-out by making a thumb print in ink in a book. This process was monitored by many international observers.

In the barrios, the voting process itself was a revolution. Previous to Chávez, the barrio inhabitants had the right to vote but there were often "technical difficulties." During the U.S.-dominated regimes which preceded Chávez, in order to vote you needed an ID card, which is still required. But before Chávez came to power, in order to get the ID card, you were required to have a permanent address, but the majority of barrio addresses were not recognized as permanent. Therefore, the barrio dwellers were prevented from voting. By legitimizing the barrios, Chávez gave these people a voice for the first time and won their fervent support.

Interviewing people on the streets, we were struck by how hopeful they were. For the first time their votes were being counted. But voting was just one of several changes. What quickly became the most striking thing was that all of these people were in school. From the youth to the senior citizens, everyone was engaged in the process of learning. Even more notable was that in order for the poorest parents to avoid the temptation to put their children to work, a monetary incentive was given to those parents who kept their children in school with regular attendance. That was, of course, another major innovation and mini-revolution. All over the Third World, children work, not because they are exploited by bad people, but because most poor parents are not able to earn enough money to support their families and, therefore, must send their children out to make money.

Throughout the day, we visited several barrios and were shown the *missiones* that were part of the *Barrio Adentro* program. In each barrio, we saw several small buildings, shaped like a pentagon, one every five to ten blocks. These were new medical centers, staffed by Cuban doctors. Early in his presidency, Chávez made a deal with the Cuban regime to exchange Venezuelan oil for Cuban teachers and doctors. For many barrio-dwellers, this would be the first doctor they had ever seen. There were two reasons they lacked medical care previously: 1) healthcare was not available and 2) the doctors, traditionally from the upper-middle class, would not agree to go into the barrios because they were afraid of the dangers and because they assumed they would never get paid. Next to these health centers we could usually find a *mercado*, a subsidized supermarket. They were usually located next to another interesting innovation: a small communication center where anyone could have access to the internet for free. In the supermarkets, organized by the Venezuelan state, staple foods were sold at prices usually discounted by 40%. On the package of each type of food, a different paragraph of the Venezuelan constitution would be printed alongside a comic or illustration, which explained to the Venezuelans, in simple terms, how their constitution was there to protect them.

Not all of these improvements radically changed the lives of barrio dwellers. They still suffer from extreme violence and many decades of neglect. Our interview with a poor woman, featured in the film, who had lost two of her sons in eruptions of violence, made plain how pervasive that violence remains. Despite that, the changes are giving them a voice in the political process and easing their situation significantly.

Later that night, we wanted to see how the results were reported on television—specifically by the international media. Around 9:00 p.m., the official results came down: 61% vote for Chávez, with a 75% turnout. The opposition party of Manuel Rosales put out its first press release claiming fraud and voter coercion. The first bulletin on CNN International did not report the official result but only the claim of fraud by the opposition. Two hours later, the opposition dropped its claim and recognized the election results. We did not see any further claims of fraud broadcast on CNN, but, notably, neither were there any reports of the election's results.

We went outside of Caracas to Vargas State, to see a relocation program of poor farmers to whom idle land on top of steep hills had been given. The three farmers or families we visited, one of whom describes his life in the film, were clearly happy with the land provided by the government. As the last interviewee explained, small farmers have been persecuted for decades. Their land had been seized many times: expropriated for the benefit of large export plantations or "development" projects. They had been forced to stop growing food, sometimes after having spent years in jail, and were forced to learn another trade like construction. This time they were not only given the land with the appropriate title but also tools and fertilizers to grow the crops of their choice. This small group of people—around twenty families—reflects the number one problem of poverty we saw throughout our travels: the land issue.

Land was confiscated during colonial times, as it was then the number one resource, to constitute what became known as *latifundios* in Latin America or large land tenures. Such giant estates created a class of local elite of landowners, mostly *mestizos*—of mixed ancestry—who were devoted to the European power from which they obtained both land and political power. In return, they supplied the needs of the colonial power. Usually, upon the country's independence, these *latifundios* remained the property of the original owner's heirs or were transferred to the local elite if they were still in foreign hands. In the vast majority of Third World countries, the descendants of the original inhabitants never got their land back, sometimes not even after violent revolutions. Political freedom sounded important at the time but it disguised the fact that, without economic freedom, the level of poverty would worsen. In most of these countries, land became not only an economic tool but a speculative one, with large land owners preferring not to grow anything on their land while waiting for its value to increase. It will take many agrarian reforms by strong-handed governments to break the de facto monopoly of land ownership. In some countries 80% of the arable land is in the hands of less than a dozen families.

Another one of the highlights of our Venezuelan journey was our visit to Maracaibo, a major area for oil exploitation. Everything there revolves around oil, which has historically been in the hands of Chavez's opposition, an upper class that has always served foreign powers. Their control of oil production made them rich, leaving the country poorer.

The upper class not only seized control of the economy but also political power. This substantiates one of Henry George's theories, which has been proven right over and over again: progress not only concentrates riches in the hands of the few but, as a direct consequence, political power, as well. When people depend on the "favors" of those who hold the keys to the economy, it is easy to understand how they will put in power the ones on whom they depend.

The key expert interviews, which would close the Venezuelan chapter and open our minds, were the ones with Edgardo Lander, professor of Social Sciences at the *Universidad Central de Venezuela* in Caracas and with Nora Castañeda, president of the Women's Bank.

We chose to interview Edgardo Lander because of his ability to explain the historical causes of the situation in South American countries today. Right away we found a common ground, as we were both great fans of Eduardo Galeano's book, *Open Veins of Latin America*. Edgardo was able eloquently to put into perspective the historical and socio-economic situations of countries like Venezuela. Moreover, he articulated the relationship between the consumption of resources and the state of the world today. He advocated radical change in consumption patterns to avoid the destruction of our planet, a point of view that became a central theme in the film.

The Women's Bank was created to answer one of the major problems in all of Latin America: that only men have access to credit, while many experiences—like those of Mohammed Yunus in Asia—have proven that giving credit to women helps sustainable development in a very efficient way. Nora Castañeda explained Venezuela's colonial historical development—from producing food exports like coffee and cacao during the Spanish colonial period to exporting oil under British, and then US, power. It is interesting to note that one of the primary methods of preventing Third World countries from developing is to force them to produce raw materials like agricultural products or mineral ones, while preventing them from refining such products and then selling them in the marketplace. The international market has long made certain that refining, packaging, and marketing of a final product increases its value far above the value of the raw material itself. That allows developed countries to obtain most of the profit. Until very recently, Venezuela was prevented from refining oil in its own refineries, in much the same way that Kenya, as we saw later, was prevented from processing and marketing its own tea.

Nora continued by explaining the disastrous effects that the twentieth century's economic tools like the IMF and the World Bank had upon her country, clearly blaming such institutions for creating poverty on a large scale. This became a central theme of the film.

Part III: Brazil

Brazil is a totally different country than Venezuela. Its size (almost as large as the United States), its multi-ethnic population, and its diverse regions in terms of geography, weather or economic development make it an extremely hard country to manage. On the other hand, Brazil shares a similar colonial history with Venezuela. It was, in 1494, a territory given by the pope to the kingdom of Portugal and became a grower of coffee, cacao and sugar cane produce, a situation that still plagues the people of Brazil five hundred years years later.

The city of Sao Paulo was the first part of the journey. It is such a gigantic metropolis with so many high-rises next to each other, that we had to go to the top of one of these buildings to truly comprehend the scope of such an area. It is a city that attracts tens of thousands of new rural poor people every year who constitute the labor reserve that companies mercilessly exploit. Visiting the *favelas,* we heard stories of people living on less than one dollar a day, families sleeping in the streets, and children dying of curable illnesses. But we also encountered a lot of hope and a lot of resilience. Hope lies primarily in their new government. Many find Lula, the former worker and now president, to be more moderate then they would like. Yet they all know that he, like his counterpart in Venezuela, created reforms and programs for the poor, including one to eradicate hunger in the short term called "Fome Zero." Some experts believe that Lula came to power with a very ambitious agenda but that the international financial institutions made very clear to him how easily they could destroy the Brazilian currency and the Brazilian economy, if they so desired. With Brazil still totally dependent on the international market, Lula was forced to compromise and since then, he has implemented rather moderate policies. The minister in charge of *Fome Zero,* Patrus Ananias de Sousa, explained the numerous programs that were implemented to reduce poverty and eliminate hunger, which only substantiated their moderate status. Although a tough decision, he did not make it into the final cut of the film!

Our visit to Brasilia, where we interviewed Ananias de Sousa and other government officials, showed us a great example of the policies created for the poor in the last century. Built over many decades by, among others, the famous architect Oscar Niemeyer, Brasilia is an ultra-modern city protected by from any outside interference by being in the middle of nowhere. The poor are kept a minimum of 10 miles from the city, hidden from any major roads. The result is a city that resembles a museum of modern art but one that is totally soulless, inspiring one to leave it as soon as possible.

Another interesting interview was with Raquel Rolnik, National Secretary of Urban Programs. She told us that poor people have been forced to live on unstable hillsides or on riverbanks that flood during the rainy season because those are the only lands available and because the middle class does not want the poor living near them and lowering their property values.

We also met with a Senator, a leader of the opposition, who told us what we heard many times—that poverty can be resolved through education. That was almost the only thing he had to say during a one-hour interview. That idea is dangerous. Of course, education is essential to pull individual people out of misery and poverty. But, to generalize that that is the solution for everyone implies that the poor, as individuals, are the ones responsible for their situation. This conveniently allows the theorist to avoid questioning the system that is actually responsible.

From Brasilia, we decided to visit the area which was, as much as the mines of Potosí in Bolivia, one of the major sources of wealth obtained by the powers of the North: the gold mines of Ouro Preto. The plundering of Brazil's gold and Bolivia's silver and tin gave enormous financial power to the North. Such power, while it allowed the northern countries to finance economic development and industrial revolutions, created in the southern countries a situation which inextricably binds them centuries later.*

Hundreds of years later in Ouro Preto you can still see the deserted mines, but more importantly, you can see the palaces that the new oligarchy built with the profits generated by such tremendous transfer of resources. This episode is also discussed in Galeano's book, *Open Veins of Latin America.*

The exploitation of underground resources by the colonizers was always coupled with an exploitation of the land itself. The colonizers profited from the exploitation of what they called "precious vegetables": tea, coffee, cocoa and sugar cane, which were grown on huge tracts of land. The original peasants were simply dispossessed and forced to work for their new masters in slave-like conditions. Millions of indigenous people died from European illnesses, horrible treatment, forced labor, and massacres. As a

---

* In the North, the Spanish and the Portuguese did not benefit as much as the British and the Dutch because, at the time, the former were largely indebted to the latter. The gold of Brazil and the silver of Bolivia transformed small countries with little or no resources like Holland and England into powerful empires, which went on to dominate the globe for centuries. The theory, derived from Max Weber's "Protestant ethic" thesis, which conveniently credits the religious system of these countries for their economic development, has long since been debunked.

result, the local population was insufficient to perform the tasks demanded by the colonizers. Thus, we can credit the system of economic exploitation with engendering the slave trade, which brought from Africa tens of millions of people—around half of whom did not survive their treatment in Africa and the voyage to South America.

Today after hundreds of years of aborted agrarian reforms, many of the lands in these countries are still organized as *latifundios* and are still controlled by only a few families from the upper class. The rural poverty that we can see today all over South America is definitely the result of such a system. Today, the large tracts of land are in the hands of agribusiness, which continues to grow products for export instead of local markets, thus forcing these countries to import the staple foods they need to survive. This unbelievable trap was first revealed to us by Joao Pedro Stedile, the national leader of the MST, the *Movimento Sem Terra*, or landless workers' movement.

The MST has been making headlines for the past decade by legally (or in some cases, illegally) seizing idle land and giving it back to landless farmers. They have also made headlines whenever their coordinators are tortured or shot by landowners. Stedile explained that a gigantic country like Brazil, with some of the best arable land in the world, still has to import rice, milk and other staple foods from other countries because most of its land is still in the hands of a few owners who work for the giant food industries which grow products for export. The ecological consequences of such international trade are devastating to the planet. It also forces millions of people to exist below the poverty line—all to satisfy the demand by the North for cheap food and other raw materials from the South. The economic tools established during the time of unrestrained neoliberalism ensure that this system of exploitation will not be easily defeated.

Today, one of the key components of this system in Brazil is sugar cane—the same "precious vegetable" that enslaved the country centuries ago. Sugar is not the only problem. The Amazon faces massive deforestation for soy farming. But sugar cane remains even more important, because ethanol can be produced from it, and that is something the international market craves today. Growing sugar cane is cheap provided that men working in slave-like conditions harvest it.

To film the harvesting of cane, we flew to to the northeast of Brazil, the state of Pernambuco. The first thing that hits you is the size of the properties, or *haciendas,* on which sugar cane is grown. They extend as far as the eye can see. Now, if you venture deeper down the tiny, dirt roads you will arrive in one of the makeshift camps built for the sugar cane cutters. These camps are not much better than the shantytowns in the poorest parts of Africa or India. The workers live sometimes in one room made from scraps of wood with a blue tarp covering and no electricity, running water, or sanitation. The good part is that some of these camps have been "taken over" by the MST which is working to relocate these landless people to a small plot of farmland.

To interview one of the local leaders of the MST, we had to undertake an epic journey. We went to a small town in the middle of nowhere. Once we arrived, we were sent by locals from one area of town to another, up and down unnamed streets, without finding him. We did this for hours. We were just about ready to give up when finally we reached a very tiny street on which sat a small concrete building surrounded by a heavy metal gate with a buzzer that did not work. After ringing for quite some time and engaging in "negotiations" with several people, we were finally ushered in. To be honest, by the time we were allowed inside, we were quite exasperated by the whole endeavor, but things quickly made sense upon meeting the occupant, Jaime de Amorim. The reason for all of this hassle stemmed from fear. He was living in hiding, afraid of being ambushed and shot by landowners in retaliation for his work with MST. His fear was justified. During the three days that we stayed in the region, three of his fellow-organizers were shot to death by landowners.

The interview with Jaime was extremely interesting. Not only did he explain to us the horrible details of how the workers live, but also how they are exploited by most of the growers. Workers come from very poor areas after having their farms seized by landowners whose actions are usually supported by corrupt local judges. The workers migrate looking for work and end up in one of these makeshift camps. The growers bring a truck into these camps very early in the morning—usually at 3:00 or 4:00 a.m.—and drive them to the fields that need to be cut. They work eight to twelve hours under the scorching sun for $2.00 to $7.00 a day, provided they have cut an immense amount of cane. If they do not reach the daily quota, they risk ending up with nothing. Sometimes, instead of money, the receive coupons redeemable for overpriced food at the shop owned by the grower. Other times, equipment rental will be deducted from this meager pay.

Jaime explained that the workers cannot survive on these wages, much less feed their families. Therefore, they have to take a second and sometimes even a third job in the cities at night and also have to force their children to work, as well, selling trinkets or, as Jaime puts it, "going into prostitution." They have no other alternatives with the region being entirely devoted to growing sugar cane, nor do they have the money to travel farther to find different work.

A few days later, we went into the fields looking for some cutters who would agree to speak to us about their conditions. That was not an easy task, as we were crossing onto private property, patrolled by armed guards. On top of that, there was a very palpable fear of retaliation on the part of the workers combined with the awareness that any time spent talking to us could possibly prevent them from making their quotas. All in all, they were very reluctant to speak to us. Finally, however, we found a group from which two men were more than happy to "explain their situation to the world" and in doing so, confirmed what Jaime had explained to us the day before. Most of these men had been cane cutters for decades, working in horrible conditions, some even barefooted because the boots they had been promised had never been sent. They told us that typically they were paid half of what had been promised to them, giving them no possibility at all to send any money to their families. The only solution was to starve themselves by eating corn or beans in order to at least bring home something at the end of the season. They had an understanding of world politics and of the enormous profits that growers were making on their backs. They concluded the interview with a pessimistic outlook, noting that the condition of people living as they do is the reason why today's world is infested with criminals.

On a more positive note, we did visit several villages built on idle land seized from speculative growers and given back to landless farmers by MST. Each farmer had a small house built of concrete with running water, electricity, and sanitation and most of all, a small plot of land on which to grow vegetables which could be sold at the local market. The striking difference about these villages was the relative peace of the people. Children were playing in the dirt streets looking properly nourished, women were attending the needs of their households, and men were ready to chat with us. That said, even if they were happy with this new living situation, they knew it would only last until the former landowner had secured a "friendly" judge who would issue a decree forcing them to vacate. And at that point they would be thrown out onto the road to once again look for a hacienda where they could go back to cutting cane.

After our visit to the northeast of Brazil, we flew back to Sao Paolo, and then on to Bolivia.

Part IV: Bolivia

We landed in La Paz after a hectic flight from Sao Paulo in an American plane from a small private company used to carry troops in Africa! The plane was rented by the Bolivian government for international flights. Bolivia once had a very good airline, but it was privatized like everything else, per the advice of none other than Jeffrey Sachs. It has since been almost totally dismantled. The pilot clearly had no concern for the comfort of his passengers and flew right through the worst storms, causing the plane to bump along through the air for hours.

La Paz airport is located in El Alto, the gigantic shantytown built on one of the high plateaus above La Paz, which is the capital city with the highest altitude in the world. El Alto is where all the poor people end up when they come from the countryside to find work. It is comprised of many square miles of makeshift housing with unpaved roads and, quite often, no sanitation. The first glimpse of the capital was no more pleasant. La Paz is an extremely polluted city where traffic jams are the way of life.

Our first interview was with Abel Mamani, the water minister. Evo Morales, when he came to power, felt the need to create a water ministry, not to control water quality, but to prevent water privatization, which had been the subject of an ongoing fight in the country for the last ten years. Mamani confirmed that the pro-US governments which had previously been in power, allied with the IMF and the World Bank, had privatized everything in the country: natural gas and oil, the electricity system, the airline, railways, TV stations, phone companies, etc. He noted that such private enterprise did not "modernize" or make these companies "profitable" as the proponents of the free market system had claimed would happen. Instead, the new owners plundered these companies, sold their assets, and left the country with no infrastructure whatsoever. Railway workers are often unpaid for months and most of the lines are no longer even serviced. His conclusion was that "privatization has destroyed the country."

That prepared us for our next stop: Cochabamba, a city deep in the country, which was the location of the siege now known as "the water war." In 2001, the government, in desperate need of a loan from the World Bank, was told that it would not receive such a loan unless its water system was privatized. This has been a common practice by the World Bank and the IMF for the last 30 years. They say, "We will help you if you open your market to foreign companies and agree to privatize your public companies." These practices have come to be known throughout the Third World by the now infamous name of "structural adjustment programs," which have ruined the economies of many of these countries, while at the same time, making northern corporations extremely wealthy.

In Cochabamba, the water was transferred to a US company: Bechtel Corporation. Bechtel promised to modernize the existing water system and bring water to those who did not have it. Within the first six months, the government and local authorities provided them with free buildings to house their operations and free equipment for their offices. But Bechtel did not keep any of its promises. Instead it started to raise the water fee by 50 to 300%, plunging some of the poorest people there into a desperate situation. Oscar Olivera and his sister, who was also involved in organizing people during the water war, told us in horrible detail how the lives of people were affected by the water laws, which even put rain and other natural sources of water into the hands of Bechtel! Led by several activists and local organizers, including Oscar Olivera, who has became a heroic figure around the world, the people refused to pay their water bills and went into the streets to protest for months, thus paralyzing the city. The government sent police reinforcements and the army to quell the revolt, but to no avail. After many months of protest and several lives lost, the government had to back down and terminate the agreement with Bechtel. Bechtel sued the government in international court for damages, despite not having spent a penny in the country, but withdrew their lawsuit once Morales was elected, realizing that they had no chance to get paid. The main reason this fight even started is because Bechtel took over a practically sacred resource in Bolivia. The appropriation of this resource, part of the *Pachamama* or mother earth, was like stepping on the culture of the indigenous people. That makes a powerful comment about the fight between modern, unrestrained capitalism and traditional cultures and values.

We met afterwards with Jim Shultz, an American writer based in Cochabamba who heads The Democracy Center, a non-profit organization. He explained to us that since the sixties, Bolivia has been the "lab rat" for the unrestrained, capitalist experiment of total privatization and, as he put it, "market fundamentalism." It is interesting to note that Milton Friedman and the Chicago school of economics, which were first to establish these theories of "market fundamentalism," used Chile under the dictatorship of Augusto Pinochet to test this policy. The short term success of this policy (based on the massive influx of capital from the initial sale of state assets) encouraged them to expand to other Latin American countries, where other US-supported dictators had already been installed.

John Perkins, who joined us in Bolivia, told us a very interesting story that confirmed all of the above. After Perkins served a long stint as an "economic hit man," the Leucadia Corporation, then in control of the privatized Bolivian power system, asked him to head this profitable activity. He would be relocated to Bolivia with his family and would be provided with several cars, chauffeurs, chefs and other luxurious amenities. His job was also a key political one, because in the event of an insurrection, he would be the one to literally cut off the power of the insurgents while ensuring that the other side, the keepers of US interests, received all the power they needed. When he presented his idea of developing the Bolivian grid so as to bring electricity to poor people all around the country, he was told that the policy of the company was not to help poor people, but to make money. Isn't this the same policy that Bechtel tried to implement 30 years later?

In a small village in the suburbs of Cochabamba, a place where the main activity consists of women making bricks on the side of the road, we interviewed a very interesting man: Eduardo Yssa. Eduardo is part of the Aymara people, a community organizer, and supposedly, a distant cousin of the president. He chose to focus the interview on the subject of colonialism, but put it in very personal terms. He explained that for the Aymara people, the arrival of Christopher Columbus was not a discovery but the worst disaster in their history. He said that Columbus's arrival was the moment that they lost their land and their livelihoods. More importantly, in his opinion, they lost their culture, their religion and, therefore, their dignity. He explained to us that they were forced to convert to Catholicism and to speak Spanish. Before that, the Aymaras had their own spoken and written language—the *Kipus*. However, Eduardo confirmed in a choked voice, today this language has completely disappeared.

We witnessed, involuntarily, a scene that could not have better illustrated Eduardo's painful explanation. We arrived in Sucre, the former Bolivian capital, on Christmas Eve and found an old city preparing for a celebration. On Christmas Day, we wandered into the main city square where a large number of people were preparing to enter the cathedral for mass. We tagged along to see that the large majority of the people inside were *mestizos* (of mixed blood from Spanish ancestors) and all were very well dressed. However, very few indigenous people were actually inside the cathedral. When I asked our fixer why, he explained that in the back of the Cathedral, a small chapel had been built during the time of colonization for the indigenous people and that they were still accustomed to practicing their new religion there. That said, a couple of old indigenous women entered the cathedral and signed themselves before they went to listen to the sermon. But to my surprise, they sat down on the ground in the aisles instead of in the pews! We proceeded to the "indigenous chapel" far in the back, which was full of people celebrating the same kind of mass, bringing very sophisticated offerings to a statue of the baby Jesus. The only difference was that the music was partly classical and partly local with a live band of young people chanting traditional indigenous songs.

On our way from Sucre to Potosí—the highest city in the world, with mines above 18,000 feet—we passed sumptuous palaces built during colonial times as well as miserable villages where extreme poverty was everywhere. It took several hours of travel through deserted land to get to the high plateau and the city of Potosí. The city was a mix of old, decadent palaces and decrepit streets and buildings. It is clear that the splendor of Potosí was long gone. During colonial times, it had become an almost mythical place, which attracted large numbers of conquistadors. The origin of the myth was the largest silver deposit ever known. The indigenous people said that *Cerro Rico* (rich mountain) was crying silver tears. Potosí, like Ouro Preto in Brazil, soon became the major source of wealth for Spain and Portugal. It created gigantic fortunes for the mother land as well as for the colonizers who had permanently established themselves to exploit these riches.

A former miner organized a visit for us through some of the tunnels that were still in use. The silver is long gone, but tin and other second grade minerals can still be exploited. We walked through these very narrow corridors—some not larger than 4x4 feet -- deep into the mountain. I should probably say that, with the high altitude and lack of oxygen, we struggled just to put one foot in front of the other. On top of that, we had to continually jump to the side of the track whenever we heard the all too recognizable sound of a cart coming toward us at full speed.

Millions of laborers died in the mines of Potosí and it is easy to understand why. Laws were created to force the indigenous people to work inside the mines for up to six months at a time. Besides being overworked and malnourished, the lack of oxygen, the dust, and the chemical process used at the time to separate silver from rocks wreaked havoc with their health. This was never of particular concern for the *conquistadors* because, according to the church, the indigenous people were inferior creatures, given by God to serve as slaves for the white man. The only thing that helped the people to cope were the coca leaves that they constantly chewed (and still do), which alleviate their hunger and boost their resistance. During colonial times, the church carved out for itself a monopoly on coca leaf sales, imposing a large tax on each transaction!

Deep inside the mine, the miners of Potosí have established a museum that retraces their history from the very beginning of the conquest. In this museum, there is a figure of a black slave, reminding us that when the conquistadors ran out of local labor, they found more on another continent, thus creating the largest population transfer ever known. The African slaves that were shipped to Bolivia died rapidly because they were unable to cope with the altitude and the cold.

The silver and tin extracted from Bolivia and the gold extracted from Brazil at that time represented the value of the European reserves many times over. Despite this, the riches from these mines did not directly benefit the kingdoms of Spain and Portugal, but their northern creditors, instead. Both kingdoms were so indebted because of the holy wars and other crusades in which they had engaged that their creditors, mainly England and Holland, were the first beneficiaries of these transfers of wealth. In the meantime, however, Potosí became the largest city in the world—larger than Paris or London.

To make sure that we truly understood the level of wealth that had been created, our miner guide took us to visit *La Casa de la Moneda* – the house where all the money of the old continent was now manufactured. It is still the largest colonial building ever built in South America. Not far from there, we visited the colonial governor's house where we were shown the underground caves in which the slaves were piled up at night and chained to the walls. Displayed in a glass case were the torture tools used to keep these "inferior creatures" under control!

Outside the mine, we conducted several interviews with miners, many of whom were no more than teenagers. They told us that they were working in the mines to supplement their families' incomes or to be able to later afford school. Others were there because their fathers, usually miners, too, had either suffered accidents which prevented them from working, or they had died prematurely from silicosis. They were usually making between five and ten dollars a day and when pressed about their future, they had really no hope that they could ever do anything better.

Upon our return to La Paz, we interviewed Miriam Campos from the ministry for indigenous people, who completed our visit to the past. For her, as for Eduardo Yssa, the arrival of the conquistadors was the beginning of the decline of Bolivian culture and the start of massive poverty. As she phrases it, "they came with a gun in one hand and a bible in the other." This is a formula that was used in other parts of the world, as well. In Bolivia, inequality was perpetuated by *latifundios*, large tracts of land that were transferred from generation to generation. The slaves, who worked on the land, carried with them the "debts" of their ancestors, thus preventing them from ever leaving the plantations. The laws that protected *latifundios* from any type of land reform are still in place. Under these laws, for example, each landowner is granted 50 hectares of land per head of cattle, while most peasants remain landless.

Campos described to us the horrific conditions in which the workers (descendants of the slaves) still live on these plantations. Most of the time they do not receive a salary for their work—only food and shelter. Children do not receive an education, and when the workers get sick, they have to find solutions on their own; the landowners never pay for any kind of health care. Campos is passionate about these issues and fights for agrarian reform. John Perkins, who conducted the interview with me, asked her what gives her such energy and courage. She answered that she will do everything to make sure that her own children never have to go through the same things that she has, and as she explained this, she started to cry.

We conducted several other interviews with government officials like Raul Manjon Ramirez, director at the planning ministry. After a very long and technical expose, Ramirez concluded by saying that the result of many decades of a free market economy, structural adjustment programs, and privatization, was that every child born in Bolivia today was already carrying a bigger part of his country's international debt than he or she could ever repay—even with an entire lifetime's salary. After handing over all state assets to foreign powers and pledging the future revenues of the nation's resources, Bolivia is now compelled to borrow more and more money from international financial institutions like the IMF and the World Bank or from international bankers. But, as John Perkins points out — that was the goal in the first place.

It is now clear why many people in Bolivia blame Jeffrey Sachs for having ruined their economy. I always wondered how such a brilliant economist could genuinely believe that the privatization of a state's assets could ulti-

21

mately be the best solution. The most amazing part is that after all these years of "let-the-market-decide-everything" and then having seen the disastrous consequences of doing so, many politicians still believe in this solution.

We went to interview Jorge "Tuto" Quiroga, the former prime minister of Bolivia and the main opponent to Evo Morales. He is in his fifties, is Harvard educated, speaks perfect English, and dresses like our US politicians. He tried to convince us that he would change the country if elected President, and more specifically—knowing that we were making a movie on poverty—that he would change the situation of the poorest people. When I asked him why he did not make these changes while he was in power the first time, he replied that the market was then too low and, therefore, he could not do anything to help. Although I was expecting a whole slew of explanations, this was not one of them. So, I asked how he would proceed now. His answer was even more interesting: now he would not take any action because the market had once again risen and, therefore, it would solve the problem all by itself! Simply put: he would not do anything either way!

A man on the opposite side of the spectrum and one who was ready to do everything was the Bolivian Vice President, Alvaro Garcia Linera. Linera was a former *guerillero* who had spent many years in jail and an intellectual who could quote Karl Marx, Rosa Luxembourg and Jean-Paul Sartre at will. He explained to us how colonialism had forced countries like Bolivia to adopt a global system, forcing them to be exporters of financial wealth. It was clear to him that the capitalist system was now coming to an end and that, together, these countries must now create a post-capitalist society in which everyone will at least have access to the most basic necessities. He concluded by warning that in a global economy, the stability that we think we have in Northern countries is actually very fragile. As long as there are people in other parts of the world who do not even have water to drink, then we should not take our own stability for granted.

Part V: Kenya

We chose to arrive in Kenya at the beginning of the World Social Forum (WSF) in January 2007. We knew the difficulty of accomplishing anything there, but we had lined up some interviews. At the WSF, we met not only experts but activists from all around the world. Among them was Miloon Kothari, the UN special *rapporteur* on housing. For a UN official, he uses very radical language to explain how our chosen economic system will lead to the death of many people, either directly or through what he calls "real estate violence," his term for land dispossession and forced evictions.

We were also able to interview John Christensen from the Tax Justice Network, a former off-shore banker. Since he realized the unfairness and artificial manipulation of the financial system, Christensen has been fighting for an international tax system that would not penalize the poor countries, but empower their people. He explained to us how the IMF and the World Bank, pushed by the international bankers and Northern governments, decided to liberalize short-term capital flows, which allows capital to be taken from poor countries overnight and put into off-shore bank accounts in order to avoid taxes. This massive transfer of funds—John provided us with astronomical numbers—deprive southern countries of the taxes they desperately need, while they enrich the international bankers and encourage corruption.

At the World Social Forum, we also met Eric Toussaint who became one of the main speakers in the film. Eric is the founder and President of the CADTM, the Belgian Committee for the Cancellation of the Third World Debt. Over the years he has become an expert on this issue and is now advising presidents and governments of poor countries which have to deal with this infamous financial tool. At the beginning I asked Eric if he would be willing to talk not only about the debt but about its historical causes, which have brought us to the point in which we find ourselves today. To my surprise, he was quite willing to give us an historical analysis that dated back to colonialism. This analysis was the perfect introduction to the reason for which we were in Kenya: to examine the consequences of colonialism in a country with only one major resource—its land.

We were helped with this task by two men: Mashengu Wa Mwachofi, a Kenyan historian and former parliamentarian, and Gitu Wa Kahengeri, a former general in the *Mau Mau* rebellion which had driven the British out of the country. Mashengu gave us a bleak account of the land dispossession in colonial times, which benefited the large number of white settlers brought there to live permanently. The natives were not recognized as human beings, but were regarded as slaves by colonial laws that required them to work on the plantations. Every male was forced to start work at the age of sixteen. To ensure that they would not escape, they were moved from one side of the country to the other, cutting them from their families, the land of their ancestors, and of course, their traditional culture. This was strikingly similar to the stories we had heard of the treatment of the indigenous people in Bolivia. Our *Mau Mau* general, a man in his eighties and admired by many, completed the overview by explaining that the *Mau Mau* movement started as a land revolt. Their main goal was to recover the stolen land because, as he put it, "we could not any more let our people starve to death." The second goal was to throw the oppressive British out of the country, which they finally succeeded in doing after many deaths and much destruction. But as Gitu was quick to add, unfortunately they did not get their land back. Upon their independence, the land was transferred from the white settlers to blacks who had been close to the colonial power. This was done in order to perpetuate the same export culture. Much of the arable land ended up in the hands of the first president, Jomo Kenyatta—whom many in the North perceived as being a liberator!—and in the hands of his family and other cronies. Gitu concluded by saying that to this day, the *Mau Mau* have still not recovered their land and are still struggling for their daily bread.

Nairobi looks a little bit like Caracas, a mix of modern buildings and housing for the poor where traffic jams are a permanent part of life. The main difference is that the shantytowns are not in the city but in the nearby suburbs. On the way to Kibera, the biggest slum in East Africa, we passed a beautiful polo field, well-watered and perfectly manicured—a remnant of British colonialism. Right behind the field, we drove down a small road and discovered a gigantic area where a million people live, practically piled one upon the other—most of them without electricity, running water or sanitation. When they need to go to the toilet, they use what they call the "flying toilets" which are small, plastic grocery bags that end up piled in the streets. All over Kibera, one can see mountains of plastic bags containing human excrement.

The pessimistic estimate places the rate of people with HIV at 70%. The people living here are mainly landless or displaced farmers—jobless people who came to the capital searching for work. We met a very interesting group of women there called STAWI They are all infected with AIDS and although most of them lost their husbands, they decided to fight the consequences of this disease. With absolutely no money—not an exaggeration—they created a myriad of programs to help the people in the community: programs for feeding AIDS orphans, pre-HIV test support, post-HIV test support. We were so incredibly moved by these women that as soon as we got back to the United States, we created a small fundraising operation called "The Filmanthropy Project" to help them as much as we could. Since then, we have financed the orphans feeding program and, through microcredits, created dozens of jobs.

We asked the STAWI women to take us to their homes and show us their lives. Apart from the founder of STAWI, who has a stable job, they all live in rooms usually no larger than 10 feet by 10 feet, sometimes with other members of their families. They survive by doing menial jobs like "going to wash clothes for richer people" or selling trinkets in the streets. They make an average of $1.00 per day, with rent for their miserable housing costing around $100 per month! In the heart of Kibera the two most common professions are prostitution and drug dealing. We visited a young man named Joseph who shares two small rooms with seven other members of his family. Most of his siblings are handicapped and only he and his mother can, as he says, "do something" to feed the family. He cannot go to school because, beyond primary education, one must pay to be educated in Kenya. This, thanks to another World Bank imposition. The good part of this story—where we see that movies can make a difference, even if on a small scale—is that a friend of mine has been sending Joseph $100 a month, as a result of watching the film. He also sent him a laptop computer to use for school. Joseph has finished school and is now a web designer with a stable job.

To understand how the inhabitants of Kibera were first displaced from their land, we interviewed H. W. O. Okoth-Ogendo, a professor who specializes in land law.* He gave us an account of how the colonizers took control of the land. It was very simple: they decided that Kenya did not have a "settled form of government." In this case, British law gave the land to the Queen of England. All land was appropriated by the British administration and handed over to white settlers. Okoth-Ogendo denounced this kind of manipulation because Kenya already had a "settled form of government" based on tribal laws, which the British conveniently failed to acknowledge!

Okoth-Ogendo also discussed the situation in Zimbabwe. The international politicians and media have held the president of Zimbabwe, Robert Mugabe, entirely responsible for the condition of his country, which is stricken by extreme poverty and hyper-inflation. However, rather than vilifying Mugabe, we in the North should recognize that the blame for what has happened in Zimbabwe can and should be traced back to the constitution the British imposed on that country, which prevented peaceful land reform. Okoth-Ogendo explained to us the history that our politicians and media have forgotten. When the British granted independence to the country, they attached a provision in the constitution that land redistribution could not

---

* Prof. Okoth-Ogendo died in April 2009 at the age of 64.

25

be implemented unless it received unanimity in parliament. But they also attached a provision saying that 20% of the seats in parliament would be reserved for white landowners. In exchange, they promised to give the new government enough money during the following ten years (!) to indemnify the white landowners for the land that was to be redistributed. Zimbabwe waited for ten years and nothing came. They waited another ten and still nothing. These essential facts about the conflict are never mentioned, not even by the serious media and even less by our favorite politicians.

Okoth-Ogendo also explained that the concept of private property was unknown to Kenyans until the British arrived. Land was available to all members of a community to use as they saw fit. Moreover, a person's children and grandchildren were guaranteed the same usage as long as they remained members of the community. This unfamiliarity with the concept of "private property" was the same throughout Africa, as well as South America and even Europe of long ago. The land was part of the "commons," meaning it was owned by all and available to all. No one could appropriate such land, and, in most instances, whatever was produced from the land was shared by everyone in the community. This prevented anyone from going hungry. If a member of a community was sick or unable to provide for himself, the community would help. And such a system was not restricted to just land. As a group of Maasai people we visited explained, when a member of the group kills one of his cows, the meat will be shared by all members of the community.

Many experts believe—as Cliff Cobb explains in the film—that the concept of private property defines not only modern times but the start of a new system called capitalism. Okoth-Ogendo told us that he has sat on many commissions at the UN and the World Bank which have begun to realize that the management of land, as it was done before by communities, is much more efficient and sustainable and that these commissions may now encourage a return to such practices!

The other side of the coin was explained by the minister of agriculture, Kipruto Arap Kirwa, who told us that his people still battle the consequences of the colonial period. Kenya is one of the best examples of the imposition of a monoculture. This imposition stems from the larger scheme of preventing the countries of the south from ever developing, as Cliff Cobb, Eric Toussaint, and Serge Latouche explain in the film. The British in India, the Dutch in Indonesia, the Belgians and the French in Africa, and the Spanish and Portuguese in South America all systematically destroyed any industry or craftsmanship that the local people mastered—even if local products were of superior quality to those made in factories of the colonial powers. Several hundred years ago, the fate of the southern countries was already established through colonization: they became the providers of agricultural or mineral raw materials. The refining and manufacturing was left to the Northern countries. The farmers of the South were prevented from making their own tools, clothes or even from growing their own food. The Europeans wanted to make sure that not only would there be no competition to their own industries, but they could also create a market for their products. By preventing the people of the South from being self-sufficient, as they had been for centuries, the Europeans forced them to become commodity buyers.

This is what happened in Kenya and it still prevents this country from developing in a sustainable way. Kenya was assigned the function of growing mainly tea and coffee for export. When the colonizers left the country, they took with them technically and legally the exclusive right to refine and sell the finished products. To this day, Kenya is not allowed to dry and package its own tea nor roast its own coffee, which is astounding in a supposedly free market world. Of course, such a practice could not still flourish without the full support of the local government which exemplifies the endemic level of corruption in a country like Kenya.

Next, we flew to Kisumu, a region in the western part of Kenya. We were brought by local NGOs to small villages on the shore of Lake Victoria which had been devastated by the arrival of the Dominion Group, a company based in Oklahoma. This company, in collusion with local officials, was given a large tract of arable land on which to grow crops for export. Intending to take control of the entire area, Dominion attempted to buy all of the land of the local farmers at an extremely low price. Most of them refused. So, Dominion built a dam which flooded the entire area and destroyed not only the culture of the local farmers, but their houses as well, forcing them to relocate to higher ground. The company sprayed pesticides by plane—as our local guide explained, "especially when people are working in their fields"—which killed most of the livestock of the communities, as well as many children. These communities have been fighting for years to be able to keep their land and to be compensated for their losses, but to no avail. Our local guide concluded his interview by lamenting the fact that his people are not even allowed to buy the produce from the crops that Dominion is growing on "their own land." The produce is instead sent directly to America!

27

This illustrates how the same practices, which started during colonial times, are still used today—and for the same purposes.

We also visited an island on Lake Victoria, home of several communities of fishermen. Here we found the same desolation, the same destruction. For most, their livelihoods have been destroyed by commercial fisheries which export the fish they catch, thus preventing these people from making a living. In addition, AIDS runs rampant there and with no health care of any kind, these people are left to die a slow death. Eric Mgendi of Action Aid confirmed that Kenya was, in fact, ordered by the World Bank to stop giving free healthcare to all, which has resulted in such devastation.

We decided to go to the heart of the problem by traveling to the Rift Valley, the location of the best arable land in Kenya, to see the tea plantations. On these rolling hills, there are tea plants in every direction as far as the eye can see. The owners of the plantations do not look as wealthy as the owners of the sugar cane plantations in Brazil, but the workers definitely look just as poor. A group of tea pickers agreed to be interviewed provided that it was not done on the plantation, but down the road. Their stories were the same as those of the sugar cane cutters: they have been tea pickers for many years, working an average of four to five months per year during the harvest, provided there is sufficient rain. If not, then they are out of a job until the rain comes. They are paid an average of $5.00 per day. During the dry season, they have to borrow food from the local store in order to survive until it rains. This store is also usually owned by the tea grower for whom they work. As soon as they get their first pay, they have to immediately reimburse the shopkeeper which leaves them with no money at all. Grace, one of the pickers interviewed, explained that it is why their stomachs are very small. They do not have food every day, but still they work an average of fourteen hours a day when they can find work.

Part VI: Tanzania

When we arrived in Tanzania from Kenya, and more specifically to Arusha, the closest city from the border, we were surprised by the difference. Even if they are neighbors and have had similar colonial history, it is clear that Kenya and Tanzania developed totally differently. The poverty was evident in Arusha compared to Kenyan cities, where it is mostly hidden in the slums. Tanzania, 50% larger than Kenya, has many mineral resources that Kenya does not have. So what happened?

Upon independence, Kenya continued policies that had been put in place by the British, mainly transferring land and political power from a white minority to a black one. Economically they continued to exploit people to grow agricultural products for export. Tanzania took a totally different turn under the leadership of Julius Nyerere, one of the fathers of the pan-africanist movement. Nyerere was a socialist who wanted the resources of his country to stay in the hands of his people. He believed that Africa would develop only if it were independent of the economic control of colonial powers. For a while the pan-africanists were definitely the best hope for Africa. But, as John Perkins and Chalmers Johnson explain in the film, the powers of the North did not let go of the resources in their former colonies. Therefore Tanzania and all other countries supporting the pan-africanist policies were ostracized and cut off from the capitalist world. So, Tanzania (like many other countries) had to turn to the USSR or China for trade and other economic help. The collapse of the Soviet Union forced Tanzania to turn to the IMF and the World Bank for help. At that point, foreign companies gained control of the resources under structural adjustment programs and other privatization policies. Twenty years later, it is clear that Tanzania is not in better shape and that development passed it by, creating major corruption and other ills.

We decided to visit Merelani, a village in the region where all the tanzanite gems come from, a couple of hours drive from Arusha. The drive took us through small, crumbling villages, stricken by extreme poverty. On the unpaved roads, it took a lot of the driver's talent to not make this several hour trip unbearable. There we found extreme poverty, coupled with rampant AIDS, malnutrition and a total lack of development. How can that be possible in a village that is among the few to mine tanzanite, which has been called the "gem of the 20th century?"

We went to interview many miners and their families. We also interviewed people in organizations that were created to defend these miners. Until the 1980s, mining was in the hands of small miners. They just had to pay a small fee to obtain a permit from the government, and they could mine wherever they wanted. It attracted a lot of people and Merelani became a prosperous town. But in the 1980s, the government was in desperate need of one of those deadly loans from an international institution. The IMF and the World Bank forced the government to open their markets to foreign corporations, which would supposedly create jobs and participate in the development of the country. Part of that opening meant transferring ownership of the tanzanite mines. Many foreign firms arrived in Merelani with powerful high-tech equipment. Little by little, legally or illegally, they took away the work from small-scale miners. As one of them pointed out: all the tanzanite veins in the ground are connected to each other, so when a company arrives at a vein that a small-scale miner is exploiting, the small miner will have to leave or "be shot." The main consequence has been extreme poverty in a previously prosperous area. As Nimrod Arachka, the president of the Tanzanian Mine Workers Development Organization made clear, the arrival of the big companies did not create jobs in the area. It impoverished the locals, and a huge amount of money has been "siphoned out of the country." Merelani provides one more proof of the results of the open-markets policies. It seems that, even if some of his policies were badly implemented, Nyerere was right. Kwame Nkrumah the first president of Ghana, and partner of Nyerere in his quest for a united Africa, freed from foreign domination, faced the same battles. Unfortunately these men were fighting against countries and corporations, which were ready to use any tools at their disposal to gain access to Africa's mineral resources, including the removal or assassination of leaders who opposed their designs. (According to William Blum, in our interview with him, Nkrumah was overthrown in 1966 by a coup that was instigated by the CIA, but carried out by the Ghanaian army. The coup was blamed publicly on the Soviet Union.)

This sad journey into African poverty did not get better when we came back to the border with Kenya. We were besieged by dozens of women and children, mainly from the Maasai tribe, trying to sell small carvings or bead necklaces. Some men were trying to sell their world famous dance to survive. Looking at them, I wondered how they feel when tourists spend a fortune in the safari lodges and give them a couple of dollars to watch them jump in the air.

Part VII: Conclusion

All of our travels and the production of the film did not answer all of our questions. I had many questions that cannot be answered apart from a global systemic analysis. For example: Why are large numbers of people in both the North and the South denied access to basic necessities, when major corporations make fortunes exploiting their natural resources? Why do shareholders pocket the profits of a company in both good times and bad? In other words, when a company becomes insolvent, why do the workers have to pay for the mistakes of managers? Why do taxpayers have to rescue banks and other financial institutions which made billions of dollars in the past? I could continue the list forever. Although the movie did not answer all of these questions, it put the global economy in perspective by ordering it from the beginning of modern times to the present. The global expansion of Europe, starting in the 15th century, saw the birth of a system that is financed by the poor. Of course, it was not that radical or simple, but we had to frame it that way to draw a simple picture.

First the poor had to give up their land and therefore their livelihood. Why? Because someone else in another country had decided that it would be so! Then they had to give up all other natural resources. Then they had to give up their personal independence and become the slaves of their new masters. They had to give up their culture, religion and identity. Little by little the guns used to control them were replaced by economic tools called open markets, monopolies, monoculture, debt, and privatization, although these policies were often implemented with violence. Gigantic inequalities were created between continents, between countries, and between the people within each country. Our ancestors thought that the best way to move forward was to separate the world between a small minority of "haves" and a large majority of "have nots." The small minority would have the land, the natural resources, the wealth and the financial and political power. Conveniently they assumed that some of the wealth in the hands of a minority would—according to a magical concept—trickle down to the majority and make everybody happy. This idea, that the poor should be grateful to eat the crumbs from the tables of the rich, was used to justify privilege and degradation for centuries, as if they arose from natural forces. But extreme inequality is not caused by nature. It is a product of laws and the exercise of power. The solution is not "trickle-down economics" but new methods of sharing the wealth.

The need to share the earth's resources has been intensified in recent decades by the realization that our present course will lead to environmental disaster. If it was ever possible to imagine that the poor could live on what was left over after the rich took what they wanted, Serge Latouche reminds us that that is pure fantasy. As he explains in the film, we are consuming 30% more than what the planet can regenerate, which means that every year we are digging a hole a little bit bigger under our feet. It also means that when we in the northern countries maintain our level of consumption, more people must plunge below the poverty line. That is why Serge Latouche became the advocate of "de-growth" or "a-growth," because "like atheism, it means exiting the religion of growth."

This no doubt will not be a very popular solution in the North. Who wants to give up the three cars in his garage or the abundance of good food. As Serge Latouche points out, we have a choice: de-growth, or finding at least 6 new planets with the same resources, so the bottom billion people can develop while we maintain our lifestyle. Let us hope we are more intelligent than to choose the latter. But the choice of de-growth probably makes the vice-president of Bolivia right. It means that we have to invent a new system, a post-capitalist system, which would sustain the current population, but not destroy the planet with pollution or resource depletion.

The current economic crisis also reveals another fundamental flaw of capitalism and endless growth. Our system is based on over-production, based in part on artificial financial tools, like mortgage-based derivatives and credit default swaps. We have reached the limits of the existing system. The only way to continue to grow or at least to maintain ourselves at this economic level is by lifting the bottom billion out of poverty, so they can buy our products and eat the food we grow that gets wasted every year. There is no alternative, from either a capitalist or a post-capitalist point of view. We will not find any solutions without taking care of the poor.

Of course redirecting the economy cannot be achieved all at once. It will take decades, perhaps centuries. But there are steps that can be taken, as Cliff Cobb explains in the film: agrarian reform, giving back—finally!—the land to the ones who work on it; ending monopolies over natural resources; canceling unconditionally Third World debt; ending unjust taxes on the poor. Beyond that, it means changing the mentality and the culture that cause us to conceive everything in individualistic terms of profits. It means re-discovering the concept of the commons, the concept of community where the resources benefit all and are shared by all, not only a few. As such, we should be able, first, to comprehend the idea of de-growth and then to implement it.

If I had to dedicate the film to some people, I would dedicate it to the innocent children of the world who suffer unjustly every day in order for other people to have a great life. I wish that the proponents of unrestrained capitalism could see the children of Kibera or El Alto, of Merelani or Recife. They are all the same, begging for some coins or for some solutions, with a desperate look in their eyes. It is why I placed them all over the film, for people to look at them. It is also why I used at the end of the film, what we could call a cheap technical effect: I slowed down the little boy holding his hand out to all of the cars who drive by on a street in Cochabamba. I want people to really look at him and try to figure out what his life is or what he is thinking and feeling, having to beg every day of his life. Nothing moves me more in the film than this little boy begging in the street and the one we see immediately before that, who carries a bag of cans twice his size. We have to understand, as John Perkins says at the end of the film, that we will never have a sane world unless every child born in Ethiopia or in Bolivia can expect to have all of the basic necessities like water and food, shelter and health care. Is it too much to ask in a world with so much wealth? The answer is in our hands.

— *Philippe Diaz*
October, 2009

Filming in Bolivia

of

"The End of Poverty?"

Written and Directed by Philippe Diaz
Narrated by Martin Sheen

Narrator

In the world where there is so much wealth, with modern cities and plentiful resources, how can we still have so much poverty? Where so many people must live on less than one dollar per day. Where entire families live in one small room in squalid informal housing settlements, far away from skyscrapers and city centers, where they do not have the means to take care of themselves.

Amartya Sen *author/Nobel Prize, economics UK*

Hobbes's statement of life being nasty, brutish, and short is a characterization of poverty. There is no reason for us to take any different view than that. It is a question of understanding what it means in today's context, given the fact there are means of enhancing wealth, means of curing illnesses and postponing death, means of making our life comfortable. Given all that, if people still suffer from deprivation, well then in the present context, we have to regard that as poverty.

Luciana Vanderlei and Husband *Recife, Brazil*

Luciana: My husband has been unemployed for 5 years. Now to survive, he is selling bottles of mineral water in the streets for 1 *Real* each [$0.50].

Husband: I used to have a job delivering gas, but they started to cut the personnel and staff. Now, I am here making a living any way I can.

Luciana: In the past we did not live here. We lived by the beach. But because of an accident, my little girl passed away at only 9 months; we had to beg for money to bury her body. Since he has been unemployed life has been very hard. We look forward to the time when we are not struggling to bring food home. If you have children, you have to fight to feed them. When they are hungry, they have to eat.

Luciana and family live in a one-room basement without sanitation, and they sleep on the floor.

35

John Perkins *author/economist, USA*

At least 24,000 people die every single day from hunger and hunger related diseases, and that does not need to happen. We have plenty of resources so that should not happen. It happens because of the system we have created. We can say, without a doubt, that this system is an absolute failure. From the most rational, objective, economic standpoint, it is a failure. Less than 5% of the world's population live in United States. We are consuming over 25% of world's resources and creating roughly 30% of its major pollution. That is a failure

Narrator

Where do we have to look to understand how it all started? Where some started to become rich and others poor?

Eric Toussaint *author/President CADTM, Belgium*

I think there is a key date: 1492. This was the start of an extremely brutal intervention by the Europeans, on what is now known as the people of the Americas. From that point on we can talk of globalization, because during the 16th century, almost all of the continents are connected together by brutal European domination, which spread progressively to Asia and Africa.

Edgardo Lander *professor/historian, Venezuela*

The construction of this global colonial system took 500 years. The capitalist system and modern times started at the moment of the Conquest, the colonization and the submission of the people of the Americas by the Spanish and the Portuguese. At that moment, a very systematic and permanent process started, which took 500 years, one of expropriation of resources and at the same time, colonization of the land and people.

Narrator

The men who would be known as the conquistadors and the colonizers came from Spain and Portugal and later from the United Kingdom and Holland. They stole all the riches of the Incas and the Mayas—all the gold and silver, religious artifacts and jewels—and then started to confiscate the land, which destroyed the natural economy of the people. Such a practice had started long before in Europe, where the upper classes seized communal land from the poor families, thus depriving them of their livelihood.

H. W. O. Okoth-Ogendo *author/law professor, Kenya*

When the British came, towards the end of the 19th century, their concern was to justify expropriation of land which did not belong to them. The way they did it was to use their own legal system. They did this, precisely, through an advice that was given to the colonial government on the 13th of December, 1897, that said that, in countries where there is no settled form of government, the land belongs to the Queen of England. Having declared that there was no settled form of government, they appropriated ultimate title to the land. They passed laws that said so, and then they were able to give settlers freehold interests, 999 year leases and other forms of leasehold.

Miriam Campos *Ministry of Indigenous People, Bolivia*

A few families own large quantities of land which do not produce anything, and in the meantime the indigenous people cannot use their own land. The reason is that by law, each head of cattle is allowed between 5 and 50 hectares of land. For one head they can justify 50 hectares of land. These are unproductive lands that have been "engrossed." It is a case where someone can profit from the land without producing anything. These are *latifundios* [large land tenures]. Major *latifundios* come from colonial times and have been perpetuated by the system

Narrator

Land was confiscated and appropriated by the conquistadors and the colonizers throughout South America, Asia, and Africa, either by force or by imposing taxes on heads and huts that the people could not pay. Today, more than 500 years later and dozens of years after the independence of their countries, people still do not have their lands back, which are still in the hands of large landowners and transnational corporations.

Joseph Ole Kishan *Maasai Tribesman*

We are Maasai people and our livelihood depends on raising animals. Livestock like cows, goats, sheep. We do not know any other way of living. Even before the colonial power came and ruled Kenya, we were living on this land. The Maasai were forced out of the Kinango Valley, to the Rift Valley where we now live. But we came back because this land belongs to us. Upon independence, our land was given to powerful people in the government. Two kinds of British came to Kenya—the ones with guns to kill and steal the land, and the ones with a Bible to deceive.

In Kenya, at the end of colonial times, the white 1% owned about 50%
of the arable land.[1]

Mashengu wa Mwachofi *former parliamentarian, Kenya*

By becoming a British colony, you actually became a property, both the country and the people. And, if you look at history, the natives were not recognized as human beings. So, all of you are total property of the Empire. In the particular district I come from, the natives refused to work on those plantations. And if they did come to work, they would come on their own time. Sometimes, they would not come. So, that is why you introduce labor laws through the "*kipande* system." The *kipande* system is a system of registration, where every male, the moment you turn 16 you have to have a labor record, and that is the one that is used for ensuring that all male laborers would work, and that is why the colonial labor laws really were slave laws.

Miriam Campos *Ministry of Indigenous People, Bolivia*

In fact, now in the 21st century, we still have families that are captive. We call them "captive" or "retained" but in fact they are slaves. This is the real world. They are slaves, because they do not receive any pay for their work. They have debts that they transfer from generation to generation. They cannot even leave the farms because they are indebted to their bosses. And it is not only individuals but whole families. The children work. They do not go to school because they have to work. Work in exchange for what? Nothing, only food.

Narrator

Having had their natural economy destroyed forced the people to work for their new masters. It is estimated that today 60 to 80 million people still live in slave-like conditions all over the world. They work sometimes with their families in rural areas on plantations and in mines, as well as in cities in exchange for food and shelter.

Maria Luisa Mendonça *Rede Social President, Brazil*

Sao Paulo is the largest state that produces ethanol in Brazil and at the same time it is the richest state. And, just to give you an example, last year 17 workers died in the space where they work— they died of exhaustion. Another 419 workers have died in consequence of their work, in addition to several cases of slave labor in the sugar cane workers that the Ministry of Labor has registered.

Jaime de Amorim *Coordinator, Landless People Movement, Brazil*

The grower sees the worker as a slave. They have not rebelled, so today growers have a much easier way to accumulate wealth than during slavery. Back then, the boss was the slave's owner. He had to take care of the slave's health and food; he had to take care of shelter even if it was the slave's quarters. Today the boss has no such concerns. He just has to drive the truck to the outskirts of the city; the truck loads up, he takes them back. No more worries. Once the cutting is done, the worker, who lives on the outskirts, has to find another way of surviving, selling popsicles or popcorn. Kids go into prostitution, into drugs; they go find other alternatives in the world of crime.

Cane Cutters *Pernambuco State, Brazil (15:00*)*

Antonio: We were given a lot of promises before we came here. We would be given everything we need: bottles, boots—a complete set. But when we got here we did not find anything. We have to wake up at 1 a.m. without even a fire. There are only four fire burners for 80 people to cook with. We need to wake up at 1 a.m. to fix breakfast; if not, we do not have breakfast.

Edinaldo: The water we use has rust in it. We take a bath today, tomorrow we are sick.

Antonio: The equipment came bit by bit. The hat first, then came the boots and even now, some work barefoot because they did not get the equipment.

Edinaldo: I have been working here for four months. They took my work permit and did not return it to me. I talked to a lot of managers who kept lying to me, without returning my permit.

Antonio: By the time we get here it is 3:30 a.m.; some get here at 4:00 but usually we arrive from our sheds at 2:30 or 3.

Edinaldo: To get a daily wage, we need to cut 40 bundles, or 32 when the cane is as hard as this. If we do not do it, we do not get paid.

Antonio: We make 12 *Reais* and 34 cents per day [$6.50].

Edinaldo: They do not pay us well here. They pay us but rob us of half.

Antonio: What we eat is cornmeal, the meal of the poor; sometimes a cookie, when we bring one, buy one, and beans.

Edinaldo: I have 6 children. What I make here, if I eat it all, I go home with nothing.

Antonio: The problem is as follows: whoever gets land, gets a home.

---

* This time code has been inserted in the transcript every fifteen minutes (approximately) to allow readers to find segments on the DVD.

Because these days, the poor who do not have a place to live, are the poor that beg. Got it? These days the poor who have a place to live—a room to sleep in, without rent to pay—can be considered rich.

Edinaldo: Working like this is no way to make a living. That is why this world is infested with thieves. That is why we have killing unemployment.

Edinaldo has been a cutter for 17 years making an average of $27.50 per month.

William Easterly *author/professor, USA*

Colonialism had very negative consequences—lasting consequences—that we still see today in countries that are poor. And colonialism is one of the big reasons that poor countries are still poor. It left a legacy of violence, the most obvious example of which is the slave trade. Millions of Africans were captured, kidnapped, and taken across the ocean under horrific conditions to be slaves for the colonial powers

Michael Watts *author/professor, USA*

I think we have to start from what the prerequisites of capitalism are. Capitalism cannot operate without free labor. Labor is a key cost of production. So, to the extent that what we are talking about here is an expansionary capitalism, it will always be looking for those circumstances.

The gap between the richest and the poorest country was:[2]
3 to 1 in 1820
35 to 1 in 1950
74 to 1 in 1997

Narrator

The European empires were built on riches stolen from the colonies and on cheap or free labor provided by the slaves. The gold mines of Brazil and the silver mines of Bolivia, like Potosí, provided the European empires with the initial capital needed to start and finance their industrial revolutions. The fortunes created were so huge, that the hill of Potosí was soon represented as the Virgin Mary in religious art. The Pope himself gave Africa to the Portuguese crown and South America to the Spanish. But the Spanish empire was so indebted because of its holy war against Islam that these riches benefited its creditors in northern Europe instead.

Edgardo Lander *professor/historian, Venezuela*

The transfer of resources that happened at that time was mainly of gold and silver, but also of the so-called "precious vegetables." Above all

40

sugar cane was the main reason for the accumulation of wealth that took place in the Netherlands and the United Kingdom. Such extraordinary wealth became the starting point for the English colonial project.

Eric Toussaint *author/President CADTM, Belgium*

Holland was a country of one million people, in a very unfavorable area with no natural resources. The theory of the neoclassicists and of the neoliberals is that if an elected people, driven by Protestantism, in very adverse conditions, can become one of the planet's richest, it means that they have adopted an economic system superior to others. What we are not told is that the Dutch were barbaric in the way they exploited their Asian colonies, and that they took from Asia everything they could. It is on the trade of products they were importing from Asia that they accumulated fabulous wealth. That is why at some point Amsterdam became the world's financial center, before that status was transferred to London.

Narrator

In Bolivia, in the bowels of the richest mine in South America, the miners of Potosí have built a museum to honor the memory of their ancestors and their loss.

Pedro Montes Coria *Miner, Bolivia*

There was a law that was imposed back then which was terrible for us which was called *La Mita*. *La Mita* forced people to work inside the mine for 6 months, without going outside. Which means for 6 months they had to sleep and eat inside the mine without going outside. It is why so many people died working in the mines. There is a writer, Eduardo Galeano, who said that, with all the silver that was taken out of Potosí, that was taken out of this hill, it would have been possible to build a bridge from Potosí to Spain. So imagine how much silver came out of this mountain. He also said that another bridge could have been built from Potosí to Spain with the bones of the people who died in the mines. According to history it is more than 8 million people—more than 8 million died here. Since they did not have dynamite back then or much technology, manual labor was very important. That is why the Spaniards started to bring black slaves from Africa, to work in the mines. They had huge problems with the altitude, the cold, hard work, and malnutrition. So the Spaniards decided to move these black slaves to the plantations around La Paz, where they produced coca leaves and fruits like bananas and oranges, as well as rice and coffee.

From 1503 to 1660, Spain took enough silver from the New World to multiply European reserves by 4.[3]

Eric Toussaint *author/President CADTM, Belgium*

The Europeans, joined early by the North Americans—and later, during the 2nd half of the 19th century, by the Japanese, who themselves became an important colonial power that was very destructive in Asia during the 20th Century—together became during the 2nd part of the 19th century what we call the "Triad," meaning Occidental Europe, Japan and North America. They start to dictate to the rest of the planet the rules of the game and impose an economic model that is capitalism.

Alvaro Garcia Linera *Vice-President, Bolivia*

First we inserted ourselves in the world market and the expansion of capitalism across the entire planet, as countries that export their financial gain. Because of colonialism, the riches generated either by human effort or from natural resources are not retained in the country, but are exported, sent to the outside. Sadly, colonialism is always part of the expansion of capitalism.

Narrator

To maintain this level of wealth extraction, the conquerors needed to keep their colonies in a state of dependency. They assigned a function to each country or region as the producer of certain minerals or a certain crop like tea, coffee, cacao or sugar cane that could be exported back to the mother country. This imposed monoculture plunged these countries into a locked economy and into a state of total dependency. The survival of their people now depended on the good will of the motherland from which they had to import food. The consequences of that practice can still be seen 500 years later.

Nora Castañeda *Women's Bank President, Venezuela*

Independence did not bring economic liberation. We stopped being a Spanish colony to become a British one, and then a colony of the United States. During the entire 19th century, Venezuela continued to be an exporter of coffee and cacao. At the end of the 19th century, the second worldwide industrial revolution took place. It was known that oil existed in Venezuela because when the conquistadors arrived they saw the natives using oil as medicine and to repair their boats. Venezuela became much more important. We stopped being an agricultural country and became an oil-mining one.

Maria Luisa Mendonça Rede Social *President, Brazil*

Our government needs to stop thinking of Brazil as a colony. You know, the policies we have right now are the same as we had in the period of colonization. You know, over and over in history, the function of Brazil in the international economy was to produce cheap goods for the North. Before, at the beginning was sugar, now we are back to the sugar cane production, then it was coffee, then it was gold. You know, we are always producing cheap basic materials for the North.

Joao Pedro Stedile *Landless Movement Leader, Brazil*

It means that the natural resources from Brazil and in fact from every country—should be used to solve the problems of nutrition of their own people, given that in Brazil we have 50 million people starving every day. And we continue to import milk from Europe, rice from Thailand, and other staple food from Argentina, Uruguay and Chile. It is a shame for the poor people of Brazil.

Venezuelan Farmer *Vargas State, Venezuela*

I am the head of a family of 8, my wife, 5 children and 3 grandchildren. The girl needs medical attention very often. She needs a special school, and where we used to live, it became impossible, because my whole life I worked and lived in agriculture. We were able to get this little piece of land over here, and little by little, I struggled to build this little house, and we started to plant fruit trees around. I have been working in agriculture for 47 years. Of these 47 years, I have been persecuted for 40 of them, because, indeed, we were persecuted by the same people in the government who would send the guards and other groups from the government. I have a lot of neighbors and colleagues who work in agriculture and who were thrown in jail like criminals for up to 48 days, for just working the land. I am telling you, we used to have 600 families here, and now only 6 remain. [The government] wanted to get rid of everything that we grew here and replace it with imports.

> *In Latin America, the richest 1% of the population receives over 400 times as much income as the poorest 1%.[4]*

Narrator *(30:00)*

Having obtained natural resources and free labor, the Europeans now needed to create new markets for their own production. They separated agriculture from industry, thus preventing the farmers from making their own tools, clothes, and other utensils and transforming them into commodity

43

buyers. All existing industries were destroyed and the colonies were forced to buy manufactured goods and equipment from their colonial masters.

Eric Toussaint *author/President CADTM, Belgium*

The Dutch destroyed the Indonesian textile industry and built a textile industry in Holland. Same for ceramics. The textiles and ceramics that we are told are Dutch are in fact made with techniques they took from Indonesia, specifically from Java. They brought them back to Holland and built a wealthy industry.

Serge Latouche *author/professor, France*

Destruction of political structures, destruction of social structures and of know-how, as well. I am thinking of the destruction of Indian craftsmanship, and Marx's famous statement describing the Ganges Plains, "whitened by the Indian weavers' bones."

Eric Toussaint *author/President CADTM, Belgium*

It is very precise that in the 18th century the Indian textiles were of a much better quality than those of the British. The British destroyed the Indian textile industry and prevented merchants within the British Empire from importing fabrics and other manufactured products from the colonies. Therefore, everything was produced in London using Indian techniques and such textiles were imported from London and forced upon India. It is a case of exploitation, a case of plundering and of destruction of what existed there.

Serge Latouche *author/professor, France*

We destroyed the social structures and we also destroyed livelihoods. I spoke earlier of Indian weavers; it is clear that in India, if one looks at the appearance of famine, it corresponds with the destruction of craftsmanship structures, of peasants' land tenure and with land reforms imposed by the British.

Kipruto Arap Kirwa *Agriculture Minister, Kenya*

Those challenges are still there. Some of the [British] settlers, when they moved from this country in 1964-65, up to 1970, now, they benchmarked [reestablished] the operations in Europe, and, therefore, we became the producers of raw materials, and they were now the agents for marketing and processing. Therefore, all the value-addition of our crops was done away from Africa. Because, like roasting of coffee, just to pick that particular crop, is done away from Kenya. In fact, you are aware that Germany, which does not have a single bush of coffee, is the largest exporter of coffee. Tea is the same. The tea that you consume in Sudan, you take it first to Europe, then, Lipton brings it back to Sudan and a number of other countries in northern Africa, and a number of other countries.

Clifford Cobb *author/historian, USA*

One of the legacies of colonialism is that the poor countries of the Third World are continuing to export raw materials and the countries of Europe and North America produce and export finished products. This stems from a practice that was developed long ago, and the intention was to make sure that the countries of the Third World remain backward and remain dependent and are never able to develop. So to this day they are continuing to survive on the export of raw materials. That has always been to the disadvantage of the country exporting the raw materials, and it gets worse each year.

Since 1960, Third World countries have suffered a 70% drop in the price of agricultural exports compared to manufactured imports.[5]

Narrator

The main legacy of the colonizers was the change in mentality, religion and culture. They came with a Bible in one hand and a rifle in the other, preaching the exclusivity of salvation and imposing Christianity by force upon all, destroying every indigenous religious item they could find.

Eduardo Yssa *Cochabamba community leader, Bolivia*

Talking about colonialism, to remember this still hurts. From that point on, we forgot our culture, and our language, verbal and written. The Aymaras existed way before the Incas; we had a very different culture and even our own writing we called *Kipus*. And now, all has been lost. We do not have it anymore. It was stolen from us. And for what? For what purpose were we robbed? To make us submit to their whims and be their servants.

Serge Latouche *author/professor, France*

The most important consequence, going back to one of the forms of colonization which was the religious conversion, the work of missionaries, was mental colonization, the colonization of the mind: the imposition of a culture, a cultural imperialism, which led to the destruction of psychological frameworks, like the concept of time and space, which, in these societies, resulted in a loss of the sense of self.

Narrator

The conquistadors and the colonizers introduced the concept of superiority in terms of race and culture, in which the indigenous people were considered objects destined by God to slave for the white man. This created millions of marginalized people who still today have not recovered their place in society. During colonial times, no equality would be tolerated between the white man and the colored one, either in church or in state. Even today, while a mass is celebrated in the Cathedral of Sucre, the former Bolivian capital, the old indigenous people who dare to enter will sit on the ground. At the same time, in the next-door chapel built for the indigenous people, a local band tries to recapture their lost culture and traditions. The belief in a collective form of social organization was the indigenous people's best protection against a commodity economy, something for which they had no desire. They believed in communal property and public utility where the assets of the group were shared by all. This is precisely what the Europeans had to replace with the concept of individualistic interest, which drove the expansion of Europe.

Clifford Cobb *author/historian, USA*

A part of the purpose of Europeans in the early age of exploration was to take Christianity to people around the world. At the same time this was developing, a new form of Christianity was emerging that was very individualistic, and this was closely associated with an individualistic view of property. There had always been some element of private use, of individual families using property, but it was always tied to some communal affiliation. With the modern idea of private property, it meant that someone could use property without any obligation or any reciprocal relationship to community. You owned it, you could use it any way you wanted and you did not owe anyone anything. In a sense, this was a system of everyone for himself and you could say this is the beginning of capitalism. So during this period we have a marriage of a religious idea of individualism with the idea of individualism in owning private property.

Amartya Sen *author/Nobel Prize, Economics UK*

You may not be able abolish poverty and usher in the golden age by just saying, "Just eradicate private property, and everything will be all right." That will not work, and you have to recognize that it will not work. The temptation to go in that direction may have to be restrained by realism, but at the same time it is important to understand that those who are asking for that were not asking out of a fad. They had a real issue in mind, that inequality of property and ownership is a cause of inequality of divided fortunes in our lives.

The richest 1% of the world's population owns 32% of the wealth.[6]

Narrator

The accumulation of resources in the northern hemisphere created this huge imbalance, making the North extremely wealthy, allowing Europe to develop its industries and to create consumer societies, while people living in the South became destitute, only able to watch their natural economy being destroyed and replaced by a commodity economy.

Michael Watts *author/professor, USA*

The preconditions for capitalism, the labor and market and strategic resources, are all about the process of "primitive accumulation." You have to dispossess in differing ways to do all of those things. You can only get someone to work in a factory if they do not have access to land. That is a dispossession. Something can only become a market if it is taken out of a non-market context. Something has to be bought and sold. It can only be a strategic resource precisely if in fact you explore that resource. Primitive accumulation is not something that happens once. It happened in this way, under specific circumstances, in Brazil in the 16th century. But, primitive accumulation is recursive, it happens time and time again under different sorts of conditions. Of course, there is an enormous amount of hype about this, but the reality is of course, we are no less dependent on key strategic resources now than we were in 1890, and it is not just about oil, it is about a whole raft of key minerals and resources that are absolutely indispensable.

H.W.O. Okoth-Ogendo *author/law professor, Kenya*

The resources of the South are fundamental to development in the North and, therefore, the manner in which access and control of those resources are determined becomes crucial for the North. That is where the battle has always been. It has been there for over a century; it continues to be there, and particularly when it comes to subterranean resources. Just look around you. Why did the Angolan war take that long? Or the Congo? Why are not we interested in what is going on in Somalia? Because there is nothing to expropriate there—but there is something to expropriate in Sudan and the Congo, in Angola and in other places. So, the resource war will continue.

Brazilian Women *Coehlo Favela, Recife, Brazil (45:00)*

Josepha: I live in this shed, and I need 2000 *Reais* [$1,100] to pay it off. I am crippled in one leg. No lies. I am a hard-working lady. Nowadays, I live here, like this. God, wherever you are, help me. I need 2,000 to pay for this shed. Before I was sleeping in the street with my children. I am a hard worker, a fighter, and I cannot pay.

Leticia: For my husband to be able to buy her [the baby] milk, he has to work the whole day in the hot sun. Some days he goes without food. We spend 25 Reais a week [$14] to buy milk, diapers, medication and things for the house. Milk costs 5 *Reais* [$2.70], 5 for milk and 5 for dough.

Maria: There are a lot of people that do not get their daily bread at home. I am a tapioca maker; I do not look like one, but I am. When it is slow I sell as little as 10 or 7, or even 2. Sometimes I come back home without having sold anything. I sell the one with coconut for 1 *Real* [$0.55].

Vera: Our lives are always like this. We do not have real work, earn very little. And it will continue like this, God willing, and those in power, too.

Today more than one billion people live in the slums of the South.[7]

Eric Toussaint *author/President CADTM, Belgium*

From the end of WWII, we began to abolish empires. The US, which had very few colonies, looked with envy at those of the British, French and Japanese and supported their independence, thinking that afterward, they would be controlled in other ways. That is effectively what is going on today. These countries are politically independent; they have their own government; but they are within an institutional system which introduces a form of neocolonialism. Many policies which are forced upon indebted countries of the South are dictated from Washington by the World Bank and the International Monetary Fund.

David Ellerman *author/ former Economic Advisor, World Bank, USA*

This sort of world order that the West, and the United States and to some extent Western Europe, have tried to maintain, it is very postcolonial in the sense of you do not try to directly politically control these countries. But we want to integrate them into an international economic and political order, and so even the very definitions of development, the very definitions of local industry and so forth is all geared in a very natural way to the needs of the North and extracting resources, extracting cheap labor, not creating genuine foreign competition. So, if you are going to have cars produced in Africa, we will come do it for you there, and we will use your workers and so forth. And so, in that sense, it is very much a subtle form of an empire, but not an old style empire. Anybody with a broad historical perspective is not surprised.

Narrator

When the countries of the South won their independence, the accumulated debts of the colonial powers used to open new markets were transferred to the newly formed governments in total violation of international laws. The only solution offered by the North was more debt with extremely high interest in order to repay the initial one. These newly formed states immediately lost their sovereignty, and became even more dependent upon the northern countries, which could then dictate policies on agriculture, trade, and customs, and give special privileges to foreign corporations, such as monopolies over mineral extraction or monoculture exploitation.

Eric Toussaint *author/President CADTM, Belgium*

From the beginning the independent states were born with a debt which allowed the World Bank to tell them: "You owe us, so you will have to follow our advice, and we will tell you how to develop." Now we are in the 1960's and the World Bank tells them: "Take more loans, to build large infrastructures to export your natural resources." McNamara, who became President of the World Bank in 1968, pushed the concept of fighting poverty. But at the same time enormous projects had to be supported, like the Inga Dam on Lower Congo—gigantic energy projects which increased the Third World debt.

John Perkins *author/economist, USA*

We will identify a country, usually a developing country that has resources we covet—our corporations covet—like oil. And then, we arrange a huge loan to that country from the World Bank or one of its sister organizations. Now, almost everybody in our country believes that that loan is going to help poor people. It is not. Most of the money never goes to the country, in fact, it goes to our own corporations, it goes to the Bechtels and the Halliburtons, and the ones we all hear about, usually led by engineering firms, but a lot of other companies are brought in and they make fortunes off building big infrastructure projects in that country. Power plants, industrial parks, ports, those types of things. The country is left holding this huge debt that it cannot possibly repay. So, at some point, we economic hitmen go back in and we say, "You know, you cannot pay your debts. You owe us a pound of flesh. You owe us a big favor. So, sell your oil real cheap to our oil companies, or vote with us on the next critical United Nations vote, or send troops in support of ours someplace in the world."

Susan George *author/ Transnational Institute Chair, France*

Let me give you just one statistic (which I worked out in minutes) because otherwise it is incomprehensible. Sub-Saharan Africa, which is the poorest part of the world, is paying $25,000 every minute to northern creditors. Well, you could build a lot of schools, a lot of hospitals, a lot of jobs— you could make a lot of job creation if you were using $25,000 a minute differently from debt repayment. So there is this drain, and I think people do not understand that it is actually the South that is financing the North. If you look at the flows of money from North to South, and then from South to North, what you find is that the South is financing the North to the tune of about $200 billion every year.

Raul Monjon Ramirez *Planning Ministry Director, Bolivia*

The only entity that can receive a loan from international organizations is the Bolivian state: the state. But when the state takes a loan, which will be well or badly utilized, it is not the government who has to pay it back, but the Bolivian people, the taxpayers. At a certain point, every child being born is already carrying a big part of the debt. Imagine for a country like ours with an accumulated debt of 7 billion dollars and with a population of 8 million. Make the calculation. It almost coincides with the gross domestic product.

Clifford Cobb *author/historian, USA*

By analyzing poverty into those three elements [trade, debt, and monopoly power over resources], I think we can also begin to understand why poverty is so much more extreme in Third World countries in the South than it is in First World countries in the North. In the North, poverty exists largely because the resources are owned by a small elite of individuals and corporations. In the South, the same is true: the resource division is equally skewed towards a small elite, but the South also faces the continuing problem of unbalanced trade and the problem of debt. Poverty exists in every country in the world, there is no denying that, but the poverty is much more extreme in the countries that are dealing with this triple problem of trade, debt, and monopoly power over resources.

The developing world spends $13 on debt repayment for every $1 it receives in grants.[8]

Narrator

By the beginning of the 20th century, the entire Third World had been split up among the powers of the North. The two world wars forced the North to create new tools to stabilize the new global economy. The IMF and the World Bank were created with such an agenda but rapidly they turned their focus toward the Third World where new leaders, trying to bring economic independence to their countries, had emerged. The reaction was swift and used all the tools available to bring these countries back to their previous role, like the loans of the World Bank and the structural adjustment programs of the IMF. These would later lead to the crisis in Latin America, Asia and Russia and plunge millions below the poverty line. This new US-born economic model became known as neo-liberalism and the set of policies used to enforce it became the Washington Consensus, which forced all economies to let the market govern everything

Edgardo Lander *professor/historian, Venezuela*

Neo-liberalism is a project which aims to profoundly transform these societies. Neo-liberalism in Latin America means a restructuring of the manufacturing sector; means a reduction in goods on the national market; means a profound process of deindustrialization. It reintegrates Latin American economies and returns Latin America to basic production. This form of reintegration is characteristic of classical imperialism in need of natural resources.

Joseph Stiglitz *Former World Bank Vice-President/Nobel Prize, Economics, USA*

The Washington Consensus was a set of policies that was a consensus between Fifteenth Street in Washington and Nineteenth Street. Fifteenth Street is where US Treasury is, Eighteenth is where the World Bank is. Nineteenth is where the IMF is. It was not a consensus among the developing countries. It was a consensus among a relatively small group of people who had a particular mindset, and a particular mindset during the period, you have to remember, that Reagan was President of the United States, Thatcher was leader in the UK, a very conservative mindset that did not reflect good economic policy, economic theory, as I would understand good economic theory. It had a particular political view of economics.

John Christensen *Director, Tax Justice Network, UK*

The Washington Consensus had four key strands. First of all, capital account liberalization, secondly, trade liberalization, thirdly, reduce your taxes, stimulate growth, follow the Laffer curve, a bit like following the yellow brick road—it led nowhere at all but tax revenues went south for most developing countries, particularly in Africa. The fourth strand of the Washington Consensus was sell off your state's assets, and in most cases they were sold off so badly and the fees that were paid to World Bank consultants and all of the Western consultants involved were so astronomical that the end prices that many developing countries got for themselves were minimal.

Susan George *author/Transnational Institute Chair, France*

All of the public companies, whether they had to do with investing in agriculture, or whether they were public telephone companies, or public whatever, roads companies, or all of that, or nearly all, has had to be privatized. So there again you get an opportunity for private companies to extract wealth. The World Bank used to publish, maybe it still does, but all through the 1980s and the early 1990s, every year it published, in microscopic print, long lists of companies that had been privatized in its member countries, under structural adjustment programs. And, every year I counted them approximately, it was sort of 1,300 to 1,500 companies a year. They were sometimes bought by local elites. They were often, particularly the larger ones, bought by our own transnational corporations.

Jim Shultz *President, The Democracy Center, Cochabamba, Bolivia*

Bolivia became the lab rat. Bolivia was absolutely the chief test lab in South America for these policies of privatization, market fundamentalism, the things that led to the water revolt, that led to all of these issues here in Bolivia. And, that is really the trajectory of how Bolivia got here historically.

Abel Mamani *Water Minister, Bolivia*

In the case of railroads they have practically disappeared since they were privatized. In the east we do not have trains anymore. They have been entirely dismantled. Last month, if I am not mistaken, workers went seven months, seven months without wages. The country has been destroyed, and that is the consequence of privatization.

Oscar Olivera *former worker/Water Defense Coordinator, Bolivia*

The Bolivian government, following a decision and an order from the World Bank, decided to privatize the water and to do so, started the following. First: they passed a law concerning drinkable water, and gave a 40-year concession to the international corporation, Bechtel.

Marcela Olivera *April foundation/Water Defense Coordinator, Bolivia (1:00:00)*

It was not the last thing to privatize here because the government before already privatized everything—railroads, airlines, telecommunications—so water was the last frontier to cross.

Pablo Fernandez *Bolivian Farmer*

Currently, I earn 35.50 per day [$4.50]. We are paid daily, each day that we work. So if I have to pay 60 *Bolivianos* [$7.50] for water only, I cannot make it. That leaves nothing to buy food or clothes for my family.

Marcela Olivera *April foundation/Water Defense Coordinator, Bolivia*

Some parts of the law said that all the water sources suddenly will not belong to the communities, or to the people, or neighborhoods. They will belong to the water company now. Suddenly, these things that were common, were not common anymore.

Jim Shultz *President, The Democracy Center, Cochabamba, Bolivia*

They came here and within a month of taking over, they raised people's water rates by an average of 50%, and in some cases double and more. People took to the streets, and said they would not take it, and faced down bullets, faced down a state of martial law.

Pablo Fernandez *Bolivian Farmer*

It did not affect only the water cooperatives and water-wells, but rainwater was included in that as well. It is why we called all the people to join. We called them through speakers and megaphones that we were able to get and also with these *potutus** that we have. *Potutus* always draw the most attention, because the majority of people are farmers, and in the country we only use *potutus*, no speakers and so on.

Oscar Olivera *former worker/Water Defense Coordinator, Bolivia*

The water war started within the rural population. It came as a result of the aggression of international capital and of the World Bank and of our neo-liberal governments toward the collective heritage of the people. It also came from the fact that this privatization is an aberration from our conception and specifically from the conception of the indigenous and farming communities that water is the blood of *Pachamama* [Mother Earth].

---

* A trumpet made of conch shell or clay.

Pablo Fernandez *Bolivian Farmer*

This war has left many memories for us because in reality there were deaths and injuries in those moments. The people were furious—it was live or die. One or the other. For me, it was not leaving my children like this, and their children as well, because we all live from water.

> *Almost a third of the world's population has no access to affordable clean water.*[9]

Joseph Stiglitz *Former World Bank Vice-President/Nobel Prize, Economics, USA*

Now, what was particularly flawed about a lot of these "theories" was they did not lead to economic growth, and that suggests, both to some extent flawed economics, but also an important role for interest. Take the most dramatic example of this, capital market liberalization—opening up capital markets, the free flow of short-term capital. You cannot build a factory on the basis of money that can come in and out of a country overnight. The IMF tried to change its charter in September of 1997 to force countries to liberalize, to open up their capital markets. At the time they did it, they had no evidence that it would promote economic growth and there was ample evidence, both in the World Bank and elsewhere, that it led to more instability. Any yet, they pursued it. In my interpretation, it is because Wall Street wanted it.

John Christensen *Director, Tax Justice Network, UK*

The IMF and the World Bank, by liberalizing capital flows, opened up a wholly new criminal environment where capital could be shifted into tax havens around the world and evade tax. And this has happened on a truly astonishing scale. To give an idea of the size of this movement, the most recent estimate of the volume of capital now held offshore by rich individuals is 11.5 trillion US dollars, a stunningly large figure. And for those people who want to tackle poverty, this raises intriguing questions because if we were able to tax that capital at even a very modest rate, at 30% on the income, we would be able to raise at least $255 billion a year of extra tax revenue around the world, which could be used for all sorts of brilliant purposes but would more than pay for the Millennium Development Goal program of tackling poverty.

Eric Toussaint *author/President CADTM, Belgium*

The World Bank and the IMF demand an increase in taxes, paid mainly by the poor; demand that the poor pay to receive an education, to receive health care. The result is a privatization of the health and education system; the result is that in many African countries, someone arrives at a hospital in need of urgent care, and he stays in a waiting room until the family raises enough money for proper treatment. One out of three people dies without having been treated.

Eric Mgendi *Communications Coordinator, Action Aid, Kenya*

The health system, where people used to get drugs free of charge, now they have to go and pay. Even where I come from, myself, I see people who are not able to go to hospital. They die of simple things like malaria, because they cannot afford to pay the small fee that is required to run the hospitals. This used to be run by the government, but the World Bank insisted that the wait bill is too high, and that the government has to reduce its expenditure, and reducing expenditure meant ignoring a majority of the people. And that is what happened that many people in Kenya do not have access to health facilities and do not have access to education.

Joseph Odhiambo *Kibera, Nairobi, Kenya*

We are three children. I am Joseph. This is my sister, she is Helen, but she is disabled, and my other brother, he is called Jos, and he is also disabled. So, among the three of us, I am the only person who, at least, can do something. I am not at school because I am supposed to pay 4,000 [$64] for the exam fees, and 10,000 [$160] for the school fees, and my mom is earning 3,000 [$48], so I am still at home, I cannot get the money. I can say life in the slum is very hard. OK, sometimes, we do go without even eating supper, now. The small bit that we have, we do share among ourselves. Some people are eating 3 meals per day, and you can just have 1 meal a day. And, also, when you go to school you have different types of people, and also, there is some discrimination there because you are not the same class as the other students. I do feel discriminated because you can find the things which they have, compared to what you have, they just laugh at you, because you are just a slum dweller. Let us say, when someone is sick, even going to the hospital, it is very hard, then, to buy the medicine. So, maybe, just stay at home and take some tablets from the shop for 100 shillings [$1.50] and you cannot afford to go to the hospital.

Joseph and his family live in a 15 square foot shack that costs one third of his mother's wages.

Clifford Cobb *author/historian, USA*

There is a great irony today that the developed countries of the world are talking about free trade as if that is the solution to the problem of poverty in the world. Much of the history of the last couple of centuries has been an effort of countries to become economically independent through tariffs, to be able to develop manufactured goods. The economies of East Asia most recently developed, in large part because of the ability to—or East Asia I should say—developed in large part because they developed behind tariffs and then, once they developed to a point where they were able to enter the world economy on the same footing as everyone else, then they removed the tariffs. Now, the United States and European powers prevented Third World countries from doing that, and in fact are imposing tariffs to prevent the import of the finished goods from Third World countries, and in fact are not practicing free trade. It is all a way of keeping the Third World countries in their place and preventing them from ever developing.

> *In 1970, 434 million people were suffering from malnutrition. Today, there are 854 million.[10]*

Joseph Stiglitz *Former World Bank Vice-President/Nobel Prize, Economics, USA*

In some countries rapid liberalization of trade has meant that corn farmers have to compete with heavily subsidized corn. Their income goes down, up to 50%, as a result of that competition. Sugar, each of the commodities we can talk about, the liberalization of the market, opening the markets to highly subsidized agriculture drives down the price and forces these farmers out of business. Or, if they stay in business, leads them to have much lower income. Another example is intellectual property. The intellectual property regime has made access to lifesaving drugs much more difficult for the poor countries. It was essentially signing a death warrant on thousands of people.

Kenyan Farmers *Kisumu Region, Kenya*

John Ayila: These people you see over here, they are pastoralists and agriculturalists. It is livestock farming that they depend on. They cultivate maize. Now, all this is gone. Now, come the year 2003, they told us that government is coming to invest here. Instead of seeing government, we saw a very unique company. This is a company from USA, Edmond, Oklahoma, USA. The company is called Dominion Group of Companies. This company is investing here. It is in collaboration with Kenya government to invest here.

Jennifer Akeiyo Chieng: When Dominion arrived here, they did not ask us anything. Their workers came onto our homesteads, making surveys, even clearing our land. Dominion started to build a dam. It overflowed and flooded all of our homes, and also our prime lands, the ones we use for agriculture.

56

Lilian Atieno: I was thrown out of my land by Dominion when they blocked the Yala River's flow which flooded everything. My home was submerged and I had to leave and go build another one.

Dalmas Ogoma: We had maize here and other crops; the water took everything away. Normally, we have beautiful crops. But now everything is rotten.

John Ayila: This company is doing aerial spraying. Now, the airplane makes a u-turn, right across our homes. And this aerial spraying is done especially when people are working; it is done twice a week. That has affected us very much. And when you go to nearby public health centers, quite a number of children have been reported dead.

Lilian Atieno: I feel very bad because I got a malaria attack because of all the mosquitoes we have now. We even have cases of typhoid and many of diarrhea. Even all my livestock died because of the flooding. I have lost all hope now.

John Ayila: And it is quite unfortunate that what he [Dominion] produces there, the legumes that he produces there, are not sold to us. They are ferried to America. They are taken back to America. So, we, the local people, the land is ours, we gain nothing from that land. It is the American government gaining, and maybe some corrupt government officials. So, we are now subjected to a life of servitude in our own ancestral land. We do not feel like moving away from this land. This is our ancestral land, and, whatsoever, we will not move out of this land.

Narrator *(1:15:00)*

Neo-liberalism managed to bankrupt many of the economies of the South, which allowed international capital to take over. This was achieved by imposing a new form of structural violence that was used for decades to maintain these countries in a state of under-development. Such violence was implemented by the dictators of the South and their repressive apparatus, which finally brought social unrest that was unkind to the free market economies. The special agents and economic hit men were born and became the new less-visible means to maintain such control over the globe's resources.

John Perkins *author/economist, USA*

If we do not like what a democratically elected leader of another country is doing—for example, opposing the exploitation of oil in his country, someone who looks like me will walk into that President's office—I had the job at one time—walks into the office and says, "And now, I just want to remind you that I can make you and your family very rich if you play my game, our game. Or, I can see to it that you are thrown out of office or assassinated if you decide to fulfill your campaign promises." Usually it is said a little more subtly than that because there may be a tape recorder listening, but they get the message, because every one of those presidents knows what happened to Arbenz of Guatemala, and Allende of Chile, and Roldos of Ecuador, and Lumumba of the Congo, and Torrijos, and on and on. The list is very long of presidents that we have had thrown out or assassinated. There is no question about that. And they all know this. So, we perpetuate the system that way. Here, you offer from this hand, from this pocket, you offer a few hundred million dollars of corruption, or from this pocket you offer subversives, jackals, to go in and overthrow the government or assassinate the president. And this has happened time, and time, and time again. Usually, the economic hit men are successful, so we do not need to send in the jackals, but on those occasions when we are not successful, as for me I was, I failed with Omar Torrijos in Panama and Jaime Roldos in Ecuador, and so the jackals were sent in and assassinated these men.

Chalmers Johnson *Author/former CIA analyst, USA*

It is fact. The CIA was the private army of the President, being used for highly dubious, virtually invariably disastrous interventions in other people's countries, starting with the overthrow of the Iranian government in 1953 for the sake of the British Petroleum Company. We declared that the elected Prime Minister of Iran, Mohammed Mosaddeq, was a communist— the Pope would have been a better candidate. That is to say, he was simply trying to regain some control over Iranian oil assets. The British wanted him out and talked Eisenhower into doing the dirty work.

John Perkins *author/economist, USA*

We did the same thing in Iraq under Qasim who was a very popular President of Iraq and decided that he wanted to get more of the profits from Iraqi oil to go to the Iraqi people, not to the foreign companies. So, we decided he had to go, he had to be assassinated. We send in an assassination team in the early 1960s, it was headed by a young man at the time who failed and got wounded in the process and had to flee the country. That was Saddam Hussein. He was our hired assassin; he failed. So, the CIA went in directly and had Qasim publicly executed on Iraqi television and put Saddam's family in power.

*Cutting global poverty in half would cost $20 billion, less than 4%
of the U.S. military budget.[11]*

Chalmers Johnson *author/former CIA analyst, USA*

There is no question that over the years the government has used its imperial apparatus for economic purposes for the advantage of American firms. Perhaps the best examples are the United Fruit Company in Central America. After the overthrow of the government of Guatemala in 1954 by brutal, very brutal means against a small and defenseless country, over the years, leading to civil war and police repression, at least 200,000 Guatemalan civilians have lost their lives. All this was done because the United Fruit Company objected to some rather modest proposals for land reform. You can carry it on to the CIA's intervention against Allende in order to bring to power probably the most odious military dictator in the Cold War period, General Pinochet. Here the interests were primarily of IT&T Company, they participated closely—that is International Telephone and Telegraph—participated closely with the CIA, financing and funding and plotting the coup against Salvador Allende. Also, equally in Chile, the mining interests of the big copper firms. American imperial power has long been used in Latin America in order to protect the interests of extractive industries, in very poor countries such as Bolivia, and places of that sort.

John Perkins *author/economist, USA*

In a very few instances, when neither the economic hit men nor the jackals are successful, then and only then do we send in the military. And this is what happened in Iraq. We, the economic hit men, were unable to bring Saddam Hussein around, the jackals were unable to take him out—he had very loyal guards and he had look alike doubles—so it was difficult to take him out. So, we sent in the military.

Michael Watts *author/professor, USA*

Iraq represents an instance of what I have called military neo-liberalism. It represents an attempt now, to push forward the American neo-liberal project, previously attempted to be secured through hegemonic consensual means, militarily. It is as if the United States is using classic late 19th century gun-boat diplomacy to break down the doors of markets, to push forward its agenda. So, that is how I see it. Not that it is about oil at all, but this is not in any simple sense about getting that black stuff.

Narrator

For decades, poverty reduction and development programs have failed to confront the different forms of power and the structural violence that hold more than two-thirds of the world in dire straits. Our chosen economic model has created a global situation in which today less than 25% of the world's population uses more than 80% of the planet's resources while creating 70% of its pollution.

Nimrod Arackha *Tanzanian Mine Workers Development Organization*

Before the big corporations amassed the huge chunk of lands that they have there, coming up with the minerals was not that hard, mining was not that difficult. The big corporations, they were given the most productive areas to mine on. So, had it not been for them coming there, then people would still be mining there and the situation, I believe, would have been different right now.

Godfrey Ngao and Aguano Nelson *Tanzanian Miners*

Godfrey Ngao: I started here in 1998. Then, I got sick, my wife got sick and died. At the beginning, I had 20 people working for me. Because I have no money to nourish them, to feed them, they went to other mines.

Aguano Nelson: The multinationals prevent us from surviving. They are hugely mechanized and have a capacity we do not have. They were given huge pieces of highly productive land by the government while we were left with only unproductive land. On top of that, here the veins interconnect underground, so when a small miner happens to work on the same vein as the big company, he'll be shot.

Nimrod Arackha *Tanzanian Mine Workers Development Organization*

When the World Bank and the IMF were really putting pressures on developing nations, they were coming with conditions: "You need to do this. You need to do this so that we can give you aid. You have to allow investors to come in and help you people to create jobs." And that is actually not giving jobs to the locals, so that is where the problem is.

Godfrey Ngao *Tanzanian Miner*

What they're trying to do is to demoralize us, to eradicate us totally from the mining sector.

Nimrod Arackha *Tanzanian Mine Workers Development Organization*

The mining fields that they are holding right now belong to the locals. So, once you take something from somebody, then you leave him with nothing.

People have been left. People are being impoverished here, severely, by the coming of the big companies here. A lot of money has been siphoned out of the country as a result of this trade. So, that money that would have been otherwise used for the locals here is being siphoned into some foreign countries.

> In Africa, in the 1990s the number of people living on less than $1 a day rose from 273 million to 328 million.[12]

Miloon Kothari *United Nations Rapporteur, India*

What I find very disturbing in all this is that there is an implicit assumption, although it is not always mentioned, that the kind of development that is taking place is going to lead to the sacrifice of some people. So, there is a very dangerous kind of an assumption and we see it actually happening on the ground that many people will have to suffer. Many people will have to be forced into homelessness, to landlessness, some will have to die, because we are following a particular economic model. We will get to those people when we will get to them. So I think the old concepts of "trickle down theory," the old concepts of growth for the sake of growth, are all very much alive. This is very disturbing because we have evidence from around the world, whether you look at Latin America or Africa or Asia, that these policies have not worked.

Clifford Cobb *author/historian, USA*

How is it possible to explain the paradox of poverty? How is it that in countries in which there is growing wealth there are actually more poor people than there were before? In short, how is it that we can explain why "trickle down economics" does not work, why doesn't wealth trickle down from the rich to the poor? There are a fixed amount of natural resources in the world and those who own the resources—land, air, water, and so on—are able to charge higher and higher prices for them as an economy develops. In order to understand that, I think it would be useful to consider a fictitious example of what would happen if we lived in a society in which there was only one oasis that had all the water, to which everyone had to come for their water supply. If a single person owned that water supply, that oasis, we would all be forced to pay as much money as we were able to for that water. Now, further imagine that if you lived in that society and you were having to pay huge amounts for some resource that could in fact be owned by all, because it came from nature, and there is no particular reason for one person to own it. After a while, or perhaps even in short order, you would begin to feel intense resentment and you would begin discussing among your fellows, "What should we do about this?" And you can imagine that there would, in fact, be an eruption of violence as people began to try to fix, to overthrow the people who owned that resource and take it.

John Perkins *author/economist, USA*

You take away their resources so you can have it, so what do they get left? And as time goes on and that resource no longer is valuable. Gold—nobody really cares that much about gold these days, which is what the conquistadors were after. But today, those same countries, a lot of them have oil. And so, we took away all their gold, we destroyed their cultures, and now we are saying, "and now oil is the big one, and we are going to take that, too." Or gas, or whatever. Or water, whatever. You perpetuate this terrible system of poverty and this system of desperation and anger.

Jerome Guillet *investment banker, energy sector, France*

Terrorism is directly linked to our policies with resources. In a number of these countries the governments are authoritarian or dictators and they are supported by the West because we think that this is the way to protect our access to their resources. For the population, they have associated "dictator" and "the West."

Joshua Farley *Professor Ecological Economics, USA (1:30:00)*

It is very interesting that if you look at the societies with the least equal distribution of income, they tend to be the most violent. There is a very small correlation between absolute poverty and crime. There is a strong correlation between unequal income distribution and crime. So, you look at the poorer societies they are not at all the ones that are the most violent, it is the ones that have the biggest discrepancy in incomes that are the most violent.

> *Of the one billion living on less than $1 a day, 162 million live on less than 50 cents a day.*[13]

Rosa Angela Graterol *La Vega Barrio, Caracas, Venezuela*

Two of my sons were killed in this barrio. One was killed on Friday, eight days ago. I am really in pain now. That is just the start. I have been living in this barrio for so long, raising my children on my own, washing, ironing and cooking empanadas for others, everything I can do for my kids so they can go to school. The one they killed had just graduated from college. My son. They took him from me on Friday, this past Friday. That one was my hope for the future, to leave this place. He was going to take me out of here. Do you understand? He did not live with me, we lived apart, but he always helped me, he would never fail me. I have always been sick and gone through life hungry, so that my kids would always be able to study. I always wanted my kids to study.

Clifford Cobb *author/historian, USA*

Poverty in the world cannot possibly be eliminated, unless the poor themselves say, "We insist on justice not charity." One example of that justice is forgiving international debt. The second element would be to change the tax system in every country of the world. Right now most taxes fall on the poor in the form of consumption taxes and taxes on wages. If justice is to be done, most of the taxes should fall on property ownership and not on wages, not on people. Third, the poor should demand agrarian reform, land reform, restoring land to the people who actually work on it, instead of a few landowners. A fourth thing is to end privatization of natural resources. We have seen in Bolivia what is possible, where the Bolivian people actually took back the water that had been given to Bechtel and they forced Bechtel out of the country. Now the Bolivian people once more own that water.

Edgardo Lander *professor/historian, Venezuela*

What is presented as a possible future for the southern countries is a fiction. And this fiction prevents people from accepting that the appropriation of resources by the part of the planet which utilizes these resources in excess of its share makes it impossible for the living conditions of the majority to reach a level of dignity.

Jerome Guillet *investment banker, energy sector, France*

As long as you can dump it, as long as you can kill Iraqis rather than increase the price of gas, and as long as you only get Bangladeshis or poor people in New Orleans to pay the price instead of you having to drive less and take the metro, or the bus or walk. Our society is geared toward this choice. The poor people and the helpless people and the unlucky to be in the places that it would be on the front line will pay that price first. Famines are effective market solutions. They reduce demand. So if we leave it to the markets, that is what we have. If there is not enough food, then some people die and that reduces demand and the market is balanced. It is an effective market solution. So if we want to avoid such radical solutions we need to find ways to redistribute and share what we have and get those that use a lot more to start using less so that there is still enough for everybody.

Clifford Cobb *author/historian, USA*

The resources of nature are given to all of us and yet a handful of people and corporations have control of them, oil companies being a prime example that everyone is familiar with. If we could enable everyone to benefit from those resources we could end poverty, and the way to do that is by restoring the idea of the commons. It means that the value that is currently gotten from those resources, that is currently being privatized, in the hands of the corporate share holders of oil companies or other mining companies or real estate syndicates, and so on—instead of it being privatized, it would be made available, be shared by all. That is basically what the commons means.

Kenyan Tea Pluckers *Great Rift Valley, Kenya*

Joseph Mugo: I am a father of 5, and in fact, we live in poverty, but we do not know how to get out of it.

Grace Wambi: I have got 6 children, 3 are boys and 3 are girls. I am working so hard, so that they do not go to bed without food.

Joseph Mugo: You can make between 3,000 [$48] and 5,000 [$80] for two weeks, depending on your energy.

Joseph Momanyi: Nowadays in Kenya when a person works a job plucking tea, he is only working a few months per year. Per year, he is getting 3 or 4 months of work at best.

Grace Wambi: When there is no rain, there is not enough food. So you must go to the shopkeeper and borrow there until the rain comes. That is why we are so behind, that when the rain comes, you must pay back that money fast, so that you can buy something to eat.

Joseph Mugo: Sometimes we do get hungry.

Grace Wambi: Our stomachs are very small, because we do not have food every day. So our stomachs are very small.

Joseph Mugo: It is now about 20 years that I have been suffering.

Grace and her co-workers labor an average of five months per year, for $100 per month.

Narrator

Our chosen economic system always was and still is financed by the poor. They did so first by giving up their land and their access to natural resources, then by financing its expansion through debt repayment, unfair trade, and unjust taxes on their labor and consumption. In addition, by forcing the poor to overpay for energy, food, and other basic necessities, the north ensures that poverty will deepen and inequalities will increase.

Rising food prices could plunge an additional 100 million people into extreme poverty.[14]

Serge Latouche *author/professor, France*

It is about exiting growth as much as underdevelopment. Of course, our "de-growth" in the sense of the reduction of our lifestyle's demands on ecosystems is a prerequisite for the underdeveloped to have an increased share. Currently, if everybody was living like the Americans we would need 6 planets. But if everybody was living like people in Burkina Faso, then one-tenth of the planet would be enough. For the Burkinabe to be able to legitimately consume a sustainable ecological share, we would have to consume less. On average, we are already consuming 30% more than what the biosphere can regenerate. Therefore, our "de-growth" is a prerequisite for them to resolve their own problems and give them a larger share of life.

Alvaro Garcia Linera *Vice-President, Bolivia*

Either we are all emancipated or none of us is. The ones who think things are fine because they have plenty of hot food and water in their house and think they have "made it" are wrong. It is only temporary and uncertain. When a lot of people do not have water to drink, one's stability is fragile. The stability of each person in your country or mine can only guarantee their continued well-being if the others' well-being is guaranteed also.

Serge Latouche *author/professor, France*

In fact, "de-growth" is mainly a reduction: reduction of ecological footprints; reduction of toxic-dependency; therefore reduction of work; rediscovery of other aspects of life; reduction of waste, reduction of trash. If we wanted to be rigorous, we should talk about "a-growth", like we talk about "a-theism," because that is what it is—exiting the religion of growth, of economy, and re-thinking a social organization. I say often "de-growth" is not one alternative, it is a matrix of alternatives. It is exiting economic totalitarianism to re-open the way to multiple histories in which each human group, each society, would define its own civilization, its own culture, its own values, reappropriating or reinventing them.

John Perkins *author/economist, USA (1:40:00)*

I know that my daughter, who is 24, and her children are not going to have a stable, sustainable, and sane world unless every child born in Ethiopia and Indonesia and Bolivia also has that expectation. This is a very small community.

16,000 children die each day from hunger or hunger-related diseases.[15]

Endnotes

1. Paul Maurice Syagga. "Land Ownership and Use in Kenya: Policy Prescriptions from an Inequality Perspective." In *Readings on Inequality in Kenya: Sectoral Dynamics and Perspectives.* Nairobi: Society for International Development, Eastern Africa Regional Office, 2006, Chapter 8: 293, 295. http://www.hackenya.org/index. php?option=com_docman&task=doc_details&gid=5706&Itemid=383

2. United Nations Development Program. *1999 Human Development Report.* http://hdr.undp.org/en/reports/global/hdr1999/

3. Earl J. Hamilton, "Imports of American Gold and Silver Into Spain, 1503-1660," *Quarterly Journal of Economics*, Vol. 43, No. 3, May 1929, p. 468.

4. Terry Lynn Karl. The Vicious Cycle of Inequality in Latin America. "In 1970, the richest 1 percent of the population earned 363 times more than the poorest 1 percent; by 1995, this had risen to a whopping 417 times." http://democracy.stanford.edu/Seminar/KarlInequality.htm

5. Food and Agricultural Organization. *The State of Agricultural Commodity Markets, 2004.* http://www.fao.org/docrep/007/y5419e/y5419e02. htm: "Between 1961 and 2001, the average prices of agricultural commodities sold by the least developed countries fell by almost 70 percent relative to the price of manufactured goods purchased from developed countries."

6. UNU-WIDER, *Estimating the Level and Distribution of Global Household Wealth.* Table 8, p. 28. http://www.wider.unu.edu/publications/working-papers/research-papers/2007/en_GB/rp2007-77/

7. *Millennium Development Goals Report 2007* http://www.un.org/millenniumgoals/pdf/mdg2007. pdf

8. World Bank, *Global Development Finance 2002: Financing the Poorest Countries,* p. 22.

9. Population Reference Bureau. http://www.prb.org/pdf05/05WorldDataSheet_Eng.pdf

10. Food and Agriculture Organization, *The State of Food Insecurity in the World* 2004 and 2006. cited at http://www.globalincome.org/English/Facts. html.

11. For $20 billion estimate: *Technical Report of the High-Level Panel on Financing for Development.* http://www.un.org/reports/financing/report_full. htm#appendix. US military spending (not including Iraq and Afghan wars) based on FY 2008 estimate of request by Pentagon of $506 billion. http://www.armscontrolcenter.org/policy/securityspending/ articles/fy09_dod_request/

12. Martin Ravallion, Shaohua Chen, and Prem Sangraula. *New Evidence on the Urbanization of Global Poverty.* World Bank Research Brief. Mar 21, 2007. http://econ.worldbank.org/external/default/main?theSitePK=46938 2&contentMDK=21268611&menuPK=574960&pagePK=64165401 &piPK=64165026

13. Akhter U. Ahmed, Ruth Vargas Hill, Lisa C. Smith, Doris M. Wiesmann, and Tim Frankenberger, *The World's Most Deprived: Characteristics and Causes of Extreme Poverty and Hunger,* International Food Policy Research Institute. 2020 Discussion Paper No. 43, page x. http://www.ifpri.org/2020/dp/vp43.asp

14. "Food costs endanger UN poverty efforts." *Los Angeles Times.* April 21, 2008: "World Bank President Robert Zoellick has warned that rising food prices could push at least 100 million people in low-income countries into poverty."

15. UNICEF, *State of the World's Children,* 2008. p. 4. 9.7 million children died in 2006 before the age of 5. According to UNICEF, State of the World's Children, 2007, "Malnutrition and hunger-related diseases cause 60 percent of the deaths." Thus, the daily death rate of children from hunger is 9.7 million x 0.6 divided by 365 = 15,945 per day. http://www.wfp.org/hunger/stats

Interviews

conducted by Philippe Diaz
for the production of

"The End of Poverty?"

Charles Abugre, *Head of Policy, Christian Aid, Ghana*

Contrary to the popular image of poor countries in the global South receiving assistance from the global North, there is a net transfer of wealth from the South to the North. In Africa alone, this amounts to $200-350 billion each year. Some of this takes the form of capital flight: corrupt leaders in the South depositing their assets in northern banks. A bigger factor is mispricing of imports and exports, including minerals exported from Africa at less than one percent of the world market price. This costs Africa about $10-15 billion per year. The failure of companies to pay their fair share of taxes and mineral royalties to African governments costs Africa more billions. Dumping practiced by the North has stifled industrial development in Africa and costs another $10 to $15 billion per year. African nations also pay interest on $280 billion on debt accrued under structural adjustment programs. The next major development in the domination of Africa is a plan to privatize the major water bodies. If this occurs, it will be a catastrophe for the people of Africa.

The South Finances the North

The popular view is that developing countries, such as those in Africa, depend on resources that come to them from the rich North, either through aid or subsidized loans or foreign direct investment. Much of the discussion between governments in the North and the South has been about facilitating resource flows to Africa, which is poor in financial resources. However, Africa has been a net capital exporter for many years. Africa transfers in net terms more money to the North than it gets. The modest estimate of the net transfer from Africa is $200 to $350 billion every year.

The transfer of wealth from South to North happens in two ways: personal transfers and mispricing of exports and imports.

First, Africans with high net worth transfer their money and their resources abroad. Some say this is proof of corruption. That may be the case, but corruption does not always lead to resources flowing out of a country. Corruption may lead to resources being sucked from state coffers into private hands. When it leaves the country, it means that either the conditions at home are not good, or the conditions abroad are attracting the capital.

Recent studies show that the conditions abroad attracting the capital are the bigger factor. This occurs mainly as a result of banking secrecy laws maintained by rich countries. Examples include the United States, the United Kingdom and some small islands. London and Switzerland are big tax havens. Banking secrecy encourages illegal movement of resources, because it makes it impossible to trace the resources. To stop the flow of personal resources out of the country, we only have to address the conditions that shield the illegal movement of resources.

The second, and bigger, part of resource transfers out of Africa is in the commercial arena. This also takes place in several ways. Big companies underprice exports from Africa and overprice imports. In this way, they declare a very small income and a very small profit. Many resources exported from Africa are heavily underpriced. The practices of companies operating in Ghana and the Democratic Republic of the Congo are typical.

Ghana exports both industrial and non-industrial diamonds. A 2004 study showed that they sold non-industrial diamonds to the United States at $6.50 per carat, but the world-price level for a similar quality of diamond was $6,250, almost one thousand times as much. This heavy underpricing cost Ghana, in diamonds alone, $350 million dollars in one year. The total reported export value of Ghana's minerals is usually $1 to $1.5 billion. So, diamonds alone would constitute about 30 percent of the official estimate of Ghana's mineral exports. If the same underpricing applies to gold, that $1.5 billion may be a fraction of what is exported.

Similarly, in 2000, the Democratic Republic of the Congo exported platinum to the US at 0.3 percent of the value of platinum in the US market.

The companies that operate in the South also heavily overprice their imports. One example was a case in Nigeria where an imported generator worth $40 was actually quoted as costing $6,500.

Between 1996 and 2005 the underpricing of exports and overpricing of imports led Africa to lose at least $45 billion to the United States market. The United States market constitutes 30 to 40 percent of Africa's exports, so you have to multiply that by 2.5 or 3.3. You are talking about $100 to $150 billion in export revenue lost in these crooked deals with transnational companies.

How Companies Avoid Taxes and Mineral Royalties

One of the aims of the Tax Justice Network, apart from ending banking secrecy, is to make financial transactions transparent. Mining companies should be required to report on all their transactions, including their imports and exports, to the tax jurisdictions in which they operate. Without that, it is impossible for poor countries to regulate and tax them.

African and other developing countries lose huge amounts from their basic exports and resources because of "tax holidays" or fiscal incentives and subsidies that are supposed to encourage foreign direct investment. Those incentives are mainly offered because of pressure from the World Bank, the IMF, and bilateral agencies.

In Ghana, Zambia, or Tanzania, companies pay very little in royalties. In the case of Ghana, it is an average of 3 percent of the total value of production of minerals. In the case of Zambia, it is only 0.6 percent of the total value of production. Zambia depends on copper for more than 75 percent of their total exports. If they do not earn foreign exchange from copper then they will hardly earn any at all. The copper companies declared in 2004 that they had exported copper to the tune of $1 billion. It could be $3 billion or $4 billion or $5 billion, but the declared value was $1 billion. The total tax take with royalties plus income taxes, with every type of tax put together, gave Zambia only $8 million in revenue.

When the IMF, the World Bank, and all of these "donors" applied pressure on African countries to reform their laws regarding natural resource extraction, the extraction companies were allowed to keep up to 80 percent of their foreign exchange earnings in their own accounts abroad. Not only do these countries not get revenue to spend on health, education and water, but they also do not get access to the foreign exchange in their own central banks, to enable their own business people to import the kinds of things they need to grow the economy.

Dumping From the North Cuts Output in the South

The race to the bottom by offering zero taxation for natural resources and the fraud involved in the import/export arena is not the whole story of how the North extracts money from the South. Add to this the cost imposed on developing economies by dumping of products in their markets.

The IMF and the World Bank pressure countries to open up their markets. That leads to a flood of imported luxury consumer goods that compete with products that might potentially be produced in these weak, small economies. Any industrial or agricultural capacity that exists in these places is wiped out. The US dumps cotton and rice on African markets by providing subsidies for farmers in the southern United States.

This dumping of products from the North reduces income in the South. Christian Aid did a calculation in 2005 and showed that the cost of trade competition from dumping in the African market was equivalent to $250 billion between 1980 and 2000. That was almost equivalent to all the aid given to Africa over that 20-year period. That includes grants, food aid, and loans.

Africa is not a net recipient of resources; it is a net exporter of resources. The situation in the Philippines and the smaller developing countries is even worse. That is why the critical question for international development and for poverty reduction is to plug the leaks.

Corruption and Lack of Accountability

The mechanisms that facilitate resource flight destabilize democracy. It is better for people to generate their own incomes and pay taxes internally. This way they can hold their governments accountable, because there is a link between taxation and democracy. When governments have to depend on foreign donors and foreign creditors, the accountability of governments cannot be to their citizens; it has to be to the foreign donors and foreign creditors. When commercial operations deprive Africans of the resources that naturally belong to them, the resulting dependency on aid is anti-democratic. It undermines the principles of democracy.

In addition, practices that transfer resources from the South to the North generate corruption. Corruption is not limited to giving and receiving bribes. Corruption occurs when the integrity of trade or the public sector is undermined. To fight corruption, we should remove banking secrecy, ensure that the transnational companies report on their operations everywhere, end tax havens, and transfer stolen resources back to the countries of origin.

Debt and Structural Adjustment

African countries had very little dependence on external aid or loans before the oil crisis of 1979. They exported natural resources and taxed their farmers. In the 1970s, commodity prices collapsed, as countries tried to produce as much as possible, and as production in the North shifted from natural materials, such as cotton, jute, and rubber, to synthetics.

The collapse in commodity prices, combined with the rise in world oil prices, forced African countries to go to the IMF. At that time, the IMF gained a new agenda: to reduce and privatize the state. Because poor countries now needed loans, the IMF and World Bank prevailed upon them to liberalize markets and privatize the state. So, African countries opened markets rapidly, which led to massive competition and stagnation of the economy. They also removed teachers from rural areas and introduced cost recovery and fees in education and health care. A continent with a low level of education and health care after colonization had made massive progress in the first 10 years of independence. Suddenly Africa had to cut back on health and education services, and to introduce user fees.

Developing countries were also asked to shift their emphasis to export production to pay back loans. A continent that started with a total debt burden in 1975 of $600 million, by 2000 was in debt by over $200 billion. Even after paying about $211 billion in debt service up to the year 2000, they still had a debt overhang of $280 billion.

Privatizing Water Resources

The privatization of water bodies is now being planned and implemented. This is being done in the name of "providing Africa with energy." The US, the World Bank, and donors, together with the New Partnership for Africa's Development, have set up a consortium to mobilize private capital for an electricity and energy generation program, and they want to control large water bodies.* To build dams, from the Democratic Republic of Congo all across Africa, they are planning to mobilize $40 to $50 billion a year in private capital.

Private capital will mean private equity ownership over water bodies that produce electricity. They are thinking of producing not only electricity, but also water services. It will include hydro-storage for dams and irrigation, and also drinking water. If this consortium takes place, another part of the commons will be owned by private companies.

There is a growing social movement in Africa to respond to these plans, because privatization of water is very clearly now at the heart of people's survival.† You can go without soap and shoes and trousers, but you cannot go without water. If you drink bad water, you will get sick and may die. Most deaths in Africa among children are not from malaria or AIDS. They

---

* Ed.: This consortium is formally called the Union of Producers, Transporters and Distributors of Electric Power in Africa (UPDEA).

† Ed.: The interview with Mr. Abugre took place at the World Social Forum, January 23, 2007. The next day, at the World Social Forum, 250 activists from 40 countries in Africa met to form the Africa Water Network to resist water privatization. See www.africawaternetwork.org. Many of those present had been active on this issue for years prior to the formation of the network.

are from water-born diseases.

Communities will fight governments and companies to get access to water. They will probably be dispossessed of their land, because the land around water bodies will be cordoned off in order to protect the water basin systems. This stage of privatization is worse than any previous stage of neocolonialism. It is ridiculous that for-profit companies effectively should own large chunks of water bodies. This is scary.

Markets As Conscious Creations

People who think markets are the solution to every problem never seem to consider that markets do not happen in a vacuum. They are shaped by laws and policies. For example, the world cotton market is deliberately shaped by the United States and Europe to subsidize cotton to keep their farmers going. They maintain that market. The same is true with the market for aircraft. Boeing and Airbus are basically supported by heavy military expenditures.

The flooding of African markets with commodities occurred because Africa was the most vulnerable. It had the smallest base of industry, education, and infrastructure at the time of independence. It was the least able to transform natural resources into finished products for international markets. African governments started to develop those capacities in the 1960s and 1970s, but structural adjustment has reversed that. Structural adjustment intervened to keep Africans commodity-dependent by giving them absolutely no space to process their natural resources, to add value to them. Africa has to be part of the market. It has to shape the market just as the Chinese have. The Chinese were heavily exporting, but heavily protecting, their markets. To date the Chinese have refused to privatize their financial services.

Africa has sold virtually every commercial bank that mobilizes savings. Africans have transferred their assets to the North, in the form of either capital flight or luxury imports from the North. Banks have nothing to do with expanding the productive capacity of Africa or the southern countries. So you see, the market has been deliberately shaped by actors who head the continent.

Christian Aid and Tax Justice Network say you have to stop forcing poor countries to liberalize; you have to stop forcing them to follow policies which you think are right and which simply serve your interests. We now know from the evidence that this hurts poor people and that it hurts the economy in general.

Jaime de Amorim, *National Coordinator, Landless Workers Movement, Brazil*

The men who work in the sugarcane fields live under slave-like conditions. Actually, their lives are worse than the lives of slaves, because bosses at least took responsibility for the health of their slaves. Workers are now used up and discarded. They start the day at around 4 a.m. On the days they work, they are trucked to the field and start working. Other days, they have no work at all. Workers have to cut a quota of 4 tons every day, compared to 3 tons in previous years. When they are paid for what they cut, the bosses cheat them. Workers are shorter and weigh less than in the past, which is a measure of their extreme poverty. Workers do not pursue their rights because the bosses kill those who complain too much. The bosses have power because they have money, connections with judges, and influence with legislatures. Change will occur only by structural reform that shifts production away from export monoculture to diversified agriculture for local consumption.

Daily Life of a Sugarcane Worker

A family that works in sugarcane lives in complete insecurity, without a secure job. The family has to compete for the job. Usually the worker wakes up at 3:30 am and at 4:30 he is already on the side of the road waiting for a truck to take him to work. When he gets to the field, he starts cutting the cane. Many times he takes his family along to help achieve the daily work quota. The older children cut the sugarcane and the small children tie the cane and pile it up. He spends all day cutting sugarcane. For lunch, he will bring along dry flour with *charque* (sun-dried bull meat). Other times he takes some other food. His workday usually lasts until 2 or 3 or 4 in the afternoon. He then returns home tired.

Some days, he meets his work quota, other days not. Some mornings, he arrives late by the side of the road and is not chosen to work, so he returns home without work. Other days he stays at the side of the road waiting for the truck, but it never comes because another one came by already filled with workers. He has to compete for work. In addition, the cane worker has to cut a minimum amount each day, which is a perverse requirement. He has to rely on the help of the youth and children in order to ensure the minimum standard of living.

He returns home. He usually lives on the edge of the city, in the outskirts, where conditions are not livable. He competes for the possibility of his children getting an education or going to a healthcare center. If he needs medicine and has no money for a doctor, he will ask for help from a local council member or the mayor to buy it.

Cutting sugarcane never pays enough for him to buy enough food for a family. But sugar growing is expanding because the government subsidizes ethanol. Rural communities are destroyed to create sugarcane plantations. This system of helping owners has survived for centuries, with workers treated as animals, supporting a system that accumulates wealth.

When a worker gets a job, he usually gets paid in money, but two forms of payment still exist. The few workers who live around the sugar mills buy food on credit throughout the year at the company store, so their wages go directly to pay what they owe there.

Those who live in a city's outskirts and do not have an employment contract are tied to the mill only through their work. This sort of worker gets paid in money, but he is also in debt at the company store. He receives cash payment at the mill on Saturday mornings.

The workers take what they produce to the scales to be weighed. They are usually robbed by being told their cane weighs less than it does. A worker may cut 5 or 6 tons a day but be paid for less. He cannot complain because of the mill's security guard and gunman at the payment stall. Workers cannot complain about any violation of their rights. If a worker cuts 3 tons a day he makes less than 10 *reais*. Normally, they cut 4.5 tons per day. But in practice nobody pays the worker the appropriate amount.

The daily work quota keeps rising. A few years ago, it was around 3 tons a day. Nowadays, it is 4 tons or more, depending on the situation. Therefore the worker is physically weaker. There are studies showing that workers are being transformed into a generation of dwarfs. In the slavery period, the average sugarcane worker weighed 80 kilos and was 1.72 m (5 ft. 8 in.). Nowadays, the average height is 1.64 m. (5 ft. 5 in.). As a result of their physical degradation, workers have to endure more to produce more than in the past.

Power of Sugar Producers

When we took over a bankrupt mill, we found documents from 1964, when the military dictatorship occurred. We found pictures of people who were tortured. We found a photo of a young man who had been assassinated and only the mill had that picture. His body had been burnt in the sugar cane field. What happened? He was about to get married in those days, and came to the mill to collect his final pay. The mill probably paid him and killed him right after to get the money back. That was the normal way things used to be done. Still today, after working 2 to 3 years at the mill, workers do not pursue their rights because they are afraid for their lives. Thus, violence is the most perverse aspect of sugar production.

Managers envision workers as slaves who have not rebelled. It is much easier for the boss to accumulate wealth than during the slave period. The boss used to be the slave's owner. He had to take care of the slave's health, food, and housing even if it was in the slave quarters. Nevertheless, he had to take care of the slaves. Nowadays, the boss has no such concerns. He pulls the truck over in the outskirts of the city and loads up the workers. At the end of the day, he takes them back. He has nothing more to worry about. Once the cane-cutting season is over, the worker who lives on the outskirts goes on making a living in other ways by selling popsicles or popcorn, while his kids go into prostitution or selling drugs, or other forms of criminality, because there is no alternative.

Meanwhile, the owner gets richer and has more political influence in the region. Since the 1500s, 18 families have dominated the region. The expansion of sugarcane to export ethanol and biodiesel reinforces a whole culture of domination, slavery, and hierarchical administration. Mechanization and technology have never benefited workers. They only increase the wealth of the elite families that dominate the area.

The power of the owner of the sugar mill or plantation is bigger than just controlling the worker. Besides controlling the worker, he has ideological control. He controls which teacher will teach in his plantation. He decides who will be the police chief in town. The town's judge is usually a friend or a family member of the sugar mill owner. The whole apparatus of the state is in the service of the owner. The owner has more than just economic power. He also has ideological and political power.

In addition to direct violence and political power, landowners also rely on judicial power, which the sugar processors largely control. With that power, they impede inspections. They can even avoid land expropriation by suspending presidential decrees. The federal government has not managed in the past year to expropriate a single area among those occupied and restored.

So we have here triple power: economic power, governmental authority—especially the ever-present police who coerce, intimidate, and repress workers—and judicial power.

Landless Workers' Movement

To change that, the Landless Workers' Movement fights for agrarian reform—to change the agrarian structure, the concentration of land in the hands of a few.* We have organized the workers who were excluded from trade unions, especially those who are just sugarcane cutters, maintenance workers, seasonal workers, or temporary paid workers who mostly live on the outskirts of the city. In contrast with the trade union movement, we have not mobilized to improve wages or working conditions. We had a few periods in which sugarcane plantations went bankrupt, from 1998 to 2002. We managed then to take over many sugar plantations.

We also propose to solve the problem of monoculture. We are working for diversification in production starting with large-scale agrarian reform. Until then, the socio-economic and political panorama of this region will not change.

Nimrod Arackha, *Tanzanian Mine Workers Development Organization*

The gemstone tanzanite is mined around Mererani, Tanzania. For a decade, local people engaged in small-scale mining. Then, under pressure from the IMF, the Tanzanian government opened up mining to foreign corporations. Those corporations evade taxes, abuse workers, change ownership to avoid responsibility, and maintain control over the market. As a result of the entry of the large corporations in the area, the small-scale miners have been impoverished. The citizens cannot expect any help from the central government, because the government has been colluding with the corporate mining interests from the beginning.

Local Struggle over Mining in Mererani, Tanzania

Immediately after the discovery of the gemstone tanzanite in 1967, there was an influx of local immigrants from neighboring places. They

---

* Ed.: As a technical matter, de Amorin notes that the government makes it hard to designate land as underutilized (and thus subject to expropriation) by failing to update land productivity indexes since 1975. The government continues to define minimum yield as 80 tons per hectare, even though the norm is now far higher than that.

started settling in Mererani for the sole purpose of mining gemstone, and the population increased. Then, in 1977, the mining policies of Tanzania changed, paving the way for big companies. Immediately after that, big companies were formed, and the locals were displaced for the construction of the mining fields of big corporations. Some people were rendered homeless and brutally dehumanized. That culminated in a war between the locals and the people hired to protect the mining area. For a long time, people have been fighting over the mining area. The government apportioned the most productive 70 percent to the big companies and only a portion of the remaining 30 percent was given to the small-scale miners That is how we started fighting for the rights of citizen mine workers.

The mission of our NGO is to strengthen the capacity of small-scale miners, so they can gain access to and benefit from the mineral wealth. Small-scale miners are not able to access the market. They do not know how tanzanite is sold. Annual turnover of tanzanite, according to statistics, is on the order of $350 million annually. Yet, here at the source of tanzanite, people are still living in abject poverty.

Around 200,000 people live in this area and depend on mining. The big companies only employ 300 people. Some who stay here still do some farming in or around Mererani, but most depend on mining, directly or indirectly. There are a lot of brokers of gemstones here. In Kijiweni, which comes from the word Kijiwe (gemstone), there are many people doing all sorts of brokerage jobs for mining. That is how they survive.

How Big Companies Create Local Poverty

The big companies have rendered many people jobless. Their mining fields once belonged to the locals. Here in Mererani, 90 percent of the locals rely on the mineral, directly or indirectly. Mining has not been that effective recently because the mineral has not been found in the areas left to local people. They are languishing in poverty.

Before the big corporations amassed huge chunks of land in the most productive areas, mining was not that difficult. Had it not been for their coming there, then people would still be mining there. A lot of money that locals would have received has been siphoned out of this country.

The big companies mining tanzanite play tricks to avoid accountability. I call them "gambling games." A company operates here for a certain number of years, but then it claims not to have any gemstones. They change the company name, but it is still the same company operating here. They end up creating new names all the time to make the government believe that they have disappeared, but they are still here. They are still working here.

AFGEM, or African Gem, is from South Africa. That is the major company that has been here for years. It has also been called many other names. Most recently, it became TanzaniteOne. There used to be another company called Kilimanjaro Mining, which formerly belonged to an Australian, and then it was with some Tanzanians. But now, they are getting together with TanzaniteOne.

Corporate Abuse of Miners

AFGEM has treated the small-scale miners very badly. Deep inside the mining field there are some interconnections between the company and the small-scale miners. They have used rubber bullets on the small-scale miners. Some electronic devices have also been used on small-scale miners, which cause some ailments and diseases later in life.

The workers who are employed by the big companies are also abused. There are cases where people have been stripped naked to inspect them after coming out of the mine to ensure that they have not hidden any mineral on them.

When the big companies were first allowed to invest, there was a lot of violence. Activism was strong then. People were maimed, disfigured, or even killed. Once, when someone was shot, the investor who shot him said he was insane at the time. That is how he defended himself, and he got away with it in court. Those are some of the atrocities that the small-scale miners have had to endure.

Collusion Between Big Companies and Government

It is hard to get any justice from the big companies, because there was a contract signed by the government when the mining laws were enacted. The government protects the big companies. A couple of weeks ago, we had a case here where someone from the government allowed an owner of one of these big companies to shoot anyone on sight who tries to penetrate his mining area. That is a blatant indication of government's involvement in protecting the big companies.

The companies are cheating the government. These people evade taxes because the government does not measure the amount of gemstone that comes out of the mines. Annually AFGEM comes up with fictitious production figures. We understand that AFGEM is the leading producer of gemstones in the world. If it is the leading producer, why is the effect not being felt by the government here?

AFGEM has imposed a monopoly on the small-scale miners.* Anyone with gemstones has to pass through AFGEM and their chain to sell gems. When you go to the market with your tanzanite, you are told to go back to the agents, because they are the ones holding the market. Technically, small-scale miners can sell wherever they want, but at the end of the day they come to find that they sold to the agents of AFGEM.

The Role of the IMF

All of this came about because of outside influence. The IMF set as a condition for aid that a country must allow foreign direct investment to help us create jobs. We did not carry out a cost-benefit analysis, because we did not know what it would cost us to have all these people here, or the benefits.

The government mining policy was therefore introduced as a structural adjustment program. The big corporations entered Mererani as investors and that is how the economy of the locals was crippled. They entered here as investors, but they did not give jobs to the locals. The government invited these people in, but it forgot what it was losing. Government policy contributed to rural poverty in this region.

John Ayila *Local Leader at Yala Swamp, Kenya*

As leader of the landowners in his village, Mr. Ayila has been faced with hazards created by the Dominion Group, an American company that was given control over the region by the Kenyan government. By blocking the local river to create hydropower for their operations, Dominion has flooded the lands and homes of the villagers, without offering any assitance or compensation. This is an example of the hidden costs of development projects, costs seldom considered by government officials.

I am a resident of this area, which is called Seje village. I am the leader of Seje landowners. The people here are a Luo tribe. We started living here in

---

* Ed.: The technical term is actually "monopsony," which means a single buyer in a market. Monopoly refers to a single seller.

1934 as pastoralists and agriculturalists. The people here in this swamp depend on livestock rearing, bee keeping, and cultivation of maize, millet, bananas, and sugar cane. Since our arrival, life here has been very smooth and good. There was an abundance of food. The livestock sustained the community. We got milk and meat. From the swamp we used to get papyrus stems to make mats and grass for thatching. The women used papyrus for mats. They made mats to earn their living. One mat, 6 feet by 6 feet costs KSh 200 [$3.00], so our woman could get over Ksh 500 [$7.50] a day from making mats.

Now all of that is gone from the swamp where we used to get it. We are subjected to total poverty. In 2003 our local politicians (county councilors, parliamentarians, administrators, chiefs, assistant chiefs and district commissioners) went door to door, making us aware of what was to happen. But they lied to us. They told us that government would invest in the trust land where the Lake Basin Development Authority operated. When Lake Basin dropped out due to financial constraints, some of us began working that land. Then they told us the government was going to invest in that area, 15 kilometers from here, but only on trust land, not on private lands. That project was supposed to sustain the whole country and give employment to the community. So we willingly left the land, because we wanted that particular development.

The Opposite of What Was Promised

Then everything changed. Instead of government machines, we saw a company arrive from Edmond, Oklahoma, USA, called the Dominion Group. This company is investing here, in cooperation with the Kenyan government. We were told the company would employ us and provide benefits. The company was going to use the trust land. Some three months later we saw tractors coming along here. The surveyors surveyed an area of 5,800 hectares: 15 kilometers from the trust land to the other end of that hill. We did not expect that.

They built a weir dam across the Yala River. It generates electricity and provides irrigation for their rice farm. It was designed to engulf the entire 5,800 hectares on both the Siaya and Bondo side. It cut off the flow of water to Lake Victoria, so there was a backflow of water that submerged private lands. A total of 210 homes were affected. Nine homesteads were totally demolished by water. The cattle dip, where we wash our cattle, was totally submerged. The water has receded a little bit, but it submerged the whole of this area and destroyed our farms. We have got nowhere now to go.

In addition, Lake Kenyaboli, a lake some 15 kilometers from here that we used to fish, has been privatized. We have been displaced from that lake, so the company could fence it to raise fish in cages. The fishermen who earned their livelihood from that lake have lost their income.

The company has cultivated some 40 hectares of rice, cotton, maize [corn], and beans. The maize and beans that the company has planted is genetically modified, which has put the company at loggerheads with NGOs and some government scientists. We buy maize from the company. There have been quite a few complaints of diarrhea, stomach pains, and skin diseases. We used to get clean water from the Yala River, but now it is inaccessible. We are subjected to stagnant water, which is full of worms. Our cattle drink from the place we get our drinking water, and the company uses the same water to wash their vehicles and tractors.

On the rice plantation, they spray every two weeks. The airplane makes a u-turn right across our homes, when people are in their farms in the middle of the day. In nearby public health centers, quite a number of children have been reported dead, some of them have skin complaints, flu, especially three days after being sprayed. Last week, the company sprayed and killed bats in the swamp, because they claimed that the bats were destroying the rice. Our dogs got a hold of these bats and ate them. So, our dogs died. A week ago, all of us lost the poultry we kept. We have no hens. They all died.

Young children cannot go to school, because it was demolished. Our children do not start school until they are twelve because they have to walk 20 kilometers to the nearest school.

The Aftermath

We now get our food supplied by the Red Cross. Two weeks ago we got some hundred bags that the Red Cross and other NGOs brought to us. We depend on that, and on the belief that this company [Dominion] would employ us. The government and the company told us that we would get employment there. But machines are there to do every kind of work. There is nothing a laborer or a skilled person can do there. It is highly mechanized, but there is no way that project will upgrade our standard of living.

The legumes produced there are not sold to us; they are ferried to America; they are taken back to America. The land is ours, and we gain nothing from that land. It is the American government [actually, the Dominion

Group] and maybe some corrupt officials in the [Kenyan] government who gain from this project. This project is not meant to develop the local poor at all. The project is meant to develop those who are in the government. But we local people will remain poorer and poorer due to this project.

This company has brought us more harm than good. The community demands, if the project is to continue, a new memorandum of understanding between the company and the local community rather than with some powerful parties in the government. We want the project to be discontinued. We also want the dam, the hydroelectric structure to be demolished, so that water can flow freely and naturally to Lake Victoria. Currently Dominion manipulates the water. Sometimes they close the doors, and the water rises and submerges our homes. At other times, they open the doors and the water recedes.

Yala Swamp contains some wild animals: crocodiles, hippopotami, the *sitatunga* [antelope], and a number of beautiful birds. The company has no regard for these wild animals. It has cut all the trees in this beautiful area. Some types of bats and other animals have disappeared. We used to pick herbs for medicine. Since we live quite a ways from hospitals, we depend on these local leaves for medicine to cure our children. Now we cannot get any because they are submerged.

We bestowed this swamp with myths, like this ancestral tree. We believe it cannot be cut down, or we will not get any rain. We used to go to that mountain over there to pray. But Dominion has put an embargo on it. Dominion insists the whole community must use one site for prayer on the other side. So now we are subjected to a life of servitude in our own ancestral land. We do not feel like moving away from that land. This is our ancestral land, and no matter what, we will not move out of this land. We are residents here. I would ask the government and NGOs to help us fight this menace. This is an egocentric company that will not benefit us. I would be very thankful if ever the officials agree to answer.

William Batt *Government Analyst (retired)*

After the tsunami struck Thailand, a second disaster befell many villagers: their land was seized by large-scale developers. This exemplifies an ongoing problem, whereby small-scale farmers sell their land to build a big house in order to gain status. But without land, they lose everything. Wherever land is treated as a commodity there is a danger that ownership of it will become concentrated, leading to higher rates of poverty, which is the absence of an opportunity for a dignified life.

At a recent UN Habitat World Urban Forum, I was reminded of my Peace Corps work in Thailand. Some families talked about the tsunami that hit southern Thailand and washed away everything many of them owned, including some of their family members. After the tsunami, a second disaster struck. During reconstruction, wealthy people seized their land to develop it for hotels, resort, whatever purposes. Many of the people who lived there had no land deeds. Their families had owned the land for centuries, but they did not have formal title to it. So there was a huge land grab. These families lost not only their family members, but their properties as well. Without property they were bereft.

My original Peace Corps service in Thailand was in 1962. I go back every ten years. It is amazing to see how many rural families in the area I lived in, have sold their land very naively, often at artificially low prices, in order to get the money to build a big house. They thought that would really set them up. They had no notion that the houses would have very little lasting value and that they would relinquish their place in the community forever because they forfeited their land.

They sold their land to gain status. Farmers have low status in Thailand. They felt that with the offers they were getting for their land they could build a big house, and that big house would give them more status in their communities. Some were my students forty years earlier. It was hard to explain that they were relinquishing something important.

Land was more important than the house because land gave them security. As farmers, they were able to produce rice to give them sustenance. After they sold their land, they became dependent on money they could earn in the city. But the land was important not only for the food they could grow and sell; it was also important for their status. Going to the city gave them higher status, but only momentarily.

Historically all of the land was owned by the king. Until the end of the 19th century, a farmer owned land as long as he farmed it continuously. In turn, the farmer owed to the king an obligation to work on the canals, the dikes, the irrigation systems, the roads. But it was his land for purposes of use, for farming. If he failed to farm for a period of three years, he forfeited the land back to the king. During the 20th century, the Western system of property ownership began to take hold. When I arrived in 1962, freehold ownership of land was well established.

Comparative Land Loss in Other Countries

Perhaps I can best explain the transition in Thailand by reference to a book by a Canadian historian, John Weaver, entitled *The Great Land Rush*. He traces how land was originally valued for its use. Later it came to be seen as a commodity, and it was valued for purposes of speculation, which meant that some people owned it who did not use it effectively. That change led to an enormous maldistribution of wealth, as people who did not understand this new economics were essentially disenfranchised.

An enormous number of people have been disenfranchised world-wide, who previously had use rights to their land. When they relinquish those rights, they have gone to the cities and become homeless or living in the favelas. The use value of land may really be of far greater consequence for economic equity than the value in the market.

Titling of land can be very helpful, because that gives a certain security to people who are using and living on the land, but title has many components. Lawyers refer to a bundle of rights. Titling not only gives security for use, but it can also be used to leverage money for purposes unrelated to use, and that is not good. The use value is lost sight of. The land simply becomes a bargaining chip or an asset to be mortgaged, and that leads to the loss of productivity and inefficiency throughout the economy.

As long as land is a commodity, many people cannot afford to purchase it and are thereby disenfranchised. That leads to greater concentration among people who can afford to purchase it. That is the source of economic injustice throughout the world and the disenfranchising of as many as two billion people.

People are simply driven off the land, but even if they are allowed to stay on the land they use, they sometimes have to pay exorbitant fees to stay on that property. That just adds to the wealth of another class. The people who could make best use of the land no longer have the security necessary to use it.

Most Americans own the land under their houses, but that is usually all they own. The most valuable land is corporate property, or property that is held out of use by speculators. The land underneath people's homes is only a fraction of the value of land downtown, in the central city, which is usually commercial property.

Poverty Related to Concentrated Land Ownership

Economic growth in a poor country frequently results from reliance on natural resources, since that is all poor countries have. They have mineral wealth, oil wealth, and agricultural wealth. That wealth becomes concentrated in a small group of people. There is a disparity between people who have title to ownership of those resources and the large majority of people who are simply the instruments of the owners. The more concentrated wealth becomes the more people are driven into poverty.

Poverty is the absence of an opportunity for a dignified life. One of the problems we have in the world today is the number of people who not only do not have food to eat, but who also do not have a stable livelihood or a place to live. Gandhi had a wonderful phrase: live simply so that other people can simply live. What we have today is a number of people who cannot simply live. Dignity is what people want. It is even more important than wealth. People trade wealth frequently for dignity.

That is what the story of the Thai villagers selling their land to build houses is all about. They see owning a big house as bringing them dignity. Whether that will bring them lasting dignity is another question. Status is another word, but dignity is all people really have to bargain with.

Richard Biddle   *Teacher*

Many of us grew up with the game of Monopoly. *We internalized ideas about the fairness of land ownership and a "winner-take-all" view of life. This orientation comes from the 1935 rules. But in the original game, dating back to 1903, the creation of monopolies and bankrupting of others was only the first part of the game. At a certain point in the play, the players could elect to change the rules and make it a cooperative game, in which real estate was shared for the benefit of everyone. That simple difference provides a clue about how to solve the problem of poverty in reality. We need to change*

the rules by which we live—from rules that allow the winner to gather a monopoly and force everyone else aside, to rules that enable everyone to win.

I was educated at the *Monopoly* board. My brother pulled me up to the Monopoly board when I was 5 years old. That is where I learned how to lie, cheat, and steal. It was very effective. I learned some math, reading, and ethics (probably not good ones), and I learned about land tenure, real estate, money, banking, and mortgages.

I realized just how much it had influenced me many years later. The seven-year-old son of a friend of mine was upset because his parents were buying the land their house was built on. He thought it immoral for people to own land, in the same way that it is immoral to own people. All of a sudden I figured out that he had never played *Monopoly*. He did not have the opportunity that I had with my brother—who beat me up every day—to learn about deeds and land speculation and our winner-take-all society. That is when I understood how much the game of *Monopoly* has shaped us.

The game most of us grew up with is winner take all, bankrupt thy neighbor, and it is the way in which the world pretty much operates today. More than 250 million copies of the game have been sold, 4 million every year. The game of *Monopoly* is itself a kind of monopoly. There are trademarks, patents, and copyrights, but the trademark is the thing that persists. That is the thing that functions like land use; it is in perpetuity.

Monopoly had an earlier history that most people are completely unaware of, and that early history goes back to 1903. It was before cars, so instead of "Free Parking" in the corner space, there was Central Park as a free space.

The rules of the game before the 1935 patent had a message that was completely different than what is taught today. The greed, backstabbing, winner-take-all, and roll of the dice were always part of the way each game started. But at a certain point in each game, after things were clearly going in a winner-take-all direction, the players could elect to switch to a second set of rules in which everyone could win. This created a sense that things really could be different—things could be better; we do not have to reside in the perverse economics of the system we started off with. So, the original game was partly an earth-sharing game, instead of the profits ending up in private pockets, as it does in the later game. The provision in the rules that allowed a switch to earth sharing showed that the values that were created by the community would come back to the community rather than end up in one player's pocket. The original values were about the good of society and the possibility of a better way of life based on fairness.

The message of the earlier game is that the poor do not necessarily need to be with us; we can all be relatively affluent. The issue is sustainability and efficiency. There is no point in trying to dampen the best competitive spirits that people have. People all around the world are seeking better opportunities. We have set up some of the worst models to follow and pursue, based on the spirit of the later game, and that is tragic.

The game we play today is the story of how poverty is created. When you bankrupt your neighbor, what does he do? Does he go away? Does he go on to do other things? Those people survive on some level. Quite a few end up in jail, both in life and in the game. It is really an issue of wealth distribution. The game shows how land ownership and land development create monopolies that impoverish most people. It shows how land markets do not work for everybody. They only benefit a few. It also teaches people that power and luck are rewarded more than hard work. There are advantages to ruthlessness, concentrating power, seeking special interests politically through legislation. We see aspects of that in Chance and Community Chest.

By 1935, the car had become popular. America was the prime producer of oil until the 1950s. The game does not deal with this, but the car destroyed public transportation. In the original one, there was a "Slambang trolley." But by the 1930s, General Motors and Standard Oil were pulling the trolley cars off the American scene in favor of buses and the automobile. The net result was that we went from about 74,000 streetcars in 1917 to 17,000 in 1948. They destroyed a very viable transportation system. That story is not part of the game, although it is part of the game's history, in a sense. Originally, you got the sense of a walkable community.

The railroads were part of the original game. The railroads were given 100 million acres in order to crisscross the country with rail lines, and that provided an opportunity for the development of what Thomas Jefferson thought would be the land that would not be developed for the next 200 years. But all of a sudden, we were enclosing the commons, the lands that had not been owned up until about 1890. And the railroads sought special favors from government. They represent a force to be reckoned with—but they were never really reckoned with.

William Blum *Historian, Author*

The US has tried to overthrow 60 governments since 1945 and intervened in many others. The purpose is to destabilize any efforts to establish a regime that resists American economic domination, or neocolonialism. Thus, it does not matter whether corporate interests are at stake. The Washington foreign policy establishment balks at having any national leaders who follow an independent course. Global poverty is not caused by lack of development, but rather by American intervention against progressive governments. Terrorism is not a product of poverty or envy. It is the result of a desire to retaliate against the suffering caused by American bombs, intervention, and torture. Latin Americans previously retaliated against American intervention in much the same way that Middle Eastern terrorists now do. Examples of US intervention are: Russia in 1918, Italy and France in 1948, Iran in 1953, Guatemala in 1954, Chile in 1973, and the ongoing harassment of Cuba. American leaders should be tried for war crimes, but they are too powerful to be brought into court. Covert operations by the CIA that are not widely reported include a case in Poland during the Cold War, US sabotage of the Chilean economy before the 1973 coup, intimidation of the Nicaraguan electorate, coups against African leaders Lumumba and Nkrumah in the early days of independence, the civil war against Neto in Angola, and the recent efforts to overthrow Hugo Chávez in Venezuela.

The main purpose of US foreign policy since World War II has been to prevent the rise of any government that offers a good alternative to the American economic model. The US has attempted to overthrow 60 governments since World War II and even more before WWII. Almost half of these attempts have been successful. We have attempted to assassinate about 50 foreign leaders. We have intervened in a serious manner probably 100 times since 1945.

The level of poverty would be much lower in many countries if the US had not overthrown governments that tried to help their own people. Whenever a government intended to work against poverty, to raise the lower classes, it was overthrown, almost without exception. The kind of leader most feared by Washington was anyone who meant to improve the lot of the poorest. Governments that have tried to make important changes have been overthrown again and again.

The actions of the US and European powers are sometimes referred to as neocolonialism. Neocolonialism consists mainly of being able to gain the same advantages economically, through financial institutions, that, before, you gained through military occupation. You do not need to occupy a country if the IMF, the World Bank, and the World Trade Organization make life impossible for a Third World country.

Foreign corporations gain full standing and full rights in countries, even more so than any native companies. They get full legal rights to operate there and compete, and the native companies or businesses cannot begin to compete with these multinational corporations. So that puts an end to homegrown industry. And that is a first step on the way downhill to a failed state: when you do not have any homegrown businesses.

Today the issue that is before the public is terrorism. The question of what causes anti-American terrorists is very important. The main motivation for anti-American terrorists is revenge or retaliation. They want to retaliate for the many bad things the US government has done in the Middle East and elsewhere.

There should be tribunals on US war crimes. The US and Britain can get away with so much that other nations cannot. There is a big movement in Lebanon and France to find the people who assassinated Rafik Harari. The US government assassinates people every day of the week in the Middle East. There is never any cry for any kind of investigation. We have planes that fire a missile into a car, killing five or six people, but sometimes the person they are aiming at is not in the car.

If a weak nation should assassinate somebody or just be accused of it, it is subjected to a tribunal set up by the powerful, such as the tribunals on Yugoslavia and Rwanda. The international tribunal on Yugoslavia has convicted and sentenced a number of people from Serbia, Croatia, and Bosnia. But Madeleine Albright and the leaders in Germany who were responsible for those wars are not being punished.

Many people know about US support for the military coup in Chile in 1973. Less well known was the CIA's covert action, for two or three years prior to the coup, to undermine the Allende government and to make life very hard for the Chilean people. The CIA and their allies in Chile caused food shortages and other shortages to make life difficult and to turn the people against Allende. When the coup was finally staged, the generals in Chile said it would end the "chaos," not mentioning it had been created by the CIA's activities.

American support for the right-wing Contras, fighting to regain control of Nicaragua, is generally known. Less known is that the Contras made it a point to assassinate teachers and medical workers to disrupt the health and medical programs of the Sandinista government. In Nicaragua in 1990, the Sandinista government lost the election because the Contra politicians, with US support, had made it very clear that, if they lost the election, the civil war would resume. The people understood that as long as the Sandinistas remained in power, the US would never relax its attempts to overthrow the government, and the violence would continue.

Kwame Nkrumah in Ghana, who coined the term "pan-African movement," was overthrown in 1966 by a CIA-staged coup. It was staged by his own military, but instigated by the US. It was blamed on the Soviet Union. Nkrumah was forced into exile, where he died a few years later. The US role is almost never mentioned in the mass media anywhere in the world. I have put together facts from several different places to form a whole. This was among the most hidden of the coups and interventions.

Chesa Boudin *Author and Activist, Caracas, Venezuela*

Oil revenue has provided the means of distributing social services to the poor in Venezuela under the Hugo Chávez administration. That was not possible before his election because a) OPEC had allowed world oil prices to drift downward, b) most of Venezuela's oil profits were distributed overseas rather than at home, because c) the executives of the national oil company (PDVSA) were more loyal to the oil industry than to Venezuela. The struggle over whether oil revenues would be reinvested or shared with the people of Venezuela was the central conflict during the early years of the Chávez era. A coup and an oil strike were both initiated to force Chávez from office, largely because he used oil royalties for the poor at home and reversed a long history of giving PDVSA complete autonomy. Both attempts to oust Chávez failed, but only after considerable damage was done to the country.

Nationalization of Oil in Venezuela

During the 1970s, oil-producing countries experienced a major oil boom. The surge in oil revenues led people in many countries to call for nationalization of oil, which Venezuela did in 1975. Officially the government gained ownership, but in practice, each multinational company simply changed its legal ownership, and little changed. Executives remained loyal to the industry and its informal social networks. Eventually, all of the companies were integrated into PDVSA [pronounced PeDeVesa], the national oil company of Venezuela. However, the major oil companies, known as the "Seven Sisters," continued to do the refining and exporting. By controlling refining and distribution, the Seven Sisters determined who received the profits. Instead of paying a lot to the producer, they claimed a glut of oil on the market lowered the price of unrefined crude. They could control where the bottleneck was in the industry and concentrate profits in their own hands.

Oil Investment Fund Scandal

In the Act of Congress that nationalized the oil industry in 1975, they provided for 10% of oil revenues to go into an investment fund for the industry, because the oil industry is very capital-intensive. PDVSA needed to invest in development of its own tankers to transport oil and to continue replacing reserves as it produced. By 1982, only 6 years after nationalization, the PDVSA investment fund had accumulated over $5 billion. But in 1982, oil prices had declined considerably and oil revenues were declining.

Meanwhile, Venezuela had borrowed heavily and needed foreign currency to service its foreign debts. Venezuela was paying foreign banks 40% of its oil revenues. So, the Venezuelan government demanded that PDVSA turn over its $5 billion investment fund. Devaluation of the currency lowered its value to $2.5 billion. Much of that was used to bail out a failed state-owned bank which caused a huge scandal.

That experience in 1982 taught PDVSA executives not to hold liquid assets that were subject to government confiscation. The government was extremely corrupt and money was squandered or embezzled. So, PDVSA executives decided to invest the money in forms the government could not touch, by creating a network of refineries around the world. That policy has left the Venezuelan government weak if it ever tried to negotiate a better price for the crude oil at home. The share of oil earnings received by the Venezuelan government fell from 70% in 1982 to 38% in 2000.

By the time President Chávez took office, PDVSA had accumulated over $10 billion in debt and acquired over 180 subsidiary companies around the world. (Heavy indebtedness would make it difficult for the Venezuelan government to sell off the subsidiaries.) There were higher revenues but they were offset by the fact that half of the revenues were being invested overseas or going to holding companies in the Caribbean which never paid taxes or royalties to the government. The PDVSA holding company based in Caracas was still remitting $500 million dollars a year to subsidiary companies overseas through transfer pricing even after Chávez was elected, before he had full control of the oil industry.* As Rafael Ramirez, the current Minister of Energy and Petroleum in Venezuela, has said, the PDVSA inherited by the Chávez government was subsidizing the government of the United States.

President Chávez Fights PDVSA for Control of Revenues

The first thing President Chávez tried to do was to bring PDVSA back under control of the government, to re-nationalize it, not by selling off the foreign assets but by making sure it was accountable to government policy. That effort met with huge resistance from PDVSA. There were three major conflicts as a result of Chávez's attempts to control PDVSA.†

The Chávez administration finally gained control of PDVSA in 2005 and uses it creatively in its foreign policy. Citgo, its US affiliate, has been offering substantial discounts on home heating oil for poor families across the United States, for Native American reservations, and for homeless shelters.

The Chávez administration has also recouped for the government a huge percentage of the revenue being generated overseas. In 2005, Citgo generated $500 million in dividends for Venezuela, due partly to rising oil prices and increased oil royalties or taxes. Much of that money has been invested in social services, such as a free health-care program in the barrios for the poorest Venezuelan citizens. Critics think transferring revenue to the government is hurting the capacity of PDVSA to compete internationally and that it will drive down the long-term production levels of PDVSA.

As President, Chávez has cut production, rather than raising it to five million barrels a day as PDVSA had planned. Prior to Chávez's election,

---

* Transfer pricing is a process that multinational companies use to avoid paying taxes to the country where their operations are held. In the case of PDVSA, they would charge a subsidiary company, such as Citgo, a price for oil below the market price. Citgo then sold it at market value for a huge profit, but PDVSA transferred the costs of production, transport and other costs to the Caracas-based holding company. While the profits stayed overseas in the U.S., Europe, or tax shelters in the Caribbean, the cost and the debt were accumulated domestically, so there were never any taxable profits in Venezuela.

† Ed.: Boudin here explains the ways PDVSA resisted efforts by Chávez to reclaim oil company revenue for the Venezuelan government, including its support for a coup attempt in 2002, followed by a strike and sabotage of petrochemical facilities (which did $20 billion in damage), followed by a recall referendum in 2004.

PDVSA had systematically oversold OPEC quotas and undermined OPEC as a cartel. Since oil represents 80% of Venezuela's export earnings, raising the price of oil was an important objective for Chávez. His diplomacy with other OPEC member-states has been a significant factor in keeping OPEC production down. The resulting high prices have allowed him to finance social services.

Miriam Campos *National Coordinator for the Empowerment of Indigenous People*

Spanish colonization of Bolivia included both military and cultural domination. They suppressed, but could not destroy, the indigenous religion. Even after independence, indigenous people were still treated as they had been under colonialism. They were allowed to vote only after 1952. One of the most important ways of subjugating the indigenous people was the latifundia system, which concentrated the ownership of land. The law still favors the rights of cattle owners over people. The Guarani people have been treated as slaves for centuries, and many are still living in slave-like conditions.

Two Kinds of Subjugation: Military and Cultural

At the time of colonization, when the Spaniards arrived and subjugated the Indians, there was a major massacre. The Ahimaras, for example, who created the Tihuanacote culture, put up resistance and were eliminated. Bolivia has 36 indigenous populations, some of which avoided contact with the Spaniards during the colonization, by distancing themselves from the centers.

But the Jesuits got them to submit after the early colonial period by introducing the idea that God was going to save them and that there was a heaven waiting for them. That is why there is a saying, "In one hand there was a cross, and in the other a rifle." The role of the Church has been crucial because the idea of an afterlife has been a repressive mechanism. People conform to the idea that in this life they are going to suffer and have a great life in heaven. Using that argument, the Church has controlled a lot of people.

A lot of indigenous leaders have rebelled and spoken out against religion. They criticize the way religion has controlled whole communities. We have our own culture that is so rich. We have an infinite variety of languages, more than thirty-six languages. Only the Ketchua and Guarani are recognized, but we also have other languages that are spoken in the Amazonian region. We are capable of resisting. Only as recently as 1952 were indigenous farmers allowed to vote. Until then, they were not citizens.

Land for Cattle, Not for People

There are about nine million people in Bolivia, but only a few families own a majority of the land. They are not even using much of it for production. This imposes a cost on the indigenous people who do not have access to the lands from which they originated. They are excluded because the law said that for every head of cattle you own, you can hold up to fifty acres of land.

So, rich people could buy cattle or hire people to place the cattle for them to comply. As a result, no more than forty or fifty families own enormous expanses of land. Some indigenous people, such as the Guarani, do not own any land, so they cannot produce anything. They have lived by working the land, and they do not know how to do anything else. If they do not have land to work on, they cannot survive.

Restoring Land to People

There are lands in Bolivia where nothing is being produced. They are called "fattening lands," where a few people enrich themselves without working the land. This *latifundio* system came into being during the colonial era, and it has continued to reproduce itself. Even now we have latifundios. The law says if they are not producing, if they do not accomplish an economic function, this land should be returned and redistributed to those who will use it.

New laws have been passed for the redistribution of the land. At least for the indigenous people, there is a very serious proposal to restore their lands by taking them from the major property owners, either by paying them off or by demonstrating that human rights have been violated. Either way, we want to return these lands to the people who originated from that area.

Guarani Treated As Slaves

The situation of the Guarani is a shame for all Bolivians. The Guarani people are considered as tools or animals. This have been devalued as human beings. Sadly, the Guarani people still see their boss or "patron" as a superior being. They consider themselves inferior, as a result of colonization and the "mestizaje" process that has taken place in our country.

In the 21st century some Guarani families are still captive—actually enslaved. They do not receive any compensation for their work. There are debts that are passed on from generation to generation, and the people cannot leave the *hacienda* because they have an ongoing debt with their boss. This applies not only to the person but to their whole families.

The children work in exchange for food and do not go to school. The women supposedly earn half as much as the men do, but it is according to accounts that they are not allowed to see. Since the majority of these people do not even know how to read or write, the payment of their wages is a unilateral decision, with the boss writing whatever he wants and saying, "I've given you rice, sugar, and clothing in exchange for your work." They have no control over it.

The *patrones* do not feel responsible for the kids. There was a boy who lost an eye when he was feeding the animals, and the *patron* did not even take him to the hospital or the doctor. He argued that nobody would take care of the bill. The *patron* obviously does not feel responsible for them. As a result, they feel like inferior human beings.

History of Resistance

My kids are the basis of my work and my inspiration. They have to live in a different world. I would like for them never to have to suffer what I had to suffer, from October to February, picking up dead people, picking up innocent children, that had to die on a terrace just because they walked outside. I hope my children will not have to relive that. I am working to ensure that they will learn to respect others and they can expect others to respect them, so that they can live as human beings, with dignity.

This whole process is a history of courage, of anonymous heroes that have died defending their identity, their customs, and their ideals, what they believed in. That is an example for us. Maybe we do not have an armed resistance, but we have a different type of resistance. But we can not let ourselves continue to be dominated by cultures that are strangers to us.

Nora Castañeda *President, Bank for the Development of Women, Caracas, Venezuela*

The Bolivarian revolution has brought progress to Venezuela, overcoming its history of slavery, export-oriented production, large-scale poverty, and loss of social identity. Cuban doctors have been hired to work in barrios where Venezuelan doctors have refused to work. Primary education has been made available to the poor. Micro-finance programs have been created, although they are not really a solution to poverty, just a way of managing it. More important are the public banks, including the Women's Development Bank, which support "development from the inside to the inside" (production of basic needs for people). Although these banks seek to recoup capital they have lent, their purpose is not to make a profit, but to promote development.

Venezuela's Social History

Venezuela is a rich country inhabited by poor people. When Spanish colonizers came to Latin America and the Caribbean in 1498, they were looking for gold and silver to sustain commercial development in Europe. There was no gold or silver here. Instead, the Spanish found land capable of growing cacao and sugar cane, so they forced the small indigenous population along the coast to work for them on plantations. The Spanish used the sword and religion to further their aims. When the indigenous people died off in large numbers from European diseases and harsh working conditions, slaves were imported to provide cheap labor for the plantations.

The Creoles, the descendants of the colonizers, turned into an oligarchy of slave owners and plantation owners. The other stratum of society was composed of indigenous people, descendants of Africans, and the *mestizos* or *pardos,* who were a mixture of European, Indian, and African ancestry. The dominated class consisted mostly of slaves. That history explains why the distribution of income is still so uneven. The Bolivarian Revolution regards greater equality of income as a central goal of its development agenda.

After independence, we stopped being a Spanish colony only to become an English colony and later a colony of the United States. During the colonial era, until 1930, Venezuela exported tropical products such as cacao and coffee. Later, we exported rubber for the automobile industry and anil for textile dyes. So Venezuela continued to be a producer of export products, functioning as an export economy. No internal market was developed during the 19th century.

Slaves were liberated at the end of the 19th century, but debt slavery continued on *latifundios* that charged workers for their presence on the land, and paid them with scrip that only circulated on the *hacienda*. Workers were tied to the land by debt. Ezequiel Zamora, a farmer, led the "federal war" (1858-1860), to give free land to free men.

At the end of the 19th century, the second industrial revolution took place. Venezuela suddenly became a supplier of petroleum after the incorporation of the internal combustion engine in trains and ships.

The Bolivarian Revolution in Action

Until 1999, the government followed the neoliberal model of limited public spending on behalf of the poor. The official estimate of Venezuela's poverty rate was 66%; the unofficial estimate was 80%. The rate declined to 56% a few years after 1999, due to increased public spending and creation of the "Sovereign People's Bank" and the "Women's Development Bank."

The poor also suffered from lack of health care. They were denied entry to hospitals. We will never know the number of people who died because of this. The government now provides medical attention within the barrios. In the past, even leaving a barrio to visit a doctor was difficult due to the high crime rate. It was better to die at home than to be killed in the street. So medical facilities were set up inside barrios, mostly with 10,000 Cuban doctors, because the local doctors were unwilling to work in barrios.

Another issue that needed to be resolved was education. Venezuela used to have fairly good education, but that was lost when public education was neglected and private education grew. The current government adopted a "Robin Hood mission." It focused on education, starting with the Bolivarian type of schooling, where you implement a few good schools that provide both education and meals for children and increase the number of them over time until all schools are Bolivarian.

Before 1999, Venezuela had lost its culturally diverse identity. We were told that Spain was our motherland. The new government created a cultural mission to improve our identity and to overcome the idea that non-European ancestry is shameful. Now we have a way to recover and appreciate our African roots. For example, yesterday, December 4, was the day of *Chango*. Previously, black people had to celebrate the day of *Santa Barbara* instead so they would not be punished, because *Chango* is an African saint, who could only be celebrated in secrecy.

Another part of our culture is our way of articulating our relationship with nature. For our indigenous people, the land is "the motherland – *pachamama.*" When women of the barrios water their plants, they talk and sing to them. Capitalism destroyed that harmonious relationship by exploiting the land. We are trying to recover our identity and our old ways.

Hegemonic International Institutions

Because of financial crises and diminished profit rates in the 1970s, the governments of developed countries formed the G-7 meeting of governments, which later became the G-8 when Russia was incorporated. They decided how to throw their crisis onto Third World countries. This led to the "package of economic standards" that guides the World Bank and IMF. The increasing poverty of our countries came as a result of an intrinsic problem of the capitalist economic cycles. At that time, inflation combined with depression. So intellectuals came up with neoliberalism. In order to reduce the crisis, they perfected the market, which caused growing poverty in developing countries and enclaves of poverty in developed nations.

Market liberalization caused a crisis in Venezuela similar to the ones in Asia and Mexico. Carlos Andres Perez took power in January 1989. In February the crisis/rebellion started, with people resisting such things as increases in prices of oil, transportation, and food, and reductions in public spending. The financial system is an instrument of economic violence to poor people, particularly women, who comprise 70% of the poor. "Informal economies" have increased, chiefly as a result of international policies that force people to live at a subsistence level.

Venezuela is not part of the free trade agreement with North America, but we are part of the WTO. It continues to hold us to treaties that have been signed in the past that tie our hands. Evidently the WTO has brought major conflicts to the structure of industrial capital: we can see that in the scarcity of investment capital for productive assets rather than speculation.[*]

Micro-finance Merely Manages Poverty

Economic organizations have promoted the creation of "micro-finance" as a way to enable the poorest of the poor, mostly women, to manage poverty. But micro-finance is aimed only at administering poverty, not overcoming it. It is one way to maintain and contain the masses of the

---

[*] Ed.: This interview was in December 2006. Two years later, the global speculative bubble tied to real estate burst, causing bank failures and depression.

world. Micro-finance expands poverty and therefore it serves the interests of the oligarchies of the world.

In Venezuela, the Bank for the Development of Women, the Bank of the Sovereign People, the Micro-Finance Fund and the micro-finance policy in general were created by President Chávez. They are not our idea. We do not want indebted women managing poverty. We want powerful and independent women who are incorporated into the development process and who benefit from it. Development should not mean women sewing at home sixteen-hour days, seven days a week. We want women to enjoy "integral health" and integral life. That is why we do not follow the saying, "It is better to teach someone to fish than to hand out the fish." We say, "No, when people live in conditions of extreme poverty, we will hand out fish and teach them how to fish."

Solution: Public Banks

The majority of the world's banks are instruments of accumulation of capital. They are mostly instruments that rely on industrial capital to exploit the workers of the world. Now, in Venezuela, national public banks have been created, so we differentiate between the public and private banking systems. The private ones support the development of capitalism and therefore the reproduction of capital.

The public banking system is obliged to serve the people-centered principles of the Bolivarian revolution. Public banks have been operating for many years. These banks are undergoing a transformation, by order of the President of the Republic. Each day more of them take actions that support indigenous development and domestic consumption needs, or "development from inside to inside." This has a lot to do with local development, which makes it similar to the import-substitution model. We want a world that is not based on the reproduction of money but on the historical experiences and communal organization of our indigenous societies, such as agricultural communities that have a personal relationship with the land. We can build it that way. Women, in particular, are involved in that system.

The Women's Development Bank differentiates itself because it is not interested in the accumulation of capital. We still recoup invested capital, but our fundamental objective is to help poor women living in extreme poverty incorporate themselves in the development process. That is what makes our women's bank distinctive. Other banks care only about loan repayment and the profit or interest margins on what they lend. For us that is least important. We want to recoup the money we lend, so we can continue lending.

When foreign banks were having problems in the early 1990s, the Central Bank of Venezuela lent them money. But after we rescued those banks, they took their profits abroad. They took all their resources and left only their buildings as assets. Since the Venezuelan state had supported them, it took possession of their buildings. Now poor women can use them.

Now we have a regulatory banking commission that serves the interests of the Venezuelan people. Those controls have not prevented us from having the biggest yearly financial gain.

Ordinarily in Venezuela, the regulations of the bank commission require that borrowers provide land as collateral for loans. At the Women's Development Bank (WDB) and the Sovereign People's Bank, we do not require that. We are not subject to the banking laws or the regulatory banking commission. We are subject to the Bolivarian revolution. The WBD does not ask a woman if she owns the land she lives on. Practically speaking, the land belongs to those who work it. So we give these micro loans to women who live on the half-acre they work on.

Shivani Chaudhry *Housing and Land Rights Network*

City officials in India order mass evictions of tens of thousands of poor people from their homes in cities every year. The driving force behind the evictions has been land speculation. The evictions are the official result of new city planning programs, carried out by private companies without citizen input. They function as land clearance programs that benefit investors in upscale shopping malls and other developments. Governments ignore the civil rights of those who are displaced. This indifference to the plight of the poor also characterizes the reconstruction of villages wiped out by the 2004 tsunami. Instead of rebuilding fishing villages along the coast, the government has relocated the people far inland, in tiny apartments, far from where the people can earn a living. Meanwhile, large tourist hotels are being built along the coast.

Mass Evictions Destroy Housing and Livelihoods

People are coming to cities because of the collapse of agrarian economies. When they arrive in cities, they work hard, but there is no subsidized housing, so they are forced to live in slums or informal settlements. When they build informal settlements, the government considers them eyesores and destroys their houses. In the last five to six years, forced evictions have been on the rise in India. This has been fueled by a combination of state policies, which are meeting the interests of private investors and of larger cities, such as Mumbai and New Delhi.[*]

In Mumbai there was a massive eviction in the year 2004: in five months 90,000 homes were demolished. Almost 400,000 people were left homeless. No alternate housing was provided. In New Delhi, similar forces are pushing evictions. The Commonwealth Games are coming up in 2010. Land is coveted for developing stadiums and housing for the event. The government is catering to this temporary population and building housing for them. The poor people who live along the Yamuna River were evicted. Of the 27,000 families evicted, only 20 percent of them have been rehabilitated and that was 40 kilometers out of the city.

The poor are working. They drive buses or auto-rickshaws. They are the ones who clean and provide basic services for the city. The livelihood of the poor is threatened when their housing is destroyed and they can no longer commute.

We need to question the political economy of evictions. The people who benefit are large land developers. The land is not being used for any equitable purpose. It is largely for developing shopping malls or housing for the rich. Eviction is creating segregation in cities. We use the term "open apartheid" to describe this, because it creates ghettoes. They build physical barriers between places where the rich and the poor live, and the poor get pushed to the peripheries of the city, far away from the places of livelihood.

Evictions and Urban Renewal

Across India evictions have occurred because the government is promoting a mission of "urban renewal" and "beautification of cities." The aim is to make mega-cities. The model planned for Mumbai is largely influenced by Shanghai, where all the poor people were kicked out of the city.

Mumbai projects are being funded by private investors. The World Bank is funding half the nearly one billion dollar cost of a large urban transportation project. There is no concern for the poor people, who are largely the ones who make the city run. A very lopsided model of development is being pushed, which ignores development for the working classes.

---

[*] Ed.: The interviewee makes references to Mumbai and Chennai. The old names for these cities are Bombay and Madras.

Land Speculation and Land Mafias

It has become extremely profitable to invest in land. Speculation artificially pumps up the prices. The more you speculate, the higher the prices are, and the less affordable housing or land becomes in urban areas.

Mumbai has the second most expensive commercial real estate in the world after Tokyo. There are only a few big builders and land developers. These conglomerates work closely together, artificially pumping up the price of land. Because it is so profitable now, the wealthiest people are investing in land and real estate. The land mafia controls prices.

Tenants suffer because rents have become unaffordable. The government does nothing to check rents. Homelessness is increasing because there is no social housing. Real estate speculation is on the rise, and there is no law to control it. There are no schemes to provide services and housing for the poor. Investors develop the land and sell it at a profit to those who can afford it. Since poor people cannot afford it, they are pushed out.

These trends regarding land need to be checked at various levels, in international advocacy as well. They exist around the world, from Barcelona to Brazil to India. There needs to be some kind of policy change to make sure that there is a check on these land cartels that are growing.

Corruption of City Planning

Foreign companies and multilateral development banks are among the large investors in these projects. Both the Asian Development Bank (ADB) and the World Bank have taken a large stake in the urban renewal mission. Civil society groups are challenging it.

City development plans are supposed to be done by the government and the people, but even city planning is being privatized. The Delhi city plan is being developed by an American multinational company, which has no idea of the social dynamics or culture of the place. People's participation is missing. Master plans for cities are looking increasingly at high-investment-oriented infrastructure development. So there are five-lane freeways and shopping malls, but no space for the urban poor.

As part of the Mumbai urban transportation project, the World Bank gave loans to the Mumbai government to invest in building roads, redo the railways, and provide some kind of housing. There is no need to take loans for such a project. India is a socialist welfare state, so it is the responsibility of government to provide these services.

We had an urban land ceiling law in India that restricted the size of landholding in urban areas. However, people believed it was not favorable for commercial or industrial development, so the law was repealed. Social justice movements are trying to get that law back in place, because at least with it, the government could control how much land was owned. Now, without that ceiling on the amount of land or housing that someone can own, many of the wealthiest can have multiple properties.

Failure of Post-Tsunami Reconstruction

Another crisis is in post-disaster reconstruction and rehabilitation. People who suffer a natural disaster on the scale of a tsunami [on December 26, 2004] lose everything. Overnight they lose their loved ones, their homes, and all their material possessions. It is a challenge to rebuild and to reconstruct. A lot of money came to India through various NGOs and the public sector. The government did not take bilateral funding.

Initially people were herded into temporary shelters, which were really worse than cattle sheds. They were built from material called tar sheeting. If you try to pull the material, it comes off in your hands. It is that bad. After two years there were a lot of agencies coming in to build permanent housing, but there was little regulation of the location and kinds of housing that should be provided.

Providing disaster victims with immediate and complete rehabilitation should have been a priority. The special needs of women and children have been neglected. Resettlement sites have been constructed far from schools, so children drop out because they cannot commute. So a lot of children just sit around, and parents do not know what to do with them. These are all factors that play into increasing cycles of poverty within communities.

The World Bank is involved in tsunami rehabilitation: rebuilding infrastructure and building housing—but without much community participation. So they have developed ridiculously small apartments of 180 square feet in four-story buildings. The fishing communities cannot be expected to dry fish or keep fishing boats in four-story apartment buildings six kilometers from the coast. In Chennai, one of the tsunami resettlement sites has become a new slum. They actually created slums for people who previously had a pretty decent standard of living. It is about ten to twelve kilometers away from the coast. The housing is extremely inadequate: the roofs leak when it rains; there is no space for children to play or for women to have any privacy. It is not even a one-bedroom. It is just a one-room structure.

105

Because it is so far from the coast, and they do not own boats, the people of this community work on other people's boats. They go to the coast, and if somebody needs extra labor, they are hired. But they are not guaranteed any work. It costs them forty *rupees* to get to the coast, but they are not sure if they are going to get a daily wage. So they cannot afford to go to the coast with that risk. No transportation is provided for them.

The conditions of poverty in this community are so bad that some women are being forced to sell their kidneys or engage in sex work. It has been two years since the tsunami, and still there is no restoration of livelihoods.

India has a coastal regulation zone, known as a CRZ, that says it limits housing within 500 meters of the coast. But fishing communities have customary rights over the coast. They have been living there for generations. So to displace them twelve kilometers inward destroys their fishing livelihood. Communities in Chennai living on Marina Beach are now being threatened with eviction. But right behind them, a "seven-star" hotel is being built in the 500 meter zone. They have been given permission to build there. Tourism is being promoted, and a lot of hotels have licenses to build along the coast, but not the fishing communities.

John Christensen *Director, Tax Justice Network*

Based on personal experiences in international banking, Christensen has observed how poor countries are deprived of the income they generate, particularly through transfer pricing. This involves a company setting up a shell corporation in a tax haven, buying goods at low prices from poor countries and selling them at high prices to rich countries. Since the profit is made in a country with little or no taxation, the company avoids paying taxes on the transaction. This kind of decep-  *tive trade practice has increased in recent decades from capital account liberalization and trade liberalization, which were promoted by the IMF and World Bank as part of the Washington Consensus. That ideologically-driven policy also encouraged poor countries to cut taxes on imports and raise taxes on domestic production, which seriously damaged weak economies. In addition, countries were forced (by debt conditionalities) to privatize their industries and services in a manner that allowed foreign investors to buy up public assets at bargain prices.*

How I Became Involved in Banking

I grew up on the island of Jersey in the 1960s. I left to study as an economist. I worked for many developing countries in my twenties on co-operative savings systems.

In the mid-1980s, I was working in Malaysia with the national government. Their banks were then very poorly regulated. Hundreds of millions of dollars of deposits had been shifted out of Malaysia into offshore accounts. That was disturbing. To shift hundreds of millions of dollars, the people who were embezzling the money were using sophisticated and secretive offshore bank accounts. I was puzzled that the bankers, lawyers, and accountants involved paid no attention to the embezzlement. None asked any questions about whether the money was legal. Much of the embezzled money came from normal deposits that were supposed to be protected by Malaysian law, but they were not.

Since some of the funds had disappeared to my native island of Jersey, my curiosity was aroused. Once I finished my job in Malaysia when I was in my mid-thirties, I decided to return to Jersey to learn about the new offshore economy that was emerging.

Capital Flow Liberalization Promotes Illegal Activity

A bit of background to the offshore economy. From the late 1970s to the middle of the 1990s, the World Bank and the IMF forced countries to adopt capital account liberalization, which enabled capital to move freely between countries without any control. This was part of the conditionality of the Washington Consensus. They ignored the fact that when capital moves freely across borders, it can be shifted into secret accounts and change its identity. There is no way of tracing that capital back to the people who own it, and that is what offshore banking does.

Capital account liberalization encouraged capital flight, the illicit movement of capital from one country to another, particularly into jurisdictions with banking secrecy, where owners could evade taxes.

The IMF and the World Bank, by liberalizing capital flows, opened up a wholly new criminal environment, where capital could be shifted into tax havens around the world and evade taxes. To give an idea of the size of this movement, the most recent estimate of the capital now held offshore by rich individuals is US$11.5 trillion. For those people who want to tackle poverty, this raises intriguing questions. If we taxed that capital at 30% on the income, we could raise $255 billion a year. That would more than pay for the Millennium Development Goal program of tackling poverty.

Offshore Banking as Tax Haven

In 1986, when I came back from Malaysia, Jersey had changed a lot. The island had become an offshore center. Lots of banks around the world were opening branches there. I took a job with a big accounting firm in a division that specialized in offshore trusts and company administration, so I was right at the heart of the beast.

I began to pick up on how it all worked. Nothing was managed through Jersey. Many of the instructions came from the City of London. Capital was coming in from all over the world and being distributed through many jurisdictions. We set up schemes which hid the ownership of money. We might establish an offshore company in Luxembourg, owned by an offshore trust in Bermuda, with trustees in New York or London or Switzerland, and a secret bank account in Luxembourg or Switzerland. With that structure, it becomes almost impossible for the authorities in any country to track it back to the real owner.

This serves anyone engaged in criminal activity, including tax evasion. Offshore tax havens like Jersey are almost exclusively and entirely used for activities that are either criminal, like tax evasion, or bordering on the criminal, because they are setting up tax avoidance strategies. Lawyers and bankers would say tax evasion is illegal but tax avoidance is okay. Some people regard it as the duty of a good citizen to avoid tax. However, if someone is avoiding tax, it means either someone else, usually a poorer person, pays more taxes, or there will be cutbacks in public services.

The African Union says that every year at least $148 billion is taken out of Africa, typically heading to either Europe or North America, and the vast majority of that capital never returns. This is a crisis for Africa in two senses. First, Africa's financial resources are literally disappearing northwards. No tax revenues flow back to Africa, even though the owners remain in Africa. Second, if that capital were invested in Africa, it would create both jobs and tax revenues. So Africa loses the capital, and the tax revenues. As dirty money from drug trafficking, embezzlement, bribes, fraud, or corrupt practices is transferred abroad, the tax burden is shifting increasingly onto middle income earners and lower income earners. That increases the gap between the rich and the poor.

Transfer Pricing and Tax Avoidance

Very often people think of bribery as the principal source of corruption, but bribery is actually a very minor part of corruption. Less than 10% of dirty money stems from bribery. The vast majority arises from commercial transactions, using what is called "transfer pricing." Typically this arises from cross-border trades where false invoicing is used to shift capital out of one country into another country, typically a tax haven, in order to avoid or evade tax.

Extreme examples of this can be found in Africa, where a lot of the mineral resources are traded on paper through tax havens like Jersey. Oil is invoiced to an offshore subsidiary in Jersey or in Switzerland. It is exported out of Africa at a very low price so that the offshore company is paying Africans way below the market price for the oil or mineral. The profits will be retained in the offshore subsidiary. The oil will be re-invoiced back to the mainstream economy where it is being sold to the end user at a high price. The difference between the low invoice price paid to Africa and the high invoice price received when the oil is sold is retained offshore in the tax-free or minimum-tax jurisdiction. That is the way the vast majority of capital flight operates.

An American researcher [at Pennsylvania State University], Simon J. Pak, has compiled examples of these practices from American customs records.* He has found bicycle tires being imported at $400 each and prefabricated houses being exported out of America to Trinidad at $1.50 each. These practices minimize taxable income in the US by raising reported costs (such as the bicycle tires) and lowering reported revenue (from the prefabricated houses).

A more elaborate example is Mobutu, the dictator-president of Zaire for many years and the pioneer of African kleptocracy. During his presidency from 1965 to 1997, his company, Gecko Mines, exported diamonds out of Zaire at about $8.55 per karat, which is far below the world market price of diamonds. Over the course of his presidency, Mobutu embezzled approximately $5 billion out of Zaire into offshore accounts using that kind of transfer pricing strategy.

Aggressive tax avoidance using transfer pricing applies across most sectors. It is not peculiar to extractive industries. It is used by pharmaceutical

---

* Simon J. Pak (2006) "Capital Movement through Trade Misinvoicing: The Case of Africa," *Journal of Financial Crime*, Vol 14, No. 4, 2007, pp 474 – 489.

industries, media, and communications. It applies to many horticultural and agricultural exports out of Africa, in fact to virtually any cross-border trades. This is very corrupting. Transfer pricing is regarded not just as normal business practice—it is regarded as good business practice. This is a challenge to companies that claim they want to be good corporate citizens. They should begin by paying the taxes that are due on the profits they generate in the countries where they operate. However, very few companies disclose what profits they earn in the jurisdictions where they operate, what taxes are due on those profits, and what taxes are paid on those profits.

One of the things that amused me about Jersey, a rather cold and wind-swept island in the middle of the English channel, is that "on paper" a lot of tropical commodities come from there, yet I never saw a banana plantation or a coffee plantation there. Many agricultural commodities coming out of Latin America and Africa are traded via tax havens like Jersey in order to shift the profits out of Latin America and Africa.

Hidden Monopoly Power

Offshore companies are also used to disguise the monopolistic positions of big companies that dominate trade in Latin America and Africa. Disclosure of beneficial ownership reveals that supposedly competing companies are in fact owned by the same company. In Kenya, for example, the cement market appears to be highly competitive between four large companies and a number of others. In fact, these four companies are not competing. The market is dominated by a major French company called La Farge, which effectively controls the market price.* The same applies to other trading sectors. Combining that with transfer pricing means very little value remains in the country of origin. It is shifted offshore. They achieve very high monopolistic prices but use all sorts of devices to shift the profits out of the country of origin into a tax haven where they pay no tax at all.

The Washington Consensus

Offshore bank accounts and offshore trusts and offshore companies have been in use since the 1920s. Concerns about this were first raised in

---

* Ed.: Lafarge has a 41 per cent stake in East Africa Portland, a 17 per cent stake in Athi River Mining Ltd., and a 58.6% controlling stake in Bamburi Cement. It also holds a majority stake in cement manufacturers in both Uganda and Tanzania. http://www.mashada.com/blogs/RIBA_CAPITAL/2007/12/10/___Lafarge_Acquires_Egypt_s_Cement_Company.

1923 with the League of Nations. The World Bank and the IMF must have been aware that capital account liberalization would increase the potential for tax evasion and aggressive tax avoidance structures. Apparently, they were so committed to the ideological agenda of the Washington Consensus that they went ahead blithely, uncaring about the consequences.

The Washington Consensus went beyond capital account liberalization because they were also pushing for trade liberalization. The idea was to create a world of free trade, so they wanted to reduce tariff barriers. They ignored the huge subsidies that are paid in the European Union and the US—so, by forcing a reduction in tariffs, they only looked at one part of the equation. At that time tariffs comprised 50 to 60 percent of government revenue in Africa and Latin America. The IMF insisted that countries substitute a value-added tax or a general sales tax. The IMF claimed the revenues lost from tariffs would be regained through a tax on consumption. Now behind this was a rather quirky economic theory devised by an economist named Arthur Laffer that if you reduce taxes, you will stimulate sufficient economic growth to recover the lost revenue.

Laffer's theory was put into practice by the Thatcher government in the UK and the Reagan government in the US, and some people claimed it had some success. More recently, it has proven to be wrong, and no economist will give it serious consideration. But the IMF pushed forward trade liberalization. IMF research in 2007 has revealed that for every $1.00 of tax revenue that governments in Africa lost through trade liberalization and cuts in tariffs, they recovered, at best, 30¢ through the new VAT regime.[†] The change in tax regimes hit the poor hardest. Whereas trade taxes are quite progressive because wealthy companies and people pay tariffs on their imports of luxury goods, general sales taxes and VAT regimes are generally quite regressive. They have a disproportionate impact on the poor. Not only did the governments of these countries lose tax revenue; their poor people had to pay more tax. Bravo IMF! Bravo World Bank! But they are still in Africa telling the African countries what is best for them.

The ideology imposed by the IMF and World Bank did not stop there. The Washington Consensus had four key strands. First, capital account liber-

† Ed.: See Thomas Baunsgaard and Michael Keen, Tax Revenue and (or?) Trade Liberalization, December 2005, IMF Fiscal Affairs Department, Working Paper WP/05/112 Washington, D.C. : International Monetary Fund. http://www.imf. org/external/pubs/ft/wp/2005/wp05112.pdf . A later version of the same paper appears at http://www.ssc.wisc.edu/~scholz/Seminar/Keen.pdf.

alization, second, trade liberalization, third, reduce your taxes and stimulate growth by following the Laffer Curve (a bit like following the "yellow brick road"—it led nowhere at all). Tax revenues declined for most developing countries, particularly in Africa.

The fourth strand of the Washington Consensus was selling off the state's assets. In most cases, they were sold off so badly and the fees that were paid to World Bank consultants and all of the Western consultants involved were so astronomical that the end price that many developing countries got for themselves was minimal. In other words, they sold the family silver and got very little in return. Worse than that, privatization in many areas, particularly in sectors like water, did not lead to new investment. It simply led to higher prices and massive profit-taking. Very often the fine print of the privatization sales involved all sorts of in-built subsidies, tax holidays, and capital depreciation allowances way beyond the norm. In short, privatization was handled in such a bad way that the vast majority of countries gained very little from it.

Debt Versus Democracy: Accountable to Whom?

Alongside faulty privatization programs, the IMF and World Bank also pushed developing countries deeper into debt. The most efficient and least expensive way of raising government revenue and financing capital expenditure is to tax. It is the cheapest way, particularly for sovereign nations with relatively good credit ratings. Borrowing externally is the most expensive option, and worse still it brings with it a whole lot of conditionalities. The IMF and World Bank have undermined the ability of many governments in Africa and Latin America to raise their own taxes. This raises a lot of very troublesome questions about the commitment the IMF and World Bank have to democracy, which depends on the ability of citizens and parliaments to raise and spend tax revenues. So the IMF and the World Bank have purposely pursued programs which undermine democracy in these countries.

African people are deeply troubled that they are accountable to external people more than to their own electorates. It is not just the World Bank and the IMF that are imposing conditions. Government aid departments, such as Britain's Department for International Development, have offered advice and imposed conditions upon their advice. In many cases, the advice has been extremely poor.

So rather than use taxes to fund expenditures on health services or education, many countries in Africa have been forced to privatize, to impose costs onto education and borrow massive debt externally. In my consultations with 18 countries in Africa, I have learned that because of the high price charged for education, most African families cannot afford to take their children through education beyond primary level. Secondary level is just too expensive. The tertiary level, higher education at university or education colleges, is beyond their means. There is wholesale under-investment in education in Africa, which will lead to lower rates of economic growth.

The World Bank and the IMF have undercut the basis of economic growth in Africa. They have created much less stable social environments in Africa. They have created the conditions in which criminality, not just bribe-taking but all sorts of other crimes, including tax evasion, has become the norm. This has led to a political environment which is a great deal less secure now than it was before the IMF and the World Bank intervened. To understand why, across Africa, Middle East and some parts of Asia you have such high levels of insecurity, resentment towards the West, and indeed terrorism, you need to understand that the West is largely responsible for the undermining of the economies here and for the social disintegration that I have seen in the last 30 years.

Cliff Cobb   *Historian, Author*

Poverty stems from inequality of power. It began with the invention of agriculture, at which point the warrior class extracted a surplus from peasants and created cities. At every point in history, when agricultural technology allowed an increase in food production, greater poverty resulted, because the surplus was taken, leaving workers and peasants worse off than before. Poverty did not slowly decline over time. Wages rose and fell in waves over hundreds of years. For example, European workers were generally better off in 1450 than in 1850. Enclosures (land  *privatization) created poverty in Europe after 1500, partially under the influence of Protestant theology, which emphasized private salvation and private property and de-emphasized social reciprocity. Colonialism carried the same ideology to the rest of the world. The same instruments that inflicted poverty on workers in Europe were used to dominate people in other countries. In addition, trade patterns in the post-colonial era have not been mutually beneficial. The countries of the South have not been allowed to use tariffs to initiate the development of manufacturing. In addition, many poor countries are still tied to the colonial pattern of exporting raw materials (agricultural products) and their relative value has declined over time. To change all of those patterns, the South must demand justice, not charity.*

Poverty Stems from Domination

I define poverty as the domination of one person over another. Poverty is thus based on social relationships. It occurs whenever one person takes part of the surplus produced by other people.

Poverty began with the advent of agriculture. Although agriculture permitted more calories to be produced per person, that did not make everyone better off. Just the opposite happened. The first agricultural revolution, about eight thousand years ago, permitted more food to be produced per worker, but absolute poverty increased. Archaeologists have shown that people became more poorly nourished with the development of agriculture. They have discovered that the average height of humans declined. Most people were not able to gain the fruits of their own labor, because there was a warrior class that was able to take the surplus away from them and use it to build cities.

A second agricultural revolution took place about 250 years ago, at the beginning of the Industrial Revolution. Once again, food output increased, but poverty increased as well. Declining nutrition caused the average height of humans in the 19th century to shrink to the lowest point in history. Even though the national wealth of Northern Europe increased, most people became poorer, precisely because of the paradox that increased wealth produces greater poverty.

The Green Revolution in the 1960s and 1970s initiated a third agricultural revolution. Grain output doubled or even tripled in many countries, and many agronomists believed that they had solved the world hunger problem. But the increase in food production made most peasants worse off. Even though average incomes rose, wealth disparities also rose. Wealthy farmers grew richer, but small-scale peasants lost their land and became tenants. They were worse off than before.

The Paradox of Poverty Amidst Plenty

How is it possible to explain the paradox of poverty? How is it that in countries in which there is growing wealth there are actually more poor people than there were before? In short, how is it that we can explain why "trickle down economics" does not work, why doesn't wealth trickle down from the rich to the poor?

This is the basic paradox of poverty. Throughout the history of civilization, whenever new technology allows an increase in productivity, the result is not prosperity for everyone, but instead, a few benefit while the majority suffer. A late 19th century economist, Henry George, offered an explanation of the poverty paradox in a book called *Progress and Poverty*. He explained why an increase in prosperity for society causes increased poverty to the majority of people. There is a fixed amount of natural resources in the world and those who own the resources: land, air, water, and so on, are able to charge higher and higher prices for them as an economy develops. Those who own land can become wealthy simply by charging more rent to the people who need to use it to live and to work. The people who have to pay the landlord more money are made worse off than they were before. That is the basic mechanism by which increased output causes most people to become poorer.

It may help to consider a fictitious example of a society in which there is only one oasis that has all the water, to which everyone has to come for their water supply. If a single person owned that water supply, that oasis, we would all be forced to pay as much money as we were able to for that water. Yet, it could in fact be owned by everyone because it came from nature. There is no particular reason for one person to own it. After a while, or perhaps even in short order, some people would begin to feel intense resentment. There might be an eruption of violence as people began to try to overthrow the people who own that resource and take it.

Waves of Poverty in European History

Most people have the impression that poverty slowly declined throughout European history as progress was made. In fact, poverty did not slowly decline. It occurred in waves. Starting in the year 800, there was gradual improvement in the lives of people for the next 400 years. After about 1200, things began to get worse. Food intake declined, and the population of Europe became less disease resistant. When the bubonic plague struck Europe in 1348, between 30 and 40 percent of the population died of disease within two or three years. During the next 150 years, from 1350 to 1500, because there were fewer peasants working the land, they were actually able to get higher wages, as were the urban workers. The period from 1400 to 1500, was a golden age for European workers. After 1500, wages declined in Europe. They did not rise to the same level as 1500 until around 1900, four centuries later.

As the economy began to grow after 1500, output and prices rose. The landowning gentry, the wealthiest people in society, were able to buy up land from small farmers. The gentry, the wealthy elite, became richer, and the peasants became poorer and lost their land. During the reign of Queen Elizabeth, poverty and landlessness became a big problem in England. There were bands of vagrants roaming the roads. There was a rise in the crime rate in England in the 1500s that resulted, very specifically, because of the increase of landlessness. That had not happened before. Poverty on that scale was a new phenomenon in Europe after 1550.

Enclosures Cause Poverty from 1500 to 1900

The decline of wages in early modern Europe happened largely because of enclosures, starting in the 16th century. The word enclosure may create the wrong impression. It does not mean putting a fence around something. Enclosure actually refers to a legal process whereby one person gains private control over a larger amount of land.

There were two categories of common lands that were enclosed. First, there were common fields that were cultivated. Each farmer in the village had individual plots or strips as his or her allotment. During a certain period of the year, the sheep would graze on this cultivated area, and their droppings would fertilize the fields. Second, there were common areas that were not cultivated, called wastelands. Those areas provided firewood, fish, and grazing land for sheep and cattle. Access to that land was very important for the subsistence of people, because the amount of grain they were growing on their land in the enclosed area was often not enough to actually feed them. They needed to catch fish and graze cattle to supplement their meager diets.

The enclosure process was two-fold, corresponding to the two types of commons. First, the landlords rescinded rights of access to the wastelands. Technically speaking, the nobility or gentry already had feudal rights over most of the land in and around the village, but they had traditionally granted the villagers rights of access to the wastelands. As the value of land rose, however, these conventional rights were denied. For example, the story of Robin Hood shows how access was denied to the forest to hunt or gather wood, because that forest belonged to the lord. The process of privatizing the common wastelands continued over the next few centuries. By the 19th century, little land was left in England for gathering food and fuel for subsistence.

Second, the enclosure of the cultivated fields required consolidation of separate strips of land. The gentry believed they could farm more productively if they had an unbroken tract of land. They consolidated strips of land either through cooperative agreements with the village or by a special Act of Parliament that gave them the authority to take over that land.

At least in theory, the new owners paid compensation, but when property was seized through eminent domain, many people felt they were not fully compensated. Even if they were compensated in one generation, the future generations of small-scale farmers lost that land, so that, over time, a smaller proportion of the population owned most of the land.

By 1700, at least one half of the land of England had been enclosed. Few independent farm operators survived the process. Millions of displaced people became dependent on someone else for work. Farm tenants had to pay full market rent for the land they cultivated, as they were no longer protected by customary rules. Day laborers received wages below subsistence. By the late 18th century, factories began to attract people from the countryside, because they paid wages slightly higher than farm wages. Since the life expectancy of factory workers was only 25 to 35 at that time, and since workers were fleeing the countryside to work in factories, living conditions in the countryside must have been worse.

Workers driven into cities by the enclosures had nothing to sell but their labor. They were at the mercy of the mill owners. As the novels of Charles Dickens show, they were paid miserably and lived very poorly. In fact, in the absence of drinking beer, most people in England would not have had enough calories to survive.* They were living at the margin of subsistence. In the 19th century, even a 5 or 6 percent excise tax on sugar or beer made the difference between getting enough to eat and slowly starving. Consumption taxes lowered the standard of living for a lot of people and probably reduced their life expectancy. They were that close to the margin.

Even though it might not be obvious, the loss of the commons is directly related to the situation we face today. Thomas Jefferson believed the backbone of modern democracy was widespread ownership of land and small businesses. He wanted to prevent big business from dominating society, because he was skeptical that democracy could function if most people worked for somebody else. The enclosure of the commons not only hurt small-scale farming, it also created economic conditions under which small business would have difficulty sustaining itself alongside big business.

We still live in an economy that allows a few large entities to engulf others. The basic problem is the lack of reciprocity. If everyone had to pay

---

* Beer provided between 20 and 30 percent of the daily calories required. Beer is a good way of storing grain, because fermentation allows it to be kept for a long time without rotting. But the necessity of drinking beer as a means of survival is an indication of the actual level of poverty for most people.

for what they took from the commons, then it would be much more difficult for anyone to amass the wealth required to absorb the property of other people. But in a society in which reciprocity breaks down, wealth becomes more concentrated, and small-scale operations are absorbed or displaced. That has been taking place for hundreds of years.

Protestantism and Privatization

Part of the reason enclosures began after 1500, is related to the Protestant Reformation that began in 1517. Protestantism was developing as a new form of Christianity that was very individualistic. For Protestants, each individual was responsible for his or her own salvation. This tied in very closely with the emerging idea of private property. Feudalism was based on the idea that if you owned something you also had a social obligation; there was a connection between owning and owing. Private possession by families had existed for centuries, but it was always tied to some communal affiliation.

Starting in the 16th century the idea arose of private ownership without any obligation to the community. That was a radical change because it meant the loss of a sense of reciprocity. Private property was based on the idea that individuals should be solely responsible and solely have claim over a particular piece of land, and would not have any obligations to the community. If you owned property, you could use it any way you wanted. It was everyone for himself. So the individualism of theology was connected with the individualism of private property ownership. Those who favored private ownership were often attracted to Protestantism. The people with an affinity for Protestantism were largely merchants and landlords who saw some advantage to them if they could break the old feudal ties and deny that they still owed something to society. They wanted a pure economic relationship of work for money, and cash payments of land rent, not the mutual obligations of feudalism.

This was the beginning of capitalism—the marriage of a religious idea of individualism and a property-owning idea of individualism. The basic idea was that you do not owe anybody anything—not the government and not your neighbor; your wealth is all yours. That has never happened completely, because there have always been taxes and regulations. But in the 21st century, when neoliberals talk about privatization, private property rights, and the poor being responsible for their own condition, they are extrapolating this logic and saying, "If I own something, I do not owe anybody anything. I do not owe taxes. You cannot regulate me. It is mine, all mine." That way of thinking is rooted in the Protestant notion of radical individualism.

The logic of academic economics reinforces that doctrine. If people are poor, they are blamed as individuals for not having invested enough in "human capital" (education). Some economists support a little charity in the form of welfare programs. But few economists speak about why ownership of property is so concentrated. Instead, they focus on education as the solution to poverty. In doing so, they distract the public from raising questions about the historic roots of inequality in the unequal distribution of property.

Colonies Make Poverty Global

One of the safety valves for European poverty in the early modern period was the possibility of migrating overseas to colonies established by Europeans. There is a direct correlation between the impoverishment of European workers and the colonization of other lands. First of all, it provided a safety valve. If colonization had not existed, revolutions would have been far more frequent in Europe than they were. Second, the same process that the European elite used to take away the land from the peasants in Europe was used in Asia, Africa and Latin America. In that way, the European elites were able to increase their power. So, even though some Europeans benefited by colonizing the rest of the world, the average European did not benefit. If European peasants and workers had benefited, average wages would have gone up, but they did not. The only people to benefit were the top 3 to 5 percent of European society. So European society, as a whole, was being treated very much like the exploited, colonized people in other parts of the world.

The Irony of the "Free Trade" Ideology

There is a great irony today that the developed countries of the world are talking about free trade as if that is the solution to the problem of poverty in the world. Historically, almost every country that developed did so by building a wall of protection around itself. England was the first country to develop an industrial structure in the eighteenth and nineteenth centuries. After they developed, they pronounced that free trade was good for everyone, when in fact it was good for England alone. One of the major reasons for the American Revolution was to enable the American colonies to develop enough economic independence behind tariff barriers so their infant industries were able to thrive. Only at that point were they able to compete with England. Much of the history of the last couple of centuries has been an effort of countries to become economically independent through tariffs, to be able to develop manufactured goods. If they fail to do that, countries become dependent on raw material exports, which is a problem. The economies of East Asia most recently developed using tariffs. Once they were able to enter the world economy on the same footing as everybody else, they removed the tariffs. But it is essential for most countries to use tariffs as a way of reaching that point. The United States and Europe have prevented Third World countries from doing that. The rich nations are not practicing free trade. They have imposed tariffs to prevent the import of finished goods from developing nations. Yet they are telling the Third World to practice free trade. There is a deep irony in all of this. That is a way of keeping Third World countries in their place and preventing them from ever developing.

Poverty and the Terms of Trade

One of the legacies of colonialism is that the poor countries of the Third World are continuing to export raw materials and the countries of Europe and North America produce and export finished products. This stems from a practice that was developed long ago, and the intention was to make sure that the countries of the Third World remain backward and remain dependent and are never able to develop. So to this day they are continuing to survive on the export of raw materials. That has always been to the disadvantage of the country exporting the raw materials, and it gets worse each year.

The terms of trade are against the exporter of raw materials. The price of raw materials has gone down over time, but the price of finished goods, which contain a lot of value added in the form of labor, rise in price each year. Third World countries pay more for what they receive in trade and they are paid less for what they export. As a result, Third World countries remain impoverished.

Justice, Not Charity

To put an end to world poverty would require three elements. First we would have to change the international trade system to make it fair for all countries. We need to end the process whereby the rich nations of the north are continually able to extract wealth from the south. The second element involves dealing with a problem that has accumulated because of the unfair trade system of the last 50 years. The accumulation of debt in most third world countries makes it impossible for them to grow out of poverty. So ending the debt by forgiving it, and forgiving it unconditionally with no strings attached is the second requirement for ending poverty in the world. The third element would be to end monopoly control of resources. The resources of nature are given to all of us and yet a handful of people and corporations have control over them, oil companies being a prime example. If we could enable everyone to benefit from those resources, we could end poverty. And the way to do that is by restoring the idea of the commons. Those resources exist for all of us in common. That does not mean we have to own a little share of each resource—an oil well or piece of a river. It means that the value of those resources that is currently privatized by corporate shareholders of oil companies, mining companies, or real estate syndicates, would be shared by all. That is what the commons means. That is what we should be aiming for if we are interested in ending poverty.

By analyzing poverty into those three elements, we can also begin to understand why poverty is so much more extreme in Third World countries of the South than it is in First World countries in the North. In the North, poverty exists largely because the resources are owned by a small elite of individuals and corporations. In the South the same is true: the resource division is equally skewed towards a small elite. But the South also faces the continuing problems of unbalanced trade and of debt. Poverty exists in every country in the world. There is no denying that. But the poverty is more extreme in the countries that are dealing with this triple problem of trade, debt and monopoly power over resources.

To summarize, poverty in the world cannot be eliminated unless the poor themselves say, "We insist on justice, not charity." One example of that justice is forgiving international debt. That is simple justice because of the corrupt way the debt was created. The second element would be to change the tax system in every country of the world. Right now most taxes fall on the poor in the form of consumption taxes and taxes on wages. If justice is to be done, most of the taxes should fall on property ownership and not on wages. Third, the poor should demand agrarian reform, land reform, restoring land to the people who actually work on it, instead of a few landowners. A fourth thing is to end privatization of natural resources. We have seen in Bolivia what is possible, where the Bolivian people took back the water that had been given to Bechtel and they forced Bechtel out of the country. Now the Bolivian people once more own that water.

George Collins   *Teacher*

Poverty is the result of monopolization of land and other resources. In Jamaica, in the 1950s, the first post-colonial government under Chief Minister Michael Manley adopted a limited program of land value taxation. Had it survived and with higher tax rates, it would have promoted increased production and reduced land hoarding. But it was whittled away through concessions during the time Manley was in office. Jamaica has become poorer since then because foreign owners of bauxite mines and tourist resorts have  *never paid their fair share of taxes and because of privatization of public services.*

The usual explanation for poverty is that people are not educated or need better training and better habits. Those are answers based simply on observation of results rather than identification of causes. The cause is essentially the maldistribution of wealth: a disproportionate amount going to those who own or control the sources of wealth, such as land and other monopolies. So land monopoly is the fundamental starting point for understanding poverty.

History of Land Taxes in Jamaica

I was born in Jamaica, and as a young man, I learned about a tool to fight monopoly. At that time, Jamaica was emerging from colonialism, and the political environment was alive with new ideas of how to operate a government and how to raise revenue. Representative government was just beginning in Jamaica.

The People's National Party, a socialist party, had as one of its planks the collection of land rent, land value taxation. This was a very radical proposition, radical insofar as it went to the root of injustice, unlike other measures that were superficial. This measure was significantly different from what the opposition was offering, or any other leader in the newly independent states of that time.

Norman Manley, the Chief Minister (the equivalent of the prime minister) had learned about this as a law student in England before World War I, when the Liberal Party was active in Britain, and Lloyd George and Winston Churchill were making grand statements about how to control land monopoly and land speculation. He brought those ideas to Jamaica. When he assumed leadership of the government in 1955, he introduced land value taxation.

In order to sell the idea to the people, he had to explain it in simple terms to a largely agricultural population. One of the pieces of campaign literature illustrates the method. There was a little pamphlet with bold red and green figures and lettering on it, and it showed a simple farmer in a straw hat working in the fields, and it said: your crops will not be taxed; your fencing will not be taxed; your barns will not be taxed; only the land will be taxed. It was offering a way out from under the burden of taxation on production. It would release the productive energies of a country by taking taxes off peoples' backs and putting it just on the land. There may not have been widespread understanding of this principle at the time of its implementation, but it was well grounded in Manley's exposure to it in Britain.

He had the land revalued, as no valuation had taken place since the 1930s. He introduced a tax rate that was initially very low. He wanted to avoid stirring up too much opposition because he knew the amount people had to pay would increase a lot as soon as the new assessment took effect.

Opposition to the land tax came, nevertheless. There was a lot of absentee ownership of large estates, and much of the land was unused. Those owners opposed the tax, and although the rate was low, many of them faced increased tax costs. So the challenge to the tax was pretty extensive. Concessions began to be made very soon. As time went on, more and more exemptions were granted. The flourishing tourist industry had the resort area lands excluded from the land tax. So its effectiveness was diminished. Gradually, over time, it became a less and less significant part of the revenue raising process.

A number of years later, in the early 1960s, when I happened to meet Prime Minister Manley in New York, I asked him why he had rescinded this measure that he considered to be an important reform measure. His answer was: "I am a politician, and as a politician I know that when something does not work, you have to try something else."

If Mr. Manley had persisted in his original efforts, the retention of the land value tax would have given the economy a tremendous boost, making possible the reduction of taxes on productive enterprises, as it was aimed at doing. The reduction of taxes on wages would have helped poor people. In addition, reduced tariffs would lowered the price of consumer goods. A land value tax would also have opened up of a lot of land and resources to more extensive and intensive production. All of these things would have stimulated the economy. The greatest benefit would have been the release of fertile land and increased production. The tourist industry would have contributed to the revenue base. Jamaica could have become one of the garden spots of the Caribbean, both for tourism and for business. It could have had good schools and maintained its status as one of the leading countries in the region.

Jamaica: Control by Mining Companies, Large Farms

Jamaica is a very poor country, with average income perhaps $100 a year. It is poor because all of the resources that it possesses are either granted or franchised to exploiters at minimal rates. It has bauxite, the basic mineral for the manufacturing of aluminum. Bauxite lands are either owned by the mining companies or leased by them on very favorable terms. The revenues to the government from those leases are far below their value. Although the bauxite mining companies are partnered with the Jamaican government on a 51/49 basis, that in itself is not the significant issue. What matters is that the revenues paid to the government are low, and the terms of the agreement are very favorable to the extracting companies.

Some local individuals own a lot of land, but the bauxite and the tourist industry are owned and controlled by outsiders. The leases and the franchises of the bauxite mining companies are very generous and yield very little revenue. The government partners with the bauxite mining companies, but it is an unequal partnership.

The taxes from the tourist industry are too low for the government to provide support to develop any sector of the economy. So over the decades, Jamaica's economy has been declining. The monopoly situation still prevails with large ownership. The agricultural sector is primarily dominated by small farmers. Many of them are not economically viable. So the government relies upon taxing imports, wages, and productive output, which stultify the economy.

Privatization in Jamaica

Jamaica has had a very difficult time with the IMF, and has sought over the last several years to cease borrowing from the IMF because it was overburdened with debt. About three years ago when I was there, the percentage of its budget that was devoted to debt payment was about 60 percent. Very stringent restrictions were imposed by the IMF since the 1970s, limiting government services. Now they have paid off much of that debt, but they are still in pretty dire straits, so they are unable to provide services or maintain basic infrastructure. Roads are in bad shape. There are frequent cuts in water and electricity service.

As a result of privatization, prices of services have either gone up or the quality of service has declined and the price remains the same. In effect, that is a price increase. A limited-access highway has been built, as a toll road. Everyone is forced to pay for this, because it is the only route from point to point. It replaced the old roads that were there. After the power company was privatized, people complained that the services were worse than when it was run by the government. The airport in Montego Bay has been privatized, and they have put in new jetways. While it is probably more convenient for tourist traffic, it is unlikely to yield a fair level of revenues to the government. So, in the absence of collecting land rent, the government is turning to other revenue streams, such as selling public enterprises with some leaseback provisions. That gives the government a lump sum, but that does not last very long.

Jose Eli da Veiga *Economics Professor, University of Sao Paulo*

Poverty in Brazil stems from the patterns of land ownership that developed in the 19th century. The poorest parts of Brazil are in the northeast, where sugar plantations dominated the economy, and there was little small-scale agriculture. The wealthier parts of the nation are in the south, where family farms were the norm. The latter form of agriculture produced food crops for Brazilians, so mining was only able to develop in regions in which small-scale agriculture was common. In the US, in contrast to Brazil, artisans emerged within a society based on small-scale farming in New England, and industry then developed from the workshops of artisans. The landlord class in Brazil, which lived on sugar exports and imported most other goods, stifled efforts to establish protective tariffs, which would have helped industry develop. The plantation owners in the southeastern US also sought to block such tariffs, but after the US Civil War the northern industrialists established high tariffs, enabling the US to industrialize. Brazil still needs agrarian reform. However, since few Brazilians are now interested in farming, agrarian reform would not help as much as it would have in the 19th century.

Widespread Poverty or Prosperity Tied to Land System

To understand the cause of poverty, we have to understand its origins. In Brazil, the states with the highest levels of poverty began with large plantations. The regions with the lowest levels of poverty—Rio Grande do Sul, southwestern Paraná, and Santa Catarina—were based on family farming. That demonstrates that the poverty problem is more related to the form or process of land appropriation than to any other factor, historically speaking. Poverty in Brazil today originated in the 19th century, not earlier. The country was not heavily populated until then, and it had conditions similar to other countries that would have made it possible to reduce poverty to minimal levels.

A century and a half ago, Brazil was dominated by a landowner class that still had strong ties to the metropolis [Portugal]. The landowning elite received most income from sugar production. Some people, particularly André Rebouças, had a clear vision that things could be different, if the abolition of slavery could be connected with access to land by workers.*However, the abolitionist movement was defeated in this broader goal by the landowning elite, which still resembled the Portuguese court.

Every place in the world where monoculture has predominated, there is a strong social contrast. For example, in Italy and Portugal, the northern regions followed a path of family farming, meaning property in land was dispersed and democratic, whereas the southern regions followed a pattern of landlord domination. In the southern regions, agriculture tended toward monoculture and laborers were excluded from property-ownership.

Plantations in the northeast of Brazil effectively prohibited family farming. Brazil is so big that there could be simultaneously a very centralized structure of monoculture, with deep social divisions in the sugar cane regions of the northeast, in what is now Pernambuco, while other areas developed family farms. The social division in the northeast developed in the late 19th century and early 20th, as Europeans went to the north and created a landownership structure that is different from the rest of the country. We can still see the repercussions of this.

Before the industrial revolution, it was very rare that any society could increase per capita income systematically. This only occurred a few times and in a few countries. Some people imagine that it happened as a result of a mineral cycle, as when people migrated to Minas Gerais. But that ignores the need for a successful farm economy around the mines that could supply miners with food. So, mining generally developed where there was an economy based on independent farmers instead of an economy of feudal landowners. The barrier to formation of an economy of independent farm-

---

* Ed.: Slavery was abolished in Brazil in 1888.

ers in Brazil has been a constant factor in our history. The central feature that affects development and poverty is whether power is democratized or not. The elite caused many regions of the Brazilian economy to be retrograde by barring access to land. That changed only ten years ago, with the National Family Agriculture Improvement Program, or PRONAF, a decree favorable to family farming.

Why Brazil and the US Developed Differently

The US gained freedom from British power early, and there was not an elite that could centralize power. Power moved permanently to Washington only after 1932. In Brazil, domination by Portugal delayed our development. Our independence was not based on a popular movement but was simply declared by the son of the king of Portugal. So, it merely transferred power to a Brazilian monarchy and a centralized elite.

Some people imagine that Brazilian industrialization was suppressed, but that is not true. Instead, the development of craftmanship was thwarted in most regions of Brazil by the lack of independent farmers. Since craftsmanship precedes industry, the latter was slow to develop. This was completely different in New England, where family farming first supported the establishment of crafts, which is why American industry first developed in that region.

In addition, Brazil's landlord class, which imported their clothes, food, utensils, and working tools, blocked the use of protective tariffs that would have enabled domestic industry to develop. This conflict also occurred in the US and was one of the biggest reasons for the Civil War. In the US, the industrialists won the war. In Brazil, the landlords who dominated the sugar and coffee economies had more power than the small group of early industrialists. Those landlords also feared possible retaliation against their exports, so they put all their strength into not allowing protectionist measures to be adopted. That is why Brazilian industrialization took a long time. The first signs of it appeared in the 1920s.[†] This was a period of "misplaced ideas." Today we normally think of industrialists as favoring free trade. But

---

[†] Ed.: Prof. Da Veiga mentioned something about Baron de Máua, who developed a ship-building and railway company in the 1840s and 1850s, but which ultimately failed as part of an international financial crisis in the period after 1864. However, he does not elaborate on the significance of this for Brazil's development in comparison with the US or explain the relation to his statement that industrialization in Brazil was delayed until the 1920s.

in the 19th century, it was the big landowners and slave-holders who were economic liberals in the sense of being against protectionism. The sides of this debate have now completely reversed.

A large group of people in Brazil—the "excluded people"—never gained a place in the economy Some migrated to take possession of unoccupied lands in sparsely populated places like Maranhão. As soon as they established themselves and made the land more valuable, a speculator would show up to take those lands. They became victims of fraudulent land appropriation or "land grabbing." Factory owners benefited by having a large contingent of workers with no opportunity to earn a living on their own. That pushed wages down during the whole industrialization process. This structure continued into the 20th century, with poverty growing worse.

During the period of slavery in the U.S, slave owners often taught their slaves to read, because they were Protestants and wanted their slaves to read the Bible. The opposite happened in Brazil, where the religion was Catholic, and the Church considered slaves to be poor souls and not worth teaching. So, there was a big delay in education.

Models of Agrarian Reform

Brazil still has not had agrarian reform despite changes in the past decade, but even if reform occurred, agricultural land does not have the decisive importance for poverty that it had in the 19th century. The people who once needed land are now in the favelas (urban squatter settlements). So the current program to promote rural resettlement is a very small part of the economy.

Why would someone today like to be a small farmer? Most people who now have access to land do not succeed, because normally they have 20 to 30 hectares. It is more difficult now to make a living on 20 hectares than to be the CEO of IBM. So it is difficult to understand that 500,000 families would like to be small farmers. They plan to provide land to 100,000 settlers, but even this goal is not attainable. Even if they were effective, it would still affect only 10 percent of the agricultural land. This is not agrarian reform. In Japan, after WWII, one third of the agricultural land of the country changed hands in two years. That is agrarian reform.

One issue related to agrarian reform is knowing the number of people involved. To determine how many people want land, the government did a survey a few years ago and asked all eligible people to go to the post office and fill out a form. Public officials and those who already own property were not eligible After all those people answered, technicians eliminated people in the same family as someone who has land from the government. When we analyzed the results, there were 300,000. However, because some people did not know about the survey and because there may be some new people who want land, we estimated the total as 500,00.

Joao Pedro Stedile, the leader of the People Without Land Movement, came up with an estimate of 11 million landless people. To calculate that, he took the census estimate of the rural population. From that, he subtracted farmers with property and administrators who are not eligible and supposed that all the others are landless. He estimated 11 million people. That is people, not families. It corresponds to about 2 million families. But 2 million is exaggerated. Most of the people I know who live in rural Brazil normally have access to television. If they have basic schooling, they want another perspective of life. Only a small part of the youth think about being a farmer. The rest say the opposite. Stedile is a friend, but we think very differently.

Another concept related to agrarian reform comes from Henry George, an important thinker because of his idea of nationalizing land for capitalism. Even if he was defeated in the countries where this debate took place, we created taxes on the land, especially when the land is not well used. If there is no stewardship in the use of land, we pay very high taxes. A less important land tax in Brazil is the Imposto Territorial Rural (ITR); it means "Rural Territorial Tax." It is very small. But even the debate about whether the thesis of Henry George was right or wrong did not take place here.

Shelton Davis *Anthropologist*

Ethnic diversity has become an important issue in efforts to reduce poverty in Latin America. During the colonial era, ethnic and racial groups were often separated and allowed to maintain their distinct identities. After independence, there was an assumption in many countries that everyone would assimilate and lose their ethnic identity. Communal land rights were ignored, making it easier to privatize land ownership. Only recently have a few nations begun to recognize communal land claims and to work on restoring those rights. But  *land rights are not enough. Indigenous peoples and Afro descendants face discrimination and high rates of poverty. At the same time, their cultures were not recognized. Only in the past decade have international agencies begun to take seriously the special needs and interests of indigenous peoples and Afro descendants. Future programs need to consider not only their human rights as individuals, but also their collective rights.*

Historical Background

Under colonialism in Latin America, indigenous peoples were set off in separate communities and the church organized them as *pueblos,* or communities, with the church in control. They maintained their collective identity. Among Afro-descendants, many escaped from slavery and set up independent communities in remote areas. In Brazil, they were called *Quilombola* communities. There were similar communities on the Pacific coast of Colombia, Ecuador, and Peru. In the Caribbean, slaves mixed with the indigenous peoples, forming communities known as *Garifuna.*

In the United States, preservation of indigenous communities was not a policy. After expanding across the western US, we privatized indigenous lands. The aim was to assimilate native populations, not to maintain their cultural identities.

Independence movements in the 19th century in Latin America claimed that they were going to make indigenous peoples citizens in their countries, but they were assimilated, not recognized. The first country to recognize the land rights of indigenous peoples was Mexico. One important change affecting indigenous peoples was the discovery of rubber on indigenous lands. Exploiting rubber meant invasion of indigenous lands.

Communal Land Rights

Indigenous peoples attempted to maintain their own communal land, but in the late 19th century, much of it was taken from them. Communal land rights were recognized only in a few countries. There were attempts to privatize land and to resettle people from highland areas into lowland areas.

Protection of communal land rights was organized in the post-World War II period by agrarian reform movements in Mexico and Bolivia and in parts of Peru and Ecuador. Peasants, not indigenous peoples, ran those reform movements. Beginning in the 1970s, indigenous peoples started their own movements, which promoted agrarian reform that was tied to cultural and identity rights.

The first international attempt to set up land rights began with an Inter-American Indigenous conference in Mexico in the 1940s. Then the International Labor Organization (ILO) set up its first convention on protecting indigenous peoples, but it was still based on assimilation, rather than cultural recognition. It was not until 1989 that the ILO held another convention to "protect their rights, provide them with the opportunity to participate in development, but recognize their cultural identities." Indigenous movements for land rights broadened into larger cultural issues.

Economic pressures on land are among the most severe problems for indigenous peoples. In the 1970s, many areas inhabited by indigenous peoples were opened to hydrocarbon development and forestry exploitation. In addition, increased sugarcane production displaced cattle ranching, which moved into areas with indigenous peoples. To protect their land, indigenous communities need credits for maintaining forests where they live.

Private landowners do not often accept communal land rights. Also areas have been set up for biodiversity and ignored indigenous-protected areas. By contrast, in Guatemala, the Maya Biosphere Reserve and the Bio-Itza Reserve are biodiversity reserves that are controlled by indigenous communities.

In Brazil in 1988 and in Colombia in 1991 and 1993, a law was passed for the rural Afro-descended communities to identify, demarcate and title their lands. Demarcation means registering communal lands and doing surveys to determine boundaries. On the Pacific coast of Colombia, even though their lands were demarcated, many were displaced by the civil war. A major issue is how to help them regain access to their lands. In Brazil, only a portion of Quilombola lands have been demarcated.

In the 1990s, the expansion of soybean production in Brazil and oil production in Peru brought an invasion of indigenous territories, so land rights issues continue. In Venezuela, their constitution did not introduce the idea of recognizing rights of Afro-Venezuelan populations until 1999.

Poverty and Human Rights of Indigenous Peoples

When there is poverty alleviation, it should take into account indigenous people and Afro-descended people. In urban areas, there is job discrimination against them. In Brazil, most indigenous migrants and Afro-descendants in urban areas have been forced to work in the informal economies.

As part of the Organization of American States (OAS), there is a convention against racial discrimination to promote judicial reform. There is also an OAS declaration on indigenous peoples that is important for fighting poverty caused by discrimination.

Poverty and human development began to be looked at in a major way in the 1990s—poverty by the World Bank and the Inter-American Development Bank and human development by the UN Development Program. Initially their work only made a distinction between rural and urban poverty. Then a discussion began of race and ethnicity. In 1994, George Psacharopolous and Harry Anthony Patrinos of the World Bank produced a book called *Indigenous Peoples and Poverty in Latin America*, which found enormous differences in poverty in rural areas between indigenous and non-indigenous peoples. By the late 1990s, a lot of work showed that Afro-descendants were generally poor. It became important to recognize their rights and assist them to become less poor, but to recognize their identities.

Recognizing Cultural Identity

It was not so long ago that no one gave any thought to multiculturalism. Dominant cultures favored assimilation and integration. It was not until 1967 that there was a convention on political and civil rights that included a special section on cultural rights and identity rights—that not only would you have human rights as individuals, but there would be cultural rights that communities could have. A book called *No Longer Invisible* was published by Minority Rights Group International in 1993. In almost all countries of Latin America and the Caribbean, Afro-descendants and indigenous people started to see themselves as distinctive in culture, spiritual beliefs, music, dance, and identities.

Museums such as the National Museum of American Indian are now run by indigenous people. We are starting an Afro-American Museum to be run by Afro-Americans. Affirmative action in the US not only gave Afro-Americans and Native Americans access to higher education; it also created the idea of Afro-American studies and Native American studies.

International Recognition of Diversity

In the UN human rights program, a special working group on indigenous peoples was started in the early 1980s. A declaration on indigenous human rights has not yet been approved. So the protection of rights was done through agrarian reform, but that does not include cultural identities. In 2004 the UN Development Program (UNDP) began to look at race, ethnicity, and inequality in its report, *Cultural Liberty In Today's Diverse World*.

The World Bank began to take diversity seriously in the late 1970s. By the early 1990s, they began to support multicultural bilingual education in Bolivia. In the late 1990s, Afro-descendants were taken into account. The issue is how to maintain that recognition.

In 2004, the World Bank published *Inequality in Latin America and the Caribbean: Breaking with History*. It concluded that reducing poverty and promoting development is not enough. New policies towards poverty reform should take into account racial and cultural diversity.

When the United Nations Millennium Development Goals were introduced, the issue of maintaining recognition of race and ethnicity was important. How was this to be done? In 2006, the UNDP and other organizations jointly published *Ethnicity and the Millennium Development Goals*, which deals with race and ethnicity. The Human Development Program seeks to ensure that the Millennium Development Goals take into account race, ethnicity, and cultural diversity. The important issue now is the promotion of actual projects that will take diversity into account.

Tourism is an important issue for indigenous peoples. How much income will indigenous communities get when tourists come to visit indigenous communities through eco-tourism and cultural tourism? There is an Afro-Peruvian museum on the coast in Peru, which is promoting tourism. In Bahia in Brazil, there has been tourism. There may be African people and Afro-Americans from the US that go to Brazil and want to visit, looking at heritage.

Will Progress Continue?

Will interest be sustained in reducing racial inequalities? Will organizations recognize that there is a racial and ethnic component of inequality and poverty? We need to promote cultural diversity, because that makes democracy possible. We need to deal with diversity as part of development and poverty reduction.

Trade agreements need to take into account not only labor rights and environmental issues; they should also take into account cultural issues, in order to reduce poverty. Before, we only looked at individual rights, but now we have begun to address collective rights, too. Immigration policies are also important. Remittances by migrants have helped communities and families to reduce poverty.

Democracy requires that social and economic rights be taken into account. Democracy will not continue unless there is reduction of poverty and inequality, as well as recognition of diversity. Many people talk about multicultural democracies as a way of promoting this.

Roland Denis *Author*

The Venezuelan state was formed under complete political dependence on the Spanish and subsequent economic control by the British. It began to evolve into a more democratic state after World War II and began to claim some control over the oil resources that had previously been ceded to foreign companies. The dependency mentality of the Venezuelan oligarchs and the small middle class that supports them has not disappeared, however. The task of the Bolivarian Revolution is not merely to provide services to the urban poor, but also to overcome this history of subservience. The recent radicalization of Latin American leaders has occurred because the US is unwilling to negotiate directly with independent states in the region.

History of State Weakness in Venezuela

The reasons behind poverty in Venezuela are peculiar. As a colonized country from the discovery of Latin America to independence, little infrastructure was developed, and only in special export zones. It was developed only for the production of cacao, sugar and coffee, which led to an export-based economy under the control of the Spanish Exporting Agency.

A whole population was subjected to exploitation through slavery and commission programs. After independence in the early 19th century, we became dependent on the most powerful empire of that time, the British. An export economy developed that repeated the colonial model. There was never any development of a working class or of urban centers from which a democratic culture might emerge.

Because Venezuela lacked a strong government, big companies were able to control the country. When Venezuela was under the dictatorship of Juan Vicente Gomez, he simply transferred control of oil to foreign powers. Huge concessions were given, with minimal benefits for the state. By the 1960s the state became strong enough to establish contracts with oil companies under which the Venezuelan government received half the profits. Nonetheless, this democratic state was dominated by an oligarchic elite.

Oligarchy and the Dependency Mentality

The conspiracy of 2001 against the Chávez government began with the fear among landowners that the state would expropriate their land. Fear united the middle class with the oligarchs, even though the struggle had nothing to do with their interests. There has been little development of a class of small business owners in Venezuela.

The Bolivarian Project is a justice and equality project that stems from the crises that the "weak state, strong oligarchs" model generates. Hugo Chávez plays the role of the leader of a "Savior Type" movement, based on that model. People maintain a negative dependency on the bureaucratic state.

Historically, patriotism was directed toward Spain, not our own country. That is why independence started as a defense of the rights of the King of Spain against the Napoleonic Invasion. Still today in school, Spain is taught to be the "Motherland."

We tore down the statue of Christopher Columbus, as a symbol of one of the worst genocides of human history in which more than 100 million people were killed. That statue was an insult to us. It is being re-installed by the office of the Mayor of Caracas, which is led by a Bolivarian. The mechanisms of subjugation are profound; they are engrained in our skin. That is where tendency of total domination begins.

In the eastern part of Caracas some people even feel more comfortable speaking English, because they deeply despise not only their skin (they think it a curse to be born with dark skin) but also their culture. You will find this in any home of the upper middle class. This cultural annexation and integration also has a material or economic component. They depend on North America for markets and for credit, because without the dollar they could not accumulate capital. They have supported the North any way they can, against social democratic processes in Venezuela. They have even supported the most oppressive elements of the North against the possibility of healthy change.

Radicalism as Reaction to Northern Intransigence

That is also the crisis of Latin America. Look at what happened in Ecuador, where Mr. Correa, a university professor who favored reforms that are not radical, became radicalized because of the anxiousness of the Northern countries. Radicals such as Evo Morales and Hugo Chávez are in the same situation as Fidel Castro was initially, when he proposed dialogue under conditions of respect and sovereignty that would allow for an equal dialogue. Castro and Cuba evolved in the direction they did, simply because the U.S. would not engage in dialogue. Now, 40 years later, the same thing is happening with Chávez. We support not only a socialist program, but a constitutional and nationalist program. We did not ask Chávez for socialism, but he ended up coming our way, becoming a spokesperson for the projects that are born from the collective vanguards that have been formed during this tough period.

Maria de Oliveira *Regional Director, INCRA (National Institute for the Agrarian Reform), Recife, Brazil*

Brazil has succeeded in becoming a major agricultural exporter, but the social system behind that success has resulted in poverty and widespread violence and lawlessness. When reforms provide land to poor households, landlords may force the poor to sell their land. Land reform has been an issue in Brazil since WWII, but since the majority of politicians are landlords, it has been difficult to gain legislative support. Only in 2002, under pressure from various social movements throughout Brazil, did genuine land reform begin, under President Lula. By 2011, his government hopes to provide land to two million families.

Injustice Breeds Violence

The producers of sugar and other agricultural products for export do not need to violate human rights and the environment. Brazilian producers were never asked to respect the environment and life. They were told only about the opportunity for large-scale production. Their exports generated international satisfaction, but the system has created a high level of poverty. Today we live a life of fear. Criminals are present in all parts of Brazil. We cannot travel, we cannot go out, and we cannot have peace in our homes. This is the result of lack of management in Brazilian agriculture. To export cane, soy, wheat, corn, and livestock, they destroy the forests, pollute rivers, promote slave labor and social exclusion. The Brazilian model of production has to be reversed. But we cannot damage commercial international relations, because we need to export.

The Brazilian model of development is an exclusionary model. It makes poor people poorer and rich people richer. More people die in Brazil [from poverty] than are killed in a war. We have to reorganize the strategy of wealth and land distribution.

We will protect agrarian reform and guarantee a place where families of rural workers can live and work. How can we guarantee that the families stay in the fields? The federal government allows the use of lands for some years, at which point, it gives the families title to the property. Then, they can sell the property. The government is now revising this law because families have been forced to sell their land to landlords. With the use of legal instruments created by agrarian reform, the registries are forbidden to register agrarian reform lands, to protect the small rural workers from being defrauded.

Since the inception of family farming, there has been no harm to large scale production in Brazil. This is the small-scale agriculture, which is not competitive with large-scale agriculture. The harsh thing is that there are some individuals in these territories [Amazonia] who own 4 million acres of land. It is impossible that one Brazilian needs 4 million acres of land where all the wealth like gold, diamonds, iron ore, and lumber is concentrated. We do not want to disorganize the country to establish agrarian reform, but we want at least, to allow the Brazilian people to use their natural wealth.

How INCRA Works

INCRA repossesses or buys land. It registers rural worker families. These families are submitted for an evaluation. The government classifies and allocates land to the families. It finances their homes and their production. It guarantees technical assistance. These families live on the lots and develop a product for a specific market. These are the agrarian reform projects.

Without training, it is not possible to guarantee good production. The federal Government buys practically all of the production from the agrarian reform projects to sustain the schools, public hospitals, and preschools. Recently, the government created the Zero Hunger program. This program guarantees food for poor families and families that live in the agrarian reform projects. There are about 50 million people that live below the poverty line. The production is financed by the agrarian reform projects, and the government buys their products to give to the people.*

The Political History of Land Reform

In 1942 we had a militia of rural workers in two states: Pernambuco and Rio Grande do Sul. In 1954, the Brazilian Communist Party tried to create an agriculture that favored small farmers. Then the military revolution

---

* Editor's note: Oliveira also explained programs to provide rural and urban jobs to the poor by offering training, as well as food until they can work.

happened in 1964. The small farmers created the National Confederation of Workers from the Field. This Confederation created a new model of agricultural management.

In 1975 the Catholic Church organized programs in the city and in the fields that addressed social exclusion. In 1979 the Church created the MST (Landless Workers' Movement) in the state of *Rio Grande do Sul*. [It eventually became a national movement.] Because of MST, the federal government created the first national plan for agrarian reform in 1985, the year after the military government ended, but it could not go forward. In 2002, the federal government developed a second national plan for agrarian reform. We aim to give land to one million families by the end of President Lula's first term in 2006, and to another million families by the end of the second term in 2011. This project was developed under pressure from social movements that protested with one hundred thousand people in Brasilia. Among these movements are the indigenous, Quilombolas, Ribeirinhos, small farmers, MST, and the Catholic Church. In Brazil we have seventy-six social movements. Several movements have created forums with the objective of re-thinking agrarian reform in Brazil. Agrarian reform in Brazil has started to occupy a positive place. In 1999, we had a soap opera about landless rural workers. Brazilians learned in detail what agrarian reform means.

The pace of agrarian reform has been slow for many decades because Brazilian politicians do not want to discuss agrarian reform. Most of them are landlords. They own extensive areas, particularly lands in the best locations, with the best climate, with the best soil—the most productive and expensive land.

For a long time, the judiciary did not discuss agrarian reform because this subject was not its responsibility. Today, judges discuss agrarian reform, and we receive support from various judges, who participate in seminars that discuss land distribution and the legal aspects of land invasion.

The federal government, represented by President Lula, made the discussion of agrarian reform possible, including criticism, proposals, and ideas on how to improve the agrarian reform process. He provided INCRA with satellite imaging that can delineate land boundaries and help the judiciary decide cases with more certainty and agility. He also hired thirteen hundred new employees. Agrarian reform in Brazil is an issue the society demands be addressed by the government. The democratization of land is a citizenship right of the Brazilian people.

Patrus Ananias de Sousa *Minister of Social*
Development and Combating Hunger, Brazil

Inequality in Brazil today, with one percent owning 50% of wealth, has historic roots in colonialism and slavery. Only in recent years has the state taken an interest in helping the poor. Under President Lula, the neoliberal ideology of reliance entirely on market decisions has been set aside in favor of social policies to help the formerly excluded. This involves programs of direct aid for the poor and programs to restore the power of the state to take action. International organizations contribute to Brazil's development, but the WTO primarily serves the interests of developed countries.

The great challenge for Brazilians is how the world's fourth or fifth richest country, with vast natural resources, can find a solution to our great social debt with the poor. We can explain this historically.

Land and Slavery in Brazil's history

The colonization process in Brazil began in the sixteenth century, with the arrival of the Portuguese and the division of Brazil into fifteen hereditary fiefdoms along Brazil's shore. Those receiving the land grants gained private benefits and also exercised state power. Through administrative, judicial, and legislative powers, they could even condemn to death slaves, Africans, Indians and the poor. They could also "exile" felons by law for up to ten years. That began the confusion between the public and the private domains. The public sector was privatized by landholders, each of whom was subordinate to a higher-level landholder. This system lasted until the 1930s.

By comparison, the land laws in the US said the occupier of land is the owner. In Brazil, which was also growing westward, the law said that the owner is whoever has the documentation for that land. So people with money would obtain documents to take the land away from Indians, former slaves, and whole communities that had occupied the land for years. The process of land concentration in Brazil still has not undergone a strong, democratic agricultural reform, to establish the Christian principles that property serves a social function and that access to property is a human right. Land rights must be subordinated to the national common welfare—to social justice and the right to life, which are essential conditions for peace.

We abolished slavery too late and failed to give former slaves the rights and duties of citizenship, nationality, and human dignity. Social exclusion and poverty have grown worse. Before 1930, a phrase was attributed to one of our presidents and it reveals a lot of the feelings at the time: "The poor are a matter for the police." Brazil incorporated social questions and labor and retirement rights only after 1930. Yet those rights did not reach rural workers and also did not change the division or structure of land ownership.

Developing Programs for the Poor

In the absence of agricultural reform or support for small and medium farmers, we had vigorous migratory flows and unplanned growth in cities during the dictatorship, in the 1960s and 1970s. By 1970, we had a very big social debt. We made a mistake by not distributing revenue or creating public policies of social inclusion to protect the poor during that period of economic growth. The 1980s and 1990s were the lost decades, with little growth and rising debt. Since 1975, our population has doubled to approximately 190 million. The decline of per capita income has aggravated the social debt.

A broadly participatory process in 1987 led to our current constitution, drafted in 1988. This constitution makes social assistance a public policy, with increasing awareness of vulnerable people. Prior to this constitution, we had laws for children and teenagers and the organic social assistance law. Then we had a period of neoliberalism, when wealth concentration was ignored, the state was viewed as an unnecessary evil, social development policies were considered hindrances to economic growth, and markets were the measure of all things. Lately, the wave of neoliberalism has passed., with its one-sided emphasis on privatization, devaluation of the state, and globalization of finance.

After the reelection of President Lula, we have sought to bring everyone to the same social, environmental, and cultural level. With the "Bolsa Familia" program and the consolidation of social assistance and nutritional programs, we are bringing Brazil to a new social level. For the first time, we have a ministry exclusively for the poor. We are trying to establish a uniform poverty line. Different programs use different measures, such as one-half or one-quarter of the minimum wage.

Excessive Wealth Concentration

One per cent of Brazil's population has more than fifty percent of the country's wealth. Profit has to have a social counterpart, and corporate earnings must be limited. After years of neoliberalism, the market has created a high social bill. The neoliberals said nongovernmental organizations could substitute for the state. We do not agree. We need a democratic state to discipline the market and promote social justice. Neoliberals were dismantling the state, making it fragile. We are rebuilding the state and semi-public organizations, such as: *Petrobrás, Banco do Brasil, Caixa Econômica Federal, Banco do Nordeste, Banco da Amazônia.*

The greatness of Europe, with all its beauty and culture, was created by the brutal exploitation of other countries. The current debt to developed countries is related to slavery, colonialism, unfair trade practices, our sale of raw materials for low prices and our purchase of industrial products for a higher price. That history damaged our development and growth, especially in Africa.

In addition to capitalist globalization, we also need globalization of social rights and the globalization of environmental action. We need international forums, because we have common challenges. But there is also a responsibility inside each country to reduce and overcome their social inequalities and create conditions to promote development, especially spiritual and ethical development.

The first condition for the emancipation of people and nations is justice. The developed countries have exploited so much already. If they really want a more balanced world, they need to make some allowances, but it looks like they do not want to. They would rather give us some marginal contributions, without letting go of their main interests in these international relations. That is why we need to affirm Brazilian interests in every forum. We cannot be naive. It has been said, "Countries do not have friends, they have interests." I do not agree much with that, but we cannot forget it. That is why each country, always thinking in terms of international relations, peace, and the great universal themes that bring us together, has a fundamental duty to protect vigorously the interests of its people.

Edward Dodson   *Manager, Fannie Mae (retired)*

Mr. Dodson worked at Fannie Mae for many years promoting affordable housing, but the market eliminated two units for every unit they helped create. The basic problem of affordability stems from high land prices, which result from wealth interests holding land out of use in expectation of higher future prices. Today even a two-income household has more difficulty buying a new house than a single-income household did a couple of generations ago. The best way to hold in check the speculative rise of land prices is to adopt a land-only property tax.

Experience at Fannie Mae

I spent most of my professional life working in the area of affordable housing. From 1984 to 2004, I worked at Fannie Mae, the largest mortgage investment firm in the US. It started out as a government agency, but then was privatized at the end of the Lyndon Johnson administration. As a private company, its stock is sold on the stock market. It buys mortgage loans from US banks and mortgage banking firms.

Within Fannie Mae, the mission included expanding home ownership by providing financing to households that could not afford to buy a home. I was part of a team that worked on private-public partnerships to finance first-time homebuyers, low-income individuals, and single heads of households. We were collectively putting our finger in the dike, because the market was moving against our objectives. For every person we managed to put into decent housing, two units of housing stock would become unlivable.

Affordable Housing Criteria

The supply of affordable housing today is inadequate. The rising cost of land and construction makes housing subsidies increasingly costly for government and private foundations. The average family is priced out of the market. People are doubling up with relatives. Those who become unemployed, get divorced, or become ill may find themselves homeless, a problem that is related to the dysfunctional land market.

In the early 1980s, I was involved in projects in places like Harlem and the Bronx in New York. Affordable housing eligibility requirements were tailored to local conditions. Working families making $75,000 a year (165% of the area-median income) still needed to be subsidized to get into a starter home, even for homes on free land, which was donated by the city.*

When I started my career in banking and affordable housing, the land cost component of an average home was probably about 15 percent. So if you paid $15,000 for a house, 15 percent of that was the land cost component. Now an average new home might have a land cost component of 40 to 50 percent. As a result, perfectly good housing is being torn down and replaced by "McMansions." When land costs $200,000 for a quarter-acre lot, a developer can make a profit only by building a house that sells for for four times that amount. That is why so many new homes cost $800,000. How many working families can afford a 30-year mortgage on that? So, low-income families are doubling up. Even young professionals are having to do that. A few years ago, half of the college graduates under the age of thirty were living with their parents.

Role of Land in Housing Crisis

The housing crisis is tied to the land market. Few people fully understand how the land market differs from labor or capital markets. When most people stop working, they have no income. They may go into bankruptcy and lose their house. Similarly, business machinery has to be maintained. It depreciates, even if it is left idle. Land is different because it does not depreciate. It can be held indefinitely without being used. Wealthy corporations and individuals can afford to hold land idle for decades, merely by paying the property tax, which is low in most cities. That practice may reduce the effective supply of privately owned land by as much as one-third.

Holding land out of use increases competition for it, and that drives up the price. Companies may relocate their production facilities to China or India to save on land costs and avoid environmental regulations. Because land is in fixed supply, raising the price does not induce an increase in supply. Instead, there are booms and busts in the land market.

Policy analysts and elected officials fail to understand the implications of tax policy on housing. So, we penalize housing construction with heavy taxes on improvements, and give land speculators and landowners a free ride.

Effects of Rising Land Prices on Working Households

Rising land costs are a major cost of doing business. That results in a shift of operations overseas, which causes structural unemployment and

---

* The city had a large inventory of land that it offered to developers for free, so the cost of housing was tied solely to the costs of construction, labor and materials.

reduced household incomes. American families now compete for shrinking job opportunities. An increasing percentage of them work intermittently or at multiple jobs.

Because of the rising concentration of wealth, the middle class is disappearing. To get people of limited means into housing has meant stretching eligibility limits. When I started out in the 1970s as a bank officer, loan officers would limit housing payments to 28 percent of gross monthly income, based on one income. The income of wives in married couples was generally disregarded, because it was assumed that most women would not continue working long. Nowadays, if both husband and wife work, even their combined incomes may just be enough to pay for an interest-only mortgage payment, such that the principal is never repaid. They may have to accept an adjustable rate mortgage. In a couple of years, if interest rates rise in credit markets, they may get a shock. Their mortgage payment may increase by a couple of hundred dollars. If their household income has not increased, they may lose their house. A serious economic downturn will cause a tremendous increase in mortgage delinquencies and foreclosures.[*] Personal bankruptcies are already at record levels, yet economists do not generally seem to think this is a serious problem.[†]

Solution: A Land-Only Property Tax

The current tax system encourages hoarding of land, which drives up the price. The remedy would be to shift to a land-only property tax to take the speculative value out of holding land. That will enable people to buy land to develop it with a house, a factory, or an office building. That not only creates employment; it also makes the land market more competitive, like the labor market or capital markets. Changing the way we raise public revenue would go a long way toward solving the problem of generational poverty, of boom and bust experiences in our economy. The business cycle is man-made. It is not natural. It is caused by bad public policy based on privilege entrenched in law.

---

[*] Ed.: This interview was conducted in September 2006. The S&P/Case-Shiller® Index of house prices peaked in May 2006 and began declining in subsequent months, confirming Dodson's prediction. [http://www2.standardandpoors.com/spf/pdf/index/082906_homeprice.pdf] Foreclosure filings rose 42% in 2006 and 75% in 2007. [http://www.realtytrac.com/ContentManagement/pressrelease.aspx?ChannelID=9 &ItemID=3988&accnt=64847]. Both websites accessed March 29, 2009.

[†] Ed.: Mr. Dodson spoke here at length about senior citizens taking cash out of their homes through reverse mortgages as a way to cope with rising prices. Other senior citizens are forced to move from their neighborhoods because of gentrification.

William Easterly *Economist, Author*

Colonialism in its early phases was a system of plunder and exploitation that left a legacy of violence and a dysfunctional nation-state system, particularly in Africa. Corruption and violence in Africa today are a product of that legacy. Although colonialism may have impoverished the people of the global South by leaving behind a social system based on exploitation rather than mutual exchange, the colonizers did not become rich by dominating the world. The Industrial Revolution occurred as a result of internal changes within Europe, not because of silver mined in Latin America. The leading colonizer, Spain, was one of the last countries of Europe to industrialize. Meanwhile, Germany and Scandanavia industrialized without the help of colonies. The main cause of poverty today is that colonialism persists in the form of paternalism. Jeffrey Sachs personifies that characteristic, as he ignores the disasters he has left in his wake in Bolivia and Russia. The IMF and World Bank have taken over from the old colonial administrators in offering bad advice and forcing poor countries to implement economic projects that benefit the North more than the South. Foreign aid fails precisely because it is paternalistic. Development can only occur under conditions that allow people to experiment, make mistakes, and find their own way forward.

Consequences of Colonialism

Colonialism had very negative and lasting consequences in poor countries. Colonialism is one reason why countries are still poor. There are two obvious things that colonialism did: a legacy of violence and a legacy of artificial states.

The most obvious example of the legacy of violence is the slave trade. Millions of Africans were captured, kidnapped, and taken across the ocean under horrific conditions to be slaves for the colonial powers. That left a horrible legacy in Africa because it created a tradition of getting rich through violence. Also, some African chiefs were involved in the slave trade. But the tradition of internal exploitation of one African by another was started by Europeans, who put in power the most unscrupulous people in Africa and gave them enormous power by arming them with guns. That is a terrible legacy for Africa, and that is one of the reasons why Africans are still poor today.

Second, colonialism left a very bad legacy of artificial states, particularly in Africa. The colonizers drew the boundaries completely on their own whim, having no respect whatsoever for the realities on the ground. The colonialists separated ethnic groups into different states and divided them with artificial boundaries. The Ewe tribe in West Africa was actually split among four different states. There are some in Ghana, some in Togo, some in Benin, and a few in Nigeria. In Europe, ethnic or linguistic groups created their own states. For the Ewe, this whole process was short-circuited by the colonizers splitting them up among four different states, and preventing them from having a natural evolution towards a coherent nation.

As a result, the corrupt African leaders who are the legacy of the slave trade can prey easily on their populations, because they rule over artificial states. Upon independence, the power of the state, the army, and the foreign aid budget were handed over to hand-picked successors.

Did Colonialism Finance the Industrial Revolution?

Spain took silver from South America, and all the colonial powers got rich through sugar plantations in the New World worked by slave labor. The Dutch took resources out of Indonesia. So, the colonies transferred a lot resources to Europe. But was that transfer enough to account for the Industrial Revolution in Europe? I do not think so.

It is true that colonialism impoverished colonies by leaving a lasting destructive legacy of inequality and class antagonism. But the wealth and industry of Spain, England, and France today are not because of colonialism.

Consider the evidence. First, Spain was the main beneficiary of the exploitation of the New World, and yet Spain did not industrialize. It remained backward until the twentieth century. Second, some European nations that industrialized had virtually no part in exploitation of the New World, like the Scandinavian nations, or Germany. Third, the size of the resource flows involved is not enough to explain how rich Europe became. The European countries never got more than a small percentage of national income from the colonies. More wealth was being created at home, because of British and French and Dutch institutions, than was coming from the colonies.

Colonialism Interfered with Local Development

Even if precious metals from South America did not make Europe rich, colonialism interfered with the development process. Colonizers blocked homegrown efforts to develop better technologies, to learn crafts, to create their own specialties, and to learn what they are good at doing. Colonies were not allowed to trade with the rest of the world. In Latin America and other colonies, domestic industries were destroyed by the Europeans. This interrupted homegrown economic evolution and development.

Another destructive feature of colonialism was the way the mother country would dictate what the colonies should produce. For example, in the fertile region around the Great Lakes of Africa, in nations like Uganda, Rwanda, and Burundi, the Europeans insisted that cotton be grown. This was a disaster for the farmers. Previously, they had a very high standard of living and a rich diet. But the heavy labor requirements for growing cotton interfered with food production, and they began starving. The nutritional content of their diet went way down. They were also inadequately compensated for the cotton they were growing.

Again and again, the same principle was at work. The colonizers forced their ideas upon the poor nations. It was almost like the IMF and World Bank structural adjustment programs that we see a hundred years later, forcing what the IMF and the World Bank experts think the countries should do to make themselves prosper.

What we see today is not so much neocolonialism as neo-paternalism. The aid donors today are the successors to the colonial ministries that existed in colonial times. The administrators who dispense foreign aid are almost as paternalistic as the colonial administrator was. It is still, "We know what is best for you. You should do x, y and z in order to profit." Some of the same specializations that were being urged and forced upon people in colonial times are now being forced upon people under the auspices of the World Bank, the IMF, the British aid agency, the US aid agency. They are the same imperial powers that existed in colonial times.

Repeated Failure of Foreign Aid: Incompetence, Not Design

The same foreign aid programs are tried over and over again, even though abundant evidence accumulates that they do not work. The Ivory Coast received 26 structural adjustment loans from 1980 to 1999 and had one of the worst economic depressions in history. That is a typical example of structural adjustment. Even worse, the Ivory Coast descended after that into civil war and anarchy, which is where it is still today. Everything went catastrophically wrong.

Structural adjustment programs, or SAPs, started around 1980. Despite overwhelming evidence that they do not promote economic growth and recovery, they still continue today in 2007. The conditional aid loans made by the IMF and the World Bank are exactly the same as the structural adjustment loans that were made in 1980. So why is this? How can anyone look at situations like the Ivory Coast and not conclude that SAPs are a disaster?

One hypothesis could be that aid programs were never really intended to work, that they were a vehicle to exploit poor countries or to keep them poor. I do not believe that. I am more convinced by the hypothesis of sheer incompetence than I am by intentional impoverishment or exploitation of poor countries.

Why can sheer incompetence persist for so long in foreign aid? Very simply, the bureaucrats and the aid agencies get to stay in power and keep their jobs, their high salaries, and their perks, whether the programs succeed or fail.

The Paternalism of Jeffrey Sachs

Jeffrey Sachs is the best possible example of modern day paternalism, which is the modern day equivalent of Rudyard Kipling's poem, "The White Man's Burden." According to that view, the white man knows best. Sachs has consistently taken that approach to every problem he has encountered in his career. With him, it has always been, "I am the expert. I will come in with my overnight solution to your problems. You have to do my ten-point program overnight, and that will fix all of your problems. Do not ask questions. Do not object. Do not give me any feedback from the people who are going to be affected by this program. Just do it, right away, and fast." So he "fixed" Bolivia by doing shock therapies to end inflation. Then, he "fixed" Poland and Russia by switching overnight from communism to capitalism, by privatizing everything and creating free markets overnight. Today, he proposes to end poverty in Africa by flying in foreign scientific experts to "fix" Africa's problems. With Sachs, it is always the same idea: the fantastically gifted, outside expert who knows the whole complex problem, who knows how to solve it, and is giving you the scientific answer: here it is.

When anything goes wrong, Sachs always has some excuse he can drag in to explain why things went wrong. Bolivia today is a disaster, and now Sachs says, "The altitude is too high." People like Sachs always have an airtight case. It is impossible to disprove what they say, because they can always come up with another hypothesis to excuse their failures. In Russia, he claimed, "Things failed because they did not do exactly what I said. They did points one through three of my ten-point program, but they neglected to do points four through ten." In Africa, if things do not work—and it is already pretty clear things are not going to work—it is because, "They did not take all of my advice, so I can only help five thousand people in one of my millennium villages. The rich nations did not give me all the money that

I asked for to implement my expert outside solution, my white-man solution for the problems of Africans."

So Jeffrey Sachs continues to thrive as a fixer for poor nations, because his mistakes never catch up with him. And no one ever seems to question this whole mentality of "the white man knows best," which is disastrous and insanely objectionable, paternalistic, and, dare we say, even a racist approach to thinking about poor people's problems.

The unwillingness to accept responsibility for failure is not a characteristic of Jeffrey Sachs alone. It is also true of the experts in the IMF and the World Bank, who forever escape blame for these failures. They are skillful at turning development economics, which should be a science, into a pseudoscience. It is so flexible that they always have some explanation for why things went wrong. For example, they say, "They followed some of our advice, but not all of it," or, "There were other bad things that happened, like the collapse of cocoa prices in the Ivory Coast." There is always some excuse that takes attention away from the failure of structural adjustment.

The tragedy is that the people in charge are never held accountable for their mistakes if things are not working. So they go on doing the things that are not working. The bureaucrats always have some explanation for why things are not working. The tragedy of efforts to help poor countries develop is that the people in charge forever escape being held accountable for their mistakes.

Success Comes from Autonomy

How did the countries that are now rich, become rich? The only common thread among the developed nations is that they themselves were responsible for their own development. They were autonomous—not subject to the whims of outside experts or bureaucrats telling them what to do. Their success was homegrown. The free market was allowed to operate in a non-exploitative way. The free market was not imposed by outside experts.

Imposing a free market is a contradiction in terms. The whole idea of freedom is that you decide what to do, and I decide what to do for myself. The most famous success stories of the recent past are China and India. No one told them what to do. They were not subject to the whims of the IMF and World Bank and structural adjustment programs. Jeffrey Sachs played no role in China and India, and yet they found, through experimentation, their own path to rapid growth and lifting hundreds of millions of people out of poverty.

What Can Be Done?

People want to know what policy or action can help poor countries develop. The first step is recognizing that that is the wrong question. There is no one simple answer. To think that an outside expert could give such an answer is an example of intellectual arrogance. So, when somebody like Jeff Sachs says, "The answer to development is mosquito nets and fertilizer," that is ridiculous on the face of it.

We can observe how countries have developed in the past, and get some general lessons. They involve things like: individual freedom, human rights, democracy, freedom to borrow, lend, and trade, and entrepreneurship. These are the building blocks of national prosperity. They do not become rich by following an expert plan, like the one Sachs wants to impose on poor countries, involving little sound bite elements like mosquito nets and fertilizer. It involves a whole society building itself through the efforts of individuals. When somebody else tries to tell you the answer and forces the answer on you, that guarantees that you will not develop.

How Real are Environmental Limits to Growth?

There are those who claim that development in the form of economic growth must stop because the resources of the planet will not permit further growth. I disagree. We have not reached the capacity of the planet. If the poor today became rich, they would not be using so many resources that we would exceed the capacity of the planet. Human beings will find ways to adapt as resources become scarcer. They will find technological solutions to substitute for resources, like water, soil, or clean air.

Environmental standards are lax now, and we are destroying the environment, because there is no pressure on anyone to conserve the environment. When we increase pressure on the environment by raising the incomes of the poor, pressure will increase to conserve and protect the environment. People will find clean technologies that economize on the use of the environment and that are not so destructive. I am more hopeful than the pessimists who say, "The only way the poor can become rich is if the rich start to become poor." There is no way that the people who are now rich are going to voluntarily reduce their incomes to enable Africa and Asia and Latin America to become rich. That is never going to happen. Instead, the poor can become rich, with adaptation to the environmental scarcity that will come with more pressure on the environment.

David Ellerman *Former World Bank Official*

Foreign aid and foreign direct investment have both tend-ed to create enclave economies that are oriented toward external exchange rather than internal, integrated devel-opment. The problem is how to avoid the extremes of autarky (going it alone as a country) and globalization. Two key elements of a solution are 1) autonomous develop-ment that focuses on creating internal exchange linkages and 2) regional trade with countries on an equal level of development, which can learn from each other. The
North, particularly the United States, has resisted efforts by developing countries to achieve a degree of autonomy. The US wants to bind other countries into a system that benefits Ameri-can interests by maintaining them in a condition of dependency. This is not the conscious intent of those in the development field, but it is the result of their development programs. Americans need to become more conscious that "help" may actually hinder.

The Paradox of Assistance that Does Not Assist

Development assistance since WWII has not really worked, and yet it continues. The countries that have developed are the countries that did not take official advice. The countries where the footprint of the big develop-ment institutions—World Bank and International Monetary Fund (IMF)—is the strongest are the ones that had the least development. So, why do they not learn? Why do these institutions not change?

They do not develop new policies because they are trying to shape the world in a way that is compatible with Western interests, more particularly American interests. The World Bank and IMF say they want development to enable countries to become more autonomous, to act independently of Western companies, and to supply primary goods to Western markets. In fact, there has been no effort to promote autonomous development. They promote a type of development in which countries are integrated into a global economy where the West and the North are in control, and develop-ing countries supply primary resources and cheap labor.

This vision of development is one that we would not want for our-selves. Japanese companies are producing in the US, controlling the technol-ogies. We are on the receiving end and should learn a lesson. We consider it natural for our factories to be in other countries and imagine that is how they develop. But we are learning that it is a very subordinated form of development when our role is to open up and let foreigners "help" us with industrial development by building their factories in our country. It is a sophisticated interference with our autonomous development.

Helping Others: Enabling Them to Help Themselves

Americans often see problems in the world and want to know how we can help. But help is not always helpful. It is not what it seems on the surface. A lot of the sort of celebrity-driven fundraising efforts are only oriented towards relief that makes us feel good about ourselves. If we really want to help, we should consider how to enable people to become more autonomous so they do not need our help in the future.

For example, we provide foreign aid and pride ourselves on feeding the hungry. But in the long-term, that often hinders the development of agricultural capacity in developing countries. Our foreign aid has never really been oriented towards helping poor farmers. It has been oriented towards helping American agribusiness by off-loading surplus production from subsidized industrialized agriculture. For any country to be able to feed itself, the farmers have to have a market for their product. Foreign aid in the form of surplus food from the North can destroy the market for the local farmers.

With foreign aid, we give other countries an incentive to become locked into our system, which means supplying us with raw materials and cheap labor, and giving up their own autonomous development. We deceive ourselves by thinking that if they just act like us and become integrated into our system, they will become rich. That is not the way history happens.

New World Order: Indirect External Control

The West tries to maintain a postcolonial world order, dominated by the West, but which does not require direct, administrative control in the manner of early 20th century colonialism. This could be seen as "neo-neocolonialism."

We attempt to integrate other countries into the system for our benefit, which affects the very definitions of development, local industry, and so forth. It is all geared in a very natural way to the needs of the North, extracting resources, extracting cheap labor, not creating genuine foreign competition.

We integrate countries into a system of domination using local counterparts. Local elites have new powers, but the cost of their loyalty to Western companies and government is that it forecloses the more solidaristic, locally-based development that we have seen in East Asia. In East Asia , you still have elites, but they do not get their legitimacy from the West. They are not doing our business. They are doing what is best for their countries. In most other countries, the elites are oriented towards being part of the global elite. They get very wealthy by selling out their countries. Relative poverty has been increasing because of this sort of collaboration.

The World Bank and IMF as American Institutions

At the end of the day, the World Bank and the IMF facilitate a system of subordination to American interests. When I was at the World Bank, we would get phone calls from US government officials, saying "Do this, do that," and people would do it, even though we were supposedly an international institution. When I started working for the World Bank, my father regarded it as a "government job." I said the World Bank is not part of the American government. It is an international organization. Ten years later I realized he was right. It is three blocks from the White House, and the president of the World Bank is always an American. In what sense is it not an American institution?

Another bit of evidence is the standard career path from IMF to Wall Street. When you are in the IMF, you do Wall Street's bidding. You bail out the companies on Wall Street that are about to get burned, and are in some debt default in the third world. When people retire, they take the "yellow brick road" from 19th street, the headquarters of the IMF, to Wall Street. A recent example is Stanley Fischer, who became the number two man at the IMF (because the head of the IMF is always a European, but the number two person is always American). When Stan Fischer retired from the IMF, he went to Wall Street to work for CitiBank. He conflicted with Joe Stiglitz, who was criticizing the IMF. Joe was then the chief economist of the World Bank, a job previously held by Stan. Joe said Stan was doing Wall Street's work. That infuriated people at the IMF. But where do they go when they leave? They go to Wall Street.

I do not think the behavior of international bureaucrats and people doing economic development is deliberately or self-consciously oriented towards domination by the North. The people are sincere about development, but it is a weird sort of sincerity. There are certain questions they do not ask themselves. They deliberately do not notice evidence that their programs are probably not in the best interests of the people they are supposed to be helping. Instead of realizing that they are harming the people they are supposedly helping, they just keep that hidden from themselves. They do not realize what they are doing, although they have many opportunities to. Living a lie, they ignore the obvious and give it another interpretation. There are enormous personal incentives not to become conflicted about this. It makes them sleep better at night. You see this in a million small ways in the way these organizations act.

Autonomous Development vs. Western Interests

The currently international system locks countries into a state of semi-development where the elites are part of the globalized elites and the poor are not doing very well at all. The question then is, how do you change that to a system where there is much more autonomous development internationally and regionally? The Western companies and governments do not want this to happen.

We had a period where the Japanese developed very autonomously, and we went along with it because Japan represented an alternative to communist development. We went along with China because we saw their industrial development with Western companies as a way of defeating communism. South Korea also developed autonomously. All of them are producing their own cars. They all wanted to learn from the West and then build their own factories instead of having Western companies operate on their soil. East Asian have developed with a model of the corporation as an extended family, in which leaders take responsibility for what happens to workers.

Latin America is a different story. Venezuelan President Hugo Chávez is seen as a rebel against the international order. He is now trying to reallocate their oil wealth to spur local development, and have regional trade agreements with other countries, and deliberately trying to leave America out of the equation. They will sell us oil, but they do not want American companies controlling their industrial development. American companies and the American government always interpret this as something terrible that we have to stop. Americans have long controlled things that happen in Latin America, but Castro took Cuba out of that system first, and now Chávez in Venezuela is doing it, and perhaps Bolivia and Argentina. The momentum is building now in Latin America for nations to become more autonomous individually and as a group in this American-dominated system.

Development through Trade Among Equals

Countries should not try to be autarchic, have no external trade. They should trade with countries that are more or less on the same level of development. Jane Jacobs said it is really beneficial when cities or countries trade with other cities or countries of roughly the same level of development. What you import from a technological equal you may then learn how to make yourself and then re-export it to some other country that has not learned yet. Imports should have the effect of spurring local development, not smothering it.

A lot of World Bank programs open markets that smother local producers who cannot immediately compete. That forecloses the possibility of local industry. But if you had the countries of Latin America trading with each other, different countries have different specialties. They can learn from other countries how to do what the other countries do well; then the trade pattern will change as they re-export. It is a process of learning from others, and sort of ratcheting up.

To climb the technological ladder a country has to start with something it can do. African countries could then trade among themselves as a primary form of international trade, and then ratchet up. I call it climbing "Jacob's ladder" (from Jane Jacobs). The best course lies between economic isolationism and globalization.

Globalization is neither good nor bad. It can mean learning from others in a globalized sense (good) or integrating people into an American-dominated system (bad). It can mean making imports compatible with self-development (good) or remaining reliant on imports (bad). Part of globalization is very compatible with poverty reduction, and part of it is keeping the poor in the situation they are in now. We need to make these kinds of distinctions. We should say "Yes" to certain types of globalization and "No" to other types of globalization.

Tariffs, Agricultural Subsidies, and Development in Africa

A debate has been going on for a few years about trying to lower the price supports for American agriculture, so that the Third World can sell agricultural products in the U.S. It is not a simple debate at all. The problem for Africa is not how to sell more raw materials to Europe and the US. That would lock them into becoming an agricultural supplier and not an industrial country. African development requires industrial development.

How do you industrialize agriculture in Africa? It will not happen by simply reducing tariffs and other trade barriers. Instead, the process needs to begin with trade between the African countries selling to each other in a much more active way; and learning agricultural practices from each other, rather than thinking that lowering trade barriers in Western Europe is a panacea. The idea of selling to Europe presupposes that you can produce the same sort of products to the same standards that European customers or consumers are accustomed to. That takes a long time.

Development Assistance vs. Autonomous Development

It is ironic when people assume development assistance from foreign sources will help the poor. The real sources of long-term poverty reduction have come historically from internally developing the middle class through industrial development. Genuine development occurs when that is done in such a way that everyone benefits, not just an elite.

In Mexico, for example, some elites are tied to the western companies, and they are not going to spur broad-based Mexican development. But there are other elites in Mexico, who are American educated and want to see Mexico develop on its own. They have their own institute, centered at Monterey, the Monterey Institute of Technology, or MIT. MIT is really driving the whole higher-educational system and technology acquisition in Mexico, and it is an entirely autonomous process. American companies are not involved.

Mexican development will eventually come from these indigenous Mexican groups that have been educated outside Mexico and then gone back. They are not working for American companies. They are working for their own companies, and they are doing a good job. The long-term development in Mexico will come from indigenous companies, like MIT. It will not come from the maquiladoras on the border, or from trade agreements with the US. Development in Mexico will come from the indigenous process of Mexicans learning internationally and then applying it in their own country. These leaders do not see their future as part of some international elite where they lose their Mexican identity. They see it as helping their own country.

Joshua Farley *Ecological Economist, International Consultant*

Poverty is not primarily about physical deprivation, although that can also arise. Relative income affects happiness and social status. Concentrated wealth undermines democracy. The amount of violence in a society is associated with wealth inequality, but not absolute levels of poverty. Property rights emerged to increase productivity, but at times they create monopolies that interfere with productivity. This is particularly true for intellectual property. Since it is a public good, intellectual property grows in value by being shared rather than hoarded. Concentrated ownership of land has the same perverse effect of hindering progress, particularly in Brazil, where landowners leave large tracts of land idle rather than risk losing it to squatters. Because subsidies and other benefits raise the price of land, many well-intentioned programs help only landowners. Taxing the value of land reduces that problem, improves equity, and also unleashes productivity by encouraging productive use of land. The same principle applies to petroleum, which would be used more efficiently if there were adequate taxes or royalties.

The Growing Wealth Gap

*There are several reasons why we should worry about the growing gap

---

* Ed.: In a later section removed due to length, Farley argues that one source of the wealth gap is privatization of knowledge in the form of patents and copyrights. Farley talks about intellectual property rights and their effects on poverty. First, 97% of patents are held by rich countries, forcing people in poor countries to pay for the use of those inventions (whereas the U.S.and Europe developed in an era when technical information flowed more freely, without concern about patents). Second, patents discourage innovation because new ideas are mostly compositions of older ideas, so development of new pharamaceuticals against tropical diseases or new strains of rice or wheat are often blocked by the intricate web of existing patents. Third, patented material may never be marketed, unless it will generate a profit to the patent holder. Farley discusses Eflornithine, a cure for African sleeping sickness, which will not be made available to dying people in Africa because the patent owner, Bristol-Myers Squibb, cannot make a profit selling it to them. Fourth, intellectual property treats knowledge as a private good, weakening the very foundations of society. Although knowledge is inherently a public good (meaning: something that does not diminish the value to the original "owner" when shared with others), it is increasingly treated as a private good (one that loses its value when shared). The privatization of knowledge via patents and copyrights destroys the social value of knowledge, in which one idea builds on another. By allowing monopoly power over each piece of new knowledge, not only do the poor suffer; society as a whole is diminished.

between rich and poor. First, economic wealth translates into political power. If we value democracy, we should be very concerned about this skewing of incomes, giving more political power to those at the top. Second, the failure to distribute wealth more equally is diminishing the quality of life. It has serious negative impacts, not only on the poor. One study shows that our well-being is reduced by the unhappiness of others. Third, when people see themselves as relatively deprived, they are less likely to respect the laws and norms and customs that bind us together as a society; there is less feeling of attachment between economic classes.

As social animals, we compare ourselves to others. Our appreciation of fairness arises from that experience. There are studies with Capuchin monkeys where they taught them how to barter wooden chips for food. They would trade them for grapes or cucumbers, but they liked grapes better. One monkey traded his chip for a grape, and the next monkey traded his chip for a cucumber. Normally the second monkey would be very happy with a cucumber, but when he sees his friend got a grape, he is furious and throws his cucumber on the floor and stomps on it. Since humans are at least as sophisticated as monkeys and since we also value fairness, it matters in our society whether everyone is treated fairly.

Inequality and Violence in Brazil

If you look at societies with the least equal distribution of income, they tend to be the most violent. The United States has probably the most unequal distribution of income amongst the developed countries, and is by far the most violent. My wife is from Brazil, which is ranked among the top one or two in terms of unequal distributions of wealth in the world. It is the fourth most violent country in the world. Rich and poor alike suffer from living in a violent society. In their pursuit of wealth, Brazilians have sacrificed their well being. Brazilians are undergoing the same obesity epidemic now as Americans largely because they are scared to walk anywhere. In the U.S., our murder rate is astronomically high. People are scared, and that undermines our quality of life. It makes our society a less desirable place to live.

A lot of the violence is generated by differences in income. I was just in Ethiopia, which is quite a safe place. There is very little violence. Poverty is very widespread, but it is shared. Brazil has far lower levels of absolute poverty than Ethiopia, but it has far higher levels of violence, because the poverty is not shared. Some people live fabulous lifestyles; other people live desperately poor lifestyles. If you aspire to greater wealth, and if you lack legal opportunities to gain that wealth, you lose respect for society and its laws. You are then more likely to turn to illegal approaches and to show your resentment towards those who have wealth. So, it is no coincidence that Colombia, Brazil, and Honduras, countries that have among the worst distributions of income, are three of the most violent countries in the world.

There is a very small correlation between absolute poverty and crime. There is strong correlation between unequal income distribution and crime. The poorest societies are not the ones that are most violent. The ones that have the biggest discrepancy in income are the most violent. In that way, accumulation of wealth by the few undermines their well being instead of enhancing it.

Concentrated Land Ownership Explains Inequality*

Inequality stems mostly from concentrated ownership of land, which deprives non-owners of a chance to earn a livelihood. (As a shorthand, we can say concentrated land ownership is "monopoly" ownership.) If a few people can monopolize land and prevent others from working it, they reduce overall production, and yet they become richer as the land goes up in value. So instead of rewarding production and hard work, society rewards speculative withholding of resources from production. That is a perverse system.

Land monopoly lowers wages for everyone. The minimum wage, when there is land available for all, is determined by the amount of money you could make working the least productive land available—either growing crops and raising animals or running a small business, if the land is in a city. (You would not work for somebody for less than what you could make working for yourself.) When a few people monopolize all of the land, it means that you can

---

* Ed.: In a section removed due to length, Farley traces the origins of inequality to the transition from hunting-gathering to the development of agriculture and associated private property in land, leading to a stratified society. Farley explains that John Locke centuries ago offered a rationale for the origins of private property in land—by mixing one's labor with the land. But Locke said that that works only if there is enough land for everyone. Property in land allows hoarding of land, so that some people become haves, and other people become have-nots. People who own land grow wealthy not from their own efforts, but by collecting money from workers and entrepreneurs who are forced to rent land to survive. Modern wealth inequality can be traced to the same division between a) property owners, who receive rent from tenants and interest on the money they lend, and b) the vast majority of people who must pay the landlord/lender for the chance to earn a living. The ownership class also dominates the political system.

not make money working for yourself because you do not have access to the space needed for production. Land monopoly removes the floor on the minimum wage. Owners can now pay workers much less than if they had alternative places to work. Unless you have access to land, you have only your labor to offer. Monopolies keep wages low by keeping people from being productive on their own, by denying them access to land, fisheries, forests, and information. To be productive, everyone requires access to those resources.

Suppressing wages by monopolizing resources is similar to putting people into slavery. In some cases, it may be worse than slavery. If you monopolize resources and keep wages low, you can pay workers less than enough to survive, as long as there is another source of workers. The difference with slavery is that the slaveholder will give the slaves enough to survive. They are one of the factors of production, and the slaveholder wants to ensure that they remain productive. If there are enough workers around without jobs or resources, you can pay them less than you would have to pay a slave. In many ways it is similar and in many ways it is worse.[*]

Concentrated Land Ownership in Brazil

The history of Brazil illustrates how extreme inequality emerged from a process of monopolizing wealth in the form of landownership. The earliest land grants gave title between two degrees of latitude from the east coast going hundreds of miles inland to the frontier.[†] No one else could work that land unless they paid the landlord for the privilege. The landowners, who received title through political connections, were able to charge people for the right to work the land.

Still today, in Brazil, a small number of people have vast land holdings, which is part of the strong concentration of wealth. If they let somebody work on their land long enough, under the Brazilian legal system, the workers gain rights to it. So, many big landowners leave some land idle, without producing anything on it. (Brazil has a law that prohibits leaving land idle, but a lot of laws are not enforced.) They can make money just by hold-

---

[*] Ed.: Farley follows with a discussion of property rights, arguing that force has never been accepted as the basis of legitimate ownership. Instead, property rights are social institutions, rooted in social values. Since society protects property owners by collectively defending their titles to land and other goods, society has a reasonable expectation of something in return.

[†] Ed.: That would be a strip of land about 140 miles north to south and an indeterminate amount from east to west, an area that could be as large as Texas.

ing the land, waiting for its value to rise, then selling it in the future. At the same time, there are a lot of poor people working very hard on small plots of land. If some of that idle land were made available to them, they could generate much higher returns than at present.

Brazilian landowners used to have a lot of workers on their land, raising rice and beans and giving their surplus to the landowner, providing the landowner with some income. Then the landowners decided they could make more money by growing soybeans, using the methods of industrial agriculture. At that point, they kicked the tenant farmers off the land. The people who were kicked off the land had to leave the area. In the south, since they did not have access to resources, they would head up to the Amazon, which has very poor quality land. They would put a huge amount of labor into working land that had very low returns by clearing the forest. That made the land more valuable because they had made it more successful for agriculture. But sadly enough, since they were squatters, they did not have legal title to the land. So the large landowners, who had political power, were able to seize the land from the people who had cleared it. They captured that new land so that now the big frontier for growing soybeans is in the Amazon.

Farm Benefits Always Captured by Landowners

The fact that landlords capture all of the benefits of technological change means that tenants have little incentive to make investments. In India, the government has funded irrigation projects on large private plots of land that were rented out to tenant farmers. Initially, increased yields on irrigated land seemed to benefit the tenant farmers. But the landlords then required the tenants to pay them higher rent. If one tenant will not pay it, another tenant will be found. This process continues until each tenant working the irrigated land pays the higher rent and leaves only as much in net wages (after paying rent) as he or she was making before, in some other occupation. As a result, the entire value of the higher yield from irrigation will be captured by the landowner. In general, technology that increases output increases the value of land. Every time the government raises productivity, it does not help the poor. Instead, it helps the landowner.

The same dynamic holds true in the United States: agricultural subsidies that make farmland more productive drive up the value of land. Someone who sees farmers making a lot of money because of the subsidies will be willing to pay more for that land. So anything that increases the profits from landownership benefits landowners. The benefits or profits are not widely distributed. So the current group of landowners benefits, and when they sell their land to a new generation of farmers, the new generation has to pay more for the land. The first landowner gets the benefits, and the next farmer goes into bigger debt. If the government removed those subsidies, the new buyer is going to collapse because he paid so much for the land to begin with, counting on the fact that he would receive those subsidies, and so he will flounder if he does not get those subsidies.

Urban Land Speculation

So far, I have been talking only about land in rural areas, but the same principles apply to urban land as well. There is a very high demand for land in cities, and there is a fixed supply. So, the value of land in cities is skyrocketing, which makes it more difficult for people to afford to live in cities. A big problem is that people are holding onto land, expecting the value to go up, and that creates a speculative demand for land. The perverse outcome of that process is that speculation may keep the land of highest value out of productive use.

Speculative hoarding of land reduces available housing in a city and interferes with the development of small business. A lot of speculators do not invest in housing or business structures. They just hold sites, waiting to sell them at a higher price, while preventing them from being used for housing or business. In developed countries, 75 percent of the population lives in cities, and they need access to that land.

de Soto's Partial Solution

Hernando de Soto said that one of the best ways to eliminate poverty in the developing nations is to give people title to land. If people have title to land, they have collateral for productive loans, which will lead to economic growth. Giving more people access to credit in that way would allow some people to pull themselves out of poverty. In that sense, giving people title to their land is a partial answer to poverty.

But there is a risk that having title will deepen poverty. Once land has solid title, it can easily be sold, which deprives original owners of access to the means of production. Once they have lost their land, perhaps for short-term gain, their offspring have no ability to produce. When people borrow money using their land as collateral, their businesses may fail. If that happens, they lose their land. Somebody else will buy that land, and inevitably the land will be concentrated again.

Taxing Land Value: A Better Solution

What is needed is a mechanism that keeps any individual from accumulating too much land, unless they are using it very productively. The value of land is created entirely by society and by nature, and some people accumulate it as a speculative investment, as a way to get more wealth without producing more. We need a way to avoid that. It is far too late to nationalize land. That would not go over well in our society.

It is appropriate to say, however, that landowners have to compensate society for the value that society adds to or creates in their land. A very simple thing to do then is to tax the value of land.* Right now, when people buy land they borrow from a bank and pay monthly interest payments on the loan. Alternatively, if land were taxed, instead of paying the bank every month, landowners would be paying the government for the right to use the land. You would own the land and you would pay the government a tax.

This arrangement would eliminate speculative demand for land. If the value of my land goes up, my tax payments go up. I will only hold land if I can use it productively. If I have more than I can use productively, I will probably sell some of it. This would guarantee that land would be held by those who produce the most on it: a person can afford to pay the taxes only by using the land productively. So, a tax on land would lead to smaller landholdings. A high tax on land would also lower the price of land dramatically, making it easier for people to purchase initially.† Instead of paying banks every month, they would be paying the government.

Taxing land values would have very dramatic impacts in Brazil. Right now, large landowners pay virtually no taxes on land in Brazil. A tax on land would suddenly cause huge landholdings to shift from being an asset to a burden. Large landowners simply would not be able to afford all the taxes;

---

* Ed.: Farley adds that taxing land is fair because land value represents the value added by society rather than the individual, so taxing land amounts to returning to society its share of economic value. In a similar way, a pollution tax is fair because it is a way of compensating for the value taken away from society by someone. In both cases, the principle of fairness is based on reciprocity.

† Ed.: The relationship between a high tax rate and a low price may not be immediately evident. However, it is the same relationship that holds with interest rates. Most people who are thinking about buying a home will be willing to pay less for it if interest rates are high. The same applies to high tax rates. Essentially, tax rates and interest rates are interchangeable. Both taxes to the government or interest to the bank lower the up-front price someone will pay for real estate.

they would be forced to sell off the land that they are not using productively. The tax would cause the price of land to go down, and idle land would become accessible to the landless, who would then be able to increase output on that land. High taxes on land create a big incentive to use land as productively as possible. Around the world small landholders tend to get more production per unit of land than the large landholders. They put more labor into it, more effort, and they know the land better. Poverty would decline because the poor would have an opportunity to work, and their wages would rise. The share of the wealth going to the poor would generally increase.

Editor's note: A long portion of the interview deals with oil and minerals and is not included here for reasons of length. Some of the key points are as follows: 1. The resource curse leaves many people poor in oil-rich countries. Examples are Nigeria and Angola. Oil wealth a) reduces the incentive to develop, b) leads to waste and violence as people fight over control of the oil, and c) encourages corruption. 2. The rising price of oil in the ground as it becomes scarcer creates a vicious circle: rising prices discourage production if owners can make greater windfall profits by leaving it in the ground to produce it later, but this reduces the supply and drives the price still higher, further discouraging production. 3. Rising oil prices will lead to a greater concentration of wealth: more in the hands of resource owners, less in the hands of productive businesses and individuals. 4. The government should charge oil companies for the value of the oil in the ground. This would lead to a more even flow of production and reduce windfall profits. 5. Oil companies have tremendous political power, which they use to avoid paying taxes or royalties. Farley concludes: "We could potentially see a movement towards feudalism, where some people control all the wealth, and the rest of us just work the land, or just work the industries. It is a fairly frightening prospect."

Luis Carlos Fazvoli *Agronomic Institute of Campinas, Southern Brazil*

Editor's note: This is an excerpt from an interview about the history of coffee in Brazil. It is included here only to present the part in italics about slavery. The way Fazvoli speaks of slavery suggests it remains a disturbing issue in Brazil today.

Coffee was introduced in Brazil in 1727, in the north of Brazil. It arrived later in Rio de Janeiro and Sao Paulo. The peak of coffee production was at the end of the 19th century, and the beginning of the 20th. Coffee used to represent 50 percent of our economy, now it represents 3 percent. From the profit made by the coffee business, Brazil developed and created its cities. This happened because of the value Europeans attributed to coffee. *It was a very profitable business because in the past the coffee lords used slave labor and they did not pay for it. I cannot talk about this. This is very embarrassing. There was a lot of slave labor.* [Interviewer encourages speaker to continue.] *At that time we used to produce more, and consequently the coffee lords made more profit because of slave labor. Coffee is a culture that requires extensive manual labor, and manual labor by slaves was very cheap. In that way, coffee generated tremendous profits for the coffee lords.*

Pablo Fernandes Huaratsi *Neighborhood Leader, Bolivia*

Mr. Fernandes discusses his life and his experiences during the water war in Cochabamba.

I live in the barrio called May First, 8 km away from Cochabamba. There are presently six people in our family. One child died. My wife is a home maker and my children are in school at the First of May School. We built this little house that we live in.

I work in a company called CEMAP. That is my main activity. I have worked 5 years as a temporary worker and one year doing micro-enterprise. We do maintenance work for an ice company and for a sewage treatment plant. We also do repair work. When people need us, they call us. We clean different parts of the sewage system of Cochabamba.

I now make 35.50 [US$4.50] per day of work. We are day-laborers. We are paid by day of work. On days we do not work, we do not get paid. We cannot make ends meet. I get 35.50 per day which comes to about 1,065 [$131] *bolivianos* per month. But after subtracting 100 for the Christmas bonus and taxes, the take-home pay is just slightly over 800 [$101] per month. This cannot meet all our needs.

Long ago, when I earned some money in Argentina, I invested it by purchasing some land. But I have had to sell plot after plot to sustain my family. I am involved in a lawsuit, which I can settle only by selling my last plot of land.* I have not yet finished building my house. I have no insur-

---

* Ed.: Apparently the lawsuit was related to debts incurred after his son was shot by a gang member in another neighborhood.

ance, no social benefits from the company. My family and I cannot stand this situation. We are not making it at all. We keep ourselves afloat by conducting a small business during the Christmas season. We have to wake up at 4:00 a.m. to do some work. My wife and children and my sister have already gone out. We have only until December 25 to complete our little tasks from which we can earn 20 bolivianos, or sometimes 30.

The Water War

In recent years, we had a water war here. It is the most vexing problem that the community has had to deal with. When we first heard about the new water company, we realized that it would affect all of us. We were disturbed to hear that the cooperatives would be deprived of water and that water rates would triple.

Up to that time, we paid 7.50 bolivians for 3 cubic meters of water, whether we used it all or not.* Because I used more, I paid around 12 bolivians. With the new company, I would have had to pay up to 60 bolivians. There was no room for vacillation, isolation or escape. This law would affect the entire country, not just Cochabamba.

So, it affected our economy to a great degree. What would become of us who earn 25 or 35 bolivians a day, doing extremely hard labor. If I had to pay 60 bolivians for water alone, where would I find the means to pay for food, clothes and other family needs? We could see ourselves already becoming enslaved.

At that time, we did not have an association. We began to have neighborhood meetings. Several leaders and I decided to make a statement. We also decided that we, as leaders, should appoint a coordinator. Later the idea of establishing a water cooperative was approved. But we still needed a legal personality and we had not yet obtained it.

Through the press and television, a call was made to the people to engage in resistance. Our local coordinator was called to a general assembly. There was a large crowd, and the decision was reached to defend ourselves in the streets. The stakes were high, for the decision on water affected not only the cooperatives, but also water wells, including rain water. We had to

---

* Ed.: One cubic meter of water contains about 270 gallons, so three cubic meters would be around 810 gallons per month. For a family of four, that would mean about 7 gallons per person per day. By comparison, American indoor water use (i.e., not including for lawn and garden) is about 70 gallons per person per day (according to the American Water Works Association).

act for the sake of our children. Otherwise, we would remain in slavery. Every living being needs water to survive on this earth.

So the crowd took to the streets. In the city we used loud speakers. In rural areas, we called people with the *potutu* (animal horn). When the *potutu* sounds, farmers understand that there is imminent danger. After gathering, we went down to begin the march. That is how the water war began.

When we reached the city, they began to use tear-gas on us to prevent us from entering the plaza. A priest told us that the problem was already resolved and that *Agua de Tunari* (the new water company) was leaving. We celebrated in the plaza and then came back here. Then we heard on the radio that *Tunari* was not leaving, that we had been fooled. A crowd of two thousand people gathered in front of the cooperative. We decided to meet again the following day. Some people went back to the plaza the same night and were tear-gassed by the police.

The next day, all the minibuses were grounded, so we walked along the Pan American Highway. We proceeded to the plaza. There was a prohibition against gathering, and there was a lot of tear-gas in the air.

For us, it was a matter life or death. For me there was no question of relenting, for the sake of my children and the children's children. We just could not abandon them to their fate. So, we were prepared to die. Five people died that day, three known to us and two unknown. We planned to kidnap some policemen. But just when we were about to do this, we noticed that the police station was set on fire. After that, the tear-gas abated, but the crowd was still enraged.

Many people were afraid to go out, because we were all being watched. Some inside informants had been bribed to distribute pamphlets to discourage people from joining the march. We tried to determine who the villains were who attempted to stop the march. Those of us who were leaders had to conquer our fear to call for the march. A lot of people were afraid. We feared the worst and so did our families. Many times, my sister and my nephews told me not to be involved for fear that I might be arrested and killed. I reassured them that it would not happen, and so far nothing serious has happened to me.

As a result of our victory, we pay the same rate as before. By decision of the general assembly, we pay 2.50 bolivians per cubic meter. The whole population approved this amount based on discussion of affordability, the quantity of water used, and how much energy is spent in its distribution. All these points were analyzed at the assembly before the decision of 2.50 bolivians was reached.

Ever since this water war, the people now have a voice and a vote. They can express their feelings and thoughts. Before now, we could not say anything. When I participated in a march some time ago, I was afraid to speak out against the President. People now have courage. During the water war, we collectively came to the conclusion that we are all equal. No one can pretend to be superior to another person, not even the President.

Four Women *In Recife, Brazil*

Life is hard for these four women. They work hard and earn little. They are very thankful for the national welfare programs established by President "Lula," one for school children, another for family assistance. Otherwise, the money they and other family members earn doing odd jobs (such as selling tapioca) are not enough to sustain them and their families. But their spirits remain strong.

Josepha: I live in this shed and I am just short of 2000 to pay it off. I am crippled in one leg. I am not lying. I am a hard-working woman. I work in different places. Nowadays, I live like this. My hope is that Lula [President of Brazil] sees me talking. God, whereever you are, help me! I only need 2000 to pay for this shed. I was sleeping in the street with my children. I am a hard worker, a fighter. If Lula were to win another time, I hope he would win a thousand times. He was so good to me and to all the people here.

Vera: Our lives are always like this. We do not have work. We earn very little. That will continue as long as God wishes, and the "big people," right? I get a subsidy for my children's school fees, and my husband does odd jobs. I wash some clothes. I get a stipend of 350 Reals because I have two kids in school. But only until they reach 15, which they are now.

Maria: Ah, my life here is a blessing. You know why? When I came to live here I liked it a lot. Where I was before, I was suffering. Thank God, Jesus, and the president. God bless him, because he sends us a family stipend. That is something marvelous because a lot of people do not get their daily bread at home, right? Thank God, with his help, 10 reals from here, 5 from here, 20 from there, you add up and bring stuff into the house. With the mercy of Jesus, I sell "tapioca." I am a tapioca maker, I do not look like one

but I am, thanks to Jesus's mercy. Tapioca is starch. The one with coconut is 1 *Real,* and the cheese with coconut is 1.50. It is delicious! People like coffee. I sell it to my customers and sit with them and chat. That way we lead our lives. I work from 4:30 until 10 at night. My customers come all in the afternoon. When (business) is slow I sell ten tapiocas or seven or two. Sometimes I do not sell any, and I return home.

Maria: I do not get a school stipend because my daughter did not get in. We get a family stipend of 65 a month, which is based on the number of people you have at home. Thank God, it is already some help, right? When the family stipend ends it will be the end for all of us.

Leticia: In order for my husband to buy her [the baby] milk, he spends all day in the hot sun. There are days he goes without food. He spends around 25 *Reais* a week to buy milk, diapers, medication, things for the house. The milk costs 5 *Reais* and the dough 5. And when we do not have enough, my father helps us. He will buy milk, dough.

Vera: My daughter, my son, my husband, and I live on my husband's retirement plan of 350 *Reais* a month. We used to live in the boss's back yard. He gave us around 2,000 *Reais* to buy this place. So I bought it. My son is 20; he studies. My daughter, 24, also studies and she is part of the "Pro-Youth" program right now. We hope things will improve in the future. Mayors here make promises. We hope the president will help us get out of this place. That is what we are waiting for.

Vera: When we do not have enough money, we eat couscous, which is the cheapest. When we have some extra money we eat bread. Bread and coffee. That is for breakfast. For lunch, we eat eggs, sausage. We only eat better quality meat on the weekends, on Sunday. I always save some money to buy meat on weekends. On weekdays, it is normal, sausage, eggs. For dinner, it is the same as in the morning. Sometimes couscous, sometimes bread. We cannot buy yams or manioc because they are expensive. We have a better breakfast only when he gets paid. The money we have is for everything: our food, medication for him, because he has a skin problem, to buy medicines and his antibiotics. We try to stretch it. There are days we sleep without eating. That is how we live until he is paid again. He cannot work with the problem he has. He is already 77 years old. His vision is already very poor. I stay home because there is no work. I only go to work when I get a cleaning job to do. Real work is hard to come by.

Vera: I hope my kids have a good life, so they can help my husband and me in the future. We are the ones helping them, but not so they can use drugs in the future. Got it? They must be good people. I am hoping they will not go through what we are going through now, because it is not very good. They know that all I want for them is the best. I hope they will also share what they make with us if they live with us.

Mason Gaffney *Economist, Author*

Foreign aid taxes poor people in rich countries to subsidize rich people in poor countries. In the donor country, workers pay most of the taxes. In the recipient country, rich landowners are the primary beneficiaries. Aid raises the wages of workers only if it increases productivity on marginal land. Otherwise, it just adds to the value of high-yielding land, which is owned by a small elite. US corporations contribute to the problem of poverty to the extent that they are landowners. In addition, they invest little of their own capital in other countries. Mostly they just reinvest profits. The system of unequal landownership in Latin America and the failure to develop productive cities is inherited from the encomienda *system in the colonial past. North America (except in the southeast) developed in a relatively egalitarian manner, and with productive cities, in large part because land was distributed more evenly than in South America. The key factor in North America was reliance on the property tax instead of taxes on labor. This was also the secret of the development of Singapore and Hong Kong.*

Foreign Aid: Reverse Robin Hood

Foreign aid is a process of taxing poor people in rich countries to subsidize rich people in poor countries. It is sold as redistributive, but that is nonsense.

The US tax system is highly regressive. In the decade after 1913, the US taxed mostly the wealthiest households and exempted the middle class. That has gradually changed over the last 90 years. The regressive payroll tax on working people now brings in more money than the corporate income tax. So, when our generous government doles out money to so-called poor countries, it comes from the bottom income earners.

In recipient countries, the primary beneficiaries of that largesse are not poor farmers or workers, but landowners. An infusion of income from outside has little impact on wages, because the standard for wages throughout an economy are determined by the wages of people on marginal land, not by the productivity of labor on the best land. So most economic advances raise the price of land and provide a windfall to wealthy landowners.

How does that work? In most Third World countries, ownership of the best land is highly concentrated. For example, in the Philippines, the mass of the people are pushed off the most productive lands into the hills. In the hill province of Baguio, farmers barely eke out a living on land so scarce that people have had to laboriously terrace the hills. By contrast, the province of Tarlac has rich, flat land where they grow sugarcane. The wage level is about the same in both places. That is because the landowner in Tarlac has to pay workers only as much as someone can earn on the worst quality land in Baguio. The difference between what the better land and the worst land yields is the economic surplus or "rent" of land. The surplus value produced by the more fertile land in the valley is pocketed by the landowners. Foreign aid, which often takes the form of roads or irrigation systems, will not raise wages unless it increases the productivity of workers in the hills. Instead, aid programs are more likely to raise output in the lowlands where export crops are grown. But unless wages are raised in areas of marginal production, such as Baguio, wages will stay the same. Rents will increase, however, which means the price of land will rise. That is why landowners are the primary beneficiaries of foreign aid.*

US Corporate Interests in Developing Countries

When American companies go into a foreign country and acquire natural resources, they do not spend much money up front to get the resources. They acquire them cheaply where tenure or title is uncertain. Then they build up assets in three ways: 1) by firming up their title to the resources, 2) by reinvesting profits rather than bringing in external financing, and 3) by

---

* Ed.: Gaffney here describes visiting a village in the Philippines at the end of WWII. Gaffney was unable in 1945 to understand the extremely deferential behavior displayed by the local population to the *patrón*, referred to as "The Spanish Master." He told them they did not need to bow and scrape in a democracy. Only later did he understand that deference was not simply a psychological issue, but rather was a direct result of being economically dependent on a landowner.

profiting from the appreciation of landholdings. The original investment or purchase price is usually the fourth and smallest item. So, US firms own valuable assets overseas, but they represent only a small flow of capital from the US. The value of assets mostly represents appropriation, appreciation, and the plow-back of profits.

Foreign investment does not relieve poverty any more than foreign aid does. The only thing that will relieve poverty is to reform the land markets in these countries. Land markets do not induce the most intensive use of land in the way economic theory predicts. In Latin America, for example, rich, fertile lands are often given over to grazing cattle or sheep, a very low-intensity use compared to cultivation. As a result, the land employs very few people.

Landownership has been likened to a great cartel that excludes people from opportunities, but then does not use those opportunities very efficiently either. Foreign corporations, like the British Vesta Corporation that owns a big chunk of Venezuela, are underutilizing land just as if they were a cartel. Many other companies make extensive, rather than intensive, use of land.

Poverty and Inequality as a Legacy of Colonialism

Landownership and power go hand and hand. To assure their control over territory, colonial powers seized land and divided it among loyal retainers. Concentration of the ownership of land among very few people has been a characteristic of Latin America ever since the Europeans moved in. That is one of the lasting effects of colonialism.

The Spaniards created an institution called the *encomienda* in both Latin America and the Philippines. It was designed to exploit the natives on plantations and to educate them and to proselytize them, all at the same time. They were to pay for their own education and for their conversion to the Spaniard's religion. The *encomienda*, like plantation agriculture in the southeastern United States, was economically sterile in terms of generating urban life, because plantations tend to be self-sufficient. That was part of the idea. Since they produced much of their own subsistence, they had less need of cities. So Latin American cities did not develop as centers of production in the way they did in more vigorous parts of the world. To the extent they did develop, it was for luxury homes of absentee owners.

The *encomienda* system left patterns of concentrated landownership that persist to this day. When wealthy people own the best land and do not use it very well, it almost seems that they are deliberately restricting output and restricting employment in order to retain power for themselves. Whether they are doing this consciously or unconsciously, the effect is the same.

To understand how colonialism impoverished South America, it may help to contrast Spanish and Portuguese colonies with the English settlements in North America, in terms of concentration of ownership. Adam Smith made that comparison in *The Wealth of Nations*. He was impressed by the vigor of the English colonies as a result of democratic patterns of land distribution and landownership. If he had gone into more detail, he would have discovered that there were marked differences inside the US as well. New Hampshire and Vermont, the most egalitarian parts of New England, contrast sharply with the Southeast, where slavery and plantations dominated the economy.

An economy based on small farmers and craftsmen in North America also created the basis for the development of productive cities, unlike in South America. In the northern and western US there was an association of people in terms of substantial equality. The cities and states in the US that were most successful economically were ones where local governments relied on property taxes, and particularly ones that imposed a higher tax on land than on buildings. Taxing land, not output or wages, was a good policy, because it encouraged building homes, businesses, and service industries. It all worked together synergistically to create a matrix in which industry could grow and cities could thrive. By contrast, the insular plantation society in South America (and in the southeastern US) discouraged the use of property taxes, thus limiting the scope of social infrastructure and the development of cities.

These structural differences explain the prosperity of North America and the poverty of South America much better than the idea that Spain's looting of precious metals impoverished Latin America. If mining gold and silver could make a nation rich, Spain should have grown wealthy, but it did not. It spoiled Spain. The Spanish economy never developed, in part because of the enormous influx of treasure from their colonies. They could get whatever they wanted by flooding the rest of Europe with gold and silver, which had the byproduct of raising price levels during the 16th century. If gaining large quantities of those metals did not generate economic development in Spain, then it follows that loss of gold and silver is not the main reason for poverty in Latin America.

Reducing Poverty

To relieve poverty, better lands need to be put to good use. This is especially important for urban land, which is our most valuable natural resource in monetary terms. One square foot in the central business district of a major city is worth as much as a whole farm or a tract of forest land. It employs lots of people, especially in high-rise office buildings or labor-intensive manufacturing.

We normally think of land reform as a process of dividing up farmland among the peasants in small plots. But that does nothing to raise the wages of people on marginal land, the wages that set the standard for the entire economy. Even if the reallocation of farmland will do some good, how can a government pay for it? It is often proposed to impose a sales tax or a value added tax, but that will stifle economic activity in cities and their ability to create jobs. The most important land reform is tax reform of the kind that helped make cities in the US more productive and spread the wealth over large populations.

The conditions for the growth of cities are both simple and complex. But let us make it simple: when you have large numbers of different industries, different people, different activities coming together under terms where they can associate on equal enough terms so that they can interact with each other, you get a tremendous creative ferment that has characterized good cities throughout history.

Taxing land instead of labor is the best way to promote that ferment and to raise wages. Taxing land encourages the highest value land to be put into intensive use, which will create jobs and have a ripple effect throughout the economy.

There are two city-states that applied those principles: Singapore and Hong Kong. When Raffles governed Singapore, he set up a system of taxing land which turned this little island into one of the world's great ports and entrepots (a place to store goods), but also a place to manufacture goods. A similar system of raising revenue from urban land accounts for the development of Hong Kong. Enlightened English administrators deserve a lot of credit for the institutions in those two city-states that made them prosper. Their policies were highly encouraging to production.

Alvaro Garcia Linera *Vice President of Bolivia (as of 2006)*

Colonialism is inherently tied to capitalism. Even if a country like Bolivia can free itself from colonialism, some other country will take its place. We should work for a different world order in which that is not necessary. Latin America has begun to create that new order in the past few years by developing alternatives to neoliberalism. One element is creating more transparency. But the changes in Latin America have generated resistance by those accustomed to privilege. In Bolivia, farmers and Indians have been willing to take to the streets to defend the government that was freely elected. One big change in Bolivia is the expansion of the power and visibility of many indigenous groups. Ultimately, what is needed is a utopian model of society that can help transform Bolivia into a truly equal and democratic society.

Colonialism and Capitalism

It is a paradox that countries with natural resources appear to be condemned to poverty. As a result of the colonial condition of our societies, we became involved in the world market and the expansion of global capitalism, exporting our economic surplus. The wealth we generate is not retained in the country; rather, it is exported for multiple reasons. Countries with natural resources export raw materials and capital and receive industrialized products. The transfer of wealth abroad amounts to the exporting of capital, not its retention.

The colonial structure can position a country within a weak network, based on dependency, or within a strong network. The latter happened, for example, in Korea and Argentina in the twentieth century. They broke out of their colonial condition, improving their position along the global assembly line. Of course there is a further emancipation process that can change the global economic order from one that reproduces colonialism. This has not happened in Bolivia, but it has in other countries.

Unfortunately, colonialism is always part of the development of capitalism. Some countries might be able to escape but at the cost of others entering colonialism. So, even if we break out of colonialism, as a country or region, other countries will inevitably fall into the grasp of a harder colonial condition. That is why a definitive rupture of colonialism requires us to imagine an economic order globalized in a different way than one regulated by the accumulation of capital. But for that, one must think, work and

175

dream for decades, perhaps even centuries.

At the beginning of the 20th century, Rosa Luxemburg, a German-Polish economist and socialist, developed the hypothesis that capitalism requires colonialism. Little countries like ours fight to try to escape, but we are stepping on someone else's head. One or two countries can benefit, but not all. We want a world with room for all, with no need to step on someone else's head.

Constructive Policies in Latin America

Since liberalism was implemented in the 1980s, previous inequalities in Latin America have been raised to intolerable levels. The continent is waking up and becoming a laboratory to explore post-neoliberal alternatives. Brazil, Argentina, and Bolivia are different forms of finding a post-liberal regime. I like the concept of a "Continent in Movement" to describe Latin America for the past five to six years. Every country has its own way of finding a way out of neoliberalism.

There are two elements in moving past neoliberalism. First, there is a re-evaluation of the state as a producer and distributor of wealth, but not as it was done in the 1930s to 1970s. During those years, the state was an inefficient producer, a bad manager, and an unfair distributor. It focused too much on the internal market, favored strong unions, and left everyone else marginalized. The new state should be a producer that searches for ties to the expanding global market, but which is capable of retaining the surplus and distributing it in a better way.

The second element of post-neoliberalism involves finding new and different ways of being transparent and redistributing what is in the public domain and in the public interest. Public affairs do not have to be closed and hidden, even for well-intentioned elites.

Transparency of Government in Latin America

Latin America is working out a "glass case" concept of public affairs for citizen participation. The vitality of social movements as forces of pressure and management, as visible forces of socialization regarding state functions, is something new. It has been seen rarely, in Bolivia, Brazil, Venezuela, and Argentina.

In the first stage, these nations serve as a laboratory for the post-neoliberal period. If this generates better growth rates, better distribution of wealth and public services, and better-regulated involvement in the world, this model could be exported.

The second mission is utopian—not simply to distribute what capitalism provides in better ways, but to go beyond capitalism. This will require social movements, political leaders, and intellectuals working together to generate a post-capitalist model.

Change and Resistance in Bolivia

Bolivia is undergoing major changes in its economy, the role of the state, and its ties with the outside world that allow us to retain our surpluses. In the past, 82% of the wealth would go abroad and 18% would remain in Bolivia. Now it is the other way around. We have turned the world around, putting it at our feet, the way it should always have been.

These are changes that affect powerful interests. Regarding land ownership, we are putting together a reform package that sanctions the speculative entrepreneur but not the productive one. Land ownership will revert to the people and indigenous communities that have too little land or unproductive land. That also affects the conservative interests of landowners who have a long history of wealth in our country.

Politically, the dominating elites of Bolivia since the formation of the republic got used to the Indians being the servants in the house. Today the Indians are governing. They are inside the palace; they are ministers, senators, and presidents. That is a strong mental shock to the colonial mentality, to certain political sectors who were used to the majority being a mass that merely served and voted. Today the indigenous majority is a voting, working, and governing force that can share power equally.

These changes generate resistance. Legitimate resistance within the democratic process, involving political fights, is normal and acceptable. But there have also been two cases of illegal resistance in the past eleven months, in which small conservative groups started to conspire against President Morales. Our insistence on the rule of law was supported with votes and with mobilization by indigenous communities that have always had resistance mechanisms. They resisted with sticks, stones and fifty-year-old shotguns, to defend their interests. So the farmers and Indians assembled to defend their government against a potential coup. I personally declared, in response to the conspiratorial attitude among conservative elites, that if they intended to harm President Morales, they would first have to destroy the indigenous movement that has always fought for its legal interests.

The Rights of the Indigenous People of Bolivia

Bolivia has 9 million habitants, of which 62% are indigenous. There are mestizos, Aymaras, Quechas, Guaranis, Mojenio, Trinitarios, 32 indigenous groups and nations. Unfortunately, in 181 years of history as a republic, the indigenous people were never recognized as citizens with collective rights.

The demographic majority was always considered a political minority, and that is intolerable, unjustifiable. Bolivia is another South Africa, the one before Mandela's presidency. Everyone who loves democracy and equality should struggele to end unjust discrimination against indigenous people. Indians and non-Indians have the same rights and obligations as citizens. President Morales belongs to an indigenous farmer organization that reclaimed the rights to equality.

I was motivated by the issue of equality from an early age. When I was 15 years old, I lived through the first blockade here in La Paz, led by Aymaran Indians, which moved me profoundly. From then on, I assumed as an intellectual challenge and a personal and political commitment to understand and participate in this fight of indigenous people. I did it through writing, researching and involving myself with a local indigenous guerilla movement. Now I do it from an academic position and eventually from the Presidency, but this desire for the equality of people and societies has been an intimate force that has guided my life. From within government, we have the opportunity to finally achieve the dreams of millions of Indians and some Mestizos who long for equality.

Alternative Vision of Globalization

I like the idea of perceiving us as a big neighborhood using new technologies. Of course there are parts of the neighborhood that are worse off than others, but a neighborhood thrives when neighbors share goods and there are no insecurities. The goal is a situation for North Americans to feel their long term well-being is tied to ours. If we succeed, we will be facing a new humanity, which is why Sartre said we should live as if the whole world depended on every action we take. The governing powers and corporations do not understand humanity like that. These are not utopian dreams. They are slowly starting to get built. Let us hope later generations can continue along this path. Marx used to say that capitalism, despite all its evils, is the economic force that allows the whole world to be interconnected. To create a material basis of universality of societies never happened before, because societies were isolated. Now the world is the sum of all societies.

The problem is that an interconnected and interdependent world is under the control of governments and corporations that are a hindrance to humanity. If we would leave them behind, we would live together in a very small home where we would be able to know and be in contact with everyone in the world.

How to take advantage of this human way—that is the big task. Capitalism has created a material basis for interconnection. The hindrance to creating a post-capitalist world is to find ways that this material basis can benefit human beings directly. But that requires a different economic and political world order, which is the challenge of our generation.

We have humbly assumed temporary leadership, not to theorize about a new platform, but to build it. We offer our small achievements to the world, hoping that other nations will harvest their own solutions because it is a universal endeavor.

The new humanity is not going to be the result of one leader or one country. The new humanity is going to be the result of a whole world. Either we are all emancipated or none of us is. The ones who think things are fine because they have plenty of hot food and water in their house and think they have "made it" are wrong. It is only temporary and uncertain. When a lot of people do not have water to drink, one's stability is fragile. The stability of each person in your country or mine can only guarantee their continued well-being if the others' well-being is guaranteed also.

In every egocentric human being, there is a universal being that is tightly wrapped, deep down inside, and it needs to be unwrapped. Maybe here in Bolivia we are doing it at a faster rate. I sincerely we hope we do it in other parts of the world.

Susan George *Author, Activist*

Rising levels of poverty and unequal wealth distribution are associated with neoliberalism. Debt and structural adjustment programs are being used as instruments to provide leverage over developing countries. Debt repayments exceed foreign aid, so the global South is financing the North, contrary to conventional wisdom. The debt was borrowed by unelected governments in the past, but poor citizens today must repay it. It is unclear why poor nations continue to repay debt that could be partially voided under the doctrine
of "odious debts." In any case, debt has given leverage to the World Bank and IMF, which have required the sale of public assets. Privatization has weakened the ability of governments to provide services to their own people. Debt hurts not only the citizens of poor nations, but everyone in the world as a result of "debt boomerangs" in the form of environmental damage, lost markets, immigration, and the drug trade. The overall solution to these problems is participatory democracy, as exemplified by the municipal budget process in Porto Alegre, Brazil. Change is possible when people are allowed to be part of the democratic process, as recent elections in Brazil, Venezuela, and Bolivia indicate. But anti-democratic institutions, such as the World Trade Organization, continue to govern without the consent of the governed. The struggle continues.*

Neoliberalism as the Source of Growing Poverty

When the market makes the major decisions, it gives to those who already have. It creates inequalities.† If you have a lot of money, you can take

---

* Ed.: In a portion of the interview removed for length, Ms. George notes that poverty is growing in rural areas around the world, particularly in Africa. Even though the middle class in China and India are growing richer, the wealth gap is widening on a global basis, including within the US.

† Ed.: At various points in the interview, Ms. George referred to statistics she did not have available. According to World Bank, *Global Development Finance 2004: Harnessing Cyclical Gains for Development*, the total debt service paid by all developing countries in 2003 was $373 billion. Official development assistance was approximately $70 billion in 2003 and $80 billion in 2004, according to the Global Policy Forum, using OECD data. (www.globalpolicy.org/ socecon/develop/oda/ tables/odahistory.htm). The IMF says that remittances to developing countries through official channels were $167 billion in 2005 but that flows through informal channels are believed to be at least 50 percent higher than recorded flows (i.e., over $200 billion). (See *Finance and Development* (IMF journal), December 2005, Volume 42, Number 4, at www.imf.org/external/pubs/ft/fandd/ 2005/12/ picture.htm.) These data confirm the accuracy of Susan George's memory.

advantage of market opportunities. But people who have no material basis are pushed further outside and further down the scale of wealth.

The idea of the market as master began after 1980, with Thatcher in Britain and Reagan in the US. Neoliberalism was then imposed or accepted throughout the world. It means, "Let the market make the decisions, without government intervention." Right-wing US foundations spent billions of dollars making people think this is normal.

This well-funded ideological offensive created inequality and drove the middle class into poverty. It was worse in poorer economies that had no social safety net. The correct recipe for society is to allow politics and society to dictate the rules to the economy, not vice versa.

Resistance to Neoliberalism

Powerful reactions against neoliberal policies have occurred, with dozens of "IMF riots" in the global South. When the International Monetary Fund (IMF) says, "No subsidized food," grain and cooking oil triple in price. Interest rates rise sky high. These changes knocked people over. That is why governments changed in Latin America. The people said, "Hello, we count too. We are the majority."

The global consequences of neoliberalism affect Americans every day but they do not pay attention. Not many in the US understand international issues, such as African debt reduction, or the unfair prices we pay Africans for raw material.

Americans are very confused about foreign aid. They think it represents 10-15% of GNP, when it is actually $1/_{10}$th of 1%. They also think aid is a very good thing. It would be, except that 1) aid recipients have to buy goods from American companies, which does not help their economies, and 2) aid is surpassed by the outflows coming from the South.

Structural Adjustment and Debt as Causes of Poverty

The blind operation of the market is not the only factor causing poverty. "Structural adjustment packages," imposed on poor indebted countries by the IMF and World Bank to extract debt repayments in hard currency, impoverish countries by privatizing everything and promoting exports. This removes resources that could be spread among the population, and sends them to Northern banks and governments. The needs of local people are neglected. Tying up capital in the export market also raises domestic interest rates, making it virtually impossible for poor people to borrow.

We have made a little progress on reducing debt, but the vast majority of indebted countries still pay huge amounts.* Sub-Saharan Africa, which is the poorest part of the world, is paying $25,000 every minute to Northern creditors. You could build a lot of schools and hospitals and create a lot of jobs if you were using $25,000 a minute differently from debt repayment.

People do not understand that the South is financing the North. Looking at flows of money from North to South, and then from South to North, the South is financing the North to the tune of about $200 billion every year. Some people say more, but $200 billion is the rock bottom estimate. There is a constant drain, a constant killing of opportunity for ordinary people in these countries. Little girls do not go to school any more because school budgets are reduced and school fees are charged. There is a vicious cycle that prevents people from working their own way out of poverty.

The Origins of Debt in the South

How did Southern countries accumulate $2.5 trillion worth of debt? It began with private banks from the North unloading money on governments or banks. A lot of it was government borrowing for public works and other government tasks. The issue is not debt *per se,* but whether the loan is used in a productive way by investing it. An investment allows more wealth creation, so that paying interest on the debt is not a hurdle. If you do not invest productively, your income will be reduced.

Everyone in the South with a debt owes the World Bank and the IMF. They are first in line for payments. Lower down, loans from individual governments are usually paid back. Then banks, which control private debt, may or may not get paid back. Many have discounted their debt. If they get $40 on $100 they loaned, they think that is great.

The debt will always hang over the heads of debtors, because it is a huge source of political control that will not be given up without a fight. The North could cancel all debts from the South tomorrow, but it would lose leverage to control votes in the UN or the South's ability to make waves about what corporations are doing in their countries.

Net Flows of Wealth from the Poor to the Rich

The flows from North to South are mostly in the form of aid, which now comes to between $70 and 80 billion (excluding US reconstruction in

---

* Only eighteen of the very poorest countries have received any debt relief. Others continue to pay, and will never get out of the debt trap.

Iraq). Foreign workers from the South, working in the North as migrant laborers, send home at least $200 billion a year. That involves the export of people who are young enough and vigorous enough to get jobs in the North. That is the money going from the North. From the South to the North, there are huge debt repayments of more than $370 billion.

Underpayment for commodities also contributes to global poverty. Developing countries have been told they must increase their exports to repay debt. But the same advice is going to everyone. The result? Overproduction of cotton, cocoa, coffee, and tea. When everybody puts more of the same goods on the market, the prices go down for everyone.

For instance, after the Vietnam War, the World Bank loaned a lot of money to Vietnam for coffee production. There was already a structural surplus of coffee in the world. So the price sank even further, hurting many coffee farmers in Brazil and Africa.

Debt: Repaying What Others Borrowed

The debt came about because of binge borrowing in the 1970s, mostly for consumption by the upper middle classes. The top people in the country sent their hard currency to Northern banks. About 20 to 25 percent of borrowing was for military products, which are inherently unproductive. Only 20 percent was actually invested in the countries concerned, and much of that was in unproductive "white elephant projects." Since the borrowed money was not invested productively, it was, in effect, wasted.

Oil prices went up, skyrocketing, from 1973 to 1975. The accumulated debt became extraordinarily expensive to pay back. The IMF said, "We have to clean this up with structural adjustment programs and austerity policies." Suddenly, poor people had to pay back what the rich had borrowed.

Privatization

Under structural adjustment, the World Bank and the IMF have insisted that everything that was public be privatized. Nearly all public companies had to be privatized.

In Niger, for example, the IMF required that everything be privatized, including a purchasing program for farmers' crops and a livestock program that controlled prices and vaccinated animals. Now, some farmers have to pay a private trucker a high fee to take the crop to market. They borrow from loan sharks before the harvest. They receive three sacks of millet and have to pay back seven or eight sacks after the harvest. These huge interest payments are a drain. Poor farmers now fail right and left. They and their families go hungry.

All through the 1980s and early 1990s, the World Bank published an annual list of companies that had been privatized in its member countries under structural adjustment programs. Every year I counted approximately 1,300 to 1,500 companies a year. Some were bought by local elites. The larger ones were bought by transnational corporations at fire-sale, rock bottom prices, especially after the 1997 Asian financial crisis. Goods in the harbor on ships could not be unloaded, because the importers lacked the cash to pay for them. Economic growth declined eight to ten percentage points in these indebted countries. But, this was a huge opportunity to buy up valuable properties on the cheap. American and Japanese companies snapped up companies which could not pay the 18% interest demanded by the IMF.

The banks in Mexico are now 95 percent American owned or controlled, even if they have Mexican names. After twenty years of these forced privatizations, anything of value has already been taken over. When the private sector takes over, consumers pay higher prices because they are not treated as public services any more.

Poverty from FLIC: Financial Low Intensity Conflict

What I call "financial low intensity conflict" has largely replaced overt forms of colonialism. Debt is a more effective tool of control than arms. You do not have to hang people or march them to the gold mines. You can control them through finances.

The South can never pay back the interest they theoretically owe from loans in the 1970s or 1980s. If Africa is supposed to pay back about twelve billion dollars a year, they can only pay back six or seven. The extra five or six gets added to the principal. Now they owe more interest because the principal is greater. They cannot win this game. For many years, I contended that this was intended, but I could not prove it. John Perkins, author of *Confessions of an Economic Hit-Man,* can prove it. He can say, "I was there; I did this on the order of so and so." We now know there was a plan for extracting resources. It is no accident that poor countries have been economically recolonized with debt.

I once asked a Brazilian minister why he did not organize other finance ministers to refuse or reduce debt payments. He said he had tried, but the two countries he contacted got phone calls from the US State Department, explaining the consequences of going along with this plan. That is how leverage works. These transactions are not visible, unlike when we send in the army. Most people are simply not aware of what goes on.

So we underpay for commodities, and we continue to extract money every year on a debt which we know will never be paid. We are selective about immigrants, but we often take the best brains and the best brawn from the South. All and all, I would say the North has more control over the South than in the nineteenth century.

The Importance of Debt Relief

There have been lots of campaigns to suspend or forgive debt. They have had a little success. Lenders could reduce interest rates or simply cancel the debt. But that would mean losing political leverage. Since 1997, when the first anti-debt campaigns really got off the ground, the IMF, the World Bank, and Northern governments have been dragging their feet. They claimed to need three years, then another three years. Even now, debt relief has been given to very few countries.

Debt relief has directly benefited the local population. In Tanzania, they eliminated school fees. The enrollment of girls in school shot up by two-thirds. When a family is poor and can only educate one kid because there are fees, they will send the boy. Yet, statistics show that three more years of education for girls reduces the birth rate.

We have been profiting from debt repayments for twenty-five years. Enough is enough. We should let those people try to develop. Debt relief would amount to hundreds of billions of dollars a year, far greater than the aid given (and without the strings attached to aid). So we could improve their life situation quite easily. African debt is peanuts for us, frankly. It is huge for them, but for us, it is very little.

Debt Boomerangs: How Debt in the South Hurts the North

I wrote a book called *The Debt Boomerang* in the early 1990s. One of those boomerangs is immigration, which is an unnatural phenomenon when it occurs on a mass scale. But if you do not allow people to make a decent living where they are, they will migrate in search of a better life. When they arrive, often transported by criminal gangs, we act surprised. But our actions have forced people to do that. A second boomerang is the environment. If you have to pay back interest, you are going to chop down trees, mine the ores, exhaust natural resources, over-fish, over-farm, and mine the soils instead of protecting them. Is this what we want? A third boomerang is in terms of drugs flowing in, because that is a very lucrative business, when most everything else is not. A fourth boomerang is on exports and, therefore, on wages in the US and Europe. If you want to export, someone has to be able pay your prices, which means they have got to earn a fair income. Trade is always a two-way street. But the repayment of debt sterilizes money and takes away income from the people who might buy our products. We are not selling what we could normally sell to these countries if they had a normal progression of wealth.

There are many impacts which are boomerangs, because they come back and hit the people who threw them to begin with. But ordinary people in the US or Europe are not responsible for this. Their governments are responsible. A very small elite has organized the debt crisis since 1982, but they keep their arrangements in the dark.

Odious Debts

When I was in Brazil last July, I asked a lot of people from the Brazilian government, who were in the same conference, if they did not consider using the doctrine of "odious debt." This legal concept, invented in the 1920s by a former Russian Tsarist economics minister, says that debts should not be paid if they were accumulated by people who were illegitimate. In Brazil, money borrowed by the generals never benefited the population. That is odious debt. The Brazilians in the finance ministry were reluctant to investigate how much of their debt was "odious." They do not want to upset the creditors. I asked the same question in Uruguay. They are not looking into the question of odious debt at all. They could distinguish odious and legitimate debts and pay interest only on the latter. But it seems they are not going to do it.

Also, these countries could jointly declare a moratorium on debt repayments. The debtors could say, "This year we will pay back twenty percent less, next year forty percent less, etc." They could give notice. But this does not happen. It is all very well in the North to push for debt reduction, but we need a little help from our friends.

Globalization and Corporations

Globalization by itself means nothing. Globalization in practice has meant neoliberal globalization or market-led globalization. So globalization has contributed to inequality.

For the first time, in about the last fifteen or twenty years, what Henry

Ford said in the US does not work any more. Henry Ford said, in the 1920s, "I pay my workers enough so they can buy my cars." That simple formula worked as long as laws were national. Globalization destroys that. When you can cross a boundary, you can find someone to produce cars at a lower wage.

With globalization you have a situation where anyone can invest anywhere. A transnational corporation is going to take advantage of this in order to get the cheapest labor with the highest qualifications. So China is turning out to be the best place to invest. Nokia, which produces mobile phones, has five research centers in China, where 900 graduates in science and technology work for 10 to 20 times less than Western scientists.

We should not globalize jobs to China, which is not only the most populous country, but also has the biggest lid on labor. It is a very repressive country. How fair is it for people who have free markets and trade unions to compete with people who have no trade unions, who are not free, and who cost twenty times less?

There are people who propose a rule that says, "Site here to sell here. You should have a plant here and sell the production of that plant. If you locate elsewhere, you cannot sell to us." Many ideas like this are floating around. Globalization has necessarily increased the power of corporations.

Wealth Distribution

Redistribution of resources is extremely important. For example, Brazil is one of the most unequal countries in the world, where there are huge landholdings and others who have nothing.* Several hundred people have been settled on the land that belonged to plantations, and they can now produce for their families, but some landless people have been killed trying to occupy land.

In other countries, including Europe, small farmers are being thrown off their land. We need to increase access to land by people. There need to be safeguards to prevent exploitation of farmers by buyers who underpay for the produce. Farmers need credit at a reasonable interest rate, not 25 or 40 percent. So land reform involves more than giving away land. It also means distributing credit and having private or public purchasing offices that are honest. It means putting in infrastructure in the countryside such as decent roads, so that a farmer can earn enough to stay on the land.

---

* Ed.: Ms. George explains the desirability of returning to a system in which progressive taxation supports various social services, similar to the New Deal and subsequent programs in the US. Neoliberalism has reduced income redistribution and fostered growing income disparities by allowing the market to decide everything.

Democracy*

When we criticize the West because of its role in oppressing the rest of the world, we should also remember that Western countries invented democracy in the 18th century. I have no problem saying that democracy, as it has been practiced for some 200 years, is a good thing for those who have been able to benefit from it.

The latest proposed constitution of the European Union seeks to put the economy first. It is as if they were saying, "Democracy was an acceptable parenthesis for 200 years, but now let us allow the experts to get on with it. Let those who have the money and influence make the decisions."

If you give people a chance to make their voices heard, they will do so, and they will make decisions which are intelligent ones for the whole society. That is why I welcome the election of Lula in Brazil, Evo Morales in Bolivia, and Hugo Chávez in Venezuela, whom the US is probably trying to get rid of, but who have been elected more times than most US politicians.

The WTO

The World Trade Organization (WTO) is another undemocratic, but very powerful organization. The WTO is based on a trade agreement that does not just cover goods. It covers services, intellectual property, pesticides on exports, and standards or regulations that are considered "technical barriers to trade." It covers all of the services, including those often considered public services. This organization, which is not even part of the UN, is extremely powerful.

Another reason the WTO is powerful is its "Dispute Resolution Mechanism." It can hear disputes between countries, and give a verdict, and then propose to the winner that they sanction the loser. For example, the US challenged Europe on hormone-fed beef, because the Europeans were refusing to import hormone-fed beef on the grounds that it might be dangerous. The US said, "This is trade restrictive, and you have not proved anything

---

* Ed.: Regarding political participation, Ms. George urges other cities around the world to follow the example of Porto Alegre, Brazil, which includes citizens directly in the budget process to minimize corruption. A lot of the corruption in the world involving misuse of funds from mineral wealth stems from lack of transparency. The World Bank or IMF could correct the present situation by making government transparency a condition for receipt of loans. But since international financial institutions are themselves opaque and governed on the basis of "one dollar, one vote," they are unlikely to promote participatory democracy.

about health." So the US won and immediately applied sanctions, including a 100% duty on Roquefort cheese. After that, there were no more American purchases of this cheese. So Roquefort farmers, sheep raisers, who live in a very poor part of France, with only sheep pastures as a source of livelihood, suddenly lost 30-50% of their sales, even though they had nothing to do with blocking hormone-fed beef. That kind of sanctioning is still going on. We need fairer trade rules that take labor rights, human rights, and environmental needs into account. That is what I am working on personally, because I think this is a hugely urgent project. Now that the talks are stalled in what is called the Doha Round, they go for bilateral agreements which may be even more demanding on partner countries. So, maybe you win one here but you lose something on the other side. It is always an uphill fight.

Eva Golinger *Author*

Venezuela has been dominated by the US for many decades. The election of Hugo Chávez in 1998 began to reverse that. Resistance by Venezuela threatens the US government by demonstrating the possibility of autonomy and the development of an alternative economic system dedicated to the welfare of the public. The most important agency involved in efforts to overthrow the Chávez regime is the National Endowment for Democracy, which has financed opposition parties, including one that participated in the coup attempt of 2002. After the coup attempt, the US increased spending on subversive political activities in Venezuela. It has also initiated a diplomatic initiative to discredit Venezuela with disinformation, a military initiative to intimidate Chávez and to assassinate him through Colombian proxies, and a campaign of psychological warfare aimed at the citizens of Venezuela. Despite these pressures, Venezuela is a leader in Latin America, both as a model of a new economic regime and as a leader in the creation of a regional trading alliance.

Most of my information about Venezuela is based on my investigations for the book I have just published, *The Chávez Code: Cracking US Intervention in Venezuela*. I have dual nationality between Venezuela, where I lived 10 to 15 years ago, and the US, where I was born and raised, so I have considerable experience in both countries.

Venezuela was never a formal colony, but the US dominated Venezuela politically and economically. Venezuela was a virtual colony, with the majority of people excluded from participation. Until Hugo Chávez became president, the government was run by a Venezuelan elite with close ties to high-level US government officials. In 1988, President Carlos Andres Perez offered to allow the US to use Venezuela to funnel money to the Contras in Nicaragua, and to serve as a façade for US intervention in other Latin American countries. When Chávez won office in 1998, the government of Venezuela was on the verge of turning over the state oil company, PDVSA, to US corporations. This would have had a dramatic effect on Venezuela, since oil had only been nationalized in 1974.

The dominance of the United States was in every sphere: commercial, economic, social, and cultural. Even 10 years ago, Venezuelan traditions, culture, music, and art were not as important as those from the United States and Europe. Listening to Venezuelan music was looked down on. There was a widespread self-hatred among Venezuelans.

Why the US Feels Threatened by Venezuela

There are three principal reasons why the US government is engaging in a war against Venezuela: one, the immense amounts of natural resources: oil, minerals, and water; two, President Chávez's leadership internationally, his integrationist model, and his alternative ideological model that promotes social welfare and development within the framework of a market economy and a democracy; and three, his resistance to domination by the United States, which is also part of that integrationist policy.

The third factor means Chávez is challenging the Monroe Doctrine. Under Chávez, Venezuela has been on a more equal level with the United States. Venezuela now has a model that completely contrasts with neoliberalism. Instead of exporting its resources, the idea now is to invest them domestically. "Food sovereignty" is one goal. Venezuela has the capacity to become almost self-sufficient, but it currently imports 80 percent of its consumer products: food and everything else. It could make plastics here. At present, Venezuela exports the raw materials, and buys finished goods at a higher price.

That type of internal development does not in any way threaten the United States or impoverish its people, because the US-Venezuelan commercial relationship has actually increased, because they find new ways to invest. The Chávez administration threatens only two things: first, the image the United States promotes around the world as the best democracy, and second, the ability of the US to subordinate all the nations in Latin America.

National Endowment For Democracy & the CIA

Nevertheless, the US government has engaged in a low-intensity conflict in Venezuela, using different strategies to try to undermine democracy in Venezuela, destabilize the government, and eventually find a way to force Chávez from power. This began in late 2000, initially through a financing mechanism. The National Endowment for Democracy (NED), an organization established in 1983 by the US Congress and funded entirely with US taxpayer dollars, allegedly has a very noble mission of promoting democracy around the world.[*] Actually, it has covertly intervened in the politics of those countries.[†]

In the case of Venezuela, the NED has been building up the opposition movement to Chávez by financing political parties that oppose Chávez. Wherever the NED is actively engaged, it works behind the scenes to form coalitions of civil society organizations, NGOs, labor unions, business unions, and private media. During the six months leading up to the 2002 coup, funding in Venezuela by NED quadrupled. The groups funded by NED executed the coup.[‡] Perhaps the NED officials could have claimed they did not know that these groups were planning a coup, and that they were working with political parties within the framework of democracy. But, two weeks after the coup, the US government increased political funding in Venezuela. The State Department gave NED a special $1 million fund for Venezuela projects to be disbursed among the very same organizations that had just executed the coup. I obtained this information from the US government, using the Freedom of Information Act.

Two months later, the US Agency for International Development (USAID) opened an Office for Transition Initiatives inside the US Embassy

---

* Ed.: Later in the interview, Gollinger said that all US agencies engaged in intervention, including NED, are facades for the CIA. NED was created when the CIA was under investigation for its covert operations. It included some former CIA operatives. NED offered a way for the CIA to continue the same activities under a new guise.

† Ed.: Gollinger later described NED activities in Bolivia in support of a separatist movement in the *Santa Cruz* region of that country. It had the potential to destabilize the Morales regime in late 2006, but since the Bolivian government survived, the NED must have been unsuccessful.

‡ Ed.: Venezuelan officials found direct links between NED and one organization behind the coup. When the attorney general of Venezuela pursued a case against that organization, the NED threatened to have the World Bank cut off funding for judicial reform programs. When the charges were not dropped, the World Bank cut off funding. That is the type of pressure the US can bring to bear.

in Caracas to administer a $10 million State Department fund, allegedly to promote democracy and help the transition in Venezuela. But there was no transition taking place. In fact, the Venezuelan people came out during the coup and blocked the coup. They rescued their president and reclaimed their constitution. An elected government had been overthrown, and the people came out and revived it.

The opening of a "transition office" demonstrated the US government intended to provoke a transition in Venezuela. The amount of funding increased after the coup, and the number of organizations being funded increased from 16 to about 75. After that, at the end of 2002, there was sabotage in the oil industry, which caused more than $10 billion dollars in damage to the economy.

The propaganda campaign subjected the Venezuelan people to severe psychological warfare. For 64 days, the private television stations gave non-stop programming over to the opposition. There were no comedies, no soap operas, no movies, not even commercials. It was a massive information manipulation and distortion campaign. Business owners hoarded their products. Some even shut down completely, or stopped food and beverage distribution. The purpose was to cause panic amongst the population, so that people would call for the resignation of Chávez.*

These tactics did not work. Nor did the sabotage of the oil industry. Although oil production was virtually halted, the Venezuelan government was able to restore it. The US intervened in the electoral process again, but that also failed, because the Venezuelan resisted.

The Role of Venezuela in the Region

Despite pressures from the US government, Venezuela has given the leadership in Latin America to a model of regional integration that would break free of domination by the US. Brazil, Argentina and Uruguay have not gone as far as Venezuela. They may not have suffered destabilizing pressures to the same extent as Venezuela, but they also do not have the oil industry that Venezuela has.

The new integrationist model in the region directly conflicts with the

---

* In 2005-2006, the US escalated the attack on President Chávez, claiming he supports terrorism and drug trafficking, trying to isolate Venezuela diplomatically, engaging in psychological warfare tactics, and sending thousands of Colombian paramilitary troops into Venezuela. Gollinger spoke with one of the latter who had direct orders to assassinate Chávez. The US has come close to naming Venezuela part of the "Axis of Evil."

US model and the US policy plan for this entire region. For example, there is a conflict between the Free Trade of the Americas Agreement (FTAA) and the ALBA, an integrationist, mutually beneficial, non-capitalist model based on barter and trade that Venezuela promotes.

Venezuela is a potent model of social transformation and change. This was a nation where nobody was interested in politics, and now you would have to look really hard to find one person who is not interested in what Chávez has to say, or in voting, or in what is going on politically in different communities throughout the country. Now this is a country where just about everybody is active in something.

Lucas Junior Gonzales *Community Activist, Coehlos Favela, Recife, Brazil*

Life in a favela is precarious. Everyone works in marginal occupations, without a regular salary. When a salaried job opens up, it is only for a few months. Basic sanitation is lacking. The people of the community want to achieve change, but they have little assistance. There is a local culture, including a "circle dance" that is being used to motivate children.

We are in downtown Recife, in the neighborhood of *Coelhos* (means: "rabbits"). Some people think this area has gangs, but, as you can see, it does not. We are in a community.

People who live here are in a precarious situation. A person may get a *bico* (a low-wage job in the informal sector), but there are no jobs with salaries, which require a work document. Occasionally, a job opens in a store or a supermarket, but they are temporary and do not require a work document. They only last three months, then they fire you. Every three months they find someone new.

Basic sanitation is missing here, even though this area is in a zone targeted for government assistance and registered by the town. Basic sanitation is all in pieces, ditches open to the sky, stagnant water in the middle.

All the people here want it to change. We all hope to see our community evolve and develop. We do not have infrastructure or assistance from people who have the means.

But still, we are rich in culture, which is forgotten by the government. We have here the *Maracatu Dona Roda* (a circle dance), which has been helping the children here get involved in things that would really motivate them to pursue a good life. But we do not get any support for this sort of thing, not even from inside the community itself. As you can see, we are in the center of the city, but people forget this place even exists.

Quisia Gonzalez   *Medical Doctor*

Poverty in Honduras cannot be separated from the land, because communal traditions are tied to the land and its productivity. As communal land becomes privatized, those traditions are breaking down, leading to urbanization, unemployment, and passivity, which takes the form of waiting for remittances from Hondurans working in the US. Corruption is becoming more rampant, as government takes over land and treats it as the private domain of officials. Better land titling might help to some extent, but a far more effective solution to the misuse of land in Honduras would be a tax on land values that would encourage productive use and discourage speculative holding of land.

Conditions in Honduras

In Honduras, there is economic development, but the majority of people live in absolute poverty. People in the street are digging in the garbage, looking for food.

I am a member of the Garífuna, a mixture of West African with Caribs and Arawaks. We have our own language, tradition, religion. We have lived on the north coast of Honduras for more than 200 years. By arrangement of the British Crown, they were established in 1797 with access to land and sea, so they had everything they needed to fulfill basic needs. They lived without poverty or malnutrition. Communities and villages developed around a common area. They have respect for the traditions of the elders, who were the main guides. Fifty years ago, the Garífuna started to migrate to the United States, and that has increased in the last 20 years. That had a great impact on our development.

Campesinos are another rural group in Honduras. They are a mixture of Spanish and indigenous people. They face evictions, because landowners are taking over their land for resource development or to grow monoculture crops. That is forcing *campesinos* to work in factories or sweat shops.

Since 1998, when Hurricane Mitch hit Honduras, the main factor in economic development has been remittances from Hondurans in the US. There is almost no production in Honduras except for some sweatshops. In my home city, the port of *La Selva,* the major livelihood is tourism. High unemployment is leading youngsters into uncontrolled gang activity. That is the result of growing inequality in Honduras.

Losing Traditions, Deteriorating Society

The rise of poverty and inequality in Honduras has historic roots. When the Garífuna people migrated to the United States, they abandoned their land, which had communal titles. None was held privately. A person would work some land and then move on and allow it to rest, giving it time for restoration. The government realized that the people of this community were not really using their land, so it could be repossessed. Also, since Hurricane Mitch, the government has sold Garífuna beaches to private developers.

All of these changes are causing the Garífuna to abandon their traditions, including the consensus of having guidance from their elders, who no longer work for the people. The elders are seeking personal profit. They have installed NGOs who claim to represent the community, but they actually get aid from other countries and do nothing to improve the lives of people.

We never had malnourishment before, but that has started. When roads and highways flood, communities are isolated. Teachers do not want to teach in rural areas. Those who do have difficulty finding teaching materials. Honduras has a very high and growing rate of HIV and AIDS. Every issue is connected to land, to the loss of livelihood. There is no substitute for a direct connection to land. The only option left is to emigrate.

The same thing is happening to the other part of the population, the poor *campesinos*. With no access to financing, they also move. Even if they have land, they cannot produce. They have problems with weather and with access to the market. So they see the US as the solution.

Free trade agreements have hurt the people of Honduras because 75 percent of Honduran production is agricultural. Agricultural products that could be produced in Honduras are more expensive in the market than imports. So people buy the imported food. The poor producers from Honduras are left outside the system because there is no market for their products. We are not an industrialized country. So what can we trade?

The free trade agreements also include provisions that allow biological information to be copyrighted. They are generally biased in favor of the US against small-scale farmers in Honduras. The agreements allow factories to pay workers 30 to 35 cents per piece. That is not fair compensation, since the final products, such as Levis jeans and clothing for the Gap, are being sold for $20 to $25. Working conditions are poor, and employees are hired on a temporary basis to avoid paying health insurance. With a low income, workers cannot pay for education or for quality nourishment or housing. It is really hard for them.

If big, beautiful houses appear in villages, the money is likely coming from drug trafficking, particularly in the the north east area of Honduras, the coastal area, where there are few police or they are corrupt. Other people become rich from cutting mahogany, because we have the second best mahogany in the world. It is being put under protection, but illegal exploitation is a problem. Rural people are being banned from using their land. Drug trafficking is there. People are confused about what to do.

In my community, they no longer recognize the importance of land, because development has distorted their thinking. They spend money they receive from the US and wait for more, without producing anything. They are abandoning their tradition of planting and growing things that they need for themselves. Now it is important to have dollars to buy Nike shoes. They think that land is something from the past, that we do not have to continue getting our hands and feet dirty, doing hard work on the land, because someone else has migrated to work in the United States, and will send dollars home.

That attitude has opened a gap. The government puts lands under total protection, so people do not have land to grow food, only a place to live. No other measure is being taken to provide for them. Education should show people that they have opportunities in front of them. They can learn to catch up with development by using land and profiting from it. People also need education to understand what politicians are offering, to recognize who will benefit from proposed arrangements.

Corruption is causing problems with communal land. When new officials take over in a village, they start selling common land to private owners, at which point it is set aside and not worked, so people have no access to the land. Some land is used by private enterprises.

Land Titles, Land Reform, Land Taxes

Our problems are tied to what has happened to land as a source of livelihood. Small-scale farmers are vulnerable because they risk their land when they borrow money for production. If they cannot repay the loan, they lose their land. Many people work on *latifundias* as share-croppers.

Land titles are manipulated to deprive people of what is theirs. On the north coast there are areas they suspect have oil. People are being evicted from that land. People are also denied access to areas where tourism can be developed. People need clear title to land so they can put up a house or grow food or go fishing. Even in the case of fishing, people are being denied access to their traditional fishing grounds, but industrialized fishing companies are being given permission to fish. But just giving people title to land, as Hernando de Soto is saying, is not enough, because it does not always give people the right to be in that area and work in that area. Sometimes getting title gives people no hope to work. That is going on in Brazil and other countries in Latin America.

Because there is a huge amount of land that is not in use, the government very often promotes land reform to give land to the people. This happened also in the 1980s. When people receive some land, they have to put it to work, and in order to work they need financing. So they go to the bank for a loan, but if they cannot keep up with the payments, they lose it again. So it is a vicious cycle: you have land; you lose it again. If that happens, the land may be used by the tourism industry, which exploits forest land that is being put under protection.

One way land reform could happen is by way of taxes. People who concentrate ownership of the most useful and fertile land would be taxed more than those who do not have worthwhile land. That would encourage owners to use land productively.

In order to fulfill the right to life, people need access to land. If someone claims ownership of land, he should put it to work, take only what he has created through his own work, and give to the community the rent of the land: the part of production that was contributed by the land and not by his work. That portion belongs to the community. We should establish a form of taxation that works for each particular country based on its development and the way land is used.

Taxing land allows private ownership, but it eliminates land speculation. That could alleviate the situation on the north coast of Honduras where vast areas are used for cattle grazing. That land is not in use, at least not totally in use. As a result, a huge amount of people have moved from the countryside to the big cities, because they lack a place to plant crops for themselves. They are living in very poor conditions, without potable water or sewers, in poorly constructed houses, along rivers where there is danger of flooding, wherever land is not being used. They do not know how to read and write and they lack skills. They know very well how to grow food, but what can they do in cities? So they build around the main cities. Poverty and crime increase there.

If land were taxed, landowners would either pay something back to the community or give the land back to the community or the government, so the government could give it to those who want to work that land and produce. Right now, Honduras has to import agricultural products because we are not growing enough food. If the tax system encouraged people to grow food, perhaps we could have enough once again.

Rosa Angela Graterol and son, Felix La Vega Barrio, Caracas, Venezuela

Soon after the murder of one of her sons, Rosa describes her despair. Now, she has lost hope of ever achieving her goals for herself and her family.

Rosa: This *barrio* has killed two of my sons. One was killed Friday, eight days ago. He was killed after work, because my son would not participate in a gun fight against the people of *Barrio Nuevo*. So his friend shot him. I am going through a big pain. I raised my children by myself, washing and ironing for others, making *empanadas,* so that my kids would study. The one they just killed had already graduated from college. He was my hope and my future, because he was going to get me out of here, you understand? He did not live with me, but he is the one who always helped me. He would never fail me. I have always been sick, and gone through life hungry, so that my kids could study. I had three kids, they have killed two. I have one left. The one who is left is a little "slow," but despite that, he graduated from high school. The one who was just killed left me with a grandson to take care of. I still have my family that helps me. I got a scholarship through the "Rivas Mission." I am studying my first year. As old as I am, I will get to 6th grade. I will fight. My classmates and friends help me out.

Felix: I sell ice-cream. I make the minimum wage. Minimum wage is not enough to buy anything. You can barely eat. (Mother interrupts to say, "Not enough to give me anything. The one that supported me was my other son.") The new ice-cream that just came out is selling pretty good. I can make about [US$8] a day, which does not buy much. I live here, near my mother. When she is sick, I stay here to take care of her. I have tried to get a stable job, but I lost my papers. There is a lot of insecurity [i.e., violence] in this area. Very soon, it will not be possible to live here.

Rosa: Even though they have killed two of my sons in this *barrio,* I do not want to leave. I have lived in much worse barrios than this one, such as *24 de Julio* and *Carpintero*. My friends here have helped me out and will continue to help me out. Whenever I am hungry, someone sends me something. I cannot complain about any of my neighbors. They have all been good people to me. The whole community should form a neighborhood committee and have the National Army roam the streets. Nobody is intimidated by the police anymore. But we have not gotten together yet, so we are not unified.

I need help so I can establish my ranch. That is what I wanted—a ranch! We have a good house, but not here. It is with my family, in Cachao.

Damon Gross *Program Director, Robert Schalkenbach Foundation*

Poverty is a function of maladjusted institutions, not personal failure. It arises when people are denied access to natural opportunities, preventing them from earning a living. When rural irrigation projects and urban renewal projects increase prosperity in an area, the only ones who benefit are landowners because the value of their property rises. The cause of unemployment has nothing to do with individual characteristics. Instead, according to Henry George it is due to the monopolization of resources. Hoarding of land is also re-  *sponsible for cycles in which great prosperity is followed by periods of high unemployment.*

Poverty not Based on Natural Limits

Poverty is a pervasive problem. It has been resistant to many efforts to get rid of it. It has many manifestations which are devastating. It is caused by maladjusted human institutions, rather than inadequacies of human beings or nature.

Eliminating poverty would reduce the level of misery and desperation, the number of people who are willing to debase themselves just to survive. There would be no involuntary employment; everyone who wants to work will have a job. People will be able to pay for the things they need like healthcare; when an emergency comes along they will have reserves.

Most people are capable of making a living. The world has natural opportunities; that is, resources do exist from which people can make their living. Those societies which have become prosperous have done it without being especially well-favored. The wealthiest nations on earth are not the nations that have the most natural resources. Thus, there is no natural limitation that prevents people from earning a living and being prosperous. Poverty is not due to natural limitations.

Why Growing Wealth Leads to Inequality

In countries well endowed with natural resources, we can expect to find a great disparity between rich and the poor, because natural resources tend to get monopolized by a minority, leaving the majority of people even poorer than they would be without those resources.

The World Bank provides funding for various projects, usually conspicuous large-scale projects that benefit the people in control of land and natural resources. Consequently those people will tend to benefit, but people who are earning their living by ordinary trades and occupations will tend not to benefit from it. They will have to compete with even better-heeled controllers of natural resources in order to get access to natural resources and good locations.

Let us consider what would happen if a village received aid from the outside in terms of financial resources to do an irrigation project? If they currently allocate plots of land at the beginning of each growing season in a relatively egalitarian manner, that system would probably begin to die. If an irrigation system raised the value of the land, the most likely outcome would be that someone from outside the village would assert ownership rights to the land, bring in tractors, and throw the villagers off the land.

The villagers might have a short run benefit because they already had crops planted when the irrigation project was completed, and so they would get a higher yield for a season. But before the next season's plantings, someone, either inside or outside of the village, would decide to exert private, exclusive ownership to a significant portion of the land. Over time, fewer and fewer people would benefit, because of the assertion of private ownership by a small number of people.

The same principle operates in cities. An example is an urban renewal project in which the land and buildings in a particular rundown area are bought up by a city government, often with federal money. That purchase benefits the owners of those lots, while the renters of the dilapidated buildings are left without housing when the buildings are demolished. Developers benefit by having the opportunity to start with a clean slate after the blight has been removed. The neighborhood down the street is next. The owners of those lots stop maintaining the buildings and wait for the urban renewal project to be expanded. The poor people wind up with no benefits. The owners of land allow each neighborhood to deteriorate and then become ready for the federal dollars to flow in, enriching the owners. Through a program that was supposed to alleviate poverty, a few wealthy people get the benefits, while the plight of the poor becomes more desperate.

The Cause of Unemployment

Unemployment also adds to the suffering of the poor. People typically explain employment based on individual attributes such as educational level, diligence, and credit history. The premise is true that those characteristics increase a person's chances of being employed, but a false conclusion is often drawn that if everyone worked harder, had more education and better credit scores, unemployment would be reduced. That conclusion is simply unwarranted. The level of unemployment is cyclical and does not respond to personal attributes, like how hardworking or well-educated people are, but those attributes do explain which people are at the top and the bottom of the ladder.

The writings of Henry George offer a different explanation of unemployment, based on the artificial monopolization of opportunity. Sometimes that involves monopolization of natural resources. At other times it involves land speculation, which causes many sites to be underused, or not used at all. These conditions reduce employment opportunities.

This Georgist explanation also fits with the cyclical nature of the unemployment rate, because land speculation is also cyclical. Unusual prosperity causes the price of land to rise. That causes land speculators to grab more land and to hold to it, instead of developing it. That, in turn, worsens the shortage of land and curtails the prosperity, which increases unemployment. Eventually the price of land will drop, which will allow more people to be employed, as startup businesses gain access to land and become successful. The new prosperity starts the cycle again. So land is involved in an observable cyclicality that explains the cyclicality of unemployment as well.

Jerome Guillet *Investment Banker, Editor,* European Tribune

Inequality is growing, but that makes the economy look stronger since extreme wealth boosts the GDP. Neoliberal ideology is based on a "winner-take-all" philosophy. It opposes redistribution to the poor. Using flawed statistics, the neoliberals criticize France for its tradition of strong government involvement in the economy. Planning and regulation are needed to maintain a healthy economy. Contrary to neoliberal propaganda, the state needs to be especially strong if deregulation occurs, because the state must still arbitrate disputes and prevent chaos. Russia and Zimbabwe are examples of pure markets without regulation. Now that we have entered an era of resource limits, economic growth cannot continue forever. We need national accounts that better reflect actual costs. Terrorism and the growth of Islam are tied to our resource policies. By installing authoritarian regimes around the world to protect American access to resources, the US has created the conditions for militant Islam to thrive. The solution to these problems is to pay the true cost of polluting activities. But so far, citizens have resisted efforts to do so, even rioting over rising fuel prices. We should not blame the oil companies. They just do our bidding. As consumers of oil, we are all to blame.

Inequality and Economic Policy

We use growth of GDP and financial numbers as the main measures of success. GDP says that the addition of Bill Gates and a worker is better than the addition of a teacher and a doctor, because the average of Bill Gates and the worker is $10 billion, and the average of a doctor and a teacher is $50 thousand. By focusing only on the sum (GDP), economics and politics favor concentrations of wealth in a few people.

There has been a big campaign saying France is stagnant and in decline. This is false. Most people are doing better in France than in liberalized economies. The only people who are doing worse in France are the very rich. If you strip them out, France is doing very well.* But since wealthy people are

---

* Ed.: Guillet elaborated in a comparison between France and England. Poverty is declining in France as a result of an active state and redistributive programs. People say young people go from Paris to London in search of work, but the statistics show the reverse. However, bankers are going to London, and they are the sort of people who matter to the press. The financial world is dominated by English and has a strong bias against French traditions of state intervention, high taxes, and redistribution. The English use flawed statistics and claim that France is on the wrong side of history by fighting a battle against poverty.

driving the economic policies, they say France is doing badly. The GDP in France is in fact lower, but only because the amount that goes to the very rich is smaller in France.

Neoliberal Ideology

We live in a political climate that values freedom, entrepreneurship, and reward for merit. This contributes to the idea that the poor people deserve what they get because they do not put in enough effort. Neoliberal ideology appeals to the idea of being rewarded for one's work and being free to do what you want. It ignores solidarity, the common good, and the institutions that underpin society. It operates according to the winner-take-all principle, and the number of winners is very small. A lot of people hope to be among the winners. Something like 30 to 40 percent of people think that they are in the top 1 or the top 5 percent of the population. It is hard to argue for helping the poor.

The financial world dominates society and pushes for efficiency, not equity. It is indeed more efficient to concentrate wealth and reward effort and entrepreneurship, because the aggregate is bigger. Redistribution goes against the idea that you should reward work. As a result, there is now more concentration of wealth in fewer hands. The top 0.1 percent have gone from 2 percent to 7 percent of income in the US in the past 25 years. Wealth is even more skewed. In countries like China, you see the same thing: the bottom 10 percent of the population has actually grown poorer in the past ten years, even as the country was growing by leaps and bounds.

The Need for Planning and Regulation

I finance energy projects. Energy is a sector where you need regulation. Infrastructure, such as transmission networks and power plants, takes many years to build. Electricity is very difficult to store, so you need to balance supply and demand at every moment. Strong regulation is needed to force producers to produce more or less at a given time and to maintain spare capacity.

Regulation and state intervention are required in the transport sector, where decisions are made about highway and rail construction. Policies to restrict emissions of carbon to deal with global warming require cooperation, which will come from the political world, not from the market. A public authority is needed to force coordination of behavior.

It is ironic that the financiers want deregulation because financial markets are among the most structured and organized markets. They have very clear rules, and rules are a way to organize and effect coordination. That is what serves the common good.

Deregulation Requires a Strong State

Ironically, when you deregulate and privatize, as the IMF has required many developing countries to do, you actually need a strong state. The state will have fewer roles, but it must do these roles better. If the state is only an arbiter, then it needs to be fair and it needs to enforce the rules. The problem in developing countries is that the state is weak and does not enforce the rules. So the strongest players behave illegally, and nobody calls them on it. In the worst cases, physical violence takes over.

The drift for the past thirty years has been 1) to say the state is not doing its work, 2) to cut taxes, and 3) to get the state out of business. That has weakened the legitimacy of the state. The parts of the state that are weakened are those that fight for the common good, because they are not protected by lobbies. The parts that are protected by lobbies, such as subsidies or policies that favor one group over another, remain entrenched. So you actually weaken the better parts of the state and you let live the more parasitic parts, like the military-industrial complex, the agro-industrial farm-subsidy complex, and public sector unions sticking to some of their privileges. Those are the parts that the parasites focus on. The parts of the state being weakened are the ones not protected: those that redistribute for the weakest and those that enforce the rules.

Those who violate rules say, "You are forcing us to shed jobs and you are cutting our profits, so we cannot invest and we are losing jobs." This argument about jobs comes up all the time. The state as the regulator is seen as the enemy of the companies, when in fact the rules are needed and the state needs to enforce them.

Companies do not like markets. They want to be left alone so they can charge a high price, become a monopoly, or engage in illegal behavior. We saw it a century ago with the trusts. You need government to make markets work. In the Western world, where governments are still powerful, liberalization can make sense in some ways. Even though there are lots of vested interests, the states are still reasonably strong and can control things.

In countries with no institutions and no strong governments, you get terrible results very quickly. Russia and Zimbabwe are the ultimate in pure markets where you have no state and no taxation and you get anarchy and chaos.

That starts a cycle. People get tired of chaos and demand an authoritarian government. Later, they get tired of a government with too much power and strip the government of power, leading once again to chaos. Strong democractic government is better than either chaos or authoritarian government.

Democracy and markets are not quite the same thing. Democracy is markets tempered by the common good, as defined by voters, and by politicians who answer to voters, not to money. Today we see that campaigns are driven mostly by money. The balance is shifting from "one person, one vote" towards "one dollar, one vote." Of course, different countries are in different places.

The Growth Issue

Elites tend to view growth of the economy, of GDP, as the solution to every problem, but we count growth improperly, because we do not count the assets that we are using up and we do not count the cost of cleaning up. We push a lot of costs into the future. Natural resources are fundamentally mispriced. In the commons, what is in the atmosphere is not priced, and what is underground is not priced. So we just take from the ground as if it were free and put it into the atmosphere, or into dumps, or into the ocean, as if this had no consequences. This is a well-known failure of market economies. Economists refer to these problems as "externalities."

Our biggest cost for oil is in the taxes we pay to sustain our military. The biggest role of our military is to protect the flow of oil. If you added the taxes used to protect the oil flows, the cost you already pay in taxes for gasoline would surprise you.* But that cost is not apparent when you drive your car. People do not want to change as long as waste can be dumped, Iraqis can be killed, or Bangladeshis or poor people in New Orleans have to pay the price [of global warming], rather than increasing the price of gas, driving less, taking the metro, or the bus, or walking. Our society is geared towards that choice. The poor, the helpless, and those unlucky enough to be on the frontline, will pay the price.

People speak of China as if it were going to grow at 10 percent per year and overtake the US economy in twenty or thirty years, but that is physically impossible. There is not enough oil or coal or other resources for them to grow that far. Before they reach these numbers in terms of GDP, we are

---

* Ed.: Amory and Hunter Lovins estimated that before the first Gulf War the price of military protection of oil supplies from the Persian Gulf was $468 per barrel, or $11 per gallon. ("Energy: The Avoidable Oil Crisis," *Atlantic Monthly,* December.1987.)

going to crash into physical limits. We have no idea how this is going to happen, and we have no idea yet how we are going to adapt.

Foolish Oppression of Islam

Terrorism is directly linked to our resource policies. A number of countries with authoritarian rulers or dictators are supported by the West, because we think this is the way to protect our access to the resources. The population thus associates dictatorship with the West. By contrast, religious groups do a lot of social work. Often they are the only groups that have been allowed to express themselves, but they are prevented from having a political role. So, in the popular mind, oppressed Islam is associated with democracy and freedom, and dictatorial government is associated with the West. That breeds resentment against the West, or even terrorism.

In a way, oppression is silly. Look at Iran. An Islamist government has been one of the most reliable suppliers of oil on the market, and they are even more open to foreign investment than Saudi Arabia. Why should we care if they are Islamists? Iran has been governed by Islamists, but the population is actually getting tired of them. If we had not given them a second life by allowing them to rally their population around nationalist and populist themes against foreign aggression, they would probably no longer be in power.

In Algeria, the Islamists were elected, and the military crushed the Islamists. A civil war killed 100,000 people. That was not a solution. Algeria is not a friendly country for oil investments, either. So, is Iran or Algeria the better example for us? Maybe we should let people choose whom they want, so they can become unhappy with Islamists and with fundamentalist Islam. They will get over it, and then we can start over. For the time being, they associate fundamentalist Islamists with democracy and the West with oppression. It is hard to fault them.

Solutions

So, what can be done? One solution is to have markets that actually work, which means to put a price on externalities. We need to price both resources and pollution properly, according to their consequences or externalities. If that were done, we would suddenly see the real price of things and realize that we are not so rich.

A hectare of tropical forest is worth so much. You could put that value on the balance sheet of a country as an asset, before it is cut. Today, if the forest is cut, no cost is recorded. If the forest had a value, than cutting it would have a price, which would mean reducing the GDP. We need to put into GDP the negative things to see where value is actually created.

Nobody has to pay the consequences of their acts directly, so we just keep burning coal as a cheap fuel. By burning coal, it looks like you are creating wealth and growth when in fact you are depleting a resource that was not priced and causing pollution and global warming. If depletion or pollution had a price, maybe we would not use coal so carelessly.

A pollution or carbon tax works by making things more expensive that cause damage. Europe taxed gas for a number of years in the late 1970s and 1980s, when car mileage was a big issue. We had smaller, more fuel-efficient cars. Then we stopped increasing the taxes, and people got used to the price of gas. So, we started having big cars, including SUVs, in Europe, because people did not notice the price of gas anymore. So you need increased gas taxes to make it apparent that gas consumption has consequences.

When we talk about a gas tax, people say it will hurt them. But they are going to hurt anyway. If you are in New Orleans, you have paid the ultimate price. If you are on a low-lying island, you will pay the ultimate price. The price is going to be paid in different ways. Either we all pay the price by accepting that energy and resources have a price and we pay it up front, or are we going to dump it on others and make them pay in indirect ways: pollution, asthma, or military conflicts.

Another way would be to coordinate. We cannot say to countries that were never developed that they should not have more. So how do we move to something that is fair and over which time frame? We need a mechanism of coordination that can be used by everybody to resolve questions of global governance. If we do not do that, if we continue to grab land and resources, issues are probably going to be resolved by military conflict.

If we do not cut our demand for oil, the supply will be cut in a very abrupt way. Famines are effective market solutions; they reduce demand. If we leave it to the markets, that is what we will have. If there is not enough food, some people will die, and that reduces the demand and the market is balanced. It is an effective market solution. To avoid such radical solutions, we need to find ways to redistribute and share what we have, and get those who use a lot more to start using less, so there is enough for everybody.

Oil Companies are Not the Enemy

Some people may regard the oil companies as the enemy, but I do not. They are our servants. They do the tough job of bringing oil that we so desperately need. We should not blame the oil companies. We should blame ourselves. Whenever you drive your car or use something that is oil based, you are part of the problem. The oil companies are just doing what we ask them to do by bringing us oil.

There were fuel riots in the UK in 2000 when taxes were going up and the price of oil rose for the first time. People picketed fuel storage stations and became militant activists to protect their access to cheap oil. That sent a very strong signal. The UK government stopped increasing gas taxes after these events, and the oil companies got the message: "Get the oil from wherever you can get it, however you can do it." We should not blame them for doing this. We are hypocrites when we do.

Contrary to popular belief, oil companies do not have such large profits. They are large in absolute amounts because the companies are big, but when you look at the scale of their business, they are not extravagant. Microsoft makes as much profit as Exxon, with one tenth of the turnover. So the numbers are very visible because there are a small number of very big companies. But in absolute terms, it is not that profitable an industry. In fact, they are the profits of a dying industry. They are making more profits because there is less oil around. For the past five years oil prices have been going up while the production of all the major oil companies has been going down. If oil prices were going up, they should be producing more, but they cannot. They are not investing in their industry. They are investing as much as they can, but mostly they are just giving back money to their shareholders via share buyouts. They are telling shareholders, in effect, "You have better things to do with your money than to invest in exploration and production of oil, despite the current high oil prices." This is a very strong signal. The oil companies do not have access to a lot more oil.

Ted Gwartney *Assessor*

As a local assessor, it is clear that taxing property, and specifically land, has many advantages. Russia could have raised its productivity with a progressive tax on resource instead of regressive taxes on wages and sales. Latvia is considering land value taxation to reduce its other taxes. Venezuela has been able to provide more public services by collecting more of their oil revenues for public purposes. Other cities and countries have

done the same. Many countries could learn from this example. Within the US there is a big difference in taxation between New England, which has relied heavily on property taxes, and the South, which has been dependent on regressive taxes.

I am the assessor for the town of Greenwich, Connecticut. The job of the assessor is to value real estate for tax purposes. About 80 percent of revenue of the town comes from property taxes. About 60 percent of the assessed value is land and 40 percent is buildings. States monitor the quality of local assessments. Property needs to be assessed frequently. In some states assessments are allowed to go unchanged for years, such as New York State where assessments are sometimes thirty years old. This breeds unfairness and dissatisfaction among property owners.

Potential Resource Taxation in Russia

During the 1990s, I visited Russia on twenty different occasions. I gave lectures before the Duma and before the municipal association on how to value and tax real estate, in particular land values. I also had the opportunity to work in Estonia and Latvia. The Latvian government is seriously considering adopting a land value tax so it can reduce the sales and income taxes.

I met with the head of the Russian National Resource Study Commission. I asked him about the value of resources that could be used for raising public revenue. He said no one had made an inventory and that they had only surveyed 12 percent of the land in Russia. He estimated that there is at least $300 trillion of value in the surveyed land, perhaps much higher. In Russia, they also could have tapped the value of rising land values in cities. In Moscow, for example, the land values rose 100 times in 10 years. They could collect much more revenue, and they could reduce more regressive taxes, such as the VAT [value added tax].

In Russia in the 1990s, there were opportunities for individuals to become very wealthy. There were multi-millionaires who simply took advantage of the fact that no one was watching. Land, enterprises, and manufacturing were given away, which created a class of wealthy people. People who could not steal from the public wound up having to work harder. Housing vouchers were distributed, but everyone sold their vouchers, and then they had no place to live.

In Latvia it was done much better. They made sure people had places to live debt free. But that country now realizes that it has to do something to stop hindering people with very high taxation. So they are trying to come up with a reform—a better way to raise revenue for public services.

Tax Resources To Increase Productivity

Poor people are helped when the government has the ability to provide services such as schools and hospitals and a social safety net. So whenever a government is able to raise revenue from natural resources, everyone benefits. By raising revenue in a neutral way, you can fund the obligations of government and provide things that are of public benefit.

There are disadvantages when governments choose regressive taxes, such as sales and income taxes, and fail to use a progressive tax, like the land value tax. It is possible to reduce taxes by raising revenue from what already exists in the public domain—land and natural resources. That it is a neutral source of revenue. Given the opportunity, people will work in a more progressive way if they are not saddled with heavy taxation. Resource taxes make people more productive by lowering other taxes. Taxation of natural resources opens up opportunities, opens up the job market, and opens up chances for everyone to benefit.

One example of a country in South America that has actually done something is Venezuela. They supply a major portion of the oil used in the United States. They have taken a lead in trying to capture more of the value of the oil for the public good. That is allowing them to be more progressive in providing public services.

The city of Long Beach, California collected for years 90 percent of the value of oil drilled offshore because it was owned by the city of Long Beach. They were able to fund municipal services largely from revenues from oil and natural resources. There are many other cities in the world that do the same thing, and certainly the Arab countries are using much of the value of the oil resources. Other countries, including the US, could derive more revenue from natural resources. Alaska has a heritage fund, and so do Saskatchewan and Alberta, where they are able to put aside money for the future from reserves of natural resources and oil.

In New Hampshire they do not have, and have never had, taxes on sales and income; they raise all their revenue from a property tax. New Hampshire is one of the more progressive, fastest growing areas. It is considered a place for entrepreneurs to do well because they are not faced with regressive taxation. This is true of most of the New England states. We see quite the opposite in some of the southern states, such as Mississippi, Louisiana, and Georgia, where more revenue is raised from regressive taxes than from progressive land and resource taxes. Opportunities for people are greater where a larger portion of revenue comes from natural resources and land as opposed to taxes on industry and business.

Matt Harris *Business Consultant*

Poverty is far more prevalent in the U.S. today than appears at first glance. Even people with stable jobs are effectively poor if they cannot afford to pay for health insurance and other necessities (such as owning a car). Poverty can be measured in either absolute or relative terms. Relative poverty has grown to extreme proportions in recent years because of the exceptionally high growth among the super-rich. A useful way to understand the wealth gap is in terms of the concept of privilege, rules granting one person exclusive rights. Although privileges are necessary for the growth of civilization, one person's privilege is the loss of freedom to someone else. Thus, those with privileges should compensate society for the losses they impose. In that way, privileges would be shared by all, and poverty could be minimized. This approach has similarities to both capitalism and socialism, but it is different from both.

Someone who says that poverty is not a problem in the United States is not very well acquainted with it. They probably have not met poor people and seen the kind of tensions that exist in life because of economic hardship. There is a tremendous amount of poverty in the US.

To understand poverty in the US, we should include middle-class poverty. You may have a middle-class income starting at around $40,000, but in order to participate in middle-class life, you have to commit 10 to 15 percent of your income to owning and operating a car. If you do not have health insurance, or if you have some that covers you poorly, you may appear to be middle class and appear to have some level of prosperity. In reality, if you consider the odds year by year, that so-called middle class family is actually living in poverty. They just have not hit bottom yet.

Privilege and Unearned Wealth

The word "privilege" comes from Latin, meaning private law. The Romans were very clear about private law. They passed laws that explicitly pertained to either single individuals or groups of people, such that they had a legal status or a legal standing that was different and distinct from others. When James Madison talked about privilege in the early days of the US, he was talking about it in the Roman context: the government allows one person or a group of people to do something and other people are not allowed to do that.

Arguably privileges—exclusive rights—are the very basis of civilization. To use of a piece of land intensively by adding labor to it, you cannot have one person sow the crop and a second one take the harvest. Privilege is what allows the first person to exclude the second one and to make productive use of resources.

In addition to ownership of land, other privileges include ownership of mineral rights, broadcast licenses (and rights to other parts of the electromagnetic spectrum), pollution permits, landing rights at airports (the time slots when a plane can take off or land), rights of way, and many other rights that have an economic value attached to them.

One way to think about privileges is that they are the opposite of freedom. If I give someone privilege, then somebody else lost freedom. If you are going to have a society where people have equal rights, a person who holds a privilege should compensate other people. If I am going to dirty the air so that you cannot breathe it and enjoy it, then I owe you something for that. If I am going to extract oil out of the ground, I owe both people here today and future generations for taking possibilities away from them. Privileges require a *quid pro quo* to have justice.

A challenge for us is to learn how to manage privileges in a way that does not create undesirable side effects, particularly related to the distribution of wealth. Privileges allow a much more intense use of natural resources, but they also distort the distribution of wealth.

The great conundrum is how to allow privileges where they help society become wealthier, but not let a small fraction of the population hijack that wealth. The answer suggests itself: we need a *quid pro quo;* we need a charge for those privileges—privileges that are rooted in government and in legal action. Congress and state legislatures create these privileges. They could also create a requirement that the person who holds a privilege make a payment back to society for that privilege. At the same time, we could get rid of other taxes that truly are injurious.

Neither Socialism nor Capitalism

Capitalism is usually referred to as the free-market system. But you cannot say that you have a free market, a free system, when a relatively small number of people hold privileges that allow them to choke labor and the productive elements in society by extracting money, just by holding a privilege. That is not freedom.

Socialism recognizes that there are systematic problems in society because the economic rules are systematically grinding a fraction of the population into poverty. But socialism fails when it wants government to control capital or try to control the details of how an economy works.

The ideas I propose do not fit readily into the categories of socialism and capitalism, both of which have a lot of contradictions underlying them. The theory of taxing privileges is really in a class by itself. I would call it a true free-market system.

Fred Harrison *Author, Journalist*

At an early stage of civilization, the economic surplus of land, also known as rent, was used to support common purposes: religion, the arts, craftsmanship, literacy. Poverty developed in ancient times when the rent was appropriated for private use by an aristocracy. As a result of that rupture, a few became very rich and powerful, and most people became poor. This process was repeated in England under Henry VIII, when land held in common was enclosed or privatized. This system of landownership was then used as a template in the colonization process, spreading the problem of poverty and inequality around the globe. Today the problem can be most readily seen in the tax system. High income taxes seem to fall heavily on the rich, but in fact, the rich are more than compensated for their income taxes by the increase in value of the property they own. Much of that increase in value comes from government spending. Thus, the rich get their taxes back through capital gains on property, while the poor, who own little or no property, bear the burden of taxation. This process could be reversed through the simple expedient of taxing land values, thereby capturing for public use the value bestowed on land owners by public spending.

Privatized Social Surplus as Origin of Poverty

At the beginning of civilization, all of the things that enrich culture (art, religion, administration) were funded out of the economic surplus or rent produced by farmers and used to pay for public services. Economic rent is both the surplus produced from land and the amount that we pay for the use of land. It is the surplus people accumulated to make civilization possible.

Poverty became built into the DNA of our social system when civilization took a wrong turn. Some groups engaged in a land grab to appropriate the rental surplus for their private benefit and become an aristocracy. They did not want to work for a living, so they rigged the rules to pocket the rent. Once the rent was privatized, societies had to begin taxing people to pay for law and order, defense of the territory, communication systems, and highways. That is when the rot set in. By hijacking the public purse, the elites, the aristocracy, set themselves apart from society. They created a competing culture and repressed the majority of people. The result was the division between rich and poor, the haves and the have-nots.

Social pathologies and dislocations all resulted from the privatization of the rental surplus from land. Today, we have a million people in Britain who do not go to work because they are clinically depressed, psychologically incapable of earning a living. This can be traced back to a time when elites grabbed the land and kept the rent for themselves, instead of sharing it to pay for common services.

In England, the rot set in about five hundred years ago, with Henry VIII's massive land grab. He closed down the monasteries, took their land, and sold it off to his favored courtiers. That began the process of privatizing land that had been held in common in England for centuries. The feudal aristocracies wanted more and more land, so they began to throw the peasants off their fields, which they had previously held and worked in common. The aristocrats enclosed that land and charged people to work on it. The aristocrats enjoyed life in London, while the peasants worked in their fields.

The enclosure movement created not only a massive dislocation of communities within England, but then spread the disease abroad. People left England and went to America, where they set up a similar system of private ownership of land and seizure of rents for themselves. They built into the New World the very disease from which they had tried to escape back in England, Scotland, and Ireland.

This massive land grab in England established an ideology of living off other people by taking the land away from them. The English led the process of globalization through the colonial project. That meant going to places like Africa and Asia, locating in territories like Kenya and India, taking the land away from the local people, forcing them to work on the new plantations owned by the absentee landlords, who were living in London. The colonizers exploited people, in order that the rents from those territories could be shipped back to England and other countries in Europe that participated in this project. As a consequence, we now have massive poverty in the Third World, which can be traced back to the process of land grabbing that originated in Europe, especially in England. It might seem that poverty is being addressed by the United Nations. We are trying to tackle debt by cancelling it. But the ideology of privatizing land, the most basic asset that we all need to share, continues to wreck the fabric of the global economy.

Taxes Discourage Employment

To exemplify how poverty is generated by the same processes today, we are standing near the Oceans Estate, a public housing project in East London. Just half a mile or so in two different directions are the City of London and Canary Wharf, two centers of high finance for the world. People there earn yearly salaries of $1 or $2 million. Within the shadow of those financial districts are families in this housing project who earn only one-quarter to one-third what the average working class family does.

Poverty is not the consequence of personal shortcomings. It is the result of two factors: 1) a tax system that discourages employment and 2) the way government spends money on behalf of the community.

About 60 percent of the people here are unemployed. They do not work, because our tax system keeps them out of the work place by raising the cost of employing people. If someone's work adds £5 an hour of value, an employer will be willing to pay that wage. But if the employer has to pay £7 or £8 an hour, because of the tax on his wages, that employee is forced out of the labor market. A person worth £5 cannot be employed at the rate of £7 or £8, so he loses his job. He goes on unemployment benefits. Employed people then pay additional taxes for people who are pushed out of work.

Government Spending Raises Land Values

The other half of this equation is the way government spending affects property values. When government invests money in infrastructure, such as a new railway, the value of land near stations rises. As a result of tax-funded public spending on schools or health facilities, the land near those public amenities rises in value. If those land values were captured and used to fund public services, it would no longer be necessary to tax the incomes of poor people or the goods they buy. It would be possible to employ them and to restore their dignity.

Our current convoluted tax system pushes people into poverty. Then we spend the taxes paid by low-income people on infrastructure, which raises land values. Those increases in land values are huge windfall gains for property owners.

How The Rich Get Their Taxes Back

The main beneficiaries of rising land values are the rich people who have very high salaried jobs. If tax-funded expenditures on infrastructure and services increase house prices by 10 percent per year, and you live in a million-dollar home, your net worth will rise by $100,000 each year, for doing nothing. If you pay $100,000 in income tax and live in a million-dollar home, the net effect is that you have not paid any taxes to the government at all. You may have technically paid an income tax, but you have clawed back that tax through the increase in the value of your property. People who do not own property, who rent their homes, do not get back a single penny through this process of rising land values. They do not share in the windfall gains that are the result of tax-funded spending programs.

So we have a system of injustice in which poverty is built into the fabric of our society: the poor people pay taxes; no matter how poor they are, they cannot get away from the taxman. Even if they are not earning income to pay income tax, they pay taxes when they buy goods. So they pay for the public services they receive.

The rich pay taxes but they get their money back. They get it back via public spending, which raises the value of their residential property. So the rich live tax-free lives. They can cash in on the increase in their property values at any time, by borrowing against it. This bias in tax policy is one reason the gap between rich and poor grows wider.

Take the case of Tony Blair and his wife Cherie, a judge, who are in the top 10 percent of income earners in this country.* They can claw back, in two or three years' worth of house price increases, their lifetime tax payments. Tony Blair and his wife can spend two or three years watching the rise in value of their five residential properties, and the result of those increases in their property assets means that, for the rest of their working lives, they effectively pay no taxes at all, because they have already been compensated for their future tax payments. They have clawed all their tax payments back in just two or three years.

---

* Editor's note: At the time of this interview in 2007, Tony Blair was still the Prime Minister of England.

What does that mean? It means that the Blair family live at the expense of the poor. The Blairs use the public highways, the public transport systems, and the other amenities funded by taxpayers, but they are not contributing to those services. The Blairs are not exceptional; they just happen to be very lucky because they own five homes. The increase in the value of their assets is enormous. Being able to live tax free all your life is something that we all would like to enjoy, but unfortunately that opportunity is denied to those who rent their homes. It is the privilege of landowners.

Cancel Debt, Tax Land, to Reduce Poverty

People seem to think that the one way to solve poverty in the world today is to cancel debts, the debts of nations. The theory is that, if we cancel debts, impoverished nations will have a better chance of investing in productive infrastructure and enterprises, creating employment, and raising living standards. Unfortunately, the debt cancellation project is a very partial one; it is not a comprehensive solution. Why not?

The idea of canceling debts to eliminate poverty goes back to biblical times, but the original debt cancellation strategy—as it appears in Leviticus 25—was only part of a two-plank strategy. The second part was to restore land to the people. Restoring land is crucial if we want to eliminate poverty in the world today. Debt cancellation, by itself, will not actually deliver the elimination of poverty in the world today.

We need a mechanism for restoring the land, or, rather, the income from land. The key is not so much giving people land itself, but letting people share in the benefits from land. Everyone would benefit if the government collected the economic rent of land in the form of a tax and used that revenue to provide public services. To see how this would work, consider the way a good school will cause property prices to rise. If we paid for new schools out of the increase in surrounding property values when they are built, we would not have to tax people's incomes, their wages, in order to fund capital investment.

So what would give low-income people a chance to earn a decent living? We would start by reducing the taxes that are imposed on low-income people. We could eliminate the income tax. We would then pay for public services with a tax on land rents instead. The people in public housing are already paying rent to the local government, whose properties they occupy, so they are already paying the land rent. That is all they ought to pay. If that were the only tax they paid, then they would become employable again. Employers would find that the costs of hiring them would be lower than they are today, and they would find work.

If we taxed the rent of land, what would be the consequences for the rich people? They would have to start paying their way through life. At the moment, because of the windfall gains that they receive through the land market, they are more than compensated for the taxes they pay. Under the system I am proposing, they would be obliged to pay for the benefits they receive. Rich people would not be financially worse off under the new system; they would just have to earn their income rather than deriving some of it at the expense of poor people.

Gilbert Herman   *Software Engineer (retired)*

Poverty is readily visible in the Philippines, particularly a large slum on the edge of Manila. The cause of poverty is the control of resources by an oligarchy that controls the economy and the government. While they grow enormously wealthy by owning the land from which gold, silver, sugar, pineapple, coconuts come, the rest of the population struggles to survive. Most efforts at reform have been misguided, such as the Huk Rebellion, because they have misdiagnosed the roots of poverty. The problem is not capitalism; it is the monopoly power of landlords.

I went to the Philippines, because my wife is from there. Our first trip together in 1972 was my first experience seeing the contrast between wealth and poverty in such a stark manner. On the train from Manila to my wife's province, I saw along the embankment thousands of tin shacks that people lived in. It was a sight I had never seen before in my life. These thousands of people were displaced from the land, because they could not eke out a living from farming. The Philippines has a large educated, English-speaking workforce, but the people cannot find jobs suitable to their training.

The Philippines is run by an oligarchy that was founded in land and resource monopolization. The elite maintain privileges based on their land and resources. Somebody once said that capitalists in Asia are largely based on the surpluses they have gotten from their land monopolization. People confuse the roles of capitalist and landowner. A lot of the radicals in the

Philippines want to get rid of capitalism.

There have been reform movements in the Philippines. Agrarian reform has been tried in the Philippines, but it has failed over the past forty years, by being co-opted by the landlords. The problem is that the political system in the Philippines is a crony system, based on who you know. The wealthy people control the political system. That is why there have not been a lot of popular movements. The last reform was called the comprehensive agrarian reform program, CARP. It failed. Landlords were supposed to disperse large landed estates among the landless people, but they used various legal and technical methods to get around those kinds of reforms.

It is the basic issue everywhere—privilege is the biggest problem. The most fundamental privilege is owning land and resources. The Philippines is basically a resource-based economy: gold, silver, sugar, pineapple, coconut—all these basic materials are owned by a few families. The other developments came from the surplus they collected from these resources. So Makati is like Wall Street—it is a beautiful development. Then you go a few miles away and you see shanty towns, people crammed in. My wife's family is struggling; they are considered middle class by Filipino standards, but they are struggling every day to make a living.

There are so many petty fees in the Philippines. You have to pay to go to school, after elementary school. All kinds of registration fees. All these petty fees are built into the system—all the fees that people have to pay to do daily activities they can hardly afford. It is incredible. And the number of children and adults in the streets selling drinks and newspapers and candy and whatever they can to eke out a living. These are people who have been displaced from their lands, who cannot make a living farming.

My brother-in-law is still a farmer. His land is scattered. I am not sure how this came about—maybe from selling lands. The divisions are done by embankments that are the boundaries. It is very scattered small-farm landownership. They own their own land and they have to pay taxes on the land. It is not worth much; it is way out in the boondocks. He scratches out a living.

I have been mainly in northern Luzon. In Mindanao there has been a civil war going on for maybe over forty years. There is a large Muslim population there, so it is part religious but it is also economic. There are a lot of pineapple plantations. The situation down there from a land point of view is even worse: more concentrated than in Luzon.

The Huk rebellion [in the 1950s and 1960s] was put down with a lot of help from Americans. The Huks had a misconception. If you want to distribute land, you cannot give everybody an opportunity to have the best land, so there must be some way to recoup the surpluses from the better land. So land distribution would not work. They should try Henry George's idea of taxing land and distributing the income, instead.

Chalmers Johnson *Political Scientist, Author*

Johnson worked as a consultant for the CIA from 1967 to 1973. After the collapse of the Soviet Union, he observed that the American military establishment sought new enemies to justify its existence. From that point on, he became a critic of American imperialism, writing three best-selling books on the subject. The far-flung network of military bases is costly to the US, causing financial stress to American taxpayers. Economic interest does not explain American imperialism, but there are still examples of an economic relationship. Japan and China have become the economic models for the rest of the world, based on their success using "industrial policy," state-directed investment in cutting-edge technology. America today is in danger of repeating the decline of the Roman Empire because the US has also created an executive branch which is unaccountable. It may be too late to bring it under control.

CIA Background: From Cold Warrior to Critic of Empire

I am a retired professor from the University of California, where I taught for well over 30 years, primarily in East Asian politics, the politics of China, Japan and the two Koreas.

I once worked as a consultant for the Office of National Estimates of the CIA from 1967 to 1973, at the invitation of the director of Central Intelligence, Richard Helms. I was brought in from the outside to review the intelligence reports the CIA produced, in order to check on myopic bureaucratism or generalized incompetence. It was interesting, but it also contributed to my view that United States did not have an intelligence service.

I came to believe that the CIA was the private army of the president, being used for highly dubious, almost invariably disastrous interventions in other people's countries. Starting with the overthrow of the Iranian government in 1953 for the sake of the British Petroleum company, we declared that the elected Prime Minister of Iran, Mohammed Mosaddeq, was a communist. The Pope would have been a better candidate [for being considered a communist]. Mossadeq was just trying to regain some control over Iranian oil assets. The British wanted him out and talked Eisenhower into doing the dirty work.

When the Soviet Union collapsed in 1991, the *raison d'etre* of the American imperial position had ended overnight. The American government instantaneously moved to find a replacement enemy: China, terrorism, drug lords, anything—even instability. The presumed threat could be anything to keep the military industrial complex working.

Starting around 1995, as I studied the 737 American military bases in other countries, I began to see the Cold War more as a cover for imperialism all along. In 1946 the British told President Truman they could no longer maintain their position in Greece. They asked us to assume that role in a seamless transfer of power among English-speaking imperialists.

This led me, in 2000, to publish *Blowback: The Costs and Consequences of American Empire*. "Blowback" is a special term of art, invented by the CIA in the after-action report on the overthrow of the Iranian government in 1953. It means retaliation for secret actions of our government. So, when the retaliation comes, Americans are unable to put it into context. They do not see cause and effect. Probably the most spectacular example of blowback we know is the Al Qaeda attacks of September 11, 2001.

This led to a book called *The Sorrows of Empire: Militarism, Secrecy and the End of the Republic* in 2004 and another one called *Nemesis: The Last Days of the American Republic*. Nemesis is the ancient Greek goddess of revenge, the punisher of a peculiarly Grecian sin, *hubris*, which is caused by arrogance and indifference to other people's needs. I concluded that *hubris* was very much associated with America after the collapse of the Soviet Union in 1991. We said we won the Cold War. We did not win it. Both sides lost it; the Soviet Union just lost it first because they were always poorer.

As I begin to study American imperialism, the issue of its origins arose. There was American imperialism during the 19th century. One cannot help but see the Mexican-American War in that way. Full-blown American imperialism burst forth at the turn of the century [1898] in the war with Spain. We used this war to further bring Latin American countries under our hegemony and exploit them mercilessly. We sought to take advantage of them economically, but we denied it. Nothing was more convenient to the United States than Fidel Castro. A wonderful way to disguise our imperialism in Latin

America was to say we were dealing with the threat of Soviet imperialism in the hemisphere.

Military Bases and the Dangers of a Standing Army

America has had hegemony over the rest of the world through an empire of military bases. Today, according to the Base Structure Report, an annual inventory report of real property owned by the Pentagon, we have 40 bases on foreign soil that are worth well over a billion and a half dollars in replacement value. It has nothing to do with American national defense; it has everything to do with the maintenance of American hegemony over the entire planet.

Until WWII, we certainly had a history of imperialism. But we did not have a huge munitions industry. There had been standing armies, but citizens were still called on to defend the country, and soldiers were demobilized as soon as the emergency was over.

Perhaps the greatest single warning we have ever had was in the first presidential Farewell Address by George Washington. He warned the country about the danger of standing armies. This is incidentally the exact same thing that destroyed the Roman army. The old Roman legions, composed of farmers in times of national emergency, gave way to long-service armies of 20 years' duty.

Foreign imperialism does not mix well with domestic democracy. You cannot have them both. You can be a domestic democracy and your empire will fall apart. If you want to keep your empire, you are going to lose your domestic democracy and turn into a tyranny.

Ambiguity of Economic Explanation of Empire

Reducing American imperialism to economic interests and corporate interests has the smell of ersatz or vulgar Marxism about it, but in the minds of many people it offers an easy, satisfactory explanation, which is corporate greed. I dislike this view because it denigrates what imperialism actually is: the impulse to maintain hegemony over other nations. Economic power is only one form of domination. We have used American military power to serve the parochial interests of American businesses and investors and to strengthen the American balance of payments. But, as a superpower, America is losing its manufacturing base rapidly and is the world's largest net debtor nation.

There are serious anomalies in an economic explanation of imperialism, though the US government has used its imperial apparatus for economic purposes, for the advantage of American firms. An example is the overthrow of the government of Guatemala in 1954 because the United Fruit Company objected to some moderate proposals for land reform. Later, International Telephone and Telegraph participated in the coup against Salvador Allende, president of Chile. More generally, American power has been used in Latin America to protect the owners of extractive industries.

East Asia: Success of Industrial Policy

After World War II, the Japanese developed industrial policy, which means economic goal setting by government. It is a form of socialism, but it is different from the European or Soviet variety of socialism, which involved state ownership of property as well as state goal setting. Reformed market socialism, in China under Deng Xiao Ping or in East Europe before the Wall came down, lowered a lot of decision making to the household unit, but it still maintained social ownership of property, which stood in the way of entrepreneurship.

The Japanese have simply reversed the usual Western category of socialism. Instead of reformed communism, with state ownership of property and private management of economy, the Japanese combined social goal setting and communal management with private ownership of property. The government supports enterprises in every possible way with inexpensive capital and guarantees against foreign competition. Industrial policy enabled Japan to succeed. It enabled them to sell us automobiles and consumer electronics. The latter killed the consumer electronics business in America.

We now have a more interesting competitor, and that is China. They have learned the Japanese lesson. They sometimes say the antidote, the singular source of data, is my book on the history of Japanese industrial policy, *MITI and the Japanese Miracle*. MITI refers to the Ministry of International Trade and Industry. It was the Ministry of Munitions during WWII. It is the command post inside the world of Japanese socialism where the Japanese squared the circle on how to produce socialism without the known consequences of socialism. They developed general goal setting, but without the inefficiencies, the waste, and the travesties that are associated with a true command economy.

East Asia as New Model for Developing Countries

Generally speaking, East Asia has become a model for the rest of the world. You will find that throughout Latin America, notably in Brazil, there is an increasing contempt for American neoliberism, for the preaching of free market virtues. It is more or less a taboo subject in the United States to point out that we are no longer a model for the world.

Europe is important and powerful, but Europe is aging. It does not have the huge manpower resources of East Asia.

The center of gravity is moving to China. By around 2025 China will be the world's most powerful country. The United States, if it still exists, may be the second; the third will probably be India. Then we would look at the European Union, instead of independent countries like Britain, France or Germany.

Economic Fragility of American Empire*

There is something intrinsically unstable about the American empire. Military Keynesianism, the devotion of masses of resources to the military, has unintended consequences. We are now spending close to a trillion dollars a year on our military establishment. That does not include money spent on nuclear weapons by the Department of Energy or on veterans' affairs, including treating our wounded from Iraq. It does not include foreign military aid by the State Department. It does not include the actual defense of the country by the Department of Homeland Security (DHS). After 9/11, we discovered that DHS has nothing to do with the defense of our country. It is busy with warfare in outer space or other useless ways to spend money.

The American Empire could come to an end very quickly if just one little thing happened: if Saudi Arabia required payment for its oil in euros instead of dollars. If the Saudis simply did that, the American stock exchange would collapse, the backing for the dollar would end. As the country with the world's largest annual trade deficit, we would be in the same fix as Germany in 1923, China in 1948, Argentina in 2001 and 2002. We are facing the possibility of national bankruptcy.

We are now on the threshold of what happened to the Soviet Union. They either had to reform or collapse, as they did in 1991. Our own collapse

---

* Ed.: In a part of the interview excised due to length, Johnson compares the American empire with the Roman Empire. Having an empire endangers democracy in the US, just as it destroyed the Roman republic. When Rome shifted from a citizen army to a professional army, it accepted militarism as the core principle of Roman society and made fighting a permanent way of life. Eventually, one general, Julius Caesar seized the opportunity to gain control and became dictator. Americans are naïve to think that democracy cannot give way to tyranny in our country.

is getting closer, but we are supremely unconscious in the face of the pressures on us today.

The Imperial Presidency

One of the serious problems in our society today and a symptom of how far gone we are is the "imperial presidency." It is as contrary to American constitutional theory and practice as one could imagine. Political leadership lies in the ability to compromise among three separate and coequal branches of government. As numerous Supreme Court Justices have said over the years, this was never intended to make for a more efficient government. It was intended as a bulwark against tyranny.

The Constitution guarantees in Article 1 that citizens of the United States will receive ultimately an accurate account of how tax dollars are spent. Americans do not yet get an accurate statement of how their tax dollars are spent. The budgets of the 16 federal intelligence agencies, particularly and notably the CIA, have been secret since the day they were created. That has turned these agencies into a private army of the president.

In the case of the Department of the Defense, 40% of the monstrous defense budget is "black," secret; it can only be seen by uniformed military officers and a couple of deeply hamstrung members of Congress.

The presidency is out of control. There is no effective oversight of it. The CIA had no oversight of any sort until the mid 1970s when the Church Committee was appointed because of the misuse of the CIA by Nixon in Watergate. They created the original Congressional Oversight Committee. These have been farcical. They do nothing. When Congressman Charlie Wilson of Texas became the Chairman of the House Oversight Committee, he rather famously called his friends at the CIA and said, " The fox is in the hen house. You can do anything you want to."

The current President's Intelligence Oversight Board is a check on misuse and illegal activities in the intelligence agencies that have worked their way through the past five presidencies. It was created by Jerry Ford. It has not actually met, done anything, requested information or anything for the first five and a half years of the George Bush administration. It has simply made itself notorious now for having defied a presidential order. The Presidential Intelligence Oversight Board was made permanent by Ronald Reagan in 1981. These are the types of things that are out of control.

The George W. Bush presidency has misused the power to issue so-called "signing statements." In signing a law, he adds to it a statement of his own that he does not agree with a provision or section and that he is not going to enforce it. Since the President does not have the authority to issue line-item vetos, this is clearly an unconstitutional assertion of executive authority, but it has not been challenged. It is hard to explain why Congress has so abdicated its role, why it has been so easily bought off and paid for, compromised.

Citizens are Kept in the Dark about Empire

You cannot get information about what our government does. The press has failed you as thoroughly as any institution could have. If you are an extremely adept user of the internet you could become better informed than someone who reads the low-brow daily newspapers of America. It is very hard to even begin to find out what is really going on. So we need a renaissance of public information, public awareness, and public attempts to hold their representatives responsible.

There seems to be a sense of powerlessness in this society today. I think the public is scared to death. They actually know we are in terrible trouble, we are heading towards a cliff, and they do not know what to do about it. Can we recreate the very structure that guaranteed our liberty at this point? We still take for granted that the police will treat us as citizens, that our rights will be observed, that we enjoy the rights of citizenship rather than simply being subjects. I am quite cynical on this subject of whether or not there is enough time left to make the changes that would be necessary.

Gitu-wa-Kahengeri *Freedom Fighter* (Mau Mau)

As a Mau Mau freedom fighter for independence, I fought the British from 1948 to 1961. The British took our land and treated us like second-class citizens who were not allowed to question their authority in any way. During the independence movement, those of us who fought risked prison or execution if we were caught. The Kenyans who did not take any risks during the uprising, who remained loyal to the British masters, are the ones who were given both offices and lands the British had stolen from us when independence came. We are still living with that vestige of British colonialism.

I joined the *Mau Mau's* fight for justice in 1948. I am here at the World Social Forum because I still believe there is much work to do to regain Kenya and to return its land to its rightful owners.

I was born during the era of the British colonialists, a time of harsh treatment. They denied our people basic human rights. The British, who were both administrators and settlers, stole the fertile land—the highlands. A British immigrant could have 2,000 to 5,000 acres while a native was left with one-half or one acre of low-value land. Our mobility was restricted. Many districts that were once open to Kenyans to pass through freely were now off limits to Kenyans. They also sent us to jail just for passing in front of one of their hotels or looking inside.

Because of our frustration with those conditions, a freedom movement arose. First, there were talks among native Kenyans about what approach we should take. Only a few were brave enough to discuss freedom with their peers and allies. Then, in 1946, political parties began to formulate ways to liberate Kenyans from oppression. Members of these political parties were imprisoned. In 1948, the *Mau Mau* formed an underground movement and decided, since they had no money or power, that they would use machetes and whatever threatening implements they could find to fight the British. Young people began to disobey the orders of colonial leaders. The *Mau Maus* hid in the forest from the British and their women took meals to them.

One event inspired me to take up arms and fight. I went with my father to a meeting held by a provincial commissioner. He was standing on top of a table with books under his arms, speaking loudly. Once the commissioner finished, my father asked a question. For that, he was forced out of the room and beaten by the guards. Why? Because no questions were allowed. That was the moment when I decided I had to fight for my country. I did not want the same thing to happen one day to my son. I decided then to die in the struggle for freedom.

Any freedom fighter who was caught was either hung or imprisoned. For example, my father and I were both imprisoned. My mother, sisters, and brother were also detained in their village. After that, my family lived in a camp where they dug a trench around their tent and implanted wooden spikes in the trench so that those who wanted to hurt them would fall in the trench and be injured.

After many years of our resistance, the British finally decided to negotiate an end to the conflict. In 1960-61, the British Colonial Secretary invited the freedom fighters to round-table talks. In 1963, independence was granted: the Union Jack was lowered and the Kenyan flag was hoisted.

Independence was a farce. The freedom fighters won the war but lost the peace. We did not benefit from independence. While the freedom movement was taking place, the British promoted their servants [administrators loyal to the British] into official positions. The servants were well taken care of and did not want to risk losing their titles and privileges, so they did not help the freedom fighters win independence. Before the British left, they transferred land titles to the servants, who then resisted any requests by the *Mau Maus* for land. The *Mau Maus* were left outside of government and without land. So, we are still living with the vestiges of colonialism.

Kipruto Arap Kirwa *Minister of Agriculture, Kenya*

Agriculture in Kenya faces many challenges. Only 20 percent of the land has adequate water, making the rest marginal. Trade barriers make it difficult for Kenyan goods to enter the world market. The legacy of colonialism ties the production of specific crops to specific communities. The colonial settlers also took their connections with the export market with them when they left after independence, leaving Kenya to supply raw materials, but Europeans to reap the higher rewards of processing and finishing agricultural products. Trade rules now prevent the government from providing much assistance to farmers. But low incomes prevent farmers from applying the optimum amount of fertilizer. Thus, food security is inhibited. Africa as a whole needs to become a more integrated market for food, selling food internally. A major obstacle is the lack of infrastructure, so food shipped within Africa is often more expensive than food imported from other continents. Exchange rate stability is important to enable Kenya to pay off its foreign debts. The most important land reform is consolidation of land parcels to enable more people to mechanize farm production. To do this, many small-scale farmers need to find other jobs in the agricultural supply chain.

The Challenges to Agriculture in Kenya

Around 80 percent of Kenyans rely on food production for their livelihoods. The portion of GDP directly derived from agriculture is 26 percent with another 27 percent derived indirectly through linkages to other sectors.

The first challenge for agriculture in Kenya is insufficient water. Lack of water resources makes 80 percent of land marginal. The challenge is to improve utilization of water through irrigation and to use rain for farming. We have also borrowed from development partners for irrigation systems.. The 20 percent of land in high-potential areas is settled. Pressure on that land is increasing, reducing productivity and making it less suitable for agriculture. We want to expand the amount of irrigated land, which produces close to three times as much as rain-fed land.

The second major challenge has been trade barriers. Those include tariffs and stringent measures imposed by buyers of our produce. The major challenge has been what we call "Euro-gap." Buyers in Europe have insisted on specific production processes. We have trained thousands of farmers to comply with them. If the European rules were imposed in good faith, we would not mind. But some are imposed by cartel buyers, who just want to make it impossible for us to penetrate their markets.

In Africa, organizing farmers to respond to changing market demands is complicated. Most farmers have only two to three hectares, and they lack the requisite training and capacity to understand world trade dynamics. A lot of money and human resources are spent trying to bring farmers up to date.

The Colonial Legacy

When the British settled here, around 1900, they displaced the population in the high-potential areas. Settled communities were dispersed. At independence in 1963, landownership started changing hands to Kenyan citizens. The Settlement Fund lent money from the British government to Africans to purchase parcels of land from white settlers. Years later, some loans have been paid, and other people are still paying. Communities settled away from each other are now mixed. In a district like Nakuru or Trans Nzoia, all communities [linguistic or ethnic groups] are represented.

The British adopted a "divide and rule" strategy. Even 42 years after independence, we still have the colonial legacy of stereotypes about other communities, more than in neighboring countries. One consequence of that legacy is prejudice. When somebody first learns your name, he has already formed an opinion of you. In addition, certain crops have been ascribed to certain communities: coffee to central Kenya, sugarcane to western Kenya and Nyanza province, maize and wheat to my community. The second component of the colonial legacy is that communities believe certain pieces of land belong to them. In some areas, Kenyans look at other Kenyans like foreigners. They call the indigenous people "residents." This creates volatility and a lot of problems. That colonial legacy has interfered with progress.

As minister of agriculture, I have been trying to change the Agriculture Act. In the middle of the last century, certain crops were not supposed to be raised by Africans, including coffee and tea. Tea cultivation was allowed to Africans on a small scale in the early 1960s, just before independence. After independence, there was a full rollout program for Africans to grow tea, with coffee allowed slightly earlier. Other crops that were allowed for Africans were basically for subsistence. The export market was dominated by British settlers. Almost 95 percent of our coffee is for export.

When white settlers moved away, from 1964 to 1970, they retained control over the operations from Europe. We became the producers of raw materials and they were now the agents for marketing and processing. They added all the value from processing away from Africa. That effectively exported jobs out of the country, as well as the expertise that is associated with certain handling of the produce.

That situation continues today. The roasting of coffee—just to pick that particular crop—is done away from Kenya. In fact, Germany, which does not have a bush of coffee, is the largest exporter of coffee. But as a country we produce the world's premium coffee, apart from Ethiopia. Tea is the same. The tea that you consume in the Sudan first goes to Europe, then Lipton brings it back to Sudan and a number of other countries.

Efforts to Assist Farmers

We are limited in what we can do for our farmers because of agreements we have signed with multinational and bilateral donors. A subsidy to farmers, including any indirect subsidy, violates the protocol. Most of our farmers are not properly organized to attain economies of scale in procurement of fertilizer or in targeting certain markets. The government still has a role to play in providing infrastructure—roads, electricity, and fertilizer at reduced rates. This allows farmers to shift from subsistence to commercial ventures. However, Kenya falls below international production figures for certain crops, because our farmers cannot afford to apply the threshold amount of fertilizer.

This vicious cycle (low income and inadequate fertilizer applications) causes Africa to suffer the problem of food insecurity. In sub-Saharan Africa, close to 300 million people go to bed every night without an adequate meal. The countries of sub-Saharan Africa cannot address this issue on their own, because of the vagaries of weather—the oscillation from drought to floods, a cycle requiring infrastructure to overcome it.

If the North wants to help sub-Saharan Africa solve this problem, the best way is to give us methods of increasing productivity: affordable credit and water resources. We need a lot of capital for conservation measures. We also need access to certain technologies. Another important issue is the volatility of markets. I appreciate supply and demand, but it should operate within limits that can allow a minimum for survival.

We need to add value here in Africa, to hold the entire supply chain in Africa. The rest of the world will then buy our product in a more refined form. This will allow us to retain some of the investment here, and also allow investment to grow in Africa.

Developing the Internal Supply of Food in Africa

Africa is a huge market. While we need to do business with the rest of the world, we also need to improve market dynamics within Africa. The trend of rains (and we are still relying on rain-fed agriculture) in Africa is that it changes: when there is a drought in East Africa, Central Africa may have a bumper harvest.

To get maize from Zambia is more expensive, in terms of the cost of transport alone, than getting the same commodity from Brazil. That is due to lack of infrastructure. If that problem were solved, some things could be evened out. We would be able to reduce the cost of food in Africa. Many people wonder why food costs so much in Africa. If Kenya does not have maize, we have to import it. The freight cost alone is more than the cost of maize if you purchase it locally. The cost of transport almost doubles the cost of the commodity if you buy from a neighboring country, such as Uganda.

Debt and Currency Stability

We hope our currencies will be slightly more stable than they have been in the past. For the last four years, our currency has been stable at around 72 shillings per dollar. With that stability, we can manage the debt. In 1992, a dollar was 25 shillings. By July 1993, a dollar was 77 shillings. That jump more than doubled the amount of debt, because we borrowed foreign currencies. We hope for currency stability. With that and recent improvements in revenue collection, we can retire the debt.

Debt cancellation might seem like a very nice option, but at times it is an option that you would not want to encourage, more so if it is laden with conditions. At times what you are told to do may not necessarily correspond with your national priorities. If the interest alone was removed from the money that we borrowed, we would be able to repay the money with the current debt portfolio.

Land Reform

This country still has people who lack access to land resources. The challenge is not only to allow people access to land through loans and so forth, but also for people to see that they do not all have to work on land to earn a living. You can work anywhere along the value chain of agricultural products, and make a decent living. You can market agricultural products, process them, or produce them.

In the long run, there should be effective land consolidation to improve the capacity to use machines. The pressure on high-potential land has reduced its productivity over the last forty years. The parcels have become so small that it is almost impossible to use machines on most of them.

The challenge is cultural. The majority of Kenyans, including me, believe that the only way to show that they belong to this country is to have their names inscribed on a land title. We must overcome this. Many Kenyans believe not having access to land is to disinherit them from their motherland. Many people believe that farming just means preserving the farm, not employing a manager who can operate the farm. We want them to realize that a block of farms under different owners can hire a manager to farm that land. They would be making better use of the land. We have so many trained people in this field of agriculture. The other challenge is to increase utilization of the land in areas that are marginal because they do not have water, not because of infertility. We are looking for a hybrid of ideas that cannot only create space in the high-potential areas, but also create opportunities in the marginal areas.

Miloon Kothari   *UN Rapporteur on Housing*

There is a worldwide crisis involving housing and land rights. The poor are being displaced and evicted by the thousands. Governments are failing to prevent the evictions, and in many cases politicians collude with developers to evict current occupants. Even then, the government does nothing to help those who are displaced. These events are justified by officials on the neoliberal grounds that government should not interfere in markets, even if they are destroying people's lives. Contrary to what many critics of neoliberalism may  *believe, colonialism, debt, or the IMF should not be blamed for government policies that deny the civil rights of the poor. There are alternatives to neoliberalism, and the example of several Latin American countries demonstrates that it is possible to partially delink local economies from the global economy.*

The Crisis of Housing and Land Rights

I work in the area of the right to adequate housing and land rights. As a UN Special *Rapporteur*, I have traveled around the world over the last seven years and heard testimony from the people who are suffering the global housing and land rights crisis. In the last 10 to 15 years, there has been an acceleration of land dispossession and forcible evictions of people and communities. That process has contributed to growing poverty.

Growing speculation in land and property is a big factor in the crisis. One can get very high returns from investing in land and property in all types of countries: in authoritarian and democratic countries and in countries of both the South and the North. People are now being forced to live in urban and rural apartheid situations, where the poor are being marginalized. Indigenous minorities and women are the most severely affected.

Governments have been unwilling to regulate the real estate market. They are not willing to change the economic system to respect human rights. There is a disconnect between social policies and economic policies. In both developed and developing countries, I see neighborhoods, villages, or an entire part of a city, in which people live in dilapidated, insecure conditions. It would take very few resources to improve the conditions of people. But instead of doing that, governments have the mindset to be a "world class" city.

In the city of Mumbai, in India, between November of 2004 and

February of 2005, around 400,000 people were evicted from their homes. American consultants came up with a plan to beautify the city for tourism and for international investment. Most of the people who were evicted had lived in their settlements for decades. When the people asked the government, "What are we supposed to do?" the governor of the state said, "Go back to your villages."

In Nairobi, the city council is helping a private landowner evict people who are on his land. Politicians collude with land mafias and cartels. The result is that people have no place to go. For displaced and homeless people on the street, there is not an office that they can go to for housing or food for their children.

Failure of Neoliberalism

What I find very disturbing in all this is the implicit assumption that development is going to lead to the sacrifice of some people. Many people will be forced into homelessness, into landlessness, and some will have to die, because we are following a particular economic model. We will get to those people when we get to them. The old "trickle-down theory" and the old concept of "growth for the sake of growth" are very much alive. This is very disturbing. We have evidence from Latin America, Africa, and Asia that these policies have not worked.

Neoliberal policies promoted by the International Monetary Fund (IMF), the World Bank, and many of the trade policies coming from the World Trade Organization have not worked. They have deepened poverty. But those policies are still prescribed by the IMF and the World Bank, and there seems to be a global consensus around them. It has coincided with the globalization of finance, trade, and investment. People lose control over their resources when large projects, such as dams or mines, are built. People, particularly indigeneous people, are forced out of their rural habitats into cities where they live in slums, where they can be evicted again.

The Real Estate Juggernaut

A real estate juggernaut has taken over. Real estate logic underlies the homeownership model and the idea that one must have investments in real estate. It drives pension funds in the United States to invest in real-state all over the world. The returns are so high that people go to great lengths to invest in housing and property. Now there are multinational real estate companies looking for investment wherever they can find it.

Economic policy in the South and the North is geared towards home ownership. The idea is that everyone should own a home. But fewer people, even those in the middle-class, can afford a home and can afford to keep up the mortgage payments. The whole economic system is based on giving tax reductions and subsidies to homeownership. But these subsidies and tax reductions actually go straight to the developer. They do not increase capital. They increase insecurity.

As a result, there is much more real estate violence than before. In Spain, real estate companies engage in "mobbing," hiring private agents to forcibly evict the elderly or others who live in prime city center areas. This is occurring in Barcelona, Madrid, and Seville. The state is not willing to challenge that, even though it is illegal. If anything, governments and political parties are colluding in this. Real estate profits are part of the funds that go to political parties.

A climate has been created where people have nowhere to go. If they are displaced from a large development project or from a city beautification scheme, they are homeless. These millions of people have fewer rights than a registered refugee would have. Market- and development-based evictions are now causing the displacement of more people every year than people who are displaced by armed and ethnic conflict. Huge numbers of people are being dislocated from their homes and from their sources of livelihood. This is a very disturbing trend.

Governments have to control the amount of rent people pay. Governments should control land prices that are mushrooming, but governments are not willing to do that. I have spoken to some finance ministers about this. They respond by saying it would destabilize the market. I have never understood that logic.

As real estate prices rise, a parallel phenomenon is the destruction of public housing. In the United States, for example, a lot of the public housing is being demolished. In Australia, social housing is being reduced. In other countries no investment is going into social housing.

So what happens to displaced people? They are forced to live in marginal areas. They are forced to live in higher and higher density conditions. All of that increases poverty. If you take away people's basic sustenance, their natural resources—their land and water—if you remove them from that, you are creating landlessness, indebtedness, migration, and very dire conditions of poverty.

Don't Blame Colonialism, Debt, or The IMF

Not all of the blame can be placed on colonial history. In India, for example, that was almost 55 years ago. We have made many of our own mistakes. Of course, there are countries that have very high debt and that is related to colonialism. Countries have had the opportunity to change the policies, yet they are unwilling to do that. In Brazil, in spite of all their social policy commitments, they are afraid of how the market will react to reform. They do everything to keep the market stable. Many countries could take social conditions into their own hands and improve the lives of the poorest 20 to 25 percent of the people.

Even the countries with large debts could do more.* They have a huge amount invested in the military, in tourism, in nuclear power, or in other large infrastructure projects. They have even had international support from bilateral agencies and from the United Nations. The money is available; it is just being misdirected. If a government spends money by subsidizing middle- and higher-income housing instead of creating social housing, that is not a shortage of funds. You cannot blame the IMF or the World Bank for that. The explanation for poverty in terms of international commitments is an excuse.

Government Choice: Help Poor or Middle Class?

Policies are geared towards the middle and higher income groups. This goes back to the original World Bank and IMF prescriptions of the 1960s that required cost-recovery: never invest unless you get a return. But with people who are homeless, hungry, and lacking health care, you cannot think of cost-recovery. They need subsidies. Governments, without saying it, are taking a position that people can fend for themselves. But people cannot.

You almost have the sense that people are considered dispensable. If you speak to a government official they will not tell you that. They will say, "It will take time." I do not accept that. Governments could protect people who are currently threatened with displacement or make sure everyone has access to potable water. But the funds are creating export-processing zones and sophisticated tourism facilities instead of helping vulnerable people and communities.

---

* Ed.: Elsewhere, Mr. Kothari added, "There are of course very highly indebted countries in sub-Saharan Africa and in other parts of the world that are very dependent. There the whole issue of debt cancellation arises."

Informal Land Rights to Formal Title: Disrupts Communities

Historically, people had collective or community rights to land, particularly in rural areas. They had common-property resources: water, forest products, fuel, fodder. There was no legal basis for that. Instead of integrating collective rights into formal systems of law, formalization of property rights has simply replaced collective systems with individual rights. When urban governments consider land policies and master plans, they do not look for collective solutions or cooperatives. They think only in terms of individual ownership. Models of collective rights and collective ownership are being ignored because they do not match neoliberal thinking. So developers and loggers say that local inhabitants do not have legal rights to the land they have occupied for many years. They negotiate with individuals and collude with the courts and politicians to dispossess people and break up communities. This has had a severe impact on small farmers, indigenous people, fisher-folk, and nomadic people.

Another way to disposses people is through a process that in India is called land-alienation. In that case, an outsider can inter-marry into a tribal indigenous family and use the land and the house or put it on the market for sale.

Alternatives to Neoliberalism

What can be done to remedy the situation that has been brought on by neoliberal thinking? Many remedies are available that have been tried in some countries.

My first recommendation is for countries to re-think the logic of the economic policies that are in place and to re-design them in such a way that there is much more symbiosis and coherence between social and economic objectives. A second remedy would be for most countries in the world to ratify international human rights instruments, which protect people's human rights to land, to housing, food, health, education, and social security. Then governments should take those obligations seriously and design their national policies and laws based on them. Third, regarding housing, the first step for any government to take is a survey of the location, size, and conditions of vulnerable groups to determine which members of those groups are more vulnerable than others. A housing and a land policy should be based on that. Fourth, there should be a separate focus on housing policy for the bottom 20 to 25 percent, and that policy should not be linked to the larger housing question in a society. Housing should be regularized for those threatened with displacement, for those being evicted from their homes because they do not have formal title. They are living there because they have no other choice, and they need protection from eviction.

Latin American Leaders Challenge Neoliberalism

One positive example of change is Brazil's progressive "right to the city" legislation, which requires municipalities to designate what they call "zones of special interest." This follows the principle of first identifying people who are vulnerable and then guaranteeing that they will be given secure rights there and that they will not be replaced. They have policies that protect people from being displaced from their homes.

Several other nations in Latin America are questioning neoliberal policies. We have seen other regimes in the past like Lula's in Brazil or Chávez's in Venezuela. It is too early to know whether they will succeed, but the signs are very promising. The main obstacles faced by the presidents who have come into power with left-leaning parties are the economic regimes that are in place. They will have to confront landowners and the big industrial companies tied to multinationals abroad, which effectively rule their countries. They need to delink from the international system by building up economies that are more self-sufficient. They have to stop listening to the prescriptions from agencies like the World Bank and the IMF and come up with homegrown economic solutions. If a country has heavy debts, it should consider the example of Brazil, which accepted funding from the IMF and the World Bank, but only after stipulating that Brazil would decide what to do with the loans. They have to show that people can participate in the decision-making that governs the country not only in terms of elections, but also in terms of involvement in neighborhood and city decisions. Without that, nothing much will change. This would be a big step forward, because in many of these countries there is no history of democratic functioning.

To find a way forward, we must look at our own histories. Independent and cooperative forms of development were occurring before the colonial period and in the immediate post colonial period. That was all abandoned because of the growing power of the international economic actors. There has to be a gradual delinking of that. But in the current global situation, you cannot completely delink from the international economy. One must be very selective about making linkages. It would be very good if leaders would engage directly in considering more cooperative strategies for development.

Edgardo Lander *Professor, Social Sciences, Venezuelan Central University, Caracas*

Poverty cannot be understood in the form of a statistical snapshot. It can only be grasped historically as a process of exclusion, stemming from colonialism. Liberal thought defines poverty in terms of a lack, which invites the expert to take control and fix the problem. But the liberal vision is responsible for the excessive consumption of resources and the destruction of the planet. It creates a zero-sum condition in which the poor are deprived of their livelihood. History is taught throughout the world from the perspective of northern Europe. It teaches that the Enlightenment brought reason to society and that the industrial revolution developed without any antecedents. The experience of the global South shows those ideas are false. The wealth of the North came from plundering the South, and the positive side of the Enlightenment in Europe was constructed on the domination of people and nature in the rest of the world. Latin America was absorbed into the world system in three phases: Spanish colonialism, British commercial domination, and North American hegemony. Latin America went through a phase of relative inclusion of the poor during the period of import substitution under populist leaders (Peron in Argentina, Vargas in Brazil, Cardenas in Mexico). That ended with the coup in Chile in 1973. Today, it remains difficult for Latin America to escape the orbit defined by neoliberalism.

There are many perspectives from which to approach the topic of poverty. They include conceptual issues related to who is defining poverty, historical themes about the modern colonial-imperial world-system, questions about various forms of exclusion, the natural condition of human beings, and inequality of resource control and use. I would like to say something about each one of these subjects.

Poverty as Exclusion

International organizations and statisticians look at poverty as a snapshot, which is absolutely un-historic. They lose sight of the manner in which historical processes have created social submission, class differentiation, and the construction of racial categories. They merely describe differences between poor countries and rich countries, ignoring the brutal processes of social differentiation produced by modern capitalism. Differences continue to accelerate with the current globalization process.

Historic processes have led to the enrichment of some and to complete plundering of power and subjectivity, which is characterized by Frantz

Fanon as the way in which an image is shaped for the colonized. That image is constructed by the colonial order by destroying subjectivities, identities, and social fabrics. It builds up European white males as superior beings with intelligence and identifies others with the body, affection, and sentimentalism.

The construction of poverty in the international system is a colonial construction that destroys identity and limits the possibility of self-definition. The World Bank defines the poor as those who have less than a $1 a day. Defining human well-being in monetary terms is a grotesque, Eurocentric, liberal construction of life as a consumer citizen. Autonomy is constructed as a pathology that requires an international expert to recommend therapies to transform deficient societies into modern societies. This vision excludes people from their own history and from their relations with power and nature.

Limits of the Liberal Vision

Most development or anti-poverty policies being pushed by international organizations are ecologically impossible. Achieving the levels of consumption for the "good life" in industrialized countries is not possible for two fundamental reasons.

First, the accumulation of wealth in North America was possible only through centuries of unequal appropriation of the planet's resources. The southern countries cannot repeat the pattern.

Second, the planet's resources cannot sustain it. The productive capacity of our planet is already over-utilized, particularly by the wealthiest 20 to 30 percent of people.

We have arrived at a zero-sum game in which increased use of resources by one part of society decreases available resources for others. If some factory ships obtain large quantities of fish off the African coast, the local African fishery will decrease.

We speak of progress, development, and investment, even as we destroy life on earth and use resources unequally. The social sciences are complicit. Economics naturalizes exclusion and ignores natural limits. Its models measure well-being in monetary terms, presuppose progress without limits, deny culture, and treat other options as anachronistic.

Liberal thought characterizes modernity only in positive terms—tolerance, abundance, and freedom. The negative side, colonialism, remains hidden. This colonial face of modernity appears as if it were prior to humanity, making it seem that what is needed is more modernity. The Enlightenment view of Hegel and Kant depicts Europe as the source of freedom, reason, and democracy. It ignores completely the abusive power that permitted the bright side to exist, while the majority of the world faced the dark side. Africa, Latin America, and southern Asia have experienced modernity as genocide, imperialism, colonialism, and racial hierarchy. Obviously the last thing we need is more modernity.

Colonialism was started in America with the aim of evangelization, to save the souls of the so-called Indians. It sometimes required killing the body to save the soul. English colonialism was based on the "White Man's Burden,"—Europe bringing civilization to the uncivilized. Then came "development," to vanquish "underdevelopment." Neoliberal logic now makes market society the model. Through permanent cultural war, the North forces the South into war (as in Iraq), free trade agreements, and foreign debt, all to impose a single market pattern.

The Origins of Capitalist Labor Relations in the New World

We cannot have a critical view of injustice, inequality, and racism today unless we understand our history. The capitalistic system and the modern era started when America was conquered, which set in motion a systematic process of exploiting resources and colonizing human beings and nature.

Capitalism has historically built labor relations as forms of expropriation: servile labor, slave labor, simple mercantile labor, and paid labor. They are products of capital relations. Atlantic slavery was a modern capitalistic type of slavery, because it defined human beings as merchandise in the international market. The forms of this historical process are not pre-capitalist or pre-modern (as social science mythology would have it); they are forms built by modernity and by the appropriation process of capital.

Even the forms of labor organization characteristic of the industrial revolution—the separation of workers, the duty to work, and the introduction of machinery—pre-existed in America on the *hacienda* and in sugar cane production. In each case, the organizing regime took place first in America and was later utilized during the industrial revolution. As a result, we lack any record of how these processes developed in some countries and then articulated a form of organization in others.

Misrepresenting the Origins of the Industrial Revolution

History is still taught from the perspective of northern Europe as if it were "universal history." In this narrative, the initiative that transformed Europe and made it the center of the modern world was the industrial revolution. That story distorts the origins of the capitalist order and the world system. Northern European development was preceded by the colonization of Latin America by southern Europe and the transfer of gold, silver, and the so-called "precious vegetables," above all, sugar cane. Because of the political and social circumstances in Spain, those resources were channeled to the north, mainly to Holland and England. This permitted them to accumulate wealth and served as the basis for English colonialism and the industrial revolution. The industrial revolution appears in the guise of "universal history" as something separate from colonialism, a sudden, unexplained emanation, like Minerva born from the head of Jupiter.

The construction of northern European societies cannot be repeated unless the historic conditions under which they flourished happen again. Yet this unhistoric and empiricist treatment of northern Europe as the ideal pattern is often used in comparing it with other societies. Using England and Holland as the norm to describe other societies as pathological, deficient, sick, or undeveloped hides the fact that wealth transfers were the basis of their industrialization.

Environmental Limits as a Zero-Sum Condition

A distorted view of history impedes recognition that overuse of resources by some makes it impossible for the majority of people to attain a level of dignity. The public debate over climate change is couched in purely technical terms, ignoring the need for a radical redistribution of the world's resources to deal with poverty. We cannot improve the living conditions of most people without radically reducing production of poisonous gases and consumption by the North of so much fish, meat, flour, and other goods. That topic is not part of the discussion, as if it had nothing to do with us, because responsibility always lies somewhere else. Taking responsibility for our overuse of resources is politically charged. It is ignored in the media, in political debates, and in recommendations of international organizations, because it would require profound political, cultural, and civil transformations.

Today we face a deep crisis regarding the destruction of the planet. We must undergo a profound transformation of consumption patterns and of our understanding of a satisfactory life. The existing ideal life pattern is only possible for a minority, and it is destroying life on this planet.

Latin America and the World System

There are three historic moments in the process of incorporating Latin America into the world system. Phase one, starting in 1492, established Iberian colonial control for 300 years. Early in the 19th century, independence movements arose as Spain and Portugal declined relative to northern Europe, and liberalism and free trade were adopted as an ideology by independence movements. That broke the commercial monopoly of Spanish colonialism.

In phase two, the presence of British capital was important. In the 19th century, the most important relations were with England and its commercial world. England did not have many colonies in Latin America, but commercial relations were dominant. The investment of capital in railroads was extremely important in the first decades of the 19th century. At the end of the 19th century, the US reasserted the Monroe Doctrine and its hegemony in the hemishere.

Phase three has been marked by the dominating presence of the US government and US corporations. This continues today, although European companies are beginning to compete with US companies in banking and public services. The US proposal for the Free Trade Area of the Americas (FTAA) has basically been defeated, but the US still pursues similar agreements one-on-one with countries in Central America. Europe is taking advantage of the absence of a hemispheric free trade area, taking the route of Mercosur to establish a liberal trade agreement.* The content is essentially the same as the one the US is promoting, involving intellectual property, investor relations, agriculture, cultural relations, government relations, and public services.

Processes of Inclusion and Exclusion in Latin America

The contemporary processes of exclusion and inequality cannot be disconnected from historic processes in Latin America. Exclusion and differentiation, the results of the neoliberal process, are superimposed on a colonial and racial process that creates profound inequality.

Latin America had a populist period in which there was a chance to reduce social inequality. That occurred under Peron in Argentina, Cardenas in Mexico, Vargas in Brazil, through import substitution and industrialization.

---

* Ed.: Mercosur is *Mercado Común del Sur,* or the Southern Common Market, a regional trade agreement.

It produced growth in the internal market, greater access to public services, increased equality, and greater political incorporation of the excluded sectors. This was denigrated as "populism" because it was not achieved via the classic liberal model. That process of inclusion did not achieve an equal society, but it moved in that direction.

The populist era was interrupted by a counter-revolution of capital in the form of a coup in Brazil and then in Chile. In Latin America, it cut short a cumulative process of democratization and increasing autonomy, resulting in defeat of changing social forces in Latin America. The governments leading the change were defeated through direct intervention by the US, which was responsible for both coups as well as the military horrors in Argentina.

In Latin America, neoliberalism is a project of profound social transformation. It has meant de-industrialization, a reduction of internal markets, and characteristically imperialist methods of relating to raw materials. The popular sectors have been politically weakened. Sectors linked to the internal market and industrialization were displaced by the sectors linked to the international market, specifically to the finance and the export of raw materials. That is why one finds apparent paradoxes in Lula's government in Brazil. Despite the accumulation of left-wing forces and union movements, economic policy there favors the export and financial sectors and perpetuates the neoliberal transformation of Brazil. This process has taken place in a very similar way in the majority of Latin America, and these are the sectors that have the most force and success.

Serge Latouche *Author*

Globalization has spread the idea of markets that govern society instead of markets imbedded in a society. The physical features of Western dominance of the planet are not as problematic as the psychological consequences of "colonization of the imagination." For example, the concept of poverty is a Western invention. Other cultures have defined deprivation in terms of losing social connections, not a personal lack of resources. Only through modernization have people in Africa learned to think of themselves as poor. Cultures have often  *been complicit in coming under the spell of Western ideas of progress. At first, it seems they can keep their culture and become wealthier through trade, but eventually, there is a cultural collapse, leading to poverty in every sense of the word. The solution to the problems of modernization is "degrowth," which involves both mental liberation from inherited patterns of Western thought and also practical efforts to get off the endless treadmill of development. The pressure to turn to "degrowth" will mount because of the limits imposed by the biosphere. Infinite growth is impossible. The economic system is headed for a breakdown, after which new opportunities will emerge for creating a wholly different kind of society.*

Globalization

For a few years, people have been talking of globalization, but for someone who has studied history, this is curious. The world has been globlized since 1492, when the stupefied Indians discovered Christopher Columbus. The term "globalization" began as a publicity slogan. I think it began with Sony, which offered a "portable culture." Other transnationals quickly picked up on it. The truth of globalization lies in a reversal: not globalization of markets, but the commodification of the world. It will finally commodify everything: the body, blood, sperm cells, genes, water, and air.

Capitalism has passed from societies with markets to a society of markets. We are moving toward a society totally defined in terms of markets. This market logic now ravages the planet, without any countervailing power. We need to re-imbed the economy in society. We will then rediscover politics in the true sense of the term.

Empires are a compromise between markets and political logic—feudal, imperial, or nationalist. The development of the nation-state enabled imperialism, in the form of colonialism, to put in place the three M's: markets, missionaries, and the military. From the 16th to the 19th centuries, there were destructive consequences to politcal structures around the world. The artisans of India were destroyed. In the famous phrase of Marx, the plains of the Ganges were white with the bones of weavers.

In Latin America, the most important colonization was religious and psychological. The colonization of the imagination imposed a foreign culture, which destroyed mental structures and conceptions of time and space. This amounted to a loss of sense, the collapse of a product of ancient empires. These were flowering, refined civilizations of great complexity, and then—nothing! A vaccuum. Their way of thinking and their culture just stopped making sense. There was no going back, so it just collapsed.

In Africa, despite the slave trade, colonization, and economic development programs, some of their social and mental structures have survived. But the media are penetrating even the most remote locations, destroying all possibility of organizing resistance. We cannot stop the spread of AIDS, at least not every aspect of it. The same is true of psychologically destructive developments in Africa, which are like an AIDS epidemic.

The process of underdevelopment is first invented in the imagination and then realized in actual events, by changing economics, property rights, courts, and politics. People are unaware of the way development creates underdevelopment.

Individualism: Land Tenure and Protestantism

It is remarkable that neither the slave trade nor colonization have destroyed the traditional land tenure systems in Africa. Traditionally, there was no private appropriation of land. There was a system of collective management within a hierarchical social order. Only since independence and the imposition of "structural adjustments" has that system of land tenure begun to be destroyed, though not totally.

Colonialism introduced something that was not part of Latin America: an individualistic imagination that is extremely destructive of the social fabric. One element of the Mexican Revolution was the restoration of rural communities, *ejidos,* with plenty of problems, no doubt. The *ejidos* system in Mexico was destroyed by NAFTA.

There have been thousands of unique cultures in human history. This is the only one where individualism developed. Why it did is a mystery, but it may be related to the idea of a private relationship with God. I find the thesis of Max Weber persuasive—that the origin of capitalism is related to the Protestant ethic. It destroyed traditional structures because it speaks to universal elements in humans, such as personal interest, the desire for happiness, and the thirst for wealth and power. It systematizes the passions that every society has had to channel, master, or limit. I am often asked what it would mean to "abandon capitalism." It would mean abandoning the spirit of capitalism, in Weber's sense. That would mean a change of consciousness—and practical changes.

Poverty as a Western Notion

Poverty does not exist until experience is thought of in those terms. Five or ten years ago, some students were funded to write a thesis on poverty in the Cameroons. They came back with reports on sorcery. When they spoke to people about "poverty," that term made no sense to people. When asked if they were poor, people said, "No, we are Cameroonians." But little by little, as a result of the influence of the IMF, the World Bank, and NGOs, people have learned to think of themselves as "poor." We imposed our economic conception of poverty on the world—both as an intellectual construct and as a reality. Poverty has been a self-fulfilling prophecy for two-thirds of the world.*

The concept of poverty is a modern, Western invention, difficult to translate into terms understood in other societies. Every society, however, has concepts related to what we traditionally thought of as "misery"—social inferiority, loss of dignity, lack of power, and lack of social supports. In most African societies, the closest equivalent to "poverty" is an expression referring to someone who lacks any form of family support, who is outside the human community —a social orphan.

Our concept of poverty makes no sense in a communal situation, even where slaves are part of the family (as with the ancient Romans). Slaves were surely in an inferior position, but they were fed and housed. So, the entire clan might be in a precarious situation because of a bad harvest—but not the individual. Solidarity functioned within a clan, lineage, tribe, or village. There are droughts and famines, which might be deemed extreme cases of poverty. There are cultures or lineages that have few cattle and cannot participate in public displays of wealth, but that has nothing to do with poverty according to some pseudo-objective criterion, such as a minimum income of $1 or $2 per day.

The idea that poverty is about an individual lacking the resources necessary to meet basic requirements implies an imaginary economy. That is found only in an individualistic society based on market exchange, in which solidarity is institutionalized through the state rather than the extended family. Historically, we can compare the emergence of negatively-valued poverty with the previous tradition of positively-valued poverty, such as the voluntary poverty of St. Francis of Assisi. The positive view was based on the idea of having necessities, but nothing more.

Europeans destroyed not only the social setting and culture of people; they also destroyed their means of subsistence. In India, the appearance of famines is associated with the destruction of the Indian weavers and other artisans as well as the property reforms imposed by the British, which

---

* Ed.: Latouche references *Learning from Ladakh,* a book by Helena Norberg Hodge, which describes the loss of local culture when a road was built, and outsiders introduced the concept of development. After markets were introduced, poverty appeared.

caused peasants to lose their land. French colonization involved imposing a head tax, which obliged peasants to produce for the market. Working for money made peasants richer in one sense, but it impoverished their lives by creating a market-oriented society.

Complicity by Victims of Domination

Societies have been destroyed without being colonized, such as China, Afghanistan, or Turkey. They were self-colonized, without violent predation.

When societies live side-by-side with different values, each may think it has the advantage over the other. In Indonesia, mountain and coastal people trade with each other, each thinking it has the upper hand. In Africa, the Bantus consider the pygmies their slaves, but the latter do not consider themselves slaves. They get iron from the Bantus. Very often, cultural relations operate reciprocally in this way. That is why those being colonized are often complicit, because they find it to their advantage. It is as if Martians arrived and began to gather sand. We would be very happy, because in exchange for sand, they might give us diamonds. When Montezuma proposed to give the Spanish a pile of gold as a ransom, it was of no value to him.

Initially, trade often results in enrichment. Tribes practicing the potlatch ceremony in British Columbia had only begun doing so recently before anthropologists encountered them. Those tribes had suddenly become very wealthy because of commerce with fur-traders. Eventually they found themselves indigent and marginalized, as they are today.

Similarly, in Africa, there were booms in cotton, cacao, and bananas. Societies or villages became wealthy in the short run, so they could import new things. But there followed a collapse of the flow of goods and they were devastated. During the transition, a society may initially keep its traditional values intact, but the process of self destruction begins when it absorbs the values of another society. Rich in their own values, they become poor by the standards of other people.

Limits of the Biosphere

The Western economic dynamic does not limit accumulation of capital or consumption. But eventually, expanding consumption (the terrorism of compound interest) encounters biospheric limits. We were warned of those limits in 1962 by Rachel Carson with *Silent Spring*. The Club of Rome report, The *Limits to Growth*, appeared in 1970. Politicians and the "man in the street" listened, but our toxic dependence on growth caused the two hemispheres of the brain to ignore each other.*

At present, if everyone lived as Americans do, it would take six planets. But if everyone lived as the people of Burkina Faso, 10% of the planet would suffice. For the people of Burkina Faso to consume the amount allowed by the ecological footprint, we would have to consume less. Globally, humans have surpassed the regenerative capacity of the biosphere by 30%.

We have to reduce our ecological footprint, the burden of our way of life on the biosphere. We can imagine sustainable societies that operate according to a different logic. Currently, each person has claim to about 1.8 hectares of bioproductive area. If we reach 9 billion people by 2050, that amount will be reduced to only 1.1 hectares per person. That is doable. We can produce almost all that is needed for a healthy life.

Natural constraints are a source of wisdom. If people have no constraints, it gives free rein to their follies. Humans are natural creatures. The Western delirium, following Descartes, is the thought of becoming the master and possessor of nature.

Degrowth

Degrowth is a provocative slogan to understand that everything must change: logic, system, culture, civilization. Everyone understands that degrowth for the sake of degrowth is absurd, but no more absurd than growth for the sake of growth. Of course, it makes sense to increase production of food for hungry people. Growth should only be a means of satisfying hunger, and then it should stop. It is not enough just to slow down. All of the talk about sustainable development consists of trying to step on the brake while the foot is still on the accelerator. We have to change direction.

Technically speaking, we should be referring to "a-growth," because

---

* Ed.: Latouche discusses a parable, borrowed from Albert Jacquard, of green algae growing in a pond, a parable similar to the one in the title of a book by Lester Brown, *The 29th Day*. If a pond fills with algae by doubling each year, and it is completely filled in the 15th year, when will it be half full? The answer is the 14th year. In Latouche's parable the pond is relatively healthy until the final doubling of the algae population, at which point, it suddenly goes from healthy to dead. Similarly, we face imminent catastrophe, because we have used up one-half the petroleum and other vital resources. We are living in the final year of the parable. Latouche compares Western society to drug addicts who cannot give up the habit until we are faced with mortal danger. The 100 transnational corporations of the World Business Council are the drug dealers.

what we propose is similar to atheism. It is about going beyond religion, growth, and economics to rethink society.* I often say that degrowth is not a single alternative. It is a matrix of alternatives. It is about leaving behind economic totalitarianism to reopen a pluralistic view of history. Every human group has to define its own civilization, culture, and values.

Degrowth is achieved pluralistically. Some people question degrowth because it would seem to deprive people who have never known growth. That is an ethnocentric view. If growth is perverse, we should dissuade others from entering into it. So, degrowth is not reactionary. It fulfills the modern promise of emancipation by dealing with the reconstruction of an autonomous society in the true sense. Modernity has pretended to emancipate humanity from tradition, transcendence, and revelation, but modernity led to the most unfree ("heteronomous") society in history, one that obeyed the dictates of financial markets, the "invisible hand," and the laws of techno-science.

As Gandhi said, "Live simply, so that others might simply live." Our degrowth, in the sense of putting less pressure on eco-systems, is the condition under which others can live. How can less than 20% of the world's population (people of the North) consume 86% of the natural resources? That is a problem of justice, of planetary equity.

Voluntary simplicity is not enough. We have to get things right at the planetary level, at each level on which people have some power to change. It is important that movements try to influence decision-makers. "No one is bound to do what is impossible." That is why I called my book *The Gamble of Degrowth*, because like all Pascalian bets, it is worth trying, but there are no guarantees.

The 8 "Rs" of Degrowth

Let us consider the eight "Rs," which are concretely utopian.† We need utopian images, but we also need objectives to give meaning to our actions.

Revaluation. The first "R" in the degrowth utopia is revaluation—questioning the values of Western development: a) by relating to nature less as a predator and more as a gardener, b) by tempering competition with

---

* Ed.: Latouche has found some senior executives of multinationals intrigued by degrowth, but their organizations are tied to the logic of expansion and cannot change. In this 2007 interview, he said that only a major economic crisis could shake the system to its core and open up new opportunities.

† Ed.: The 8 Rs are revalue, reconceptualize, restructure (all to decolonize the mind), redistribute, relocalize, reduce, reuse, and recycle.

cooperation, and c) by mixing a bit of altruism with individualistic egoism.

Reconceptualization. We should strive to achieve reconceptualization or "the decolonization of the imagination" through mental resistance to the spirit of economics. That would reorient our conception of what is real. It involves recognizing noneconomic and nonmaterial forms of wealth. Ivan Illich spoke of the "intoxicating joy of austerity" and of "shared frugality." We need to recapture that sensibility. Illich also questioned the concept of "scarcity" in economics. Scarcity was invented as the commons were being privatized.[‡]

Relocalization. The 8 Rs form a unity, but three are fundamental: 1) revaluation, because everything is affected by values, 2) relocalization, because every concrete event must be local somewhere, and 3) reduction, because degrowth involves reducing our ecological footprint, dependence on toxics, obsession with work (offset by rediscovery of other dimensions of life), and junk and waste. Relocalization plays a strategic role. At the local level, you can start to change something and hope it catches on and spreads.

Globalization began a gigantic and unprecedented deterritorialization in the 1980s and 1990s. We shifted from an economy of relative national self-sufficiency (trade less than 20% of GDP) to a totally extraverted economy. Every day, 4,000 trucks pass Pertus [French-Spanish border town], taking tomatoes from Andalusia to the Netherlands and other tomatos from the Netherlands to Andalusia. That is a fantastic waste of energy.

Recycle and Reuse. Recycling and reuse help overcome a fantastic squandering of resources through planned obsolescence, whereby most things have shorter life-spans to enable more to be produced. There is also extraordinary pollution. Every month 300 boatloads of out-of-date computers leave the US for Nigeria as pollutants, although they could play a positive role as resources. Toxic waste is a form of criminal capitalism. It cannot even be reused. An autonomous, degrowth society is one in which reuse is the final objective. To construct a degrowth society, we have to cut waste production, which is proportional to the cube of the output, or at least to the square of it.

To reduce waste production, we need to apply the principle that comes from Arthur Pigou's book *The Economics of Welfare* almost a century ago. We

---

‡ Ed.: Regarding the commons, Latouche describes genetically modified organisms as an effort to privatize the commons by monopolizing nature's fecundity. He also observes that a great battle is coming over the privatization of water, which is the way an abundant resource is made artificially scarce.

can correct economic logic by internalizing externalities. We would make the polluters pay—all of the costs of pollution, including those born by nature and by future generations. Pigouvian taxes are extremely reformist in theory but profoundly subversive in practice. If economic actors had to pay for the consequences of their actions, then growth would not be profitable. Insurance companies have raised the alarm about climate change because they are afraid of having to pay not only for damage from hurricanes and other looming problems. They rightly refuse to insure risks that could become too costly—such as nuclear power, genetically modified organisms, and nanotechnology.

When companies cannot earn a profit because of regulations, they try to put the burden on the back of someone else.* That is also a form of imperialism.

Breakdown of the System

Even if we continue to grow at an extremely modest rate, by 2050, it would take six planets, or thirty if we live by American standards. That is impossible. The pressure of necessity contributes to the struggle to reverse the system.† A crisis in the economic and financial system will present new opporunties. The crash will bring enormous chaos in its wake, including the end of globablization. There will probably be wars. But it will also be an opportunity to reopen a new historical path of new experiences and to rediscover constraints. This mega-machine has to break to make it possible to reopen the space of a new adventure. We just have to hope that in breaking, it does not destroy the planet or humanity. There is a great risk. It is a big gamble, but I am always an optimist.

———————————————

* Ed.: Latouche describes cigarette companies increasing sales ten-fold in Africa after lawsuits were filed against them in the US.
† Ed.: In this interview in early 2007, Latouche foretold the crash that occurred in 2008, based largely on the "the pyramid of credit in the US"—the high ratio of debt to income. He did not predict what would trigger the collapse. He said it could even be an earthquake in California that would disrupt the US stock market.

Odenda Lumumba *Director, Kenya Land Alliance*

The Maasai are pastoralists in Kenya who were displaced from their ancestral lands. Since one of the areas they lost is the capital city, Nairobi, returning their original land would today displace even more people. The solution proposed is to compensate them by helping them develop, such as by building abattoirs in their areas. In general, it is improper to think of groups that previously lost land (including those along the coast) as "absentee landlords." That way of understanding land tenure opens the door to squatter settlements, which would be disruptive and threaten national security. Thus, it is important to respect land titles. A huge, but unknown, amount of land in Kenya is left idle and not used for farming, grazing, or other purposes. That occurs because many city dwellers own land in the country as a form of security, but they do not use it. This pattern undermines the development of Kenya.

Origins of Maasai Displacement

The Maasai loss of land is a well-documented injustice. The Maasai occupied a great rangeland from Tanzania almost to western and central Kenya. The British limited Maasai use of some of lands the British wanted for agriculture. The Maasai were not allowed to move north of the Uganda railway. That pushed the Maasai clan in Laikipia out of their rangelands. Infighting between Maasai clans followed.

Although land redistribution occurred after independence, the Anglo-Maasai agreements did not enable the Maasai to recover their lands. Their numbers have increased, and many Maasai have moved to the south. In Laikipia district, 62 percent of the land is occupied by big ranchers, most of whom are foreign to that district. Some are Kenyan; some are not. The Laikipia district yields little. People fence their ranches with electric fencing.

The Maasai are forced to live with their herds in a small, rocky place without water. Every time the drought hits them, they see their animals die, literally, for lack of fodder for their animals. They have risked walking long distances along the corridor road open to them up to the Mount Kenya forest to graze. But they end up losing their animals due to the high altitude and coldness of that area.

The Maasai are vulnerable to market forces, such as selling off their land cheaply, which makes them destitute. When they sell land, they expect to rent it back for a period of time, but the new owners fence off the land

and deny the Maasai access to water or salt licks for their animals.

National parks and game reserves, such as Maasai Mara, have been declared in a number of places inhabited by the Maasai peoples. The Maasai way of life is endangered because of tourism, which fences the Maasai out of the land they need. That is worsening the historical dispossession of the Maasai.

Maasai Need Compensation for Lost Territory

Further international treaties may push Kenya to revisit the issue of Maasai land. It is in the interest of Kenya and the region to do so. It is not a question of restitution of land, as many people think. It is more a matter of helping the Maasai develop, within a given non-territorial space and keep their community intact.

The Maasai may not necessarily require all the land that was expropriated from them. Compensatory mechanisms are now needed for them in the form of development ventures. That would be in place of restoring all of the Maasai land. The Maasai will still practice nomadic pastoralism as a way of life. But they need education and infrastructure such as roads and electricity. The Maasai interact with industries. They already have leverage. There are a few Maasai elites that dot our space. We are proud of some of them.*

Some people are concerned that giving the Maasai economic assistance rather than land may be destroying their culture. Tourism depends on the Maasai. If you do away with their culture, you do away with the Maasai. However, no people have maintained a culture unchanged in the modern world. The Maasai need a territory, because no nationality can be a nationality without a territorial base. So, the Maasai will occupy some territory, but they need a development package because of their loss of a much larger territory.

You have to be reasonable. The traditional Maasai territory is today occupied by other interests. Restoring all land to the Maasai would undo Kenya, because virtually half of Kenya would belong to the Maasai or other nomads. One of the territories that they have lost includes Nairobi. How would you restrict Nairobi to the Maasai? Nairobi is the hub of economic enterprise in Kenya. You can only say that in lieu of the loss, the Maasai will get compensation.

---

* Ed.: Mr. Lumumba gives an example of a Maasai manager working for Kenya Airways to demonstrate that the Maasai have entrepreneurial skills and can succeed in business and industry, not merely in their traditional cattle herding.

Squatters Should Not Be Allowed to Occupy the Coast

Another example is the nine coastal communities of Kenya. They lost their land initially to the Sultan of Zanzibar, then to the British, and eventually to the Kenyan elites that colonized the "ten mile coastal strip." In one town, titles were given as far back as 1908 to absentee landlords. Personally I do not believe that owners of titles can be called "absentee landlords." There is no policy statement or legal framework requiring owners of land to be occupants. Therefore anybody can occupy land; anybody can have title.

What should not be allowed is for a whole community to occupy the coastal strip as squatters. Although they consider the territory as their homeland, they lack legal title to it. This historical claim to the coastal communities of Kenya threatens to tear up the most lucrative tourist industry in Kenya. Second, the landlocked countries of Uganda, Burundi, Rwanda, up to Congo, depend on the entry port of Mombasa. Allowing squatters to claim the territory would put Kenya's role at risk.

The other thing that could easily be endangered are the security interests of the Kenyan coast. When the people who occupy the coastal strip are insecure, because they do not have certainty of property ownership, then you allow the vagaries of manipulation in security. Therefore the coast is already marked as a potential world terrorist zone. This threat has not been realized yet, but the coast is majority Islamic, and Islam has its own history and geopolitical battles. But it is enough that the squatters have nothing to lose. That sets a dangerous precedent. So, the historic imbalance in ownership of land along the coast must be addressed as an important land issue in Kenya.

Tea and Livestock Regulations

Returning to the pastoralists, one of the economic problems they face is related to processing of livestock. The livestock industry accounts for 12.5 percent of the Kenyan national income.[†] The livestock of many pastoralists are not accepted by the Kenyan Meat Commission. The Commission accepts for slaughter only animals that weigh 300 kilograms or more. Many of the animals in the pastoralist areas weigh less than that. The pastoralists are demanding abattoirs in their areas other than the ones operated by the

---

† Ed.: Mr. Lumumba mentions that the Kenyan Meat Commission (KMC) was defunct from the late 1980s to 2006, preventing the measure of meat exports, both legal and smuggled. The KMC has been revived.

Kenya Meat Commission, so they can also process their animals.

Kenya recently started exporting camels to other countries. If we can really promote the marketing of livestock, we will see a clear quantifiable improvement. If Kenya lost the contribution of beef by the pastoralists, that would be a serious problem. Kenya cannot afford to import meat. To date Kenyans can have meat on their table, the Rift Valley Fever notwithstanding.

Another major agricultural export product from Kenya is tea. In Africa, Kenya is the leading exporter of tea. It is the second-highest earner of foreign exchange in Kenya. It was overtaken by tourism in the recent past. Horticulture products (including meat) now compete with it. Tea production has been dominated by foreign interests. The Kenyan small-scale growers are just beginning to follow up. A lot of the tea companies in Kenya are multinationals. So a lot of the packaged tea cannot be traced back to where it was grown. Tea was based on plantation production within the settler economy, which has become the elite economy. Tea plantations never augured well for the people, because the plantations dispossessed local communities. There is a hidden story behind the sweet story about Kenyan tea.

Idle Land Needs to Be Developed

In addition to land dispossession, Kenya also has a lot of idle land. The amount of such land has been called "the 6 million dollar question." Nobody has quantified it. Given the skewed nature of land distribution, there is quite a lot of land lying fallow that should be maximally used. Landowners have fenced off huge chunks of land, but they are busy doing other things. So, their land is lying fallow. Those who own the land could make a difference by leasing it out to users for a season.

It appears in Kenya that we have an exclusive, rather than inclusive, notion of land use. So when you have your portion of land, it is to the exclusion of others, regardless of whether it is in use or not. That is detrimental to our development. There are a lot of "telephone farmers" based in Nairobi and elsewhere who are not using their land. Meanwhile small-scale farmers miss out on the same land.

Kenyans hold their wealth in land, but they do not use the land. This question of how much Kenyan land is idle requires clear research. We have considered taxing idle land. But how do you define idle land in the absence of a National Land Use policy? When do you declare my land idle? I could be keeping one rabbit or a few trees on it, which I think are commensurate uses. So it would be crucial, as we formulate a National Land Use policy, to assess how much of our land is lying fallow.

There are places like Kisumu in Nyanza where a lot of lands are idle because the men migrated to urban areas. They are living in slums, not getting clear employment. Their wives remain behind, and they cannot use land equitably. A lot of communities have succumbed to HIV/AIDS, and therefore land has been left lying idle. Nobody has useful figures to date, but it is imperative to compile them, because we have never used our land optimally despite the land question.

Abel Mamani *Water Minister, Bolivia*

Privatization had devastating consequences on Bolivia and other Latin American countries in the 1990s, eliminating public services, reducing employment opportunties, and giving foreign interests the power to control Bolivia. The promised foreign investment never materialized. One year after the Morales government took over, Bolivia had achieved financial stability and a budget surplus. That is because the new government is defending the interests of the Bolivian people, not foreign corporate interests. The election of Morales came at the end of several years of popular uprisings throughout Bolivia in which citizens risked their lives to protest foreign control of their national resources—water, petroleum, and natural gas. Because similar social movements are taking place in other countries of Latin America, the new popular governments have a chance to work together to develop an effective alternative to neoliberalism.

Consequences of Privatization

Privatization of capital assets from 1987 to 1997—in basic services, in oil and natural gas, and in other strategic sectors—did not work out. When the mines were closed in 1987 by President Sanchez de Lozada, there was massive unemployment. When the railroads were privatized, some were dismantled. We do not have trains in eastern Bolivia any more. Last month, we had hundreds of employees with salaries that had not been paid for seven months! As a result of giving away our public assets, we do not even have an airline. When we sold our water to La Suez, a company based in Atlanta, they served private interests instead of giving everyone access to drinking water.

The country has been torn to pieces by privatization. It failed also in

Argentina, Uruguay, and Chile. We should ask whether private companies invested in Bolivia or whether they simply came to manage us. In telecommunications, little was invested in one of the most profitable companies.

Success of the Morales Government

For the first time in many years, the new Morales government has achieved financial stability in Bolivia, produced a budget surplus, and made big public investments, after just eleven months in office. In my sector (water administration), $200 million will be invested. When there is transparent administration with absolute responsibility, it is possible to achieve national stability. Bolivia is now paying back loans. Dependency causes harm, both bilateral agreements and dependency on financial institutions. It is different from doing collaborative work with the multinationals, as an equal partner.

The multilateral organizations and financing institutions can no longer dictate terms to us and force us to accept their consultants. Today we approach the financing organizations and guarantee their investments will be repaid. But the Bolivian government and its people now require sovereignty over the use of our resources.

Social Movements in Bolivia

The mobilization that occurred here in Bolivia was not a result of a political movement. It was simply caused by the masses rising together and thinking together about water. This experience is unique. It occurred in 2000 in Cochabamba. Both urban and rural Cochabambans rose together seven to eight months after the public company that provided drinking water and sewer services in Cochabamba had been privatized by Bechtel. That was the beginning of rising awareness within social movements, the need to take a stand and create a counterforce to capitalism and the privatization process.

In February 2003 there were a series of revolts in La Paz. There were many deaths and injuries, and public institutions were burnt. Then in October 2003, the issue of oil and natural gas provoked a mass movement in the middle of the country, in El Alto. In 2004, social movements identified a key strategic topic related to water, here in El Alto and in La Paz, connected with a company called "Aguas de Miliman."

Last year (2005) was the year of movements. In January there was a strong movement about the water issue in El Alto. That paralyzed El Alto and La Paz for 3 days. In April, more movements developed over water and oil and natural gas. It concluded with a 23-day mobilization in El Alto that paralyzed the city. I'm not that proud of that one, but it resulted in the people defending what is theirs: water, oil and gas, land, and employment. Then the government of Sanchez de Lozada was impeached last May, resulting in elections in December that brought the new government into office.

The Movement throughout Latin America

Throughout South America we have allowed our resources to be looted. The same people and institutions have contributed to this, and we clearly realize now who they are. All these movements have opened the way to the election of presidents. In Venezuela, President Chávez has been re-elected; in Nicaragua, Ortega has won; in Ecuador, we also have a colleague as president, and even Peru is having a lot to think about with Garcia. Argentina, Uruguay, and Paraguay give us great examples about how to govern. Just as globalization, capitalism, and neoliberalism had their time to show how they would work, today the masses have the opportunity, through governments that emerged from social movements.

This is a historical situation. In Cochabamba, during the "South America Summit," a lot was said about consolidation along the lines of the European Union. We are also talking about a South American Parliament, which is the vision for the people and masses that our heroes of the past envisioned.

John McArthur *Deputy Director, UN Millennium Project, Earth Institute, Columbia Univerity*

Editor's note: This interview is distinctive because it reflects a mainstream view of poverty, similar to that held by Jeffrey Sachs, author of *The End of Poverty*. Sachs agreed to be interviewed but was unable to find a suitable time, so McArthur agreed to be interviewed. *Since the film The End of Poverty? Think Again and this book are partially intended as a response to Jeffrey Sachs, the* interview with McArthur sets other interviews in this book in clear relief, revealing contrasting points of view. McArthur 1) treats foreign aid as the primary solution to extreme poverty, 2) explicitly endorses trickle-down economics (the idea that the poor eventually benefit from economic growth), 3) regards the IMF's structural adjustment programs as necessary, but not sufficient, 4) recognizes that unequal ownership of land may be related to poverty, but considers it too controversial to discuss, 5) applauds the role of multinational companies in Africa, including mining companies, and 6) generally ignores the kinds of problems discussed by other interviewees (neocolonialism, unfair trade practices, corporate transfer pricing, land hoarding and speculation, market distortions from asymmetric power, debt repayments in excess of foreign aid, toppling of reform governments by the CIA, and other issues).

The UN Millennium Project aims to reduce by half the number of people in absolute poverty (below $1 per day). It is different from previous efforts because it offers an operational framework and a comprehensive approach, including education, health care, farming (fertilizer and new seed varieties), disease prevention (mosquito nets), roads, drinking water, and every element required for economic and social development. Foreign aid has failed in the past only for lack of trying. There was never enough to get the job done. But still, most of the rich nations are providing less than half the assitance they have promised (0.3% of GDP, instead of 0.7%). The World Bank and IMF would help more, but they get their investment funds from their members. Debt is a problem, but the heavily indebted poor country initiative (HIPC) is solving it. Inequality of land tenure is one source of inequality, but it is hard to solve this problem, because it is highly contentious. In any case, what is most needed is for rich countries to give more foreign aid. Control of markets and domestic economies of poor countries by multinational corporations might be a problem in some places, but not everywhere. Some mining companies in Africa have signed an agreement to be transparent in their accounting and operations.

Origins of UN Millennium Project and Goals*

The United Nations Millennium Project was established in 2002 as an independent advisory body to the UN Secretary General. The Millennium Development Goals were set at the UN Millennium Summit in September 2000. In itself this was a watershed event, where world leaders set clear and coherent goals for tackling extreme poverty. The Secretary General commissioned the UN Millennium project as an independent advisory body to put forward practical recommendations.

The Millennium Development Goals are about cutting in half the

---

* Ed.: In the interview, which has been edited for length, McArthur returned to two themes perhaps a dozen times: inadequate levels of aid, and the failure of piecemeal programs. He argues that rich countries can solve the problem of global poverty if they will simply a) increase their assistance to poor countries, and b) target their assistance to comprehensive development programs. These themes are discussed below, but the emphasis on them in the original interview may not be evident.

proportion of people in the world living in extreme poverty, which means people living below a dollar a day. About 1.1 billion people in the world are living at the edge of existence. The goals are about making globalization work by improving life for those people who are outside the benefits of globalization. That involves getting those people on the first rung of the ladder out of extreme poverty.

So the Millennium Project identifies goals in an operational framework, and then translates global targets into practical national-level budgeting processes. That means connecting decisions made in national capitals to the villages of Africa where the majority of the people in extreme poverty live today.

Globalization is working to an enormous extent. In the past couple of decades, we have seen hundreds of millions of people lifted out of the depths of extreme poverty. That tells us it is possible. There are lessons to be learned on the practical steps that were taken in China, in India, in other parts of Asia, where we have seen some of the fastest rates of progress in human history.

Is this campaign against poverty just another version of the story we have all heard before? It might seem that way, but there was very little practical effort over the past generation. There was no systematic goal-oriented effort to end extreme poverty or to cut it in half. That has never existed. The Millennium Development Goals are new.

The Situation in Africa

Sub-Saharan Africa, the epicenter of poverty, has not only extreme poverty but also the most concentrated and severe aspects of extreme poverty. First, they have an extremely high endemic disease burden in rural areas. Malaria, if left untreated, is probably the greatest killer in human history. At least 2 million people a year are dying right now, 95% of them children, and the vast majority in Africa. This disease is entirely preventable.

A second issue is agriculture. Africa did not have a Green Revolution similar to the one in Asia in the 1960s and 70s. African agriculture is based on rain-fed crops as opposed to irrigated crops. Africa also lacked the transportation infrastructure required to provide the necessary inputs to farmers. Nevertheless, in the 1980s, the scientific breakthroughs for an African Green Revolution were developed, with the high yield types of crops that are relevant to Africa. This a new boost to the potential of what we can see in the next several years.

Millennium Development Goals: Comprehensive Vision

At the UN Millennium Project, when we look at basic practical solutions, we have evidence that things could be done. We simply have not had the resources and the concerted effort and attention required. There is a lot of work that needs to be done to get malaria under control, to get the fertilizer out and the new seeds out, and to actually start to take on these new challenges in Africa.

The Millennium Development Goals were quite special because we did not have this coherent vision previously to guide the international system. Since the 1960s, we had a decade of health, a decade of water, a year of the child, and all sorts of initiatives that were competing for the same small pot of resources. The Goals put these pieces together to create the conditions for those economies to grow.

Never Enough Foreign Aid!

One might ask whether foreign aid works and whether it is enough. There is a difference between what is necessary and what is sufficient. Success depends on practical plans with practical strategies and the resources to back those strategies. Countless strategies in poor countries sit on shelves collecting dust because of lack of resources. The poor countries get blamed for not implementing them. That is crazy. The countries are desperate. Many of them are heroically governed, with the most admirable bureaucracies and political leaders.

We need to be quite specific about what has and has not worked.

A lot of line items in rich country budgets, under the heading of foreign aid, were meant for political support during the Cold War or other political purposes. Not much money was involved—maybe $14 or $16 of foreign aid per capita, not much in terms of the basics of investment that are needed.

A lot of foreign aid was put into workshops, but that is not a very effective strategy for getting fertilizer out. Maybe you need some meetings, but too little is typically allocated to practical investments.

Foreign aid does work—in the form of practical things, such as immunization or bed netting or fertilizer. Let us take the substantive investments and scale those up. The Carter Center has practically eradicated guinea worm through foreign aid. Countries like Botswana and South Korea were successful because concerted government effort was not just left on its own but got foreign aid from the rest of the world.

It is still difficult to get people to take the goals seriously. Rich countries have been promising for 35 years to allocate 0.7% of national income to support development in the poorest countries, but they give less than 0.3%, not even half of what they have promised. A target of 0.7% of gross national income for support of developing countries has been around for 35 years. Only 5 countries—Norway, Sweden, Luxembourg, Netherlands and Belgium—have met this goal so far. We have seen 11 countries now sign on to do this. It is an enormous boost to have G8 countries starting to do this. The governments of the United Kingdom and France are committed to reach that target by 2012, Germany by 2015. As of 2006, 16 of the 22 so-called rich countries have all signed on to meet that target by 2015. That does not provide us enough resources yet to achieve the Millennium Development Goals but that is a huge boost. Six countries—Australia, Canada, New Zealand, Japan, Switzerland and the United States—agreed in principle in 2002 and again in 2005 at the UN World Summit, to contribute 0.7%, but they have not yet set their timetable to follow through.

Investment is far short of what it needs to be to achieve the Millennium Development Goals and to have a much more stable, global political context. We spend roughly a trillion dollars a year on the military globally, and a hundred billion dollars a year on aid, a ten-to-one ratio. Even that is based on an inflated number for aid, because a lot of that is just wiping money off the debt ledger.

I have great respect for my military colleagues for their efficiency and planning. We need to have the same sort of seriousness and professionalism to save lives through development programs.

IMF and World Bank Programs: Good, But Insufficient

Price stability is the core point of structural adjustment.[*] In the 1980s there was a strong conception that development can be achieved by getting the macroeconomics right, getting the prices right, getting the institutions aligned, getting the budget deficits under control, and letting markets thrive. I support market-based development. Yet, price stability and getting prices

---

* Ed.: The term "structural adjustment" refers to the policies whereby the IMF required countries quickly to sell off state assets, end subsidies of food, fuel, and housing, increase the saving rate, eliminate protective tariffs, and impose constraints on government spending. Proponents of structural adjustments claimed that these stringent measures would reinvigorate domestic and international markets, bringing growth and prosperity.

right is not enough. Markets are important, but they are not enough. There are no markets in places that are too poor to even have cash, which is a huge part of the world.

When you are stuck in extreme poverty, you are much more vulnerable to macroeconomic crisis because, if the rains fail one year and you get no crops, there is nothing else in the rural areas. That is a macroeconomic crisis in human terms for the rural farmers in the poorest parts of the world. If there are no crops, that might represent a 15% drop in GNP for 1 year. The failure of rains in Africa is statistically linked to a much higher prevalence of conflict.

What poor countries ultimately need is investments to get on a long-term path to economic development. The IMF is recognizing this in their statements. The Managing Director has agreed that the IMF has a role to play in supporting, through the macroeconomic side, the investments needed for the Millennium Development Goals. But the IMF is a shareholder-held institution with resources governed by how much it gets from the donor countries. Similarly, the World Bank has resources but it gets its resources from somewhere.

We cannot accept the policy mistake of expecting the poorest people in the world to pay $10 a year for their children to go to school. There was recognition of the need to abolish school fees in places like Tanzania, Malawi, and Kenya. We saw millions of children show up for school overnight because fees that were $8 per year were cut. We are seeing the convergence among international financial institutions on the abolition of school fees, led by the World Bank staff, to their credit.

Foreign Aid as Investment in the Future

The return on the investment in foreign aid may not be apparent to everyone, but it is there.

First, as in a rich country, we do not justify the investment in public education or public health based solely on each individual's return on that investment. We think of that as a basic element of a productive society, to ensure that everyone has an equal opportunity to flourish.

Second, investment in protection against global spread of disease benefits everyone in the world. In terms of pure self-interest, we care about things that could affect us directly, for example, the SARS pandemic or the Avian flu. These are just the ones we are thinking about right now. There are going to many more of these threats over the long term. That starts with basic health systems and epidemiological surveillance in the poorest countries.

Third, development aid enhances global stability. We are spending about a trillion dollars a year on military expenses around the world. We are spending around a 100 billion a year on development, maybe half of that on practical investments. The CIA task force on state failure in the 1990s found that the number one predictor of state failure is child mortality. The number one cause of child mortality in the poorest countries is malaria. This is not a complicated equation.

Why a Fight against Poverty Can Succeed Now

There are several reasons to believe that a serious fight against poverty can occur today compared to 1950 or 1970 or even 1980.

First, the rich world is much richer than it has ever been before.

Second, we have learned a lot about what works in the past few decades. We have a much better sense of the types of programs that can work and we have seen what success looks like.

A third difference from previous decades is that there are a lot of new technologies. There is a new technology in anti-malaria bed nets where they put the insecticide straight into the thread in the manufacturing process. This costs about $7 and it lasts 5 years. Similarly, new seed varieties have been developed that could triple crop yields in a year or two with basic inputs. HIV/AIDS antiretroviral treatment came into development in 1996 when it was introduced in the rich countries. Now we have more than a million people in poor countries on anti-retroviral treatment due to some very ambitious programs.

A fourth factor is the change in geopolitics. We have the development of NEPAD, the New Partnership for Africa's Development. It took the European community decades to develop its baseline for cooperation out of the European coal and steel community. We see Africa aspiring to the same types of political, economic and cultural cooperation.

Finally, there is a lot more recognition today than 20 or 30 years ago how closely our fates are all interconnected. Wherever you live, it matters if Afghanistan is a failed state. It matters if we see more failed states. There is also a broad recognition that every life has an enormous value and that practical things are feasible. There is a deep desire and almost visceral need by the public to do more.

Trade, Debt, and the Poor

To tackle the problems of the poor, we also need to think about trade and debt. Countries need to be able to trade much more openly, but opening your markets does not fix your health care system automatically. Trade is crop-specific for agriculture, so the countries of West Africa that export cotton are affected very differently from the countries of East Africa that import food. So trade liberalization helps the countries of West Africa immediately by boosting the export prices of the goods they sell. It has a much more complicated set of implications for a country that would have to pay more to import its food because it cannot produce enough food.

Debt is another issue that people raise. Cancel the debt. That is very simple and straightforward. We saw the Heavily Indebted Poor Country initiative (HIPC), that in 1999 started to cancel bilateral debts owed to countries. But that was only about two-thirds of the story. In 2005 we saw multilateral debt relief for those same countries. So they have made great progress in the last year canceling the debts of those countries. Again it is a bit of basic algebra or arithmetic. If we think about a country owing $100 million a year of debt-service payments, that should be cancelled if they cannot afford to pay that. Does that obviate the need for helping them build their health system? No. Canceling debt servicing often distracts from the need for the extra assistance that is needed.

Reducing Inequality Requires Increasing Productivity

Some people think poverty is related to inequality, particularly inequality of land distribution. Land tenure systems are very controversial, and one should not be seen as supporting more conflict by raising a red flag issue. The role of property rights and land tenure systems is very complicated and much debated. There are arguments around communal ownership and how that might make a difference. But quite frankly, I am not an expert on these very intricate questions.

There is a trend of expanding inequalities in some societies. In some countries in Latin America, the poor may get the absolute basics, but economic growth often occurs only for a subset of a society. Others are not seeing any progress. Globally there is economic divergence, when rich countries grow quite reliably at about 2% a year due to endogenous growth, while other countries stagnate.

Still, a key point is that equality requires productivity. You cannot share the fruits of a boosted crop yield until the yields are boosted. If one farmer increases productivity and crop yields rise, others can benefit if that farmer hires them to work on the land. That is the starting point.

Increases in productivity explain why, globally, extreme poverty came down since 1990, but it has been very different by region. In Asia we saw an overall improvement as hundreds of millions of people were lifted out of extreme poverty. In Sub-Saharan Africa we actually saw an increase in the number of people living in extreme poverty, below the so-called benchmark of $1 a day.

Comprehensive vs. Piecemeal Aid

Often in development assistance a road might be built or a water pump installed, and it stops working a few years later. Some complain that these projects failed. But it actually failed because no money was allocated for maintenance, on the assumption that local people would provide for that. Development assistance can be enormously effective, but just solving a piece of the puzzle does not work. The piecemeal approach to development is not enough. We just need to do so much more to solve problems.

When all of the pieces of the puzzle are not in place, it can be difficult to know how to proceed. Maybe you have fertilizer, but no extension workers to train farmers how to use it. In Africa, there is a shortage of one million health care workers, but where are the training programs? It keeps coming back to whether we are treating symptoms or causes. The question should not be how to squeeze an extra dollar of efficiency out of a clinic with no medicine. Rather we should ask how many dollars are needed to put medicine in the clinic.

In-Country Resources Insufficient

It is clear that the Millennium Development Goals cannot be achieved based solely on the domestic tax base of poor countries. There are two reasons. One factor is that countries in extreme poverty have very low incomes. If GNP per capita is only $200, the average person earns roughly 60 cents a day. Raising taxes is like squeezing blood from a stone. We recommend that developing countries increase their domestic revenues by 4 percentage points of GNP. That might just be too hard, but this has to be a stretch game for everyone.

The second reason is historical. The share of national income that can be collected in taxes goes through a natural rate of increase. As countries become richer, they can start to collect more money in taxes. Over the long-term, countries get up to 30% or 40% of GNP collected in tax revenues. So that is part of the broad dynamics that one needs to keep in mind. With enough aid today, they may not need any support in 5 or 10 years. They can kick-start their own markets and then let the markets grow on their own time. So, we say give aid to end aid.

The Role of Multinationals

Some people imagine that multinationals are controlling everything in poor countries, but that is not true, particularly in Africa. There is very little foreign investment in Africa because there is no return on the investment. Foreign investors do not want to go to a place where no one can afford to buy their products and where people are sick or poorly educated.

It is a common misunderstanding that there is so much foreign investment and that it controls local economies. That does not hold everywhere. There are places with natural resources in Africa where foreign investment works very well. Managing the transparency of those investments is important. The Extractive Industries Transparency Initiative (EITI) was begun in 2002 and has started to gain some traction. Some leading mineral mining companies are taking leadership roles in this. Many mining companies make basic investments in the communities in which they are operating because they want to be good citizens and to support economic development.

The challenge is to create healthy, educated people and infrastructure that works so that these places can not only attract the foreign investment but also build indigenous companies that can compete on the world market. We are not just talking about supporting social services. We are talking about support for economic infrastructure, such as roads, electricity, and ports.

Almeri Mello *Anti-poverty Activist, Brazil*

Work among the poor in several countries of Africa revealed poverty to be less a condition of physical deprivation and more a matter of economic and social conditions that destroy dignity. The feeling of being exploited is one of those conditions. In Brazil, poverty results from inequality and social exclusion. Brazil is a rich country. It should not need economic assistance. But poverty grew in Brazil until recently because of political decisions by elites who seem not to care about the problem of poverty. As a result, Brazil has a continuing problem of violence, which will not be resolved until the nation faces the problem of extreme inequality.

I began as a Catholic student activist in Brazil. In that role, I learned about the importance of political engagement. After 1965, I went to France and became involved in liberation movements in Portuguese Africa (Angola, Mozambique, Guinea Bissau). In Angola, I discovered that self-respect is possible even in the midst of poverty and war. I also spent time in Algeria and Senegal. Spending time among the poor in Algeria, I learned that they perceive poverty primarily in terms of a passion for dignity, not a concern about the lack of material possessions. Those lessons have stayed with me.

With UNICEF, I went to Senegal, where we conducted a survey on poverty. It revealed that the foremost marker of poverty is the feeling of being excluded from the community. There is a solidarity among the poor based on their desire to overcome the exploitation they experience at the hands of the middle class.

Later, in Brazil, as in Africa, I once again learned that poverty has many faces, many meanings. For example, among the Indians of the Amazon, there is a certain nobility and dignity, even though they have little in the way of possessions. This is a challenge to conventional ways of thinking of poverty. It reinforced the sense I got from work in Africa that poverty consists of conditions that deprive people of dignity.

Poverty and Violence

When I returned to Brazil, after many years abroad, I was invited by the governor of Pernambuco State to work for him on projects related to abandoned children, focusing on the problem of criminality. That was in the 1990s. At that time, children were being imprisoned for as long as 18 years. As far as I was concerned, the biggest crime is the abandonment of children and the economic conditions that lead parents to do that. When you work with abandoned children, you soon discover that they have not given up hope: they still think about family ties even when there are none that are visible to them.

The Brazilian economy was originally built on slavery, and to some extent, it still functions that way. It is true of the sugar plantations of Pernambuco. A few generations ago, it seemed that labor might be able to organize and improve the lives of workers. The permanent workers on plantations at least had some use rights to land to have their own gardens. After the coup in 1965, things changed. There was a kind of reverse agrarian reform. The plantation owners were able to expand their holdings by taking land away from the workers and the the small-scale farmers in the area. They forced the permanent plantation workers off the land, so they would have to live in *favelas* (urban slums) and commute from urban areas to rural plantations. These actions aggravated the conditions of the poor.

The leftist government that came in with the election of Lula has not been able to change basic conditions. There was agrarian reform that set up camps for workers. But there are still large landowners. The elites grow richer, and their behavior is shocking. For example, the Senate increased their salaries by 100%. How can Brazil justify receiving aid when it is a rich country? The problem in Brazil is the distribution of wealth, not the lack of wealth. The nation is badly managed. Poverty is caused by a political failure.

Violence is a growing problem, particularly in the big cities. We live in a culture that breeds violence. In Pernambuco, children become gangsters because there is a lack of wholesome activities for them. We need reforms to enable more children to go to school and to provide more after-school activities for them. But any sort of reform is difficult because the middle class is not concerned about the problem of poverty. They ignore it. They just want the police to protect them from the consequences of extreme poverty and inequality. The police treat the poor badly. They give good speeches, but they are all hollow. All of this is aggravated by ostentatious displays of wealth. By emphasizing economic differences, the elites make kids cynical and tempted to steal to have wealth for themselves. Until we can create a society of relative equality, in which everyone is treated with respect, the violence will continue.

Maria Luisa Mendonça *Director, Rede Social, Sao Paulo*

The victims of human rights violations in Brazil are primarily the poor. Both justice and education are needed to give them a future. Agrarian reform is important to protect the rights of landless laborers. Sugarcane workers are particularly exploited. Many of them are virtually slaves. The World Bank and other global institutions are nominally set up to help alleviate poverty. Actually, their mission is to open the markets of countries like Brazil to multinational corporations. Brazil needs to concentrate on developing food self-sufficiency, not increasing exports of food to other countries. However, Lula has not promoted the kinds of reforms that other Latin American leaders have. Reformers in Brazil are disappointed by Lula.

Need for Agrarian Reform

The victims of human rights violations, including economic rights, are mostly poor people. We need structural changes to correct those violations. To deal with hunger and violence, it is not enough to work on the surface, by giving people food. We need to implement agrarian reform. In the urban areas, we need to create jobs. We need a massive educational program, to give young people a future. We need to change macroeconomic policies.

Brazil is one of the few countries in the world that has never had agrarian reform. Since we have about 5 million landless families in the country, there is a lot of struggle for land. The Landless Workers Movement has helped some families gain access to land. We have a very high land concentration. One percent of the Brazilian population controls over 50 percent of all agricultural lands.

Private militia groups or even the military police expel families from their land. Several landless people have been killed, and dozens are arbitrarily arrested every year. The same happens with indigenous people. No government has ever taken care of the historical problem of indigenous people in Brazil, guaranteeing their right to land.

Brazil has plenty of unused agricultural land. Our constitution says that if rural land is not producing food, it can be expropriated for agrarian reform. There is legislation for that also. What we need is political will on the part of our government to implement it. That remains a big problem because large landowners are powerful. They usually elect representatives to the National Congress and to state and local government. They have strong links with the judiciary. Power and wealth concentration lead to violence and oppression. The police and private militias kill people who fight for land. Last year a 73-year-old American nun, Sister Dorothy Stang, was killed. In the Amazon, she was fighting for defense of the forest and for the human rights of peasants there.

I have personally been working in the countryside as a human rights activist for the past twelve years. I have seen the changes achieved by the Landless Workers Movement. It is no longer only the men who fight for land. Today whole families, with women and children, fight for land. I have met hundreds of families in this situation.

When people leave the shantytowns and go back to the countryside, or if they are being exploited in the countryside, they can now recover their dignity. In spite of the difficult life in an encampment, they have hope. The organization of an encampment means that everyone in the community is responsible for taking care not only of their own families, but of the whole community. They usually organize groups to take care of security, food production, health care, and education for the kids. In the struggle for land, they also build other kinds of relationships and other aspects of a community.

Sugar: Exploitation of Workers and Environmental Harm

Right now there is a lot of propaganda about ethanol production, and the Brazilian government promotes it. Agro-business in Brazil seems efficient because it exploits workers and destroys the environment with monoculture production, which requires a lot of pesticides. Burning the sugar at harvest produces a lot of air pollution and raises the level of humidity by ten percent in nearby cities. Sao Paulo accounts for 60 percent of the ethanol produced in Brazil.

We monitor human rights violations against workers in the sugarcane industry. For example, last year seventeen of them died in the space where they work. They died of exhaustion, because each worker has to cut between ten and twelve tons of sugarcane a day. In addition to the seventeen workers who died while at work, another 419 workers died as a consequence of their work. In addition, there are several cases of slave labor among the sugarcane workers that the Ministry of Labor has registered. So the situation of workers in the sugarcane fields is horrible. The government does too little to protect the workers.

The government subsidizes the production of ethanol in the private sector. We denounce expansion of ethanol exports, especially to Europe. There is propaganda that ethanol is "clean energy," but we see workers rights violations and the destruction of the environment.

An oligarchy of very large landowners has controlled the production of sugar since the colonial era in Brazil. It now controls ethanol production. More recently, foreign companies have invested, some French corporations. We even heard that Bill Gates wants to invest in bio-energy. We need to show that the concept of clean energy based on sugarcane production is a big lie.

Any policy that gives priority to monoculture production for export will violate the basic right of people to produce food. The Brazilian government says it wants to deal with the problem of hunger, but policies that emphasize production for export contradict that. The government should prioritize food production for the internal market, not production of ethanol, eucalyptus, or orange juice.

The Problem of Slavery

Some groups connected to the Ministry of Labor monitor human rights violations. When they investigate a reported violation, they sometimes find conditions of slave work. They can sue the company, but the Ministry of Labor lacks the support to deal with the problem.

Slaves are usually migrant workers who come from poor regions to other regions to work, usually in the sugarcane or timber industries. They usually have to pay for their own transportation. They have to pay for their working tools, their housing, and their food. So they start work with a debt and cannot leave work. They are so far away from their homes, it is hard to go back. So they have to work for low pay, in horrible conditions. They lack decent housing; they have to find wood and cook whatever they find. Sometimes they get food stamps. They buy overpriced food from a store owned by a big landowner. A whole mafia exploits workers in Brazil. In urban areas the same thing occurs, usually with Bolivian immigrants making cheap clothes in sweatshops. They cannot leave. Because they do not have papers, they are afraid to tell the police about the situation. This is known in Brazil as slave work.

The International Labor Organization estimates there are about 40,000 people living in slave-like situations in the Amazon region, mostly cutting timber. Their estimate is based on the total amount cut in a given period and knowledge of how much a worker can cut every day. In the sugar industry, just in the state of Sao Paulo, we estimate there are about 60,000 slave-workers. In urban areas, one pastor who helps exploited immigrant workers from Bolivia attended to about 12,000 workers this year alone. So the number of slaves is very high.

Human Rights Violations and Global Institutions

We want to understand the causes of human rights violations, particularly causes related to economic policies influenced by international financial institutions (IFIs). For example, one World Bank program provides loans for workers to buy land. This violates the constitutional provision that is supposed to make land available without imposing the burden of debt on workers. Over 60 percent of workers cannot even produce food to eat based on this project, let alone pay back a loan with interest.

Two policies of the World Bank and the International Monetary Fund (IMF) directly affect human rights. One is the privatization of basic services, such as health and education. The other is debt repayment. Brazil pays

273

about 10 billion *Reais* per month in interest on the debts, money that could pay for social programs.

The World Trade Organization (WTO) also affects people's lives by imposing rules to force countries like Brazil to open their markets to cheap imports. That is complicated for a country trying to build an industrial sector. The WTO is also involved in services, which are actually just basic rights. We resist when they talk about privatizing health care and education, or about protecting intellectual property that interferes with our right to produce cheap medicine. The WTO wants to put basic economic rights, like health, education, food, and medication, into the spectrum of commodities that can be controlled by multinational corporations.

The World Bank might seem to have failed in its mission to alleviate poverty, in which case it should have closed its doors. But the real objective of the World Bank and the IMF is not to fight against poverty. Their interest is to open markets to benefit multinational corporations. By that standard, they are succeeding, and our governments have been accepting these types of policies.

The so-called G-20 group was supposedly about defending the rights of Third World countries to export more to the North. This group put pressure on the European Union and the United States to open their markets. But even that type of policy does not benefit small farmers or reduce hunger in Brazil. We do not want market access in the North. We want food sovereignty.

Escaping the Colonial Mindset

Our government needs to stop thinking of Brazil as a colony. The policies we have right now are the same as we had in the period of colonization. Over and over in history the function of Brazil in the international economy was to produce cheap goods for the North. At the beginning, it was sugar, and now we are back to sugar cane production. Then it was coffee, then gold. We are always producing cheap, basic materials for the North.

We need to think as a nation. We have all the resources we need. We have natural resources, industry, infrastructure, and a large internal market. The countries in the North developed by not following the new liberal economic rules. The New Deal in the US was the opposite of neoliberal policies. We need a new project that prioritizes the needs of our people. Then we need to create international relationships that make sense for us, not based on the priorities of foreign corporations or countries.

Lula Less Courageous than Other Latin Leaders

The Lula government lacks the courage to change. Of course there are powerful interests involved in government decisions, but Lula has grassroots support and legitimacy. We expect more from him, including large structural changes to our economy.

Despite the damage done by neoliberalism and privatization, Lula has a lot of power. He could implement agrarian reform and deal with the historical demands of indigenous people for land, and protect our environment from GMOs [genetically modified organisms]. I think Lula has enough grassroots support to confront the national oligarchy and multinational corporations. When Kirchner was elected in Argentina, for instance, he helped educate the people in Argentina about the debt. Why has Lula not done that in Brazil? Lula could explain to the people why he would renegotiate with the IMF. He needs to trust the Brazilian people more. He does not need to give in to the interests of the powerful elites in Brazil or the multinational corporations.

In Venezuela, Hugo Chávez is helping to politicize the people. That is why he was able to get control over natural resources, the PDVSA [national oil company] and invest in massive social programs in the shantytowns. Chávez also created a new constitution, which formed the basis for making deep changes. This is what we have not seen in Brazil. If Lula were moving towards those types of social changes, we would not be so critical of him. He should at least educate our people about these issues.

I just came back from an event in Bolivia, an event with 40,000 people celebrating government control over the natural resources of the country. They fought against multinational corporations, even against *Petrobras,* the Bolivian national oil industry. That is an example that Lula needs to follow. Lula needs to trust the support of the Brazilian people more, even on these controversial issues.

Eric Mgendi *Communications Coordinator, Action Aid, Kenya*

Poverty is growing in East Africa. Foreign investment is supposed to help the poor, but even if it raises national income, it hurts the poor by displacing them from their land. An example is the Dominion Farms project. Privatization could help Kenya, but only if it gives control of resources to people themselves. Land reform is useful. One method is a tax on idle land, which owners would then give back to the government, if they do not want to pay. The Maasai have been treated unjustly. They have never been compensated for the ecological services they provide, which benefit all people.

In East Africa the majority of people live in poverty. In Kenya, a little over half the population is below the poverty line. That is also true of Uganda and Tanzania. Poverty arises because economic growth benefits only the elites, not peasant farmers, landless farmers who are squatters, and pastoralist communities that keep livestock.

Cost-sharing policies of the World Bank have caused a decline in literacy in East Africa, because people are now required to pay to attend public schools. In Tanzania, the literacy rate fell from 80 percent to 60 percent. The government health system, which was previously well respected, provided drugs free of charge. People now die of simple things like malaria because they cannot afford to pay the small fee required by the World Bank. So, many people lack access to health facilities and to education.

The Problem with Foreign Investment

Foreign direct investment in East Africa does not benefit poor people. Each government wants to produce statistics showing economic growth, but behind those statistics, there are gross violations of human rights. In agriculture, foreign investors prefer a plantation model. They take the land and the profits for themselves.

African economists argue that foreign investment brings in business, but for the poor, the new business just makes the situation worse. Suppose a widow survives on one hectare [2.4 acres] of farmland. Economists may calculate that a foreigner can use technologies to earn more income from that land. But who receives that income? The foreigner. The central government gets some revenue, but that does not reach the poor person. The only benefit the poor people might have is employment, but work on a plantation amounts to exploitation. So the people are net losers.

276

As an example, a Canadian firm is seeking a license to mine titanium in Kwale, Kenya. Initially, they offered little compensation to people evicted from their land. Then some civil society organizations intervened. After that, the company offered KSh 90,000 [$1,200] for every hectare of land. According to the law, they are also supposed to be given land elsewhere. People cannot buy land and put up shelter with $1,200. Clearly that is a case of the well-to-do benefiting more than the poor people.

A second battle is going on between Dominion Farms and the people in western Kenya. Some people are complaining that they were arm-twisted. They were evicted from their land, and received only KSh 45,000 [$6,000] per hectare, which is still too little compensation to buy land elsewhere and build a house. The company's assessment of the value of land in that place ignores the ecological benefits of the wetland. Dominion considered only what people were earning at that particular time.

Foreign investment might mean higher recorded economic growth on the one hand, but it means increasing poverty on the other hand. That is why we have very high inequality: people who are very rich and people who are also very poor. So the model that we have promotes 30 million beggars and a few million rich people. We are increasing poverty in the name of increasing economic growth.

Small-scale Farming and Co-ops

About 70 percent of the people living in rural areas depend on subsistence farming: they raise their own livestock and grow maize and other crops. We need to follow a model that empowers the small-scale farmer—something like a China model. We cannot compare ourselves with Europe and the US. A more useful comparison is with China, which starts by producing enough to feed their nation. If you produce for export and become a consumer economy, then the people you import from can hold you at ransom.

To have a model that works, we should make people a part of the revenue sharing—have a nucleus [cooperative] model. We have one [co-op] in Kenya where farmers grow the rice that is in supermarkets and another that produces sugar, called Mumias Sugar. They have a nucleus model where farmers are invited to have shares in their company. They are co-owners in the business.

In recent years, we have had a big rural-urban migration. People move to the cities in search of jobs, because that is where most of the investments are made. In the city, they cannot afford housing, so they end up in informal settlements. If we want to turn that process around, we must decentralize investments by empowering small-scale farmers at the grassroots to participate in the growth of the economy.

Natural Resources and Privatization

The number of people who really control Kenya's economy is less than 1 percent. Almost all of Taita district is owned by two people, and half of it is the national park—that is, Tsavo East and Tsavo West, so that tells you where people are concentrating.

The problem of land here in Kenya is very complex because when we got independence and the president was given some money to buy the white lands and reallocate to the people, he ended up allocating it to himself and his own family. No one knows what happened to that money and how that land was redistributed. That is where the injustices started from.

I would like us to have a clear natural resources policy. We are closely following in the footsteps of Nigeria where they battle over resources. If we do not have a clear policy stating the revenue-sharing arrangement, it is a recipe for conflict. There should be a clause that states the percentage of wealth that must remain in the area from which wealth is being extracted, so the people affected become beneficiaries. We should not only produce for export. Let us first feed our own nations, then we can export the surplus.

Western countries keep on insisting that we open our market, that we privatize. Most governments want to privatize to fill a deficit in the budget. That is a bad reason. Privatizing so that locals have their share of Kenya—that is a good reason. The people who want us to privatize have hidden agendas. They want other people to own our country. If we must privatize then let us do it through our Nairobi stock exchange, so that local people can become co-owners of our resources. Also, privatization should be for a short period to transfer skills, with a clause that Kenyans would then take over.

The government can also efficiently run some enterprises, such as providing water. I do not believe in privatization of water from the source to the piping system. Maybe you can commercialize the billing system, as Kenya has done, but it does not augur well to privatize the source of water so that a foreign company can hold you at ransom.

Foreign aid makes us completely vulnerable to manipulation. Recently, when there was a budget deficit, the different parts of the government were working at cross purposes. On the one hand, the Minister for Trade was negotiating with the World Trade Organization to protect maize farmers from globalization, but on the other hand the Finance Minister was negotiating with the World Bank to get a loan, on the condition that we remove protections for our farmers. So the two of them were not working in tandem.

We need to remove ourselves from foreign debt. Then foreigners will listen to us, because they know we are independent. As long as we continue being dependent on Western countries, we are vulnerable to their manipulation.

When our government privatized the electricity generation company, they fetched over KSh 23 billion through the stock exchange. Kenyans can finance our own projects.

Land Reform

A land reform process is going on. They have begun with the coastal part of Kenya where an 8-mile strip along the coast which runs up to Zanzibar is owned by a sultan. The government wants to allocate that land to local people. That is what we need. There are people who own huge chunks of land in the country that they are not using. This land can be given to the local people. There are many ways to do that. One way would be to introduce a tax on land that is idle. The government would be able to take back that land within a very short time because they will not be able to pay their taxes. But land reform is not as simple as I am saying because it is a governance issue. Some of the wealthiest people are politicians.*

Private ownership of land has driven many people off the land, because a private developer can buy huge chunks of land. That has opened up avenues for corruption, and displacement of people from their land. So it becomes an economy for rich people. If you are politically connected, if you have the money, you will be able to be a player in the market. If you do not have money and connections, your goods cannot even reach the market.

Lack of Fertilizers

We used to have a Kenya Farmers Association, before it collapsed, it used to supply fertilizer inputs at controlled prices. One of the biggest problems for farmers is the cost of fertilizers. It is expensive because it must be imported. Because of that, our maize farmers cannot compete with neighboring Uganda. However, a lot of the cost of fertilizer is related to what

---

* Ed.: Presumably, he is implying that land turned over to the government because of failure by owners to pay their taxes would never end up in the hands of citizens. Instead, it would be added to the estates of wealthy government officials.

happens after it arrives in our country. The cost of fertilizer when it reaches the farms is much higher than when it arrives at the port in Mombassa.

If farmers became self-sufficient using organic manure from animals, that has the potential for increased food production. But this is tied to the lack of extension services. In rural areas, the most common problem is lack of skills and better farming methods. As a result of World Bank cost-sharing policies, there are no extension services for farmers. Pastoralists cannot sell their livestock because they have not been taught the international standards and cannot export their beef.

Dominion Farms

I mentioned Dominion Farms earlier. That American company entered an agreement with the Lake Basin Development Authority to lease out 3,700 hectares of land. The transfer arrangement and the amount of land Dominion claims to own are both shrouded in secrecy. It should be adequately discussed with the public. They put up an environmental impact notice, but they did not wait for the 60-day period after notification to begin operations. They had already started producing electricity for their farm by constructing a weir that blocks a river feeding into Lake Victoria. They have flooded people's private homesteads. They merely told the local people to move out. No negotiation was done. People have been forced off their private land

It was a common grazing ground for cattle. There were over 1,500 cattle there every day. It was a common resource where they also used to get mudfish. So hundreds of people are being affected.

Unjust Treatment of the Maasai

The historical injustice regarding land began when the Maasai were pushed out, and private businesses were started in those areas. Their only livelihood was grazing. They know no other means of earning a livelihood. When they had no place to graze, that was the source of conflict.

We have wildlife today in Kenya because the Maasais respected it. Their culture forbids eating game meat, which is why we have wildlife in Kenya. Yet they get no benefits from the Maasai Mara [game park for tourists]. Nothing! If a person's property [e.g., Maasai cattle] is destroyed by wildlife, there is no compensation. For loss of life, compensation has been provided only recently. That was why there were cases of human-wildlife conflict. The bigger problem was the lack of revenue-sharing with the Maasais, who should benefit from having maintained wildlife. Over 60 percent of wildlife are outside gated areas and yet the people who have maintained that ecosystem do not benefit.

Pedro Montes Coria *Miner, Potosí, Bolivia*

Working in a silver mine himself, Pedro explains the history of the mines of Potosí and their role in the transfer of mineral wealth to Europe. These days, even though working conditions are better in private mines, most miners prefer to work in cooperative mines that let them set their own work hours.

A writer by the name of Eduardo Galeano says that with all the silver that came from Potosí, from this mountain, it would have been possible to build a bridge from Potosí to Spain. Imagine then how much silver was mined from this place. The same author goes on to say that it would have been possible to build another bridge with the bones of those who died. More than eight million people died working inside or outside the mines, using mercury, a most dangerous reagent.

Since there was no dynamite in those days, mining was done purely by human labor. The Spaniards brought in black slaves from Africa to work in the mines. However, they had problems with high altitude, cold weather, and malnutrition. So, the Spaniards put the black slaves to work in the jungles of La Paz growing coca leaves, fruit, rice, and coffee. That's why there are no descendants of black slaves in Potosí, even though we have a statue of a black slave here in the mine.

Not all the silver from Potosí went to Spain. As Galeano says: "They had the cow, but the pirates drank the milk." The Spaniards transported silver in galleons. The pirates who came from Holland, England, and France used to attack these galleons to steal their contents. That is why a lot of the silver ended up in Holland, England, and France. Sir Francis Drake was the most famous pirate. He worked with Queen Elizabeth of England, splitting the loot 50-50.

Tin mining was also important here. Here we have a statue representing the three "Tin Barons." They came to Potosí after the Spaniards had left, after the silver deposits had been depleted. So they concentrated on mining tin. Simon Iturre Patiño was the most famous of the three. Patiño was born in Cochabamba and later came to work at the mines of Potosí. He struck upon one of the richest deposits of tin in the world and became an expert in tin mining. He bought many mines and became owner of many places on the mountain. He also had many mines in Southern Potosí. Afterwards, he went to France, Portugal, Asia, and the United States.

When Viceroy Francisco de Toledo came to Potosí, he gave orders for the city to be renovated, including the destruction of some houses to build better streets. He also ordered the construction of artificial lakes, which took twenty thousand workers to accomplish. The water from these reservoirs was needed to power the mineral refineries. There was no electricity, so the heavy machinery had to be moved by the force generated by a waterfall. He was also responsible for the use of mercury for metal refining, a process called "amalgamation." Many people died because of the use of mercury.

The Viceroy also promulgated a law called *la mita* which turned out to be disastrous for us. This law required miners to work for six months without coming outside. People had to sleep, eat, and work inside the mine without ever coming outside. That is why so many people died working in the mines. He was a bastard of a man. I think we should dynamite him!

These days, private mines are usually larger and more mechanized than cooperative mines, and they are even ventilated inside with oxygen. These miners work eight hours per day and six days per week. They earn from one thousand to two thousand *bolivianos* per month, depending upon the mine. They have health insurance, life insurance, and a fixed salary.

The situation in cooperative mines is quite different. If a miner needs a mask or a helmet, he must buy it with his own money. The miners earn money based on the amount of mineral they can extract. The working conditions are not as good as the private mines.

Yet most miners would rather work in the cooperative mines than in the private mines. In the cooperative mines, they can decide on how many hours and days to work. If they work more hours, they can earn more money. If they are lucky and strike a good vein of the mineral, they can earn pretty good money. Though their earning power may be limited, the most important factor for them is that they can determine how much time to work: 5, 6, or 7 days per week, and 6 or 8 hours per day. Sometimes they can decide to work 24 hours per day, which we call "double." It's really up to them to decide.

Mashengu Wa Mwachofi *Member Of Kenyan Parliament, 1979 - 1988*

Because land is tied to all aspects of culture in Africa, including religion, the colonial disruption of the land rights system is still a problem in Kenya. The British took land from the natives to set up plantations and mines. Then they created a labor force to work for them with a labor registration system that required every 16-year-old male to work away from home. The British transported work groups to other parts of Kenya, away from their ancestral lands. This led to the continuing problem of homeless, landless squatters who have been displaced. It also led to a pattern of women being responsible for all work in the village, in terms of raising food for the family. Many who fought against the British expected to return to the old land system after independence, but instead an elite group of Kenyans merely took over the land from the British and continued the colonial system of land tenure. Reforms are needed not only in the control of land but also in governance systems.

Colonialism and Poverty

Kenya and many other countries are poor because resources are not optimally utilized. Ownership of land and other resources is not in the hands of the communities, as it was in the pre-colonial setting. Colonial governance enabled the white settlers to benefit and impoverished local communities.

Poverty begins with colonialism. You cannot grab wealth from people in a democratic manner. The struggle for independence, for liberation, is always a struggle to be free to manage and control your resources. With freedom, you can use resources to create wealth and distribute them equitably.

Prior to colonization in East Africa, there were basically two types of communities: pastoralists and agriculturalists. The question of landownership was in the hands of communities. They had governance systems in place ensuring everybody use of their labor in combination with land and water. Wealth was distributed equally. There was never total starvation or people who were sick and suffering. Everyone had enough, barring natural calamities and occasional clashes over resources between communities. Those clashes were dramatized in colonial history, but really there was calm.

283

From Slavery to Colonialism

The slave trade destabilized the whole system. Then, at the end of four or five centuries of it, as people were beginning to get organized, colonialism came in with similar devastating effects, dividing people against each other. That is why tribal clashes today originate over resource use. Resources are in abundance, and the long experience of the African was one of equality—access by everybody.

As colonization came, Britain declared this area their own. We became property, both the country and the people. The natives were not recognized as human beings, so all of us were property of the empire. The British allocated the best lands to the incoming foreign settlers, and they gave access to mineral deposits to Europeans. The new economy was controlled by dictatorial governance, which enabled them to extract wealth. The most backward laws were land and labor laws. By displacing people from their traditional home grounds, the British created the phenomenon of the squatter, a person who is landless. That is still the reality.

Labor laws took away all youthful, energetic men to work on plantations and in mines. Only women were left to carry out their own roles, and the roles that had been carried out by their husbands. If men were exploited on the plantations, the women were doubly exploited. They had to provide both for their family unit and carry out all the work. Men on plantations were paid a subsistence wage, a slave wage. The traditional economy, operated by women, sustained the larger foreign economy.

In my thesis, I was surprised to see that formal [European] education went first to boys. Initially, it was rejected. Later, a few boys began going to school, because those who were literate got better jobs on plantations, and earned a little bit more. When the traditional economy could no longer sustain families, women began looking for paid employment, and girls started going to school. Hence, the gap in education between boys and girls. It is falsely assumed internationally that Africans are anti-women, but the culture responsible was the colonial economy that put women in charge of both domestic work and production for the family unit. Men are seen as instruments for creating wealth for somebody else. Poverty exists today because those structures of governance persist. All efforts to end poverty, including foreign aid, will not solve the basic problem until the governance system is changed and resources are returned to communities.

What 20th century Western anthropologists have labeled acephalous [headless] or government-less societies do not exist. It is a big lie. Instead, there have been well-organized societies, practicing participatory democracy without centralized governance.* Even where feudal systems began to emerge in Uganda and the Congo, they were always flattened by some other action.

Colonialism interfered by creating a new culture based on competition, resource exhaustion, land grabbing, and indifference to the poverty of others. We have inherited structures of injustice, like the centralized dictatorship, under Moi, Kenyatta, and Mwai Kibaki. A few, both local and international, are able to reap the wealth of this country in their own interests, without caring for the preservation of Kenya. The government holds the people down. That is why social reform in the Third World is key, because structural changes must come.

Squatters

Land is a central part of social reform. The condition of squatters began with alienation of land: giving the best land to white settlers and relegating native people to "native reserves." Once land was distributed to settlers, native reserves were created for each ethnic group. They were not big enough to accommodate the people there. Since some families did not have land, newly landless people were "allowed" to live on the lands of white farmers to provide labor.

That is how squatting began. Tabitha Konogo has examined this in her book, *Squatters and the Roots of Mau Mau*. There were many different types of people living as squatters in what was later designated the White Highlands. Their labor was unpaid. In return for being allowed to live there and practice their own economy, they had to provide male labor to the white-owned

---

* Ed.: Mwachofi later discussed extensively the organization of life among the Taita community of which he is a part. All land belonged to all people, but different clans or groups used different areas. Land was governed communally to determine who could work on it and when cultivation would begin. "Nobody begins alone." Harvesting required ceremonies and sacrifices. Separate areas were designated for cultivation, hunting, grazing, and gathering (for building materials). Some areas were taboo for particular purposes, and some game animals were considered sacred. Harvesting trees high in the hills was forbidden by custom. "If you cut a tree in a place where it is prohibited, your arm might become paralyzed. The whole thing is tied also to the religion and the belief systems of the people." There was some division of labor among farmers, craftsmen, and religious leaders. There was democratic governance through councils of elders. Everyone except the very old and very young had work to do, but even the very old had a role as teachers of both language and custom.

farms at given periods. The Kikuyu in Central Province were the most affected by that. They moved into the Rift Valley to work on the farms of settlers there.

Colonial Labor Laws

In the area from which I come the local people were removed from the plains to create a sisal plantation. Sisal is a fiber for making twines and bags. In my district, the natives refused to work on the sisal plantation on a consistent basis. So labor laws were introduced, through the *kipande* system. The *kipande* system required registration of every male. The moment you turned sixteen, you had to have a labor record.

The colonial labor laws really were slave laws. Everyone had a duty to work on those farms. Then, for the convenience of the settler, to be able to retain labor, the British introduced a system of long-distance migration. Those who lived in the extreme west were forced to work in the east, along the coast. Migrants had no way of returning home, so the British could keep them there for a long time. As the migrants stayed in place, their communities grew, but without land. They became another class of landless people. They produced for others in the new economy.

Uhuru: Struggle For Land and Freedom

The struggle for independence was really a struggle for land and justice within labor. The leadership of political struggles during the first five decades of colonialism was always trade unions, such as Machan Singh and Chege Kebachia. It was also a struggle by persons wanting their land back. After WWII, returning Kenyan soldiers had learned that liberation can be achieved by force. So, during the late 1940s and early 1950s there was a movement to get the white settlers out. They wanted to return to how Kenya always was.

There was a struggle for land and freedom, called "freedom and land" *uhuru.* We wanted freedom to control the land, to govern ourselves. But in 1963, when we were creating a constitution, those who benefited from the system were not willing to allow change. So we had to accept a constitution that allowed native leadership, but which allowed economic structures to remain the same.

In the first five years after independence, people were completely disillusioned. In the first two years, freedom fighters were coming out of the bush, but they were not being given any land. Populations that had been displaced had no place to go. So, as early as 1964 and 1965, they merged as an unregistered organization, called KKM, *Kiama kia Muingi*, the People's Organization. They thought the only thing to do was to go back to the bush and fight again for a new government.

That threat of renewed conflict pushed Kenyatta and his reform team to come up with settlement schemes: buying out some white settlers, settling squatters on farms, or creating settlement schemes in unoccupied areas like Lamu. It was done in a haphazard manner. Communities were brought into areas occupied by other communities without any consultation at all. That created animosity and prepared the ground for tribal clashes in the longer term.

Skewed Land Distribution

In Nairobi, about one percent of the population occupies 90 percent of the land; and slightly over 90 percent occupies less than 10 percent. That is why you have urban squatter settlements. Slightly more than 70 percent of the Nairobi population lives crammed in Kibera, Korogocho, and Mathare. Korogocho is one square kilometer and has probably a tenth of the population of the entire city. The so-called "slum people" account for close to 50 percent of the population. Another 20 percent live in areas that are not that bad, but they are also crowded. Only a very small proportion lives in the posh areas, with one individual occupying up to one square kilometer. Land in Korogocho is occupied by 90,000 people. In Langata, it is occupied by one person.

Consider rural areas. The Taita-Taveta District, where I come from, is 16,000 square kilometers, of which 14,000 are state land, and less than 2,000 are occupied by the residents. Of the 14,000 that are state land, 10,000 are national parks, and the other 4,000 are leased to rich individuals, including Jomo Kenyatta and his family. There is also a sisal plantation and some ranching. The people who used to use that place are crowded together and food deficient. Their traditional ways of soil conservation are gone, because crowded people cannot practice proper rules. Sustainable use of resources could not happen there.

In 1979, in my first motion in Parliament, I proposed to change the landownership pattern in Taita District. There is plenty of spring water in that district. If some were used for irrigation, that could increase the area of arable land and promote development. But nobody liked to hear that in government, because I was advancing a people's agenda. The people in power have interests, such as gemstone mining or large-scale farming. Providing the means to improve food production and reduce poverty were not useful to the individuals in power. The arrangement we have today is the same colonial arrangement, only instead of a governor, we have a president. The situation remains the same, and poverty continues.

Need for Governance Reform

The question of constitutional reform is crucial, because we want a completely new system, where power resides below in accordance with the principle of subsidiarity.

Our biggest weakness in the pre-colonial setting was the lack of centralized defense. We need centralization, but only if it is in the interests of the smaller people.

In this country, land is vested in the president. The theory was that the president would take care of the communities, but the reverse has proved to be true. Moi gave land as gifts for political support and used it as a tool for creating money for elections. He gave his supporters land where people had been removed from their plots. The people who received the land became part of the government.

Most citizens focus on the corruption of particular individuals. But poverty is a structural thing. It is okay for people in the North to feel some responsibility and to come and help, but it is more important for people in the North to realize that their ancestors caused the problem. We need new programs to enable people to take over their governance. There is a need to establish links between the poor and the marginalized in the North with the poor and the marginalized in the South, for a better world. Look at Wangari Maathai, the renowned Nobel Prize Winner. She has suffered for many years just for advocating green ideas. Everybody seems to recognize what she is doing, but she was never honored until the other day, and even now she is still just an assistant minister.

We have a long way to go. The civil society organizations I work with believe that change will come from below. We have to organize communities to be in charge of their own governance systems and to render useless the instruments of governance from above. People in Korogocho can reorganize themselves. One handicap is space. There is not even enough space to create sewage systems. That again leads to the political question: how do we get more space? Those who are in charge will not let us have it because they are gaining from it. So it is really a question of greed.

Godfrey Ngao *Mine Operator, Tanzania*

As a small entrepreneur, Godfrey Ngao has learned that the government helps big corporations rather than small businesses. Living with hostility and manipulation by the government, the mining company, the marketing agents, and the World Bank, he and his workers face long odds of ever being successful.

I started here in 1998. Then I got sick. After that, my wife got sick and died. I stopped mining, but I am still paying rent. For the moment, I am living on what I had before. I have another mine, not a Tanzanite mine.

We have a very small area to mine: only 50 [meters] by 30 by 38. When I get an investor I cannot do anything. The large-scale miners can produce more gemstones than we have. They can control the market.

To start mining, you have to pay TZS50,000 [50,000 Tanzanian shillings [or US$40] up front to the government. You also have to pay TZS20,000 [US$16] in annual rent. When you produce some gems, 20 percent is guaranteed to the miners and 80 percent is for the mine owner, who pays for all the mining equipment and food, social services and everything.

History

Tanzanite was discovered in 1967 by Ali Juuyawatu and Manuel de Souza and some others. Then it was nationalized by 1970. National mining corporations came here. They never did anything but research. In 1988, indigenous miners came here and began illegal mining, including this mine. After that, we were invaded by the government and forced out. In 1995, the division of the blocks started, which is when we got this legally.

In 1996, we were legalized and licensed. At the beginning I had 20 people working with me here. We never found any gems here. So the miners went to other mines, because I have no money to nourish them, to feed them. So no one is working in it. There are only two people guarding it.

Different Treatment of Large and Small Operations

The big corporations try to demoralize us, to eradicate us totally from the mining sector and to monopolize the whole land. They also monopolize the market. When my friend gets some products, he helps me with blastings and other mining instruments. The big corporations do not help us with anything.

We sell what we produce in the mines to the licensed brokers and master dealers. But we have learned that most of the master dealers are agents of the big-scale miners. We have no direct market to the US. Tiffany and Company came here from the US after our President visited there, but I have never seen anything they have done for small-scale miners, and we are not allowed to know what is going on.

The big companies get loans from the World Bank, the African Development Bank, and the IMF. The government also supports only the large-scale miners. They finance the big mines to grow, which is killing us! If they lacked that financial support, they could never do this. We are never given any aid by the government or by the banks. They do not help small-scale, artisan miners. In addition, if we produce anything, they rush in for taxes, a 30 percent tax on gross revenue. You have to give them 30 percent, without any consideration of how much you invested. So, I am stranded. I cannot get financing. I am looking to sell my mines. I am also farming.

We would like foreigners to stop the IMF and the World Bank from financing foreign mining companies. That kind of investment is not good for us. They are looting our natural resources. We can work with these natural resources ourselves. The international bodies should buy from us, but not be allowed to operate mines here. This applies both to tanzanite and to gold. Maybe we need foreign companies to extract petroleum or gas, but not gemstones and the gold. We can do that. The natural resources that were given to us by God could help us develop our country rather than other countries.

In addition, the big mining operations do not really benefit our country or our government, because the tanzanite is taken to South Africa, where it is sold to the US. The South African government is benefiting from our natural resources. We are suffering.

All the tanzanite in the world is only produced here. Any tanzanite you find in any shop anywhere in the world comes from here. It all comes from these 8.5 square kilometers. Of that 8.5 square kilometers, the multinationals were given more than 6 square kilometers. The law does not say that. What has been done is contrary to the mining law. This is another problem.

Bruce Oatman *Social Worker*

Poverty in an affluent society is unconscionable. It occurs because a portion of the value created by working people is siphoned off by an elite class that owns most of the land and can live without working. In 2006, the economic rent of land was about $2.5 trillion, or 20% of GDP. If that annual amount (nearly $30,000 per family of four) were collected from landowners and shared equally, poverty could be eliminated. In addition, the power of the elite to control the political system would be vastly reduced. The main reason this transformation does not occur is that this unfair treatment of workers is invisible, so it is accepted as inevitable. But it could change if enough people have the imagination to recognize the situation we are in.

Invisible Injustice

Almost 250 years after the industrial revolution, 85 percent of the American population still feels constantly pressed every day about how to pay medical bills, rent, gasoline and car payments. Affluence should have eliminated those sorts of anxieties.

What went wrong? The answer is simple. So much of the wealth in the US goes into the pockets of people who had nothing to do with creating it. Most people who work get back much less than they contribute, but they do not realize it. The average wage in this country is $15 an hour and for 80 percent of the population that is considered a good wage. How can you live in New York City on that? But this situation is just accepted by most people.

Solution: Neither Capitalism nor Socialism

That does not mean we should opt for socialism. Socialism has no more chance of working than capitalism as a complete system. Each system has certain virtues; each has certain vices. The main vice of present-day capitalism is that 20 percent of the nation's $13 trillion income, or about $2.5 trillion, goes into the pockets of people who did not earn it. So most people cannot do much more than juggle one bill against another. Socialism has its own irreconcilable disaster. Socialist societies produce little wealth, so even with equitable distribution, there would not be enough to go around. Ideally, the virtues of both systems might be brought together some day.

That ideal could be achieved if the annual unearned income of $2.5 tril-

291

lion were distributed evenly to the entire population. If that were done, each person's spendable and savable income would increase each year. Over the course of a generation or so there would be an enormous efflorescence of production, without destroying the environment. Each family could maintain itself and actually have money in the bank, thereby avoiding the terrible family dilemmas that occur when choices have to be made among necessities.

Unearned Gains from Landownership

What is the source of that $2.5 trillion? It represents ground rent, that portion of annual product that is generated by active workers, but which is collected by passive landowners.

Currently, much land is held for speculative gain, which is why around 10 percent of the population owns around 90 percent of the land. The 10 percenters, as we might call the small class of owners, never have to work. All they have to do is own land and their needs will be quite well taken care of. They not only can live in idleness; they can also become so wealthy that they can buy legislators to defend their interests for them.

Urban locations are now the primary sources of land value. How much do you think the land under Rockefeller Center is worth? Or the land under the Chrysler building, which helps support a college downtown? Or the land under the major office districts? Land everywhere is the major contributor along with human labor to everything that we hold dear. None of it is possible without land.

Owning land does not contribute to production. It is simply an inherited claim against wealth produced by others on the land one happens to own. Landowners, without doing anything productive, gain the excess production of the community as a whole. To capture this for public use is simply the community taking back for itself that which it created. It would be theft if someone made something and another person snatches it. But if one takes back socially-created value from non-producers, that is not theft.

My landlord in Manhattan could collect from me, if he chose to, six times the rent that I was paying him 20 years ago. That would seem to him like a windfall. Most landlords in New York City think they have earned that increase. They tell themselves they had the foresight and intelligence to know where to buy, and that they should be rewarded for all the gains in value that come from owning a building here. But the value actually came from public activity, not from their efforts.

Solution: Not Land Redistribution, but Sharing of Land Value

Does this mean land should be owned communally or distributed to everyone in equal shares? No. Neither of those is a reasonable solution. Take a country like Zimbabwe, where hard-line Marxists would like to take over the land. They believe that all the natural resources should be shared and governed by a national elite. President Mugabe pretends that he is in favor of land distribution. He is breaking up the large farms and distributing the land among the people he calls the veterans of the civil war, which ended in 1980. But even if the land were equitably distributed to people who need it, what happens in the next generation, when the population has grown? There will be a need for equitable redistribution again. Moreover, better farmers will earn more money and buy the land of other farmers, and the situation will return in which a handful of people own most of the land and others own nothing.

Much better than physical redistribution of land would be a system in which the rental value of the land were to be paid back to the community. That value is established in the marketplace. If I own a piece of land worth $5,000 a year, that is the annual value of the monopoly privilege of owning that land—the economic rent. If that money, that rental value, were to be paid to the community as a whole, then that would be a way of giving the landless equal access to it—financially, but not physically.

This method would split up the monopoly privileges that land owners hold without taking the land away from them. In this way, land can be redistributed without violent revolution. Producers would still own the land. It is not taken away. But the owners would no longer be permitted to take that part of the national wealth which others have created, which comes to them from collecting rent. Instead the community will be able to collect rent from landowners. The universal sharing of economic rent will raise everyone's income and provide each person some security.

Economic Growth Benefits Landowners

About two years ago The *New York Times* had an article about the development of farming in Colombia. The gist of the article is that farming is so wonderful now compared to fifty years ago. Modern techniques and the willingness of urban banks to invest have caused a big increase in productivity. The pictures that accompany the story are revealing. The first picture, from the late 1940s or early 1950s, is of the grandfather of the present owner and the people who worked with him—twenty peasant farmers sitting in a row, smiling. The farmer looked nice, but all of his workers appeared in rags, with missing teeth, and they were not particularly clean. The story tells how difficult life was then. The next photographs show the marvelous changes in Colombian agriculture in the present. The grandson is now a handsome young man in a necktie and jacket, living in one of the larger cities in Colombia, no longer on the farm. He flies to the farm, partly because there are left- and right-wing groups who might shoot at him on the road. In one picture, he is lined up, also with his twenty workers, and next to him there are two fairly well-dressed younger men, described as graduates of agricultural colleges. They now run the day-to-day operations. Then there are eighteen or so workers. Their clothes are ragged; they are missing teeth, and they are not particularly clean. The situation has improved for the owner and a few young agronomists, but the abysmal condition of workers has not changed in fifty years.

That is the story of who benefits from the advance of a modern economy, whether in rural Colombia or in the urban centers of the United States.

Joseph Odhiambo and Family *Kibera (Nairobi), Kenya*

I was born here in 1987. We are three children. I am Joseph. This is my sister, Helen. She is disabled, and my other brother is also disabled. So among the three of us I am the only one who can at least do something. But life is hard because my mother is just a cook, and she earns Ks 3,000 [$48]. School fees are high compared to the salary she is getting. I go to school but now I am not at school because I am supposed to pay 4,000 [$64] for the exam fees, and 10,000 [$160] for the school fees, and my mom is earning 3,000 [$48], so I am still at home. I cannot get the money. Sometimes we go without even eating supper, now. The small bit that we have, we share among ourselves.

When someone is sick, going to the hospital is very hard. So, we just stay at home and take some tablets from the shop. We cannot afford to go to the hospital. Sometimes we cannot have breakfast, just some lunch. Breakfast is hard because we are many and you know for breakfast you must have something. We can just have one meal a day. When we go to school, there is some discrimination there because we are not the same class as the other students. I do feel discriminated against because the things which they have, compared to what we have, they just laugh at us, because we are just slum dwellers. You cannot tell them anything.

Dr. H.W.O. Okoth-Ogendo *Author, Law Professor*

Prior to colonialism, there were indigenous land laws in Africa. Land tenure was communal, rather than individual. Individuals were automatically entitled to land for household use simply by being members of a community, but individuals could not transfer those rights to outsiders. British colonial law imposed a system of private land tenure, which continues to pose  *problems, because African culture is still oriented toward communal ownership. Efforts are under way to restore some elements of indigenous land laws to Africa, but there is little international understanding or support for such changes.*

Transition from African to Colonial Land Tenure

Land has always been central to the economic, cultural and spiritual organization of African communities. It is the basis of livelihood. For that reason, access to land has always been universal as long as you are a member of a community, by birth, marriage, or other attachment. Land is also regarded as the spiritual basis for human existence, but colonialism transformed land from a social, cultural and economic asset to a purely investment asset, and the subject of private property.

Colonialism was concerned with the expropriation of natural resources, and in Kenya that was in the form of agricultural development. When the British came, towards the end of the nineteenth century, their concern was to justify expropriation of land. They used their own legal system to acquire a legal basis for holding land. On December 13, 1897, the British government formally advised the colonial government that in countries where there is no settled form of government, the land belongs to the Queen of England. The British declared that there was no settled form of government in East Africa, because there was no sovereign and no system of administration. Having declared that there was no settled form of government, they appropriated ultimate title to the land. They passed laws and then gave settlers freehold interests, 999-year leases, and other forms of leasehold.* They disinherited African communities under the misconceived notion that there was no ownership, no title to land by the people themselves. Most of the land laws in this country are based on that misconception. There was a judgment of the high court in Kenya in 1915 that declared Africans to be tenants-at-will of the British Crown.

Pre-colonial Use Rights in Communal Land

The ownership laws imposed by the British in their colonies began with the notion that communities do not own land. The British legal system recognized only private ownership.[†] They did not understand our system, under which a whole community can own land and act as a juridical person that manages property rights. Property could be sold or transferred within the group but not outside the group. External transfer would exploit the rights of future generations. Indigenous land law protected the rights of the unborn and provided a sustainable basis for livelihood. We had a developed system of land law.

The European idea of private ownership is an alien concept. It is an instrument of exploitation of land. The market principle says that whoever purchases land is free of obligations. Landowners argued that private title to land gave them control over its use, without regulations or state interference. Eventually the state asserted some control in response to the abuse of property rights.

The British held a deliberate misconception of indigenous practice, so they could seize land "legally." The British public wanted to know whether the seizure was carried out according to British jurisprudence.[‡] The colonial administrators said, "First, Africans do not understand what ownership is; second, they cannot control land directly; and third, they do not have the

---

* Ed.: Okoth-Ogendo discussed later in this interview the British recognition of sovereign ownership of Buganda land by the Kabaka (military leader) but not of similar sovereign claims in Zimbabwe, South Africa, or Swaziland. The British negotiated with a sovereign for land rights or not, as it suited them.

† Ed.: As Okoth-Ogendo said later in the interview, "The European idea of private ownership is an alien concept. The market principle says that whoever purchases land is free of obligations, without regulations or state interference."

‡ Ed.: Okoth-Ogendo discussed the feudal origins of English law, whereby sovereignty implies ownership, land titles derive from the sovereign, and freehold interest meant being free of taxes or duties.

technology to develop it. Therefore we will expropriate title and give the land to settlers." The British put areas occupied by indigenous communities under trust. They argued the natives could not hold them as juridical persons. Even today, land not registered in individual names is held by county councils as trustees.

Under pre-colonial law, people who held use rights in land under communal ownership had definite, transmissible use rights that could not be abrogated. Security of tenure depended on continuous use of land. The system was complex, because different people could exercise different use rights over the same piece of land. Some people had the right to graze on it, others to build on it, others to cultivate it, and others to transit over it. All that was managed through a community hierarchy from the family to the lineage to a wider territorial body. The British did not bother to find out how this was done. They simply assumed that without a sovereign, without private property and land registries, colonized people do not know about ownership.

Land tenure before colonialism was democratic in the sense that everybody who needed land had access to it. Every member of a particular group had access to that group's land. Community institutions allocated, transferred, managed, and administered land. No one could be deprived of land based on some arbitrary decision. Security depended on being able to use the land for the assigned purposes. A person who lost rights by not using the land could later regain access.

Ironically, indigenous practices are taken seriously now. When land privatization started in 1955, the colonial government incorrectly anticipated there would be no indigenous property system in twenty years. The indigenous system is not going to die. We have to provide a framework for its evolution so that it develops in response to population pressure and other changes.

Land Tenure after Independence

Private property is a means by which the elite appropriates what little community land is left. Landlessness increases as people are evicted through private registration. The people who took over in Kenya in 1963 wanted to get into the shoes of colonial property holders. They declared existing property rights sacrosanct. They then proceeded to buy property that had been held mostly by settlers.

When Zimbabwe got independence in 1980, 75 percent of all land was held by whites. The constitution prohibited expropriation of property, and changing the constitution required a unanimous vote of parliament, which included twenty white settlers. After ten years, the British and the Americans offered money to buy land for redistribution, but they never gave them the money. That is how the land invasions [under Robert Mugabe] started. I was there on two U.N. missions on land.

In Kenya, the 1960 independence constitution guaranteed property rights in the the human rights section. Those provisions on human rights are extremely difficult to get rid of. They do not allow you to touch private property except through compulsory acquisition, and upon full and prompt compensation.* At least in Kenya, the British gave us money to buy out settlers, but the political elites are the ones who ended up with the land.

Land Tenure and Land Policy†

Land tenure issues are closely related to poverty because about eighty or eighty-five percent of Kenyans draw their living from the land. For small-scale farmers, land issues are at the heart of poverty reduction. Historically, the colonial government provided infrastructure, credit, and services to settlers, not to Africans. The formal part of the economy was developed by underdeveloping the African part. That process continues to create poverty. Poverty eradication requires both land and services provided by the state.

Nearly all African countries are now reviewing their land policy frameworks. In Kenya, we want to restore the cultural importance of land: the identity, the ontological principles that surround land. We are concerned with *kires,* which are places of worship for people. We want to reorganize rural settlements so that there can be enough land for agriculture. We need to review the laws that govern the ownership, use and management of land in order ensure they respect African traditions and culture.

In southern Sudan, the land sector could be reorganized without expropriation by investors. However, there are no laws governing this, so people are staking claims to land, cutting down forests, and looking for oil without regard to indigenous systems of control. The government is seeking to address these injustices.

---

* Ed.: Okoth-Ogendo noted that similar provisions for compensation imposed burdens on the government in Zimbabwe and South Africa.
† Ed.: Okoth-Ogendo discussed the special needs of pastoralists. Their land was declared trust land; it is still managed by county councils, which abuse their power. He wants the government to work with the people to ensure that resources are used for public benefit, not the benefit of private investors.

In the rest of Africa, policy reforms have been seriously considered only recently, starting with Tanzania in 1990. This is a paradigm shift. The judicial process is also coming to terms with some colonial injustices. South Africa has just delivered a judgment restoring to communities land expropriated in the mid-1940s. The High Court of Botswana has just delivered a judgment saying the San people are entitled to their cultural land in the Kalahari Desert from which the government had ejected them. So there is a ray of hope.

International Policies Regarding African Land

The future for Africa lies in strengthening indigenous institutions, rather than destroying them further. This is what the international community must understand.

The World Bank is beginning to appreciate the ambiguities and limitations of private property. They used to argue that private ownership is necessary for development, but they have found that customary rules and norms continue to determine the way people relate to land. The World Bank is asking how to make those customs part of the modern legal system. At least they have produced a number of publications that are more sympathetic to customary land use systems than in the 1970s or 1980s.

The driving force of colonialism has always been the control of resources. The resources of the global South are fundamental to development in the North. The battle is for the South to develop its own systems of access and control and to be able to bargain with the North. That is where the battle has been for over a century, particularly for subterranean resources. Why did the Angolan war last so long? Or the Congo? That might tell us. Why are we not interested in what is going on in Somalia? Because there is nothing to expropriate there. But there is something to expropriate in Sudan, the Congo, and Angola. So we need to strengthen our own legal systems of access, control, management and use in Africa, rather than borrowing from Europe. Anglo-European property law works against us.

The African Union has started an initiative to develop land policy guidelines for Africa. Those guidelines may provide guidance for African countries regarding the control and management of property. So at least the continent is addressing that question. I am hopeful that in the next ten or twenty years, there can be some dramatic changes. I put a lot of faith in the African Union initiative.

Marcela Olivera *Activist, Coalition for the Defense of Water and Life, Bolivia*

The local water company of Cochabamba (SEMAPA) was tranferred to a private consortium, partially owned by Bechtel, on extremely favorable terms. This transfer of public assets was part of a larger program of privatization of the public sector throughout Latin America, beginning in 1986. Prior efforts to privatize railroads and airlines ended in bankruptcy. After the water wars and the restoration of the water company to the public, the central government sought to create problems. The Inter-American Development Bank has lent money, but they want to control the company. Aid agencies say they want to help, but they actually want to steer the company back toward privatization. Finally, the lesson of Cochabamba is not about water, but about democracy and whether people in poor countries will be able to take control of their own lives.

Privatization of the Cochabamba Water System

A problem for Cochabamba today is providing water in a way that serves the people. When Bechtel bought the local water company (SEMAPA), the Bolivian government agreed to cover the debt. For Bechtel, getting a debt-free company was like starting again. The government did everything for Bechtel to allow them to make 16 percent annual profit on a 40-year contract. Bechtel is a private company. They want profits. They do not want to serve the public; they do not want to make children happy. If they wanted to do that, they would be a church.

Actually, the private water company was a consortium called Aquas del Tunari. We refer to Bechtel as a short-hand way of describing its ownership, because 51 percent was held by International Water Ltd., which is owned by Bechtel. There were several companies. About 20 percent was owned by Bolivian investors. One of them has a Burger King franchise. Around 25 percent was owned by *Abengoa,* a Spanish corporation. Another part was held by Edison, an Italian company.

When the water company came back into our hands, it came back with the old debt. That is why the company now has serious problems. We cannot deal with the debt. We need more money to invest in water infrastructure, and we do not have the money.

A Wave of Privatization throughout Latin America

The transfer of the water system to Bechtel on favorable terms is part of a much larger pattern that started many years ago. Privatization of publicly-owned projects began in 1986, when structural adjustment programs began. In 1986, our railroads, electric power telecommunications, and national airline were privatized. At first, it was called "capitalization" instead of "privatization." That meant the state would still own part of the company and the private partner would make investments. But it was just privatization because no money was invested.

With a few exceptions, the privatized companies failed. For example, only one part of the rail system is still working. The valuable parts of the airline company were extracted, leaving the airline in bad shape. It happened like that in other sectors as well. The last wave of privatization involved water, and it came directly. It was imposed by the World Bank and the Inter-American Development Bank. They said there should not be any more subsidies to water.

The state-owned companies were not good before, but with privatization, they became even worse. When they were state-owned, you could at least tell them what they were doing wrong. When a company is private you do not have the opportunity to make your voice heard.

In fact, when a company is privately owned, ownership is shrouded in secrecy. In the case of the *Aquas del Tunari* consortium, we needed help to find out who they were. The contracts are not transparent. We did not know who was buying whom. The Bolivian part of the consortium was people inside government. It may have been people who were in power at that moment, but we could hardly see; the contracts were not open to the public.

Restoring the Water Company to the Public

After the water company was returned to the people, a transition directory was created. The *Coordinadora* (Coalition for the Defense of Water and Life) was part of that directory. We held many neighborhood workshops to figure out a plan. We did not want the company to go back to the state. Both state ownership and privatization had not worked. We wanted something truly "public," not just state managed. People wanted something that was really public.

Two years later, we negotiated a proposal with the mayor, because the mayor had become part of the directory. Three people were elected by district voting to the new directory. Other people represented workers, the Union of Professionals, and two represented the mayor. They have run the company for several years. The company still has serious problems. There is no money to invest to provide more water to the neighborhoods.

Central Government Undermines Water Company

The government wanted to make the water company fail. So, it reimposed the debt that it had removed from the private company. If we run the company well as a cooperative, we can ask for other companies that have been privatized, too. The government did not want that and so there was a continuous boycott.

That was when people realized we must change other things to find a solution to the water problem. To create a social work plan for the company, we have to get approval from the government, but it will not approve something that is managed by the people. So the company is not working well.

Financing from the IDB

We had to extend our hands again to the banks that had pushed for privatization, like the IDB [Inter-American Devlopment Bank]. The IDB is again making loans, but the money goes first to the government, which pays the IDB 1 percent interest. The government charges us 4 percent. The 3 percent difference feeds the awful state bureaucracy.

The IDB also imposes conditions. They focus on technical, banking things to measure financial conditions. They look at the leaks in the water system. They should also look at public participation and social control inside the company or the number of complaints from customers. They do not. They just have an economic point of view. Banks should also look at social indicators to judge our success.

We have learned that there are no international financial institutions that give loans just thinking of people and not of financial conditions or their positions. So it is still hard.

Continuing Struggle to Provide Water to the People

Outsiders think the water war ended in April. It started then. The real water war is right now. It is not like what happened in the streets. It is about how to provide water to the people. Stopping privatization was just one step. The next step is to provide water in a good way. We could stop the privatizations, but we have not been able to build an alternative to the privatization.

That is very sad.

Others continue to try to impose privatization, not just big financial institutions like the World Bank or the IMF. Agencies of cooperation, like GTZ, tried to impose privatization on us. GTZ is a Dutch corporation.* It is the same as USAID [US Agency for International Development). It is exactly the same but from the Dutch government. They called it a "public-private partnership." But it is privatization in other clothing.

Aid Agencies Promote Privatization

After the water wars, GTZ wanted to impose public-private partnerships in other areas of the country—in rural areas or small towns. They tried to build a strange model that was still just privatization. They came here to impose their ideas. For example, if we had to hire another company to do a technical study in some area, they told us which company we had to hire. They would not let us look for alternatives. In the case of SEMAPA, our water company, we wanted to work with Corsan, the water company in Porto Alegre, Brazil. They have a good working model. But GTZ preferred to pay other companies that lack any social sense of the issues. They are just economic, or very technical. So, it seems that some of the aid agencies are worse than the IMF. They are linked to the World Water Forum, which is an association of organizations supposedly created to provide water to the people, but they actually just make deals with private companies. At this point, they are even more powerful than the World Bank and the IMF. The World Bank is not very involved right now in Bolivia. The ones that are providing money right now for water infrastructure are the IDB and these cooperative agencies.

The future struggle against privatization and for justice cannot just be about water. To talk about water justice, you have to look at the big picture—at how democracy works. Who makes the decisions about natural resources? When you change that, you are going to be changing all the other things, including the distribution of water and natural resources. Do the corporations decide about water, gas, and the other things that are the wealth of your country, or do you make the decisions?

When you change that frame—that system—that is when you make real changes. Right now that is what is happening here in Bolivia. People are not just focusing on issues like water or gas or coca. We have to focus on

---

* Ed.: GTZ is German government-owned Gesellschaft fur Technische Zusammenarbeit, GmbH or German Technical Cooperation, LLC.

who makes the decisions about these issues. The government? Ourselves? The corporations? We want to make the decisions because we are all owners of the country's resources. So that is where our struggle should go—changing democracy in our countries.

Oscar Olivera *Leader, La Coordinadora de la Defense del Agua, Bolivia*

The water war in Bolivia in 1999 was not merely about rapidly rising rates when the water system was privatized. It was also a popular rejection of the idea that anyone can privatize the gifts of nature, referred to as Pachamama. *In that regard, neoliberalism is an attack on Latin American culture, because it seeks to displace communal values of reciprocity and hospitality with individualism. As a result of the water war, a number of countries in Latin America have engaged in "de-privatization," but most of their economies are still closely tied to multinational corporations. A new model of development is needed that does not merely share the value taken from the earth more equitably, but which also recovers the wisdom of the ancestors. The control of land or territory, which is a precondition for change, will not take place, without a show of force by the people, organized for that purpose.*

Origin of the Water War

In 1999, under pressure from the World Bank, the Bolivian government decided to privatize the water sector. It signed a forty-year concessionary contract with the transnational company Bechtel, which was given a monopoly.

This decision seriously affected the daily life of the people. Water rates rose to a point that families had to pay 20 to 25% of their income just for water. Moreover, the older water systems, including the network of local wells dug by local cooperatives, became the property of Bechtel. The local company had only been able to distribute water to half the population.

Privatization damaged the system of common ownership and management of water supplies, inherited from ancestral times, which was replaced by a water market in which the sources of water could be used for personal gain—in tourism, electricity production, or mining. The water that used to sustain the life of the community now disappeared.

In that sense, the water war was not solely about the rate increase. It arose, above all, because privatization violates the ancestral concept in indigenous and rural communities that water is the lifeblood of *Pachamama*. According to this cultural and mystical concept, water is a generous gift of mother earth, a gift to all living beings and not only to the human species. Since water is a gift to no particular individual, no one may appropriate it for himself as private property.

As a result of the economic and cultural aggression against the life of the people, they began to organize themselves. A neighborhood-level information campaign developed to help people understand the meaning of the contract with Bechtel. The government scorned the people's voice on these issues. That haughty attitude was the determining factor in the people's resolve for self-organization.

The people decided, through a participatory process, to oppose the privatization of water and the subjugation of social relations to the market. They opposed the transfer of water rights to Bechtel, and they insisted that the people should decide how to manage water.

This mobilization, from December 1999 to April 2000, prompted people to occupy and block roads and plazas. The government sent the army to subdue them. Five thousand people were killed and one hundred wounded in Cochabamba and among the Aymaras in the altiplano (high plain).

As a result of this uprising, Bechtel was expelled, and the law restored traditional use rights to water as well as the people's ability to take care of their collective gift from *Pachamama*. The political victory gave the people a renewed sense of their voice and their power. That changed the history of Bolivia. Much of our country's water, oil, and mineral wealth is still held by large economic interests and transnational companies. However, the recovery of popular sovereignty in the water war was a step toward the election as President of an indigenous leader, Evo Morales.

Significance Beyond Bolivia

The struggle of the Bolivian people can be compared to the biblical story of David defeating the giant Goliath. The struggle had two effects at the global level.

First, it forced the World Bank and others to rethink privatization. Since 2000, there has been a move toward "de-privatization" of water services in Latin America—in Argentina, Uruguay, Chile, Ecuador, Colombia, and Brazil. Other nations are forcing the World Bank and the IMF to rethink this process of privatization. They recognize the need to incorporate a management process that is public and participatory.*

Secondly, the struggle in Cochabamba has generated hope and inspiration in social movements around the world. People, however impoverished or invisible or unknown, can defeat the powers that be. It is possible to defeat alike the financial power, the police, the military, and the political power and establish, instead, a true power of the people.

The water revolt in Bolivia is not an isolated case. There are common struggles in similar movements around the world. In Latin America, we have struggled against the Spanish, Portuguese, and British invasions, and now the North American invasion. All of these struggles were for the recovery of our territories, our values, and our culture. Cultural aggression is now in the foreground. The value of individualism that they wish to impose on us with neoliberalism clashes with our ancestral values of reciprocity, hospitality, and equality among all.

The internet has become instrumental in broadcasting widely the information about the common struggles for water, land, seeds, and territory. It facilitates the establishment of networks that help us show that the same enemies are everywhere. Bechtel is not only in Bolivia; it is also in Ecuador and Iraq and other countries. The same principle applies to mining companies, electric companies, and banks.

The new governments in Brazil, Argentina, Uruguay, and Ecuador are controlled by people who have come out of the process of struggle, and not merely out of the process of propaganda or electoral campaigns. But, even these governments are setting up development plans that are hurting people's lives. In Brazil, they are planning on building immense dams which will displace many communities when the waters begin to rise. The installation of paper factories in Uruguay will cause severe contamination. In Bolivia, the mining policy is still based on the neoliberal economic model. The government may gain a larger share of the profits, but exclusivist, contaminating and predatory modes of production remain untouched.

We want to change that, so the people will determine the type of development to adopt, the institutional and participatory forms we want in place, and ways to live a better life in harmony with nature and under new forms of social relations.

---

* Ed.: However, Olivera contradicts this by noting that GTZ, or *Gesellschaft fur Technische Zusammenarbeit,* still subtly promotes privatization in Latin America.

Needed: A New Vision of Development

The struggle for the survival of our people demands a new vision of development. The capitalist form of development is of no use. Our leftist governments are only putting on the brakes to slow down the destruction. For if all they do is substitute the government for a corporation, we may disappear at a slower pace, but in the end, the capitalist model of development will lead us to destruction. So, in this struggle we are talking about perpetuating life with dignity, over against a development model that means death, sickness, and exile for our marginalized people.

Change for our people will not come from the government, from a messiah, or from a general. People need space from which to reconstitute their own conditions of power, where they can manage their lives, as long as they recognize the spaces needed by others. We need to recover the wisdom of our forefathers to live by ancestral values that emphasize reciprocity, equality, transparency, solidarity and a relation with *Pachamama* in which nothing that she offers us generously is turned into merchandise. That is our most important task.

I have learned all of these things from personal experience. I went to work in a factory at the age of sixteen. I was nurtured in the values of a working class culture with organization and solidarity. I learned the same at home about the lives of Tupac Atari, Bartolomeo Siso, Federico Escobar, Zapata, Che Guevara, and other people around the world. These persons were products of the collective effort of the people. I intend always to be with the people, for that is where true power to transform things resides.

Loss of Land and Culture: Growing Response

Poverty in Latin America does not stem solely from recent neoliberal policies. There has been a brutal policy of impoverishment of our people for five hundred years. Our people have been providers of natural resources which have served to enrich other countries. Tons of silver, oil, saltpeter, and tin have enriched European and North American economies. That wealth, all that generosity extended by *Pachamama*, has not benefited our people. International looting continues in the form of a) territorial occupation by transnational companies, b) protected by legal systems they have imposed on us, c) accompanied by military deployment to safeguard those interests. What we regard as common goods or our people's heritage, they regard as

307

resources to be looted. This policy of looting has driven our people to the edge of death.

In the eastern part of Bolivia, where the land is best, it has been proven that entire communities and populations work as slaves and are property of the large estates. This gives us an idea of the true problem of land in Bolivia.

Colonialism and neoliberalism have caused the displacement of many communities and the fragmentation of populations that formerly were united, thus breaking apart cultures and languages. Indigenous communities are organizing themselves against processes of exclusion and against the appropriation of extensive areas of territory. The land issue is, for indigenous communities, a concept that cannot be separated from other types of common goods. The recovery of territory also means the recovery of culture and the reuniting of people who have been divided by processes of fragmentation.

The problem of indigenous land rights is not going to be solved either by a new law or by an indigenous leader as president. It is going to happen only by a show of force. Those who illegitimately and illegally occupy the territories that formerly belonged to indigenous communities are not going to relinquish those possessions willingly.

They will abandon their privileges and their properties only by force, as a result of the people of the communities.

There have been some organized groups ready to eliminate people physically and to intimidate the legitimate protests for social demands in the city and in the countryside. That is concrete evidence that the economic interests of landlords, businessmen, politicians and the media are being infringed upon and that they stand ready to eliminate anything that is perceived as a threat to their interests. In view of this situation, we must preserve the spokespersons of the communities. In order to do that, we must organize ourselves for our own defense against their planned attacks.

Juan Patricio Quispe *Leader, Association of Families for The Defense of Gas, 2003 (La Paz, Bolivia)*

The Gas War occurred in Bolivia in 2003 to protest a one-sided contract that allowed an oil company to reap most of the profits from the export of gas and oil. Citizens were killed during the protests, but that did not deter people from marching. These events raised awareness of the way Bolivia was being exploited. As a result, a new President was elected, who has negotiated an oil and gas contract that is much more favorable to the people of Bolivia. Although the United States claims to be on the side of democracy, it is actually on the side of the multinational companies.

I come from the Andes Province, from a small town called Cucarane. I came here to El Alto when I was 7 years old, so I have been living here for maybe 25 years. I came for work, because land in the Altiplano has been subdivided into very small parcels, not like in Santa Cruz where they are broad. Also, in the Altiplano, the weather is very dry, so it does not support many families. People migrate here to work in El Alto. Some do better than others. I cannot say I live in the streets, but I am not awash in money, either. I am somewhere in between. I stay afloat. We who come from the Altiplano are trying to grow, to improve ourselves, because we did not go to school, because there are no high schools, and particularly no universities.

Cause of the Uprising

The government's policy was to give away all the resources that our country had to transnational companies or to other countries that control the resources. We were waiting for the government to listen, but it does not listen. It was 2003 when the hardest social battles took place. We ended up with a tragedy, 67 people dead, more than 400 injured due to bullet injuries. That generated a social change in our country. It has elevated our consciousness about how to benefit the entire Bolivian society. Everything that happened was a result of Sanchez de Lozada's whim. He wanted to export gas through the Chilean harbors to Mexico at minimal prices, with 18% of the proceeds for the country and 82% for the oil companies. That was something terrible that angered us and triggered what happened that day.

Events of the Gas War

It generated a social compulsion, beginning with a relatively small march from El Alto to La Paz. Then the farmers showed up who were on a "hunger strike" until the 17th of September. On September 20, the first 4 deaths were registered in Sorata, and then 3 people perished in Huarisata, among them an 8-year-old girl, who was shot through her mouth while looking out the window as she was taking care of her mother in her house. That generated an even greater repercussion. After that, we continued marching in the city. On October 9, the first miner was killed, coming from Oruro in a protest march.

Then more deaths occurred as they tried to stop these marches. The La Paz fuel supply was exhausted, since we were holding the fuel at a storage site. They ordered us to release the fuel. The government of Sanchez de Lozada published a decree saying it would avoid future loss of personal property or life by transporting the oil to La Paz at all costs. Under that decree, the police and the army took over responsibility for fuel transportation. To counter this, the people went into the streets, while the police and the army started shooting left and right. On October 11, 15 to 17 people died along the highway. The next day, the conflict was more concentrated in the "Chua district," in the north, where the authorities tried to clear the road, acting as if people's demands were not real. That is Lozada's style, trying to generate fear. By the Rio Seco bridge, another 25 people were killed by gun shots, again under the October 11 decree.

The government refused to pay any attention to the people's petition for nationalization of oil companies and reduced fuel prices. We went into the streets and we were shot at. That had a greater cost to Lozada, and will continue to cost him. People were still being killed on October 13, but now at the center of the city. A 5-year-old boy, Alex Ijito was killed by gunshot at Bridge Bolivia, in the city of El Alto. They shot from the bridge while he was playing on the terrace of his house. That is very sad, something to protest. Killing children angers us a lot. It is terrible. For six months afterwards, the wounded continued to die. Even this year (2006) two people died of complications of gun shots.

There is a personal side for me of the "gas war" of 2003.* My brother was found on October 12, on the northern side of the city of El Alto, wounded by a bullet that had gone through his back and destroyed everything, his intestines, bladder, everything. When I found him, his intestines

---

* Ed.: The next segment of the interview (not reproduced here) takes place in a cemetery. Patricio describes various people buried there who died in the uprisings. In the mausoleum is a painting that depicts the US as an eagle trying to take the resources away and the peasants willing to die to protect their country against foreign control and repressive military juntas.

were scattered all over. He lived for three days and then died at the hospital. For me it was very sad. Remembering that makes us want to fight for justice. That is what we ask for.

Changes under the Morales Government

The Evo Morales government makes us optimistic. Recovering our resources has allowed us to attend to education and health issues. It satisfies us that we have finally arrived at this point. It should have arrived a long time ago. We have seen a lot of accomplishments by the Morales government in mining and fossil fuels, which are the most important ones for Bolivia. From now on, we will be the ones being paid 82%, and they will receive 18%. We hope the income these resources generate will help us overcome poverty.

John Perkins Author, Confessions of an Economic Hitman

Poverty arises when a few people become rich at the expense of the many. This serves the interests of a global "corporatocracy" that operates behind the scenes. We live in an empire, with the US at the center. We are all complicit in the work of the corporatocracy, but we have the power to change. We should not criticize corruption in other countries because it is largely a product of the influence of "economic hitmen" (such as Perkins) who bribed national leaders and threatened them with assassination unless they accepted a bad bargain. This is the hidden face of modern imperialism. Seemingly neutral or benign consulting firms have provided misleading economic forecasts with the intent of persuading poor nations to take on more debt than they can handle by financing projects that do little to promote genuine development. Debt creates dependency, which makes poor nations compliant with the demands of the US and the corporatocracy. The participants in this charade justify the system to themselves, but only by remaining blind to the consequences of their actions. Debt forgiveness is a sham, imposing new conditionalities. The greatest hope lies in the resistance of a new genre of leaders, such as those found in Latin America.

The Condition of Poverty

To address the issue of poverty, we have to look at who benefits from poverty: wealthy folks. The problem is not so much poverty, as it is wealth, when wealth is used as the measure of value. In order for a relatively small percentage of the population to have a lot of wealth, a large percentage of the population has to act as slaves.* They have to be impoverished. As long as we live in a system that requires what amounts to slavery, we are going to have poverty. It is to the advantage of "the corporatocracy," the people who control our biggest businesses and corporations, to have a mass of poor people around the world. The wealthy can draw on the poor for labor and steal their resources, whether oil or diamonds or coltan.† The poor remain at the mercy of those of us with wealth, and we get to exploit them.

A lot of today's problems stem from the history of taking resources from the poor for the benefit of the rich. When you do that to someone you put them in a desperate situation. You take away their resources so you can have them, so what do they have left? As time goes on, that resource is no longer valuable. Gold? Nobody really cares that much about gold these days, which is what the conquistadors were after. But today, some of those same countries, a lot of them, have oil. Now oil is the big one and we are going to take that, too, or gas, or whatever, or water. You perpetuate this terrible system of poverty, and this system of desperation and anger.

Some people claim that foreign investment helps poor countries climb out of poverty. Nothing could be further from the truth. Investing money in poor countries has made the corporatocracy richer, but it has also increased poverty. Investing more money in development projects or providing more fertilizer or better technology is not the solution. Anybody who tells you that those projects help the poor is deceiving himself or herself,

---

* Ed.: Perkins noted that 19th century slave owners took better care of their slaves than they do of their slave-like employees today. "Most of the plantation owners realized that their slaves were valuable property. They gave them enough food and clothing and shelter at least to keep them alive because slaves were recognized as valuable resources. In sweatshops today, those people are not even seen as resources, they are seen as cogs. They do not get enough money to provide for their families. If they get sick, they are turned out. Workers are treated as an expendable resource, because business owners know they can go out and recruit others."

† Ed.: Coltan is the colloquial African name for columbite-tantalite, a mineral required for capacitors used in computers, DVD players, digital cameras, and many other consumer electronic devices. Mining of coltan by Rwandan forces, Western-owned companies, and various militias operating inside the Democratic Republic of the Congo has sustained warfare in that region since 1998, with war financed by more than $500 million extracted by illegal mining operations in the Congo. See http://en.wikipedia.org/wiki/Coltan

because the facts show the opposite.

The gap between rich and poor is twice as wide as it was back in the 1970s, when I was an economic hit man. Today more than half the world's population lives on less than two dollars a day, which is not enough for anyone to live a decent life. It is a slave wage. We have portrayed the period since 1970 as a time of development, when the developed world invested huge amounts to benefit the developing world, but none of that has happened. We in the developed world are at the heart of an empire that has gotten richer, while the developing world has become poorer. The major cities of developing countries are deceptive because they have incredible skyscrapers. What you do not see is that there are a lot more poor people there than before.

The Corporatocracy

To change the system that creates poverty, we must first understand who foments the system. If we are an empire, where is the emperor? The equivalent to the emperor of the world today is what I call the corporatocracy, which consists of a very few people, primarily men, who run our biggest corporations. They control the world. In the United States, it does not matter whether we have a Republican or Democratic president or which party controls Congress. Those are details that make a difference, but from the standpoint of expanding the empire, it happens under both regimes.

Today the real geopolitics of this planet has little to do with nation-states. It might be better envisioned as huge clouds encircling that globe, and those clouds are the big corporations. They really are the ones that run this planet, and if we want to believe in democracy and transparency, then those institutions, the corporations, must become democratic and transparent, and we the people have to make that happen.

The corporatocracy controls the system, and the rest of us in the US participate in it because it provides us material prosperity. Even the poor in the US benefit compared to the poor in Africa. We all buy into the idea that we want the cheapest clothes, even if they are made in sweat shops. We have accepted sending our economic hit men off to other countries to exploit them and to get cheap resources. If the price of oil or some other raw material starts to go up, we get upset. The corporatocracy feeds that. They want us to be upset. They want us to complain.

So the system of global wealth and poverty is perpetuated, first, by the corporatocracy, the modern equivalent of the emperor, and second, by the subjects. We continue to buy bottled water, even though we know that bottling water is destructive to the environment and to the areas it comes from. We use more and more oil, knowing what a terrible thing that is. We wear diamonds, knowing that mining diamonds creates slavery.

In the US, corporations have been given the legal status of a person. They have all the rights of an individual, but none of the responsibilities. An individual is expected to be a good citizen. If not, then he is put in jail and punished. But if a corporation is not a good citizen, it gets a little slap on the wrist.

To understand how the corporatocracy work behind the scenes, we have to look at the history of global institutions that serve as the surrogates of economic interests.

The Hidden Face of Imperialism

When we emerged from WWII, we created the World Bank to reconstruct a devastated Europe, the International Monetary Fund (IMF), and the United Nations. The mission statements of these organizations enunciated good principles that would still hold today. But when Western countries saw the new enemy as communism, the new institutions focused on convincing developing countries to align themselves with the capitalist West, not with the Soviet Union. The institutions developed a cozy relationship with big corporations. This tie became stronger during the 1950s and 1960s.

At the same time, we claimed to have an aversion to colonialism, imperialism, and fascism. We began to look back and criticize the conquistadors as well as British and French colonialism. But we were still living in that system. When Mossadegh was elected democratically as president of Iran in the early 1950s and began to nationalize oil companies, we did not like that. We sent in a CIA agent, Kermit Roosevelt, Teddy Roosevelt's grandson, to get rid of him. With a few million dollars, he carried out a silent campaign against Mossadegh without much violence, and without the risk of war with the Soviet Union. He replaced him with a terrible dictator, the Shah.

This sent out a very strong message: this is the new way to build empire—use economic hit men. Kermit Roosevelt was the first economic hit man. He was also a jackal; he was the two combined. But he was a CIA agent, a card-carrying government employee. What if he had been caught? We would have looked pretty bad. So we developed a new class of people, who were like me. We worked for private companies, consulting firms, and we were economic hit men. In essence we worked for the corporatocracy, the government. But we are not paid directly by them; we are paid by consulting firms to serve their interests.

Consulting Firms as Tools of Corporatocracy

As an economic hit man, I worked in a big consulting firm that gave advice to countries on economic issues. Our job was not to offer unbiased advice. Our job was to produce economic reports that would justify loans for big infrastructure projects. To justify a loan for a power system, for example, we developed hugely inflated forecasts about the resulting economic growth. Modern econometrics and mathematical modeling made it quite easy to do this.

My bosses put tremendous pressure on me to skew forecasts to justify more loans. My predecessor was determined to have integrity in his work and not tweak the forecasts, so he was fired. I knew why he was fired, and I knew that if I wanted to progress within my company, I would have to tweak the forecasts. I later had several dozen very highly skilled economists and financial experts working for me. They all knew that their bonuses and raises depended on going along with this system. When we took these forecasts to the World Bank, the Inter-American Development Bank, or the Asian Development Bank, their specialists were supposed to check our forecasts and be sure we are not tweaking the results. Some had integrity. When I stood before a committee at one of those banks, their junior analysts would pick holes in my forecasts. Some saw through what I was doing. But their bosses also knew exactly what was going on, and they were determined that the loan would be approved. It was all a charade, even though we might have to spend several months justifying, debating, and tweaking some more. But we always won, ultimately.*

So, we justified huge projects based on claims that they would result in economic growth, although often they did not. Even if the projects resulted in economic growth, they only affected the people wealthy enough to take advantage of the airports, the industrial parks, the electric facilities, and so on. They did not reach the poor people, who are left holding a huge debt that would have to be paid off later.

---

* Another aspect of forecasting is that we usually had a lot more money. There might be one or two experts at the bank, but I could draw on a staff of 30 or 40 people to come up with very complex econometric forecasts and computerized databases. They did not have the funds to compete. The system was rigged in my favor. Since my book has come out, I have talked with people at the World Bank and its sister organizations who tell me that they know how the system works and what is going on. It disgusts them, but they do not know what to do about it.

315

Debt-Based Economic Domination

So, how did those loans tie into the system of economic control by the corporatocracy? Start with a developing country that has been identified as having resources, such as oil. With justification provided by a consulting firm, a huge loan to that country is arranged from the World Bank or one of its sister organizations. Many people in the US believe the loan helps poor people. It does not. Most of the money never goes to the country. It pays contractors like Bechtel, Halliburton, other engineering firms, and subcontractors. They make fortunes building infrastructure projects—power plants, industrial parks, ports, and other structures that do not benefit poor people at all. The poor are not connected to the electrical grid. They do not get jobs in the industrial parks.

Borrowing to pay for this infrastructure, the country goes deep into debt. A few of its wealthy people get very rich in the process. They own the big industries that benefit from the ports, the highways, the industrial parks, and the electricity. They make a lot of money and transfer it overseas. If something goes wrong, they just leave the country.

Countries are left holding a huge debt they cannot repay. This process does not occur by accident. When countries are encouraged to incur debt they cannot repay, it is not a mistake. It is a policy designed to control poor countries.

If I lend somebody a lot of money knowing they cannot repay it because I want to get a favor from them later, that is illegal. But when I do it to a country as an economic hit man or as the World Bank, it is not illegal. But it is wrong.

After the debt has grown for awhile, we economic hit men go in and we say, "You cannot pay your debts. You owe us a pound of flesh. You owe us a big favor, so sell your oil real cheap to our oil companies, or vote with us on the next critical United Nations vote, or send troops in support of ours to Iraq." Also, since they are heavily indebted, they cannot afford to pay for public services. So we go back to offer another loan to privatize their education system, or to develop their sanitation system. And the process is repeated and repeated.

We benefit from every step of this process. Our corporations get most of the money we loan to the developing country. Then we use the debt to enslave those countries, to imprison them, to get them to agree to sell off their resources cheap. It is an amazing system.

With this economic and financial subterfuge, we have created an empire, the largest empire in the history of the world. We have done it in secret for the most part, without most citizens knowing that it ever happened. In fact, most citizens believe we have done a great thing by building electrical systems, industrial parks, and so forth. They think we have given some country a huge gift, and the truth of the matter is exactly the opposite of that. We have put that country in a terrible predicament.

Most Americans have no idea that we have created this empire. That is a terrible threat to democracy, which is based on an informed electorate. If the electorate has no idea about this basic aspect of foreign policy, than how can we be a democracy?

How Economic Hitmen Promote Corruption

Corrupt governments and companies in the Third World are often blamed for the system of exploitation. There is a tremendous amount of corruption, but we are the ones doing most of it, particularly in countries with resources our corporations covet. We do not like it when a democratically elected leader, like Chávez in Venezuela or Morales in Bolivia, opposes foreign exploitation of oil or gas in that country. So we try to corrupt people into going back to the old system.

In South America in recent elections, seven countries representing over eighty percent of South American population elected presidents that ran on an anti-corporatocracy platform. These presidents did not run on an anti-American or an anti-European policy. If I as an American go to any one of these countries, I will be embraced with open arms. They love our principles. They love our Declaration of Independence, but they hate having their resources exploited by us. So they ran against the corporatocracy.

Once these presidents are elected, someone who looks like me will walk into that president's office. I had the job at one time. I speak Spanish. That person walks in and says, "Congratulations, Mr. President," or in the case of Chile, "Ms. President." "I just want to remind you that I can make you and your family very, very rich if you play our game, or I can see to it that you are thrown out of office or assassinated if you decide to fulfill your campaign promises." Usually it is said a little more subtly, because the conversation may be recorded. But they get the message, because every one of those presidents knows what happened to Arbenz of Guatemala and Allende of Chile and Roldós of Ecuador and Lumumba of the Congo and Torrijos and so on.

The list is very long of presidents that we have had thrown out or assassinated. They all know this. So we perpetuate the system that way. From one pocket we offer a few hundred million dollars—corruption. From another pocket, we threaten them with subversives or jackals, who will go in and overthrow the government or assassinate the president. If I am the president, and even if I am very right-minded, and I really believe in what I have said I will do, what am I going to do? I know they can do this. I am very tempted to accept the corruption, because if I do not, I am going to be taken out. If I am taken out, what is the next guy going to do? He is going to be scared to death. I talked about this on a presidential level, but it happens all the way down through the ranks. It happens at every governmental level, and it happens in the corporations in those countries and it happens throughout the whole system.

In Iran, with Mossadegh, we overthrew a leader, a democratically elected leader, because he wanted more profits from Iranian oil to go to the Iranian people. We did the same thing in Iraq, under Qasim, who was a very popular president of Iraq, and decided that he wanted more of the profits from Iraqi oil to go to Iraqi people rather than foreign companies. So, we decided that he had to go, that he had to be assassinated. We sent in an assassination team in the early sixties. It was headed by a young man who failed and got wounded in the process and had to flee the country. That was Saddam Hussein. He was our hired assassin. He failed, so the CIA went in directly and had Qasim publicly executed on Iraqi television and put Saddam's family in power. We have done this time after time.

If the corporatocracy does not like what is going on in Nigeria or Botswana or Thailand, or any other country, they send people like me in. They send economic hit men in and we try to corrupt the system. We offer the bribe and, at the same time, the threat. If the leader does not buy, then, in fact, we do send in what we call the jackals, and they overthrow the government or assassinate the leader. Usually the economic hit men are successful, so we do not need to send in the jackals. But, on those occasions when we were not successful—I failed with Omar Torrijos in Panama and Jaime Roldós in Ecuador—the jackals were sent in and assassinated these men. In the very few instances when neither the economic hit men nor the jackals are successful, then and only then do we send in the military.

This is what happened in Iraq. The economic hit men were unable to bring Saddam Hussein around. The jackals were unable to take him out. He had very loyal guards, and he had look-alike doubles, so it was difficult to take him out. So we sent in the military. The first time [1991], we could have taken Saddam out, but we did not want to. He was the type of strongman that the corporatocracy loves. He could keep Iranians in their borders, and keep Kurds under control, and keep pumping oil to us. We figured in 1991, when we took his military out, that we had sufficiently chastised him, that now he would come around, but he did not. When the economic hit men returned in the 1990s, he still refused and the jackals were again unable to take him out. So we sent in the military to take him out.

Justifying the System to Ourselves

How do the people who participate in this system of domination and exploitation justify what they are doing to themselves?

If you are an economist, you cannot get a better job. Working for the World Bank or a consulting firm is a wonderful job, professionally speaking. You are making a lot of money, and you live in the best suburbs of Washington DC. You are on top of the world. So you want to believe that what you are doing is good. You want to keep your job and you want to justify it. The system conspires to perpetuate itself and to make it easy for the people within it to keep up the subterfuge.

People at the World Bank or other agencies convince themselves that they are doing a good thing. But anybody who really pays attention knows what is going on and knows it is wrong. Everyone working for these agencies gets a good salary. They are able to give their kids good educations. So there are two factors working. They are prospering and philosophically they can justify it.

It is easy to feel justified, because graduate schools teach that investing in infrastructure is the way to make development and economic growth happen. But in most countries only a very few people benefit from the formal economy. Everybody else is in the informal economy, living subsistence lives.

The system demands that the people who participate in it do not ask themselves too many questions. My father-in-law was chief architect for Bechtel. He designed the big cities in Saudi Arabia, and Bechtel made a fortune. I had put the deal together, but I did not know that he was doing really bad stuff. He was blinded to this. He would say it was his last job as an architect, and what a wonderful job to have all the money in the world to create cities out of the desert. But they were Westernized cities, a terribly corrupting influence on Saudi Arabia. He never thought about it that way. He is a very liberal guy actually, a very liberal Democrat. He only thought about it from an architect's standpoint and from the perspective of a man whose family was happy.

The Illusion of Debt Forgiveness

Recently there has been a lot of talk about debt forgiveness. Eighteen countries were singled out as ones that were in line to have their debt forgiven. I wish that would happen. I am totally for debt forgiveness, but it has to be unconditional and unfortunately none of this is unconditional.

The round of debt forgiveness that has been proposed is an incredible subterfuge. It is one of the best economic hit man tricks I have heard to date. So each one of these eighteen countries will have to agree to conditionalities that benefit the corporatocracy. A big one is they have to privatize. Another one is that they will not be able to export products that threaten ours (such as agricultural goods); they will have to accept restrictions on what they can sell to the United States and the G-8 countries. It is a very rigged system.

We need to understand that these countries did not take on this debt themselves, ever, in any way. We imposed it on them. We bribed and corrupted some of their officials to accept it. Those officials got very rich in the process. The people in those countries never agreed to that debt, but they are the ones that are stuck with it. It needs to be forgiven, because it is illegal debt anyway.

The Deception of Foreign Aid

It is unfortunate that most people feel that foreign aid is altruistic and helps other countries. It almost never does. There are some exceptions after a tsunami or a great natural disaster. Immediately some foreign aid goes in to put up tents to bring in food and water and so forth. Very soon, that gets corrupted, to build big hotels owned by the big international chains, not helping the mom-and-pop organizations. But we do not hear that. Foreign aid is not altruistic. It is only there to help the corporatocracy.

I would like to see foreign aid really work. We could do some really great things with that. Or even better just leave people alone. As I travel around Latin America, I hear that leaders there are not looking to us for any kind of help at all.

A whole new genre of leaders is emerging who are saying, "Let us use our own resources to pull our people up by their bootstraps. We can do it. Just do not steal our resources any more." I think symptomatic of that is what Evo Morales has done with the gas companies. His actions have created some problems between him and some of his neighbors, like Argentina and Brazil, but he is saying, "The companies used to get eighty percent of the profits and Bolivians got eighteen percent. I want to reverse that. Let the companies get eighteen percent and let the people who own the land the gas is coming from, the Bolivian people, get eighty percent." He he has done that and the companies are still there. Eighteen percent is not a bad profit. Morales said (and I think it makes total sense), "If people invest money, they should get a return back, a decent return, not windfall profits."

Companies and private investors in the stock market, in Europe and the United States, have come to expect windfall profits. They should be happy to get three or four percentage points above inflation. That is pretty good. That is better than what I get from the bank. Why do I demand twenty to forty percent above inflation? That is usury. But we have come into that system. The message is coming through from many leaders, like Morales in Bolivia, "Let us get back to a reasonable approach. Yes, we want help. We want investment. But we want to control where it goes, and we just want to pay a reasonable return, not to be exploited."

Change is Possible

It is time now to reverse the process of wealth concentration. At the core of our country are some incredible principles of equality and sustainability and stability. In the Declaration of Independence, we talk about a government of the people, by the people, and for the people, and the right to life, liberty and the pursuit of happiness. That value system is very different from the one that created the division between wealth and poverty. The world loves these ideas. The revolutions in South America today reflect that. These countries are saying they want to live by those ideals.

Three things have happened to make change possible. First, we have created a global empire, with the US as the leader, and with allies in Europe and Japan. Even though the empire is not a good thing, in the process of building it, we have created systems of communication, so that we can reach everybody on the planet.

Second, there are now enough resources in the world that nobody needs to starve. At least 24,000 people die every day of hunger and hunger-related diseases, and that does not need to happen. We have plenty of resources, so that should not happen. It happens because of the system we have created. But we now have resources that can stop that.

Third, we realize we live on a very small planet. We are one community. If we did not already know it, 9/11 taught us that. Our cities are vulnerable to people in Afghanistan. We live on a very small planet. I know that my daughter who is 24 and her children are not going to have a stable, sustainable and sane world, unless every child born in Ethiopia, in Indonesia, in Bolivia, also has that expectation.

These three elements at play right now could enable us to narrow the gap between rich and poor. We can break the 3,000-year-old pattern of wealth and poverty.

We need to move from imperialistic capitalism, where a few people make all the decisions and most of the money, to democratic capitalism, where everybody gets involved in the decision-making process, and everybody shares in the benefits. We need to go from corporations that are secret, to ones that are transparent. Corporate executives say countries need to be more democratic and transparent, but in fact, corporations are neither of those things.

Certain organizations, such as Rainforest Action Network, Amnesty International, Move On, and the *Pachamama* Alliance, have forced corporations to change their policies in specific areas, such as logging in rainforests. More than that, we need to convince the corporatocracy to change their basic attitude, their basic premise of why corporations exist. Today they are there to make wealthy people wealthier.

The only way we are going to have a sane and stable and sustainable world is by helping developing countries do what they need to do themselves, giving them the power to determine their own future. We need to pull the corporations off them, to stop exploiting them. In fact, we need to turn it around, so that corporations and all of our institutions truly embrace them. If Nike is going to have factories in Indonesia, the workers in those factories need to have a say, and they need to have a share. Their best interests need to be the first thing that Nike or any corporation looks to. Only by our taking a stance that we are not going to buy the products from any company that does not do that, are we going to pull ourselves out of this. That is the real secret to changing this world. We must change course and we must change the whole paradigm by which we look at the world.*

The corporatocracy is behind the resource grabs and exploitation today, and we must change it. We must have the courage to do that. We must look back to the people who lost their lives fighting tyranny and who made

---

* Ed.: In the interview, Perkins discussed at great length the virtues of ancestors who fought and died in the American Revolution and World War II to create a better world for us. In this final section, he calls on each of us to make a personal sacrifice.

sacrifices for us, and say, "I will stick my head in a noose, because it is that important. I will make sacrifices. I will use less gas. I will pay more for my clothes to ensure that they are not made in sweatshops by slave labor. I am willing to die to make this happen." I do not want to be on my deathbed and to think that my grandchildren are going to look back and say, "Why didn't they do something? Why didn't they take to the streets? Why did they allow these people to destroy the planet? Why did they allow these people to exploit others around the world and make them miserable and desperate? Why did they allow this to happen?"

Heather Remoff *Anthropologist, Author*

Poverty stems from concentrated ownership of natural resources, which forces everyone else to pay a high price for life's necessities: land, air, water, oil. For nations, however, having resources can be a curse, as evidenced by what has happened in Nigeria. One of the worst features of colonialism was the way Europeans divided the land, taking the best for themselves and then criticizing the local people for their farming practices. What is needed to create a fair economy is for the value of natural resources to be shared among all people. Nothing is going to be done about poverty and the high costs of housing until philanthropists and ordinary people understand the role of resource monopolies in maintaining economic privilege. The key question is how to shake prosperous people from complacency.

Monopoly as the Primary Source of Poverty

There is something wrong with our major economic systems: both socialism and capitalism. There is a horrible flaw or knot in the distributive function of any economy that cannot provide people a basic sense of security in their being, and their ability to provide for their families. The challenge is to find out what that flaw is.

The main knot or kink in the distributive function has to do with monopoly holdings. We once had antitrust laws that were taken seriously. That is no longer so. I am even more concerned about a deeper kind of monopoly that is the root cause of poverty, namely, the monopoly over natural resources, the gifts of nature.

323

The Resource Curse in Nigeria

Nigeria is an example of what has been called "the resource curse." Oil has definitely been a curse for Nigeria, because the effort to control it led to corruption, war and environmental damage. How did that happen?

Historically, colonial powers looked at Nigeria and other colonies as resources, and imposed European systems of land ownership, replacing traditional ways of guaranteeing that everyone had access to land. The guarantees might be through patrilineal systems in which certain family lineages were given the right to work pieces of land, and it might be the ancestors who were responsible for the distribution of land. In a polygamous society it was understood that a man with more than one wife needed a bit more land. That was an African system of responsibility and obligation to the land.

Once Europeans replaced the pre-colonial systems of land tenure with a European system of absolute rights, the stage was set for the multinational oil companies to negotiate a very sweet deal. It is difficult to negotiate contracts with a large number of people. So usually those contracts are negotiated with just a few top government officials. They give lip service to giving some of the oil royalties to the people, but in practice that is not what happens. Too often the revenues go into the pockets of a few government officials and their corrupt cronies, and just as often, they are deposited in foreign bank accounts.

The youth of Nigeria are feeling excluded from the benefits of oil. They steal from the oil pipelines just for their own families or sometimes to resell, and they risk being massacred. It is harsh. The environment has been totally destroyed. All the lip service about providing schools and roads has been only minimally attended to. Because of the oil wealth, Nigeria's human resource has been neglected: its well educated, multilingual population.

Colonialism and Agriculture

To understand how colonialism changed the African approach to land, we must first recognize that the colonizers neither understood nor cared to understand the cultures they were interfering with.

Rwanda was a case in point. The country was divided, with the most fertile land being given to the white settlers, and the infertile land being given to the traditional African farmers. It was partitioned in that way. When the African farmers used their traditional methods of slash and burn, the Europeans looked on in horror, and said: "Oh no, how could they use those traditional methods! They are terrible! We will come in and teach them to farm in the European style!" That made the Africans dependent on fertilizers and irrigation. The Africans had been doing just fine prior to the disruption in their access to the fertile land. When land is fertile, and they can let it lie fallow, the slash-and-burn method works. It can lie fallow for a while, and then they can move to something else.

The Europeans arrogantly assumed their knowledge was superior. They also felt they had a right to the resources there. The agricultural crops that Europeans introduced tended to be monoculture crops, designed for export. Prior to the colonial influence, there was a richly varied diet in Africa, very healthy, healthier than most Europeans eat. With the advent of monoculture and export crops, imposed by the Europeans, the dietary standard of the indigenous population diminished. I worry that there will be a Green Revolution in Africa by introducing "superior" farming techniques and bioengineered grains. That frightens me, because it holds the promise of disrupting systems that work.

Sharing Natural Wealth

The wealth that results from that progress should be more fairly distributed. That starts with distributing equitably the value from naturally occurring wealth, by collecting royalties or fees for the use of land, clean water, clear air, mineral rights, and the electromagnetic spectrum. Those royalties or fees could fund government services and eliminate the need for other taxes, to some extent.

We have to make a distinction between human endeavors and natural resources. We have to allow people to keep what their labor creates, but create a system that shares the value of resources. That is best done by charging adequate royalties.

Whatever you may think of Hugo Chávez, at least he is collecting royalties from the oil that is drilled in Venezuela, and he is using those royalties for social services, schools, roads, hospitals. That is where I would like to see oil royalties go. I am just enough of a renegade that I will not buy any gasoline except for Citgo gasoline because I know it is from Venezuelan oil. I do not want the profit from the gasoline that I put in my car to go into the pockets of the multi-national oil companies who will keep it for themselves. So my husband does not like to travel with me, because we are in danger of running out of gas unless there is a Citgo station on the horizon. I have vowed that I will walk before I put anything other than Citgo gas in my car, and he knows me just well enough to figure he might be walking with me.

Looking for Root Causes of Poverty Means Questioning the System

I have observed that compassionate people, such as Bill Gates, Bono and Warren Buffet, who are concerned about African poverty, are giving humanitarian aid to solve the problem. I do not want them to stop funding projects in the developing world to promote agriculture or to provide people with mosquito netting or irrigation systems or computer equipment. But I wish they would also look for the root causes of poverty. Their current efforts are similar to lifting drowning babies out of a river when what is most needed is to go upstream to stop the babies from being thrown in the water. To the people rescuing babies, it might seem that the person who runs upstream is abandoning the effort to save them, but clearly stopping the problem at its source is the best solution.

So, I wish that the big foundations would devote at least some of their vast wealth to studying the root causes of suffering. They mostly just treat symptoms of poverty now. I wish Bill Gates would recognize that all the effort he is putting into helping Africans is really just treating symptoms. I would like to make him curious about the causes.

Upton Sinclair said, "It is very difficult to get a man to understand something when his salary depends on his not understanding it." That is the brick wall I run up against in trying to convince my friends of the need to find an economic system that falls somewhere between capitalism and socialism, takes the best of each and creates a new and vibrant system in which we can take care of everybody. No one needs to be poor. But shifting to a system in which everyone has the same privileges and opportunities will require us to change ourselves and own behavior. That is difficult to do.

Land Monopoly and the Cost of Housing

Land monopolies make some people wealthy and impoverish others. This occurs because a few people with large real estate holdings in a city withhold some land from use, waiting for the speculative gain from an increase in land values. This artificial scarcity of urban land drives the price of housing up, forcing everyone to pay a larger portion of their monthly income for housing. If you allow private ownership of land, without collecting an annual user fee for the land being withheld from use, housing costs will skyrocket.

In Barbara Ehrenreich's book, *Nickel and Dimed,* she writes about trying to get by on what she could earn as a regular wage-earner waitress. When she went to areas where the wages were higher, her housing costs were higher still. So in the end she made out less well in areas with high wages. She did not make this point in her book, but as someone who is concerned about the relationship beween wages and land values, it screamed out at me on every page. Land monopoly effectively raises the cost of renting an apartment. In Silicon Valley, for example, wages are especially high, but workers have to commute long hours because they can not afford to buy or rent housing near their jobs. It is not the house that is expensive; it is the land under it. Land monopoly really does have an impact on the affordability of housing.

Because I keep using the word "monopoly," I need to be clear that I use that term to mean "highly concentrated ownership." Many people think that there is no monopoly in land because a little over 60% of households in the U.S. own a house and a small amount of land. What is not so obvious is that a small percentage of the people in this country own a very large percentage of the privately owned land. Five percent of the population owns something like ninety percent. That is a huge monopoly, which of course drives land prices up everywhere. That condition could be corrected by changing our tax code. Our tax code rewards withholding land from use, and it causes sprawl, and it causes all kinds of horrible things. We could change it merely by taxing the privilege of holding land.

Raquel Rolnik *Secretary of Urban Programs, Ministry of Cities, Brazil*

The central issue for Brazil's cities is a tradition of dual development: formal middle-class neighborhoods alongside vast informal settlements that often lack basic services (i.e., water, schools, police, and parks). The President ("Lula") campaigned on a new urban policy that would integrate cities, and make the poor, who inhabat the favelas, *into full citizens. The Ministry of Cities is charged with implementing that policy. Elites, playing of fears of urban*  *violence, have opposed integration strategies, preferring to promote gated communities and separatism as the solution. Thus, the problems of regularizing the living conditions of those who are in informal settlements are not merely technical and administrative; they are also intensely political.*

Housing Policy

A local strategy to open access to good urban land, not marginal land, to the poor is very important. It starts by including the poor from irregular settlements in the development of local master plans that envision an inclusionary city.

Irregular settlements are legally ambiguous. Nobody knows if the settlements are legal or not. The inhabitants must constantly negotiate their rights, such as investments in neighborhood infrastructure or school services. Brazilian politics lives on granting favors and getting votes in return. The urban political machine depends on regressive policies that exclude the poor and maintain concentrated income and power.

Up to the 1940s, most people lived at the subsistence level in rural areas. Then we had state-led, capitalist economic growth from 1960 to 1980 under military rule. There was migration from the countryside to employment centers in the south. From 1950 to 1980, we passed from 70 percent rural to 80 percent urban. Poverty became concentrated in metropolitan centers, and many small cities were emptied.

Now we have growing cities without increasing infrastructure or services. This was a political choice. The "Brazilian Miracle" did not include income redistribution or adequate housing for 70 percent of workers. The cost of housing was not factored into wages, so workers produced their own housing on unused land on steep slopes, along riverbanks subject to flooding, or in distant peripheries of cities, where there are no cultural opportunities. Housing policy from 1960 to 1990 reinforced the idea of the poor being on the urban periphery. Why are the poor on unwanted land? It protected the value and the constant appreciation of value of land in the formal part of the city. Despite the presence of so many poor in the cities, the policy of segregating the poor prevented the loss of real estate value, and even permitted appreciation of value.

To change that housing policy, we have to do two things. First, we must integrate what is not integrated, and invest in infrastructure and services where the poor live. Second, we need to transform planning policy to provide a proper, integrated place for the poor.

Migration and Demographic Change

Migration to cities occurred because agribusiness displaced subsistence farmers who possessed land but did not own it. Rural people were also drawn to cities in pursuit of education and health care. Trying for a better life is a big part of migration.

In 1970 Brazil had 90 million people; now we have 180 million. We will not double again in the next 30 years. That has ended. Brazil is passing through a demographic transition. The birthrate has declined because of rising literacy, universal primary education, health care for pregnant women and infants, and the influence of the media. Massive migration from the countryside ended already in the southeast and northeast. It continues in the center, west and north, on the frontier.

Sao Paulo and Rio are not growing, but their peripheral cities and *favelas* [irregular settlements] are. So metropolitan Sao Paulo is still growing by five percent per year.

Urban Integration Strategies

The social integration of cities has been the goal of the Urban Reform Agenda. It would mean having one building of low-income housing inside each block, mixed with middle class. In the 1970s, some Catholic parishes and some neighborhood associations began to press for more recognition of *favelas*. Before the new constitution in 1988, a coalition of neighborhood associations and professionals denounced the urban model. They opposed land speculation and favored recognition of the rights of the poor. The National Forum for Urban Reform (NFUR) presented a constitutional amendment to require democratic management of the city.

After negotiation with conservatives, a chapter on urban policy was included in the new constitution with provisions: 1) to affirm the social function of urban property, 2) to declare housing a fundamental right, and 3) to expropriate property that is not achieving its social function. The master plan in every city is supposed to define the social function of each property.

Urban Reform under the 1988 Constitution

After the constitution of 1988, the NFUR struggled to approve the City Statute. Before it was adopted, cities carried out local experiments, many of which entered into the City Statute in 2001. In 2002 and 2003, the National Movement for Urban Reform was part of the coalition that sustained Lula's campaign for the presidency. People living in the *favelas* and landless people occupying land were represented by the Urban Landless Movement.

Part of the agenda of Lula's campaign was to create a single agency that would integrate urban policy: the Ministry of Cities. I am a Secretary in that Ministry. We promote recognition of housing rights and prevent evictions. We also promote the use of empty land and empty buildings to offer more alternatives for popular housing. Also, through the master plan and municipal planning, we develop instruments to capture the rise in real-estate values in formal areas to invest in informal areas. We also seek methods of social integration of the city.

Conservatives and elites in Brazil have benefited from the segregated city. They do not want to open the city, to distribute wealth and access. They favor gated communities, but there really are no safe places in cities. The dual-city model does not work. The solution to fear (and we are all afraid) is not to hide the problem. But the more they show violence on TV, the more they sell gated communities, even in places without violence, like the hinterland of Brazil. The problem of violence in Brazil's cities is pervasive. It has almost become a civil war. But taking the poor away from our neighborhoods is not the solution. The solution is trying to integrate broadly and to reduce the poverty and ambiguity of irregular settlements.

We have increased the credit available to the poor. We also need to increase their access to land. If you do not match those two elements (credit and land), that will reproduce the model of the 1960s, which did not solve the main problem.

The City and the Country

The urban problem will not be solved by investing in rural areas in an effort to promote migration from city to country. Urban problems do not arise from the failure of rural areas. Most international organizations still have this in mind, and it is wrong. People go to cities for opportunities. We have to ameliorate conditions in the countryside and improve urban areas. We need cities to lead growth, and we need an improved countryside.

Migration is not primarily from countryside to city, but from small city to big city. So, we should improve the educational system of small cities. We need a network of small to medium-size cities that work together well regionally. A similar strategy regarding university-level education is the decentralization of campuses to regional centers instead of to capitals. If campuses are in regional centers, students can live in their own cities and study at the regional campus. This strategy promotes the economy of small- and medium-size cities. We also have to face the problem of big cities. We have to revive Sao Paulo, Rio, and Belo Horizonte. We have to invest in cities of all sizes.

Land Titles and Property Rights

We have three legal instruments to recognize land rights in informal settlements. 1) On private land up to 250 m2, we recognize squatters' rights if a family has occupied land for more than five years without a reaction from the owner. 2) The City Statute permits these rights to be granted collectively, not family by family. 3) If public land is occupied, there is a Special Housing Concession—an administrative, not a judicial, procedure. The city, the state, or the union can give title and proper registration.

These policies still have not been implemented. It is almost impossible to reach the end of the procedures: filing of documents, meeting environmental standards, and so on. For example, the national law of parceling sets a minimum width of a street. The rules make it impossible to legalize something that is illegal. So, the process of legalizing land that is occupied sometimes seems impossible. It is a vicious cycle.

We need a national law for regularizing land titles, a new parceling law, simpler registry procedures, all of which are being discussed and voted on in the Congress. Title registration is currently very difficult, but we decided not to create a separate parallel system of registering those lands. We do not want to have dual systems any more! The systems should be the same for the formal and informal land markets. The point is not to create a parallel system, but to open the existing one to include informal settlements. With federal money, we hope to promote local processes of land regularization, cartography, documentation, judicial work, and all that. We could, in three years, start regularizing more than one million households in irregular settlements. Already 300,000 families have titles.

Land regularization requires 1) streets, public spaces, infrastructure, and environmental sanitation; 2) standards to prevent acute environmental damage; 3) administrative procedures to make settlements part of the city records, with street names and house numbers; and 4) land titles in the name of the occupying family. We suggest that title be in the name of mothers, because they are generally responsible for the households.

We are investing in all four elements. There will be no more ambiguity about whether the settlement is there or not, whether it is there to stay or not. It is a part of the city, like any other, with the same rights.

Remaking the City

In every city, there are central areas devoid of activities and people.

The middle class migrated to other neighborhoods. In Sao Paulo, Rio, Salvador, there are several industrial areas from the 1930s, where there are empty warehouses near the center of the city. In the ports, like Rio and Recife, the port system logistics were re-engineered, leaving empty spaces. Those spaces could be transformed into cities with middle-class housing, popular housing, public spaces, and cultural spaces. This urban transformation should not follow the North American model in Baltimore or the European model in Barcelona, where old spaces were re-designed just to attract tourists. The inhabitants of those cities already had a proper place to live, which is completely different from our context.

We are experimenting with a new model of integrated life in urban centers in at least seven cities in Brazil. We are promoting rehabilitation projects, including popular housing. It is very difficult to do that, but I hope in the next four to five years we are going to start seeing some results from these strategies.

Amartya Sen *Nobel Laureate Economist, Author*

Poverty can be understood as absolute deprivation of basic necessities of life. In that sense, it is as old as our species. But poverty is also related to inequality, or relative deprivation, and that is caused by human institutions. A market economy is highly productive, but markets fail by increasing inequality and by not producing enough public goods. Relative poverty arises in a market because those who have nothing to exchange in a market are excluded and impoverished. In severe cases, relative poverty amounts to absolute deprivation.

Markets also do not provide incentives for private agents to produce enough goods that are shared by everyone, such as defense, public health, and education. So, the state must provide those goods. The fight against poverty is not helped by simplistic solutions such as the abolition of private property or getting rid of markets. Instead, what is needed is a balanced approach involving public provision of education, health care, anti-viral drugs, micro-credit programs, land reform, and infrastructure development. Democracy is also crucial because finding solutions requires public reasoning and debate. Although a few jurisdictions have made improvements in people's lives, such as China and the state of Kerala in India, no country has found such a good approach that it can serve as a model for others to follow.

Poverty as Deprivation

Poverty is the state in which humanity has lived ever since it emerged from its earlier apehood. Poverty is the inability to do minimum things that we regard to be important for a good human life. Poverty is an understanding of deprivation. Deprivation would be to die prematurely, to suffer from illness and pain, to be unable to take part in the life of the community.

Poverty is a matter of interest to everyone, and we have to bear in mind that mankind has lived in a state of great deprivation and poverty throughout its existence. People died in their twenties. They suffered from illnesses that are curable. Hobbes's statement of life's being "nasty, brutish, and short" is a characterization of poverty. There is no reason for us to take any different view than that. It is a question of understanding what it means in today's context, given the fact that there are means of enhancing wealth, means of curing illnesses and postponing death, means of making our lives comfortable. Given all of that, people still suffer from deprivation and poverty.

Poverty means deprivation of the basic minimal forms of existence that we should have in a fairly decent human life. So that is the territory. On one side, it requires us to avoid romanticism about the past, that poverty is some very recent phenomenon. On the other side, we have to avoid the complacency of those who say, "Now that we have technology and huge production possibilities, poverty is a thing of the past." Aggregate wealth may be very large, and the opportunity for changing peoples' lives may be enormous, and yet a huge proportion of the population of the world does not benefit from it adequately. So that is the context—neither romanticism about the past nor complacency about the present.

Wealth Production in a Market Economy

Today we live in a society that is primarily dominated by the market economy. That is not a reason for deep depression, because the market economy has in fact been largely responsible for the spread of technology, for modern methods of production, and for trade. It has been one of the creators of wealth across the world. The creation of wealth is much easier today than in the past, but there is no way of separating out the creation of wealth from enjoyment of the fruits of wealth, namely, the distribution of wealth generated.

The market economy's main force of strength is that, through exchange, you can have economies of scale. Production can be carried out on a big scale. That is a point that Adam Smith emphasized. If I had to produce everything that I wear, I would not be able to do that. On the other hand, I could produce a lot of things of the kind that I am able to do, like giving lectures. We can specialize, and that allows an enormous expansion of productivity. That productivity expansion is the central message of a market.

But the market economy comes as a package. It opens up opportunities for wealth creation, while consolidating the reasons why inequality survives. Inequality arises from lack of resources, differences in the ownership of resources that people have. With the development of modern finance, markets, trade, and the movement of capital from one part of the world to another, a lot of people have immense power to earn high income, while others are really tossed around like little straws in the wind, in a world not of their making.

Market Failure #1: Inequality And Poverty

The failures of the market economy are straightforward. If a system operates on the basis of exchange, then some people have nothing to exchange. Deprived people do not receive anything unless they have something with market value to offer as a salable commodity. That is the market's basic failure. The same institutional structure, like the market, can both generate a lot of wealth and also consolidate the inequality of rewards.

Productivity expansion can help prevent some kinds of deprivation, like hunger, undernourishment, and dying of illnesses. These deprivations are connected with absolute standards of living. So there are absolute elements and relative elements determining poverty. But even if you define poverty, as I would, as absolute deprivation of some basic capabilities, like being able to be well-nourished, well fed, literate, mobile, and participating in the life of the community, then you have to see that in terms of causation. Some parts of it will relate directly to inequality, like participating in the life of the community, and other parts will have a more absolutist origin, namely, to what extent you have the schools and hospital facilities and drugs. Here, too, inequality comes in, because very often these facilities are very unequally divided.

The thing to understand is how some people end up getting so much and others get so little. If we are going to live in a market economy, that raises the issue about what we have to sell in the market. For many people, it is nothing other than their labor power, their ability to work. For some others, they inherited wealth or acquired wealth of one kind or another. So we have to see the basic differences of ownership. Then, with what we own, can we actually sell it? If labor power is the only thing on which you live, then unemployment will condemn you to poverty. Looking beyond that, we have to consider the ownership pattern of land for those in agriculture and the results of very unequal ownership.

Inequality and poverty are completely linked, and yet they are distinct concepts. Inequality is a relative position. Poverty is in some respect an absolute deprivation. But absolute deprivation is very often linked with relative deprivation. This is a point that Adam Smith made with compelling clarity. He said that if you were living in a rich country, the ability to participate in the life of the community would require you to be dressed as other people are dressed. You might need more clothing if you are living in countries where people are more affluent and have a lot of clothing. Being way behind others in a community would be a reason for you to have a genuine sense of deprivation.

Market Failure #2: Underproduction of Public Goods

The market economy caters to goods that are privately owned, like toothbrushes or shoes. Most of the things on which life depends, however, are collective or public goods, like public health. If children are not vaccinated, they are exposed to illnesses, but infectious illness will affect other people, too. Other examples are defense, policing, basic education, basic health care, epidemiology, roads, and water. Public goods are shared; they have a me and you quality. The market economy does not address the production of collective or public goods. It fails to produce enough of them.

That failure affects the level of poverty in society. If the state builds hospitals and schools and takes steps to eliminate epidemics, unequal suffering from illnesses and illiteracy can be substantially reduced.

Avoiding Simplistic Solutions

The solution to all human problems depends on clarity of understanding what is causing the problem, and what, if anything, we can do about it. There is no magic bullet in solving poverty. Some people suggest getting back to old communities. Others say,* "Let us give people title to what they

---

Ed.: This appears to be a reference to Hernando DeSoto, who proposes in his book *The Mystery of Capital* that poverty can be overcome by granting people in informal settlements clear title to the land they occupy. By borrowing against those land titles, DeSoto asserts that the poor can transform their small real estate assets into working capital and start their own businesses. DeSoto is remarkably silent about what happens to people whose businesses then go bankrupt, causing families to lose the little security they have.

already own." No solution by itself is going to solve the problem. You have to deal with poverty with the respect that it demands. It is a complex problem. We have to understand what causes it, what sustains it, what increases it, and what, happily, reduces it.

An immediate solution to the problem of inequality may come to one's mind, namely to abolish all property, and then everything will be fine. People have suggested that in the past, but nearly every experiment in doing that has ended up producing a disastrous economic failure. So that is not going to work. In similar fashion, some people are tempted to just say, "Let's get rid of the market economy; everything will be all right." That is not a solution either.

But inequality does exist, and we have to address it. You may not be able to usher in the golden age by eradicating private property or the market economy. That will not work. We have to recognize that it will not work and that there is a temptation to go in that direction. We have to be restrained by realism. But at the same time it is important to understand that those who have asked for that were not asking out of a fad. They had a real issue in mind.

Inequality of property and ownership is a cause of inequality, of divided fortunes in our lives, and that problem has to be addressed. It cannot be addressed by simplistic solutions. We have to see what is the role of the state, what is the role of the society, what are the ways of affecting the market mechanism, whether there is democracy, and which non-governmental organizations are active. We must consider the extent to which the broadening of the institutional structure can address the problem. We have to see how to initiate institutional enrichment, as well as development of human values, respect for each other, and the cooperative spirit, which has been one of the big things that humanity has always relied on.

Some anti-poverty programs do not cost very much money. Land reform, for example, does not cost very much, unless you want to pay such exorbitant compensation, in which case the land reform would be quite useless, because that is the way the market economy is functioning anyway. The whole purpose of land reform is to do something which the market economy is not accomplishing. The role of non-market operators, namely, the state, society, and NGOs, is to supplement the market economy—in some cases, in some small respects, even to supplant it. It is not wise generally to supplant the market system, but we can supplant it in specific areas where its functioning is not good.

Kerala and China

An example of an area where the market has been supplemented and, to some extent, supplanted, is Kerala, a state in India with about 30 million people. It was never part of the British Empire. Two large parts of modern Kerala were Travancore and Cochin—independent native kingdoms. The British controlled their external relations but they had internal policies, which were very pro-education as early as 1816, with an emphasis on female education. Because of its long history of public education and health care, Kerala has achieved a high degree of equality. The literacy rate is close to 100 percent. Undernourishment is low. Kerala is more radical than other states in India.[*] As a result, the level of income per capita is low because of its deep suspicion of the market economy.[†]

China had some similarities with Kerala from 1949 to 1979. However, after China embraced marketization in 1979, per capita income rose and a lot of people were pulled out of poverty. This was accompanied by a large increase in income inequality. So there was a tradeoff. Incomes rose, but social indicators did not keep pace. Whereas infant mortality in Kerala fell from 37 to 12 from 1979 to the present, in China it fell from 37 to only 29, only about one-third as much. China's slow improvement in social indicators since 1979 could have been avoided by having a democratic system to supplement the market economy in a healthy way.

We need to look for the right balance in solving the poverty problem. No country has got the right balance. We cannot take any of these places, such as China or Kerala, as a perfect model; all of them have a lot of defects. It is a question of our being able to take a critical view of what we want and what we have reason not to want.

The Importance of Balance in Anti-poverty Programs

People often ask whether some particular policy is the best approach

---

[*] The anti-upper class movement was well developed in the 19th century, followed by the Communist Party in the 20th century. About 20% of the population is Christian. In addition, the Nair, one of the Hindu castes, which comprise another 20% of the population, have matrilineal property rights, giving women greater voice than elsewhere. Life expectancy in Kerala has been higher not only than the rest of India, but also higher than China (except for wealthy cities such as Shanghai and Beijing).

[†] Kerala has tended to rely on earning income by people going abroad and working, rather than developing domestic industries in the way China has. Kerala has something to learn from China.

to poverty. I do not think that is the right way of understanding it. Poverty elimination requires action on many different fronts. It requires land reform, education, health care, epidemiology, microcredit, development of social infrastructure, and development of physical infrastructure—roads, water, electricity, communication, and so on. It is not a question of one right approach. It is never going to be like that. We have to see what is the right balance of these things.

Sometimes people ask whether microcredit will eliminate poverty. Of course it will not. Will it help eliminate poverty? Of course it will. But you need other things. You need schooling, you need hospitals, you need roads and power and communication, and all those things. You can do a lot to reduce wealth inequality. For those who cultivate land, land ownership and credit are very important. Similarly, if you want to enter business but you have no capital, then microcredit could be very important. So it is a question of putting all these in a big picture.

Democracy is favorable to poverty elimination. We can never find a lasting solution to poverty without the public having a clear comprehension of what poverty is, why it arises, what we can do about it. It is that understanding that makes elimination of poverty possible. Democracy is primarily a method of public reasoning, and we have to reason about these things, which is why the clarity of understanding is so important. There is no way of being sure that we are doing the right thing unless the public knows what we are doing, why we are doing it, and why there is a case for us to do it. That participatory democratic solution is ultimately the way to eradicate poverty in a lasting, deep-seated way.

Jim Shultz Executive Director, Democracy Center

The Bechtel Corporation took over the water company of Cochabamba as part of a general pattern of privatization in Bolivia. After Bechtel raised water rates rapidly, the people revolted, and the water company was returned to the public. Privatization does not simply reflect self-interest. Instead, it derives from bad "economic theology," which claims that the "free market" can solve all problems, but which actually disempowers the poor. The revolt was as much a reaction to that disempowerment as it was to water rates. It was an act of resistance to the foreign institutions that have long controlled

Bolivia and other countries. The revolt in Cochabamba is a global symbol because it demonstrates that citizens can reclaim power. Progressive governments in Latin America now have a brief window of opportunity to prove they can achieve results. If they do not succeed, historic patterns suggest there may be a return to dictatorships.

Background to the Water War

A country's public policies are a big part of what helps it move out of poverty. In Bolivia the most important public policy decisions were largely taken out of the people's hands. Water, the gas and oil industry, the national airline, and the trains were all privatized. There can be a reasonable debate about whether these things should be public or private, but the people who have to live with those decisions should be able to make them. In Bolivia, those decisions have largely been taken out of people's hands by international financial institutions (IFIs) led by the World Bank and the International Monetary Fund (IMF).

Dependent countries become indebted to these lenders. To service that debt, they have to deal with "conditionalities," conditions imposed by the lender, such as privatization of public assets.

In the United States we have publicly debated whether health care, social security, and education should be public or private. The World Bank and the IMF took those decisions out of the hands of the Bolivians and made them behind closed doors with a bunch of economists in Washington DC. The results in Bolivia did not turn out so well.

One result was the famous water revolt in Cochabamba, a city of 500,000 that had doubled in the last 15 years. Expanding the water system to low-income neighborhoods was going to be expensive. Foreign aid was needed. The World Bank told Bolivia in 1997: "If you want money to extend water services in Cochabamba, or anywhere in Bolivia, you will privatize the water system of Cochabamba." So, in 1999, the government gave a 40-year lease to the Bechtel Corporation, one of the world's largest corporations. The water system never would have been privatized and certainly not in the way that it was, unless the World Bank had ordered it.

Bechtel is politically connected. Along with Halliburton, they got a no-bid contract for the reconstruction of Iraq. They came to Cochabamba and, within a month, they raised people's water rates by an average of 50 percent and in some cases double and more. People took to the streets and said they would not take it. They faced down bullets and faced down a state of martial law and faced down one of the most powerful corporations in the world.

They kicked Bechtel out and retook the public water system.

The IMF and Bolivia's Deficit

In February 2003, the IMF, told the Bolivian government: "Your public deficit is much too high." As a percentage of its budget, the Bolivian deficit was much smaller than the Bush administration's deficit. The IMF said, "Cut your deficit by 250 million dollars or we will reduce your foreign aid."

The Bolivian government scrambled. There was a proposal to raise the taxes on foreign oil companies, but the president did not want to risk scaring them away. Instead, the government imposed a tax on working people, even people who earned only $100 a month. The reaction was heated. For a day there was a shooting war on the steps of the presidential palace, between the national police and the army. The police sided with the social movements, against the tax increase. The army was sent to stop the protests. During the course of two days, 34 people were killed. That crisis is directly the result of what the IMF did here.

So these are two examples of foreign institutions dictating policy to Bolivia and creating havoc. The officials of those institutions assume they know how the world works from theoretical papers. But it does not work that way on the ground. They tell a country to reduce its deficit, and 34 people die. They say, "It was not our fault. You must have just implemented it wrong." They say to a country, "Privatize your water system." Then people earning $100 a month are asked to spend $15 for water, and the World Bank says, "We did not mean it to be like that. You must have implemented it wrong." They think there is nothing wrong with the theory; the implementation is wrong. No, it is the theory. This commands from outside economists have not worked out well in Bolivia.

Faulty Economic Theology

Some people imagine that economic self-interest drives the system. But you can confront and manipulate self-interest. The problem is more dangerous. It is theology, economic theology. In the 1980s, the US and England were overtaken by an economic theology full of self-interest. It was about "how the world works." The IMF and the World Bank became the foreign missionaries, and "conditionalities" became the bible they used to impose that theology.

It is a mistake to dismiss this ideology as an effort to defend the interests of foreign corporations. Yes, those interests exist, but in some ways economic theology is more dangerous. I call it theology because people believe in it as an act of faith, without proof and do not allow it to be challenged. Imposing that ideological vision of what it takes to combat poverty—that a free market will make everybody better off—is failed theology.

The reason people in poor countries reject these policies is not ideological. Poor people cannot afford economic theology. It is a luxury. They want clean water, good teachers for their kids, access to health care, passable roads, and access to markets. If the free market theories had worked, people would have embraced them. People reject these theories and the Washington Consensus because they failed. The people have made it clear, in elections and rebellions, that these policies do not work for them. Policy makers should start to figure out that the protestors, whether in the streets or at the ballot box, know what they are talking about.

When people with power get invested in a theory, they lose the ability to admit when it has gone wrong. George Bush still believes the war in Iraq is right. It is hard for powerful people to say, "I was completely wrong." That level of humility and introspection is rare. That is why it takes protests to change policies.

Authority and Arrogance

One definition of democracy is that people with authority are directly accountable to the people over whom they have authority. The IMF and the World Bank have no accountability to the Bolivian people. How is a woman who knits baby clothes for a living, who gets stuck with a catastrophic water bill, supposed to influence the World Bank? She can influence the mayor, or the governor, or the president, but not the IMF or World Bank. So, why should they be the government of Bolivia? For two decades they essentially have been a completely unelected, unaccountable government of Bolivia.

Is economic self-interest a factor in all of this? Yes.* But more powerful than self-interest is the arrogance of US officials thinking they are capable of managing the world without listening to the people who are affected. This arrogance of power is one reason why a global movement of young people has challenged these global bullies. They smell the arrogance of power first, because they are so used to it.

---

* Ed.: Shultz points out that foreign aid benefits American companies that sell $3 in goods for every $1 the World Bank invests in developing countries.

Privatization and Resistance

Bolivia has become an inspiration, a symbol all over the world, by showing that "the empire has no clothes." After the 1980s, the IFIs developed a new mission to lend money to poor countries to support their budgets (IMF) or infrastructure projects (the World Bank). Bolivia became the lab rat. Bolivia was the chief test rat in South America for the policies of privatization and market fundamentalism, which led to the water revolt and other issues here in Bolivia.

In Bolivia, the IMF promoted privatization of natural gas, the national airlines, and water. The gas industry was sold at bargain-basement prices to Shell, British Petroleum, Petrogas of Brazil, and Repsol of Spain. Water was traded away to Suez of France and Bechtel of the US. The national airline, LAB, was transferred first to some Brazilian investors, and then to a wealthy businessman who completely screwed it up. Now he is not permitted to reenter the country without being prosecuted.

But privatization has created global resistance. The water revolt in Cochabamba was always an international story, because the World Bank set the chain of events in motion. There there are three reasons the story got global recognition. First, it was just a very compelling story, like David and Goliath. Second, it occurred in 2000, soon after the Internet had become a common tool among activists. I was in Washington DC just after the water revolt ended, sitting in Dupont Circle, and some young women from Oberlin College in Ohio approached me about the protests against the World Bank. They asked where I was from. When I said, "Cochabamba," they knew everything, even knew the names of the people I interviewed. That is when I realized the power of the Internet. Third, it was an accident of timing. Three days after the water revolt, tens of thousands of people gathered in Washington DC to protest the policies of the World Bank and the IMF. It was the first protest of its kind after Seattle in 1999. The water revolt was iconic, as was its spokesman—a former factory worker, Oscar Olivera.

But the work of the water revolt is only half done. Yes, the people of Cochabamba removed a foreign corporation from ownership of their water. But they are still trying to build an honest, effcient, and publicly responsive water company. That work still needs to be done. People should be cautious about putting the water revolt too much on a pedestal.

Power is largely psychological. We have been hypnotized by media, governments and coporations to believe that economic justice is not achievable in this world. They limit our imagination about what is possible. The people of Cochabamba overcame those powerful messages and did the impossible: they reversed water privatization. When people demonstrate that kind of courage and win, it communicates to people all over the world that another world is possible. That is why the water revolt in Cochabamba is invoked again and again.

I recently asked a group of college students from the US why they came to Bolivia. One said, "Because Bolivia is right now what I wish my country would be." Bolivia is like the younger sibling who amazes her family with her courage and inspires the world by just being who she is.

The Future of the Left in Latin America

Progressive social movements have been given a chance to prove themselves, now that they are in power in several countries in Latin America. If they can deliver needed public services and create jobs—they will have a long run of support. If they fail, they will have a short run. In the 1960s and 1970s, there were right-wing dictatorships with left-wing insurgencies, followed by peace agreements that put into office people as conservative as the dictatorships. In Bolivia, for example, the new governments abided by conservative, market-oriented, Washington Consensus economic policies.

At that point, the Left split its attention, with half forming social movements and half forming left political parties. Subsequently, the conservative elected governments have fallen in Argentina, Brazil, Bolivia, Chile, and Venezuela. The new left-leaning governments must succeed, not just to keep the Left alive, but also because poor people in those countries need economic advancement.

A transformation of economic, political and social power does not happen smoothly or overnight. I just hope it happens nonviolently. Bolivia looks at South Africa as an inspiration. This same kind of thing happens when you have a marginalized ethnic majority that finally has found its place in taking on political power and is working out what that means.

Joao Pedro Stedile *National Coordinator, Landless Workers' Movement, Brazil*

The MST or Landless Workers' Movement in Brazil does more than fight to redistribute land to laborers who have none. It also seeks to 1) shift agricultural production from exports to satisfying domestic needs for food, 2) improve education for the poor, 3) replace chemically-based agriculture with ecological agriculture, and 4) provide workers with leisure time for self-development. The conflict in the countryside is no longer only with the rural oligarchy, as in the past. Now, the landless must also organize to fight against multinationals, which control world trade and the methods of agricultural production. For example, they occupied land on which Cigenta was illegally growing transgenic corn seeds. Poverty remains a big problem throughout Brazil. The landless are only one segment of the poor. The hope for the future lies with urban youth.

The MST (*Movimiento Sem Terra*—Landless Workers' Movement) seeks to enforce the agricultural reform law, which permits the government to take unproductive land from the big landowners and redistribute it to the landless.

Agricultural labor is very hard. Families earn less than 100 dollars a month and lack basic necessities. Every morning the workers ride in the back of trucks to the big plantations that grow export crops, such as cotton, sugarcane, soybeans, and coffee. Generally, they work as share-croppers. After the harvest they pay part of their production to the landowner. Many poor farmers own around 5 or 10 acres. When their children become adults, they cannot afford to buy land. It is too expensive. Landless workers generally have work only in periods of planting and harvesting, perhaps six months of the year. After that, they migrate to other regions, or they have no work.

Agricultural Reform: Moving Beyond the Fields

Agricultural land redistribution does not work any more. We propose popular agricultural reform. The first characteristic of this reform is that poor farmers need to organize themselves in cooperatives and shift production from exports to the internal market—producing food for own people. In Brazil, 50 million people are starving every day. We import milk from Europe, rice from Thailand, and other consumption items from Argentina, Uruguay and Chile. The second characteristic of popular agricultural reform is education. Currently, farmers only have access to four years of

344

school. Around 65% of landless adults are illiterate. Knowledge, not property in land, is what sets people free. The third characteristic is that we need to develop ecological agriculture, without poisons. Fourth, cooperative production will create a division of labor and give people more free time. This will set them free as human beings.

Fighting Against Multinationals

Multinational corporations, like Cargil, Nestle, Monsanto, Parmalat, Bungee, and Unilever, control the world's agricultural markets and prices. Farmers all over the world feel exploited by them. We organized the *viacampesina*, which represents all the farmer movements in the whole world. The farmers and people who are exploited by these corporations are intensifying their actions against transgenics, chemicals, and price exploitation, confronting corporations on an international level. We do not expect the Brazilian government to support changes. Governments always defend economic interests, even they are elected with leftist speeches. We have no illusions. We want to organize the people, so they can fight for change. In Latin America, unfortunately, we are in a period of decline in the base of the social movements. This contrasts with other periods, such as the 1960s, when base movements were growing. But the domination of neoliberalism is ending, which will lead to renewed growth of base movements. The rise of base movements will oblige governments to abandon the neoliberal and pro-imperialist project and to organize the economy in favor to the people.

Before 1930, the rural oligarchy dominated Brazil. After 1930, the industrial bourgeoisie gained control. Recently, an alliance developed between the rural oligarchs who control the land and the multinationals that control world markets. In Brazil, Bungee, Cargil, Monsanto, and Du Pont export soybeans. Cargil and Du Pont export corn. Anderson Claitho, Unilever, and Monsanto export cotton.

As a result, the fight for the agricultural reform is not just an effort to defeat the rural oligarchy. It is also a fight against the neoliberal model, against imperialism, and against the multinationals. That is why MST became politicized. To have real agricultural reform in Brazil, we need to expel Monsanto, Bungee, Cargil, Cigenta, and all of the multinational corporations that control Brazilian agriculture.[*]

---

[*] In the past, it was said that when a multinational corporation was expelled from a country, the Americans would send in the Marines. We do not believe anymore in the petulance of the American military. They are being expelled from Iraq, will be

During the1990s, Latin America exported 1 trillion dollars to the US in the form of profit remittances, royalties, and service payments. That is the exploitation we need to break. The US government uses agricultural subsides in order to generate unfair price competition. This is their problem. What we have to think about is our country. And our territory. Some Latin American countries, like Uruguay, Guatemala, Chile, are too small and specialized in their agriculture to be set free from North American exploitation. That is where the project to liberate Latin America comes in. Larger countries can organize their economies to be free from the multinationals, and Latin American economies can become more integrated. That is Hugo Chávez's project.

Our fight for agricultural reform in Brazil involves more than occupying plantations. That remains important, and we will keep doing it. But our focus is now on fighting the multinational corporations that dominate the market and exploit farmers with chemicals and transgenic seeds. For example, farmwomen occupied the eucalyptus fields of a big Norwegian corporation called Aracruz in Brazil. They destroyed the seedlings. Eight million eucalyptus seedlings were destroyed in one night to protest the monoculture of eucalyptus, which exports cellulose, and leaves all the pollution in Brazil.

A second example was our fight against Cigenta Seeds, which controls the transgenic corn, cotton, and soy seeds. In Brazil, it is still prohibited to have transgenic corn seeds. Only soy and cotton seeds are allowed. This corporation had a small corn seed farm in Paraná, where they were committing two offenses. First, they were multiplying corn seeds. Second, they were doing this in a farm very close to the Iguaçu National Reserve Park. MST occupied this farm to denounce their illegal activities. A judge demanded that Cigenta close the facility, and imposed a fine on the local government if it failed to evict the corporation from those lands. The Brazilian government changed the law, to allow Cigenta to grow these seeds near the national park, but the law has still not been approved. Shortly after the elections, the government of Paraná expelled Cigenta from those lands and created an ecological agriculture research and develop center.

Poverty and Inequality in Brazil

Poverty and social inequality are two problems we have inherited from

expelled from Afghanistan, and certainly all the intellectuals, like Chomsky and others in the US, are predicting the end of the American empire. As we light fireworks for the death of Pinochet, we will do it for the end of the empire.

the past. Whereas the wealthiest 1% of the population holds almost 50% of the country's wealth, 48% of the Brazilian population is classified as poor. Multinationals and neoliberalism have made these two problems worse. São Paulo is second only to New York City in helicopter consumption. It is also the city with the largest number of prisoners: 150,000 in jail. They are mostly in jail for petty theft, crimes committed so they will not starve to death. Unemployment is now at the highest level in Brazil's history, with 25% of the adult population unemployed, almost half of them between 16 and 24 years old. Only 8% of youth old enough to go to university can afford to enter Brazilian universities. This is a shame. In Bolivia, which is even poorer than Brazil, 20% of the youth attend university. In Korea, that has a smaller gross domestic product than Brazil, 97% of the youth attend university. In the medium term, this denial of a future to the youth of Brazil will generate a popular rebellion.

We hope our youth will have the energy to solve this problem that the neoliberal model and the multinationals brought. The landless are a small percentage of this. We represent only 10% of the Brazilian population. We are among the poorest, but we believe that the real changes in Brazil will come from the young population that live in the cities.

Squatters *Northern Brazil*

Editor's note: These are parts of interviews with two families that live on land in northern Brazil that was occupied by the MST, the Landless Workers' Movement. Under Brazilian law, land-occupiers may claim unused land if they squat on the land and if the owner does not make adequate use of it. This practice leads to conflict and violence, as revealed in the interviews.

Squatter #1: I arrived here on January 20, 1996 when the militants of the Landless Workers' Movement (MST) called me to join them occupying some land. So I quit my job at a factory and I came to the camp along with my *companheiros.* They had already been evicted once when they staged a protest. They lay on the ground for an hour at noon on a hot day. Over 700 police showed up and the *companheiros* had to run to avoid being arrested or killed. The *companheiros* went away for 60 days and after that they returned and occupied the heart of a large estate. On this occasion, I was with them. We were evicted. We went to a farming village in Retiro, and the State government gave a piece of land to some of my friends. To make the story short, we were evicted four times by the court and three times by gunmen and the police. We resisted. With the help of friends and politicians, we gained control of the land on February 18, 1997, but even as we were celebrating the victory, the landlord appealed to a higher court in Brasilia.

In May (2006), some of us participated in a meeting with national president of INCRA [the National Institute for the Agrarian Reform]. We were celebrating a new victory, but we found out that our case was in court again, because the landlords were claiming the land. We [the occupiers] were desperate; we did not know what to do. We were still on the land, but we knew if we did not leave, there would be a massacre. But we are not going to give the land back so easily after 12 years of resistance. Fifty-nine *companheiros* here have already gotten houses. When we acquire land through resistance, the rich people do not want us to have dignity, or to be free. We are still fighting, and we are not going to stop. The *companheiros* have the right to have land.

If someone comes to remove us from our house, we say that we are not going to leave, because we have been here for 12 years and not 12 days. We are going to reclaim what is ours. The landlord's gunmen and the police come. The police are paid off by the landlords. They come to confront us and to do a massacre. If the children are in front, they will be massacred. They like to attack during the night. Once they came during the night and attacked us, and we had to run with the children to avoid a massacre. They kill in cold blood. They do a massacre in cold blood.

Squatter #2: I began cutting sugarcane when I was eight years old and did that until I was thirty five.

The work was terrible. Every morning at three o'clock, we left the house to walk five kilometers to work. At work, they exploited us by not weighing the sugar properly. They stole from us. The managers were very violent. They treated us like dogs. We had little food to eat: some yucca, sometimes manioca flour, a few sardines, but they were not real sardines. There were 14 people in our family. Everybody had to work just to get that food. Sometimes other families came to our house that had no food at all. We had to feed them all.

When I was 35, I almost got in a fight with the manager, so I went to tell the boss about it. He gave me some money and told me to leave.

I moved to San Paulo. I got a very good job in the oil business, but I missed my family so I came back to Recife. Also, I did not like construction work. I prefer farmwork.

348

At first, in Recife, I did not find any work, but then in 1995, my companions called me to occupy this land near Recife. The landlords lied to the judge about the land we occupied, which is why they won in court. So now we are expecting at any moment that men will come with guns to throw us off the land. They are already invading the land we have planted with their machines. They are doing anything they can to get rid of us.

Joseph Stiglitz *Former Chief Economist, World Bank*

Northern countries dominate decision-making processes that are part of gloablization, and the rules they establish are unfair to developing countries. The rich countries subsidize their own farmers and impose tariffs on manufactured goods from the global South. Both actions impede development. The Washington Consensus caused policies to be imposed on developing countries that were harmful, particularly the liberalization of short-term capital investment, which has destabilized economies. The key principle of development is "balance." That includes a balance between government and markets, a balance between growth and equity, a balance between pragmatism and ideology. There is no single solution to the problem of development.

The False Promise of Globalization

In the beginning of the modern era of globalization it was hoped that a rising tide would lift all boats. We did not have to worry about the problems of inequality. We were told that globalization would lead to more growth and everybody would benefit. A more apt metaphor is to say a riptide knocks down some of the smaller boats, and if you do not have life vests you drown. Globalization has exposed countries and individuals to new risks, new challenges. Predictably, some people have been made worse off. The theory predicted that the winners could compensate the losers, that there would be huge gains to offset the losses. In fact, the winners have not compensated the losers. Too often globalization has been used as an excuse to weaken social protections and to lower taxes in order to compete. As that happens, the underlying problems represented by the economic disparities are exacerbated.

Globalization has been mismanaged at two different levels: 1) the rules of the game have not been fair to the developing countries and 2) the advice that has been given by the International Monetary Fund (IMF) and the World Bank has also increased the vulnerabilities of the most vulnerable.

The fact that the rules of the game have been unfair is exemplified by the trade agreement that was signed in 1994 in Marrakesh. The poorest countries of the world, particularly in Africa, were made worse off. Everybody had expected the United States and the European Union to get the lion's share of the gain, but they had not really expected that they would force an agreement on the poorer countries that was so asymmetric that the poorest countries were actually worse off.

The IMF and the World Bank foist policies on developing countries based on a commitment to an ideology, a flawed ideology that says markets will solve all problems, that puts little or no emphasis on problems of inequality. That ideology has pushed policies like liberalization and privatization. In some cases they have led to growth. In others they have not. But in many cases, even when they have led to growth, they have led to some groups in the society being exposed to new risks, some groups in societies being pushed into poverty, and there have not been the concomitant social safety nets to protect those who have been made worse off.

Northern Agriculture Subsidies Depress Southern Prices

That is an example of how the rules of the game are stacked against the developing countries. The developed countries have kept their subsidies on agriculture, on cotton, on corn and other crops, and at the same time have forced the developing countries to take away their subsidies, open up their markets. The result has been that the price of agricultural goods is depressed. This is so important for developing countries because 70% of the people depend directly or indirectly on agriculture.

In the United States, farmers are richer than average. Three to four billion dollars a year is divided among 25,000 rich American cotton farmers. As a result of these cotton subsidies, they are encouraged to produce more. As they produce more it drives down the global price of cotton. Without those subsidies, America would not be exporting cotton at all. With these subsidies, America is the largest cotton producer in the world. As the price gets lower and lower, approximately ten million sub-Saharan cotton farmers are made worse off. Many of them live on the verge of subsistence, and so when you make the prices lower and their incomes lower it can have a devastating effect. That is an example of how the rules of the game are stacked against the developing countries.

Flawed Thinking Behind Globalization

I know some people who believed that globalization would make everybody better off. They believed in trickle down economics. They believed that if you only made the economy grow, everybody would benefit. But growth alone does not raise people out of poverty.

What was particularly flawed about a lot of these theories of globalization was that they did not lead to economic growth. That suggests to some extent flawed economics but also an important role for interest. Take the most dramatic example of this, capital market liberalization, opening up capital markets to the free flow of short-term capital. Everybody thought it was important to open up markets to foreign direct investment. But you cannot build a factory on the basis of money that can come in and out of a country overnight. The IMF tried to change its charter in September of 1997 to force countries to liberalize, to open up their capital markets. At the time they did it, they had no evidence that it would promote economic growth, and there was ample evidence, both in the World Bank and elsewhere, that it would lead to more instability. And yet they pursued it. My interpretation is that Wall Street wanted it. Later on they began to look at the evidence and they concluded that its effects are, at best, ambiguous and, in the case of many developing countries, significantly adverse.

World Bank, IMF as Rich-Nation Clubs

The IMF was established with the World Bank at the end of World War II. They are called the Bretton Woods organizations because they were established at an international conference at Bretton Woods, New Hampshire in 1944. At that time, most of the developing countries were colonies. The IMF and World Bank formed a club of the rich countries that would pursue their own interests.

At the IMF, there is only one country that has the veto power and that is the United States. The G7, the richest industrial countries, collectively get more than 50% of the vote. The head of the IMF is chosen by a European, by convention. The head of the World Bank is always chosen by the American President. When the World Bank recently had to choose a new leader, the person chosen had no experience as an economist, even though the major objective of that institution is promoting economic growth.

It is not surprising, given the problems of governance, that the effectiveness of the institutions is often limited. For instance, there is a lack of transparency. After some of us criticized them for lack of transparency, there were better websites. But that is not what people meant by transparency. They meant participation, understanding of decisions before they get made, not afterwards. International institutions are dominated by special interests within the rich countries that shape an agenda that advances their interests at the expense of the least developed countries and the poorest peoples in these countries.

Those special interests put their own interests over those of their own country, let alone over the world. So, for instance, if you look at the structure of tariffs that are imposed by the United States and the EU, not only do they have the effect of discriminating against the developing countries, the tariffs of the developed countries against the developing countries are four times higher than they are against other developed countries. So it is really discriminatory. The structure of those tariffs has the effect of impeding industrialization. There are much higher tariffs on finished goods than on less finished goods. These tariffs prevent the development in poor countries of the first stage of natural industrialization, by protecting the industries in the US and EU that process raw agricultural goods.

Comparing Latin America and East Asia in Terms of the Washington Consensus

The Washington consensus was a set of policies that was a consensus between Fifteenth Street in Washington and Nineteenth Street. Fifteenth Street is where US Treasury is, Eighteenth is the World Bank, Nineteenth is the IMF. It was not a consensus among the developing countries. It was a consensus among a relatively small group of people who had a particular mindset. You have to remember that Reagan was President of the United States, Thatcher was leader in the UK. It was a very conservative mindset that did not reflect good economic policy or economic theory as I would understand those terms. It had a particular political view of economics, one that voters in both the United States and the UK rejected in elections at the end of the 1980s and the beginning of the 1990s. But ironically, as voters in these democracies rejected this particular set of flawed economic policies, it remained in place at these international economic institutions. They continued to push these policies through.

Latin America was the best student of the IMF, of the Washington Consensus policies that focused on price stability, privatization, and liberalization. Argentina was the A+ student within Latin America. And we know these policies have failed. Growth in the 1990s, the decade in which they fully absorbed these lessons, was just over half what it was in the 1950s, 1960s, and 1970s before we taught it how to grow. Not only has growth been lower, it has also been less stable.

East Asia followed a very different model. They focused on macro stability but they meant not just price stability but also real stability, full employment. But they did not focus on privatization and liberalization. When they were forced to, as Korea was when they rapidly liberalized their capital markets, they did run into trouble. But what they did focus on were policies to promote equity, fairness, making sure that the fruits of growth were widely shared, that everybody was educated and in good health. They also focused on technology and on education—to avoid a disparity in knowledge.

The critical difference between East Asia and Latin America was that East Asian countries managed globalization in their own terms.[*] They were not ideologically driven. Latin America followed the IMF prescriptions. Some of the prescriptions were right but some of the prescriptions were clearly wrong. By following that package they had a disastrous record.

The Situation in Africa

Africa, in many ways, is the saddest story of development. Africa today has twice the number of people in poverty than it had twenty years ago. In the case of Africa, globalization is partly accountable for its low economic growth. The rest of the world took advantage of Africa's natural resources in ways that did not fairly compensate these countries, but which did contribute to corruption.

Corruption not only has an adverse economic effect. It also undermines completely the politics of these countries. But it makes sense for a business. If you can bribe a government official, pay him ten million dollars, and get the resources at half value, your profits will be higher. That is the same logic used by advocates of free markets, without government regulation. They say, "Our responsibility is to our shareholders. Our shareholders are better off if we bribe, because we get the raw materials at lower prices

---

[*] Ed.: Elsewhere in the interview, not reported here, Stiglitz emphasized that government has played a strong role in the development of every successful national economy One role of the state is to provide a social insurance system. He explained that Argentina created a massive budget deficit by privatizing its social insurance system under IMF orders, leading to a financial crisis. Americans wisely rejected privatization.

and it increases our profits. What do you expect of us? Isn't this a market economy, what capitalism is all about?"

If globalization is to work we have to have rules and regulations to make it work fairly for the countries of Africa, the poorest countries of the world. So this is an example of one of the ways in which globalization has actually had a negative effect on Africa.

Both in Africa and other developing countries, problems of globalization have mainly stemmed from letting free markets rip without taking into account the asymmetries of power relationships, the asymmetries of economic relationships. For example, when mineral or oil extraction contracts were signed, they often had clauses protecting oil or companies against falling prices of oil. But when oil prices rose from $20 to $80 a barrel, there were no clauses that took more of the revenue for the nation. No one gave developing countries advice about designing contracts that would benefit the people.

Trade Liberalization has Damaged Farmers

In some countries rapid liberalization of trade has meant that corn farmers have to compete with heavily subsidized corn. Their income goes down by as much as fifty per cent as a result of that competition. In each of the commodities we can talk about, opening the markets to highly subsidized agriculture drives down the price and forces farmers out of business or, if they stay in business, leads them to have much lower income. And these are often among the poorest people in the country. So, that is an example where there is a direct link between the policies and the particular people who are suffering.

The IMF would say trade liberalization is going to create new jobs. IMF policies were very effective in causing jobs to disappear, but they did not have the concomitant policies that led to more job creation. People went from low productivity jobs, not to high productivity export industries, but to zero productivity unemployment.

Capital Market Liberalization

The IMF often pushed capital market liberalization, opening up markets to speculative capital flows. You cannot build factories with money that can come in and out overnight. But what you can do is expose a country to enormous instability. Those policies were not sustainable, so the country went into a recession or depression. Unemployment soared. In Indonesia, at one point it was estimated 40 per cent of the people of the island of Java were unemployed, 16 per cent of the people in the country as a whole. In other countries, unemployment would be 10 to 15 per cent. That results in enormous distress and increasing poverty for these people. The effects can be long lasting. When children are put out of school, they typically do not go back again when the economy recovers. So you have a whole cohort of people whose education has been stymied. Malnutrition increased and that can leave a lifelong effect. The final effect is lack of growth. In Latin America, growth was half of what it was in the 1950s, 1960s, and 1970s. In the span of twenty years that kind of discrepancy mounts up and that means incomes are substantially lower than they otherwise would have been. As a result, there are more people in poverty and more suffering than there otherwise would have been.

Can Globalization Work?

There is no single recipe for making globalization work. I have criticized the simplistic policies of the past where they have looked for a magic bullet. There are two things we need to do. We have to become more aware of these adverse effects of globalization on developing countries, such as rising inequality, and we have to improve our political institutions to make them more democratic.

We tempered capitalism in the early twentieth century because we had democracies. In the nineteenth century in many places living standards were dismal. Democracy said we cannot go on this way. It checked unfettered capitalism. In globalization we have not yet done that. We have not learned how to temper globalization. So in my mind the most important thing is to increase the democratic nature of globalization to temper it.

In *Making Globalization Work* I have a whole host of specific reform proposals affecting each of the major areas: intellectual property, trade, natural resources (to make sure countries get paid more for their natural resources), multinational corporations, environment, global financial markets. It is a rich agenda that extends over a whole variety of areas. Let me just mention two areas.

1) After the riots in Seattle at the beginning of a new trade round, the developing countries said we do not want any more of this, because last time we were made worse off. The developed countries came back and said, "Trust us." In November of 2001, they signed an agreement, it was called the Development Round, to remedy the past and help the developing countries. The

United States and the EU reneged on the promises they made. So, one of the things is to go back and renew those promises, but this time to mean it. In *Making Globalization Work,* I offer a comprehensive agenda of a true development round—reforms that could actually help developing countries.

2) Another example is intellectual property. The intellectual property regime has made access to life-saving drugs much more difficult for the poor countries. Taking generics off the market was essentially signing a death warrant for thousands of people who could not afford the medicines. The developing countries have demanded a development-oriented intellectual property regime. What separates the developed and the less developed countries is not just the disparity of resources but a disparity of knowledge. The latter need access to knowledge to overcome the terrible burdens that they face.

The US and the Debt Problem

Repayment of international debt imposes a massive burden on developing countries. In Moldova, a former Soviet republic, the move to a market led to a 70 per cent decline in GDP. When I visited, 75 per cent of that country's budget was being devoted to servicing the foreign debt. It could not afford roads, lighting. We could see the process of de-development in process. The consequences were clearly devastating for the country.

In *Making Globalization Work* I try to identify why the brunt of global instability is felt by the developing countries. Having diagnosed the sources of the problem, I propose concrete solutions to reduce volatility and shift more of its burden to the advanced industrial countries.

The United States is now borrowing three billion dollars a day from countries that are much poorer and still lecturing them about their responsibility. Money that goes to the United States is not available to other countries to promote their development. In the long run, most economists would predict that that would lead to higher interest rates. In the short run, there is this high level of low risk premium that most people in the markets simply cannot understand. When the risk premiums come down, interest rates will rise and the poorer developing countries with high levels of indebtness will face a very serious problem. In short, the imbalances that derive from America's huge government debt are contributing to global financial instability.

Rethinking Development Models

When I was at the World Bank we tried to approach development from a comprehensive point of view. We wanted to avoid the piecemeal way, such as liberalizing trade before you create jobs—a policy that creates unemployment and poverty; not growth and prosperity. The comprehensive approach naturally leads you to think about what are important ingredients to successful development. One of my concerns is always to help strengthen communities, not weaken them. A second ingredient is people, not only in terms of human capital—the instruments of growth—but also in terms of their general well-being—the beneficiaries of growth. Education improves both sides of that equation: improving productivity and improving lives. Education makes their lives richer. Amartya Sen talked about enriching their lives, development as freedom. It is that broader sense of development that I emphasize.

Development requires you to balance between the market and the government. Both have played an important role in every successful economy. In some parts of the world government has been very strong and markets very weak. And so in those countries there has to be an increase in the role of markets. China and Vietnam are examples. But in many other cases, the problem is that the government is weak. Failing states are countries where the government is not doing what it is supposed to do.

The size of government is not as important as what and how the government does what it does. In some cases, it is doing what it should not be doing and not doing what it should be doing. I see success in countries that have done what they should have done, done it well, and the benefits have redounded to everybody in society. Getting the right balance between the role of market, the role of government, and the role of civil society more broadly is absolutely essential for successful development. The attempt to force a simple-minded recipe on all the countries has been a failure.

The Role of Land Tenure and Land Reform

There are two ways in which land is important in connection with poverty. First, there are large numbers of landless workers who have to work as tenants, often on the fringes of society. There is a long history of studies showing that farmers who own their own plots often do better than under sharecropping or as wage laborers. So the lack of ownership of land is a problem. Land reform has been at the beginning of many of the most successful developments. Japan, Korea, Taiwan all began with very important land reforms. So redistributing land is important.

Second, some people have emphasized that titling is important and gone on to argue that it is important because it allows people to borrow against the land and that makes markets more efficient. First, that is not the most important problem in many countries. In Brazil, for instance, people can find access to capital without ownership. Second, there is a problem that if you give land title and people borrow against that land to pay for health care or a wedding, they will not be able to repay easily. Then you will wind up with a large supply of landless workers. Some countries are considering allowing people to borrow against the fruit of the land, against their crop, but not against the land. They have title to the crop so they can borrow some money to pay for seed and fertilizer, but not so much to have a consumption binge. You have to look at this systemically and look at it with caution. Making capital markets work better is a potential source of increased efficiency. But in the long run, if we wind up with more landless people, we will have an economy marked by more poverty.

Taquiro *Farmer, Venezuela*

Taquiro used to work along the coast as a farmer for twelve years. Then the government decided to force the farmers off the land because it wanted the irrigation water for urban uses. Now, he is working a fertile plot of land farther inland, where he is able to raise enough crops to feed his family and to provide for his daughter's special medical needs. In the past, he was persecuted by government. The new government is helping him and other farmers.

Working on His Own Farm

As a youth I worked with my father. At age twenty-five, I got married and went to work alone. I have raised a family, and my wife and I have been married for twenty-eight years now. Thanks to God, here we are, living in peace and always farming the land.

From my farm here, I get our subsistence: the expenses for my daughter, my wife and myself, plus five children and three grandchildren. I have been their life support and they are all in school. I have been working here for a little less than two years. Around the house, we have compacted the soil with feet and bamboo. After adding a bit of cement to it, one treads it under foot to prevent roaches and other insects from nesting too close by.

Thanks to God, after five months here, I was already harvesting enough food from all the plots by planting minor crops, such as cilantro, small onions, garlic, leeks, and other vegetables. As of now, I have enough to last me from December until March. After this I will have other harvests that will give me sufficient merchandise to last until next August. I plant every month of the year. Throughout the year, crops appear, one today, another next week, and they accumulate. So you sell the fruit of your labor at a good price.

When we came here, or rather, when I sought this piece of land here, it was primarily because of my daughter's illness, for she needs a special school. Where we used to live this was nearly impossible to do. For I have always worked and lived as a farmer.

So when we managed to get this little piece of land, little by little, we built this little house. We have planted fruit trees and a few other things. But at least we have some government aid; we have some credit that allows us to move forward. At least now we have something that helps us improve our lives. Moreover, we have received plenty of help from Don Omar, our neighbor here below. We have also received help and support from all the other neighbors. We are making progress little by little. The main thing is that we are here and that they have given us support just as the government has done.

It is now the season to plant a hectare of lemon trees. I need permission from OEA to level some land for planting. For you advance as you plant; you clear away and you plant. Since they do not want idle land, one must at least clear it. To merely plant a grove and then let it stand is not a good idea. In addition to avocado, lemon, and fig trees, we also planted smaller bushy plants. Harvesting the crop from these smaller plants before the lemon harvest helps us maintain a good cash flow. When the lemon trees begin to give fruit, we will have an income throughout the whole year for current expenses. The income from the plants and minor produce is for the occasional purchases of medicines, shoes and clothes. The soil here is so fertile that one hardly needs fertilizers to yield an abundant crop.

Getting Title to the Land

It was extremely important for us to obtain title to this land. It attests to the fact that we are farming the land and that it has been specifically assigned to us for farming. No one can come here and take it away from us by forcing us to move out. The deed was acquired by our own efforts.

To get a property deed for the land was not really difficult. The *Instituto Nacional de Tierra* saw that we were working hard and that our daughter had a very serious condition. At first, they withheld their consent, because I have another plot of land, but it is far away, near the coast. But since my daughter needs medical attention and a special school, which was not available over there, we finally won their attention and received a lot of help. The land title was given to my wife: she is officially the owner of the plot. They could not give it to me. According to the Department of Agriculture, no one may own two pieces of land, especially if they are close to each other.

If we leave land idle, it will be taken away. Although the large landlords do own several properties, things have changed with the recently approved law. According to this new law, anyone holding idle land will lose it to someone who really needs it.

Former Persecution as a Farmer

I like this new policy. I have been a farmer for 47 years. I was persecuted during all those years except for the last 7 years. We have endured great persecution at the hands of the old government, which used used to send the state police or someone from the Department of the Environment. Many of my neighbors and companions engaged in farming were detained as common delinquents and put in the worst and most dangerous jail. Eleven years ago, some friends and relatives of mine were put in jail for 48 days, just for farming the land.

Under the old government, they wanted to do away with all agricultural activities in order to support urban development plans, even though that meant importing our food. The water basins with abundant capacity were to serve the needs of growing towns and cities. Water became scarce. Near the coast where we used to farm, the rivers had plenty of water. But, in accordance with their urban development plans, they kicked people out and used the water for the urban needs. We lost a lot of crop over there for we did not have the means to harvest it on time. We lost millions upon millions of kilos of lettuce, to say the least of yucca roots. I worked over there near the coast for 12 years. But these 12 years were a total loss to me. I had to abandon my farm there, because we were chased out without any compensation. I could no longer afford to feed my family or to take my daughter to the doctor. I ended up trying to catch fish. From there I came here. They did not give us a single *bolivar*—nothing! Out of 600 families that used to live in that area, there are only 6 left.

Under the new government, we have not been persecuted. Rather, we have received help. The present government cares not only for the poor, but for everyone. Thanks to the new president, no one is forcing farmers off their land. Also the new government has built beautifully paved roads linking Macuto, Caracas and Potrillo. Now there is tourism that brings value and work. People have been receiving credit since the last tragedy that struck the area in 1999, when a great landslide left numerous families desolate. The government helped them with credit, seeds for planting, and the offer to rebuild their houses. No one had ever seen such a thing here. Never. In my 53 years, I finally get to see it happening now with the arrival of this president.

I vote for the PPT, the *Patria Para Todos* ("party for all")—for mayor, governor, and president. I voted for the Fifth Republic. This party wants a country for everybody, for all the Venezuelans, for you and me, and for all the non-Venezuelans. We all belong there together in love and affection.

Eric Toussaint *Author, Activist*

Global poverty today arose from domination by Europe, North America, and Japan over the rest of the world. It continues to be based on exploitation, both within countries and between countries. Examples of policies that perpetuate poverty are 1) imposing taxes (VAT) on the poor that hardly touch the rich, 2) imposing school and medical fees on the indigent, and 3) breaking up systems of communal land tenure. The wealth of Europe is not based on its internal de-velopment, but rather on a) stifling production of textiles and  *ceramics in Asia, b) copying their techniques, and c) building up European industries that then sold products in Asia at a profit. Europeans also dispossessed their own workers and exploited them as well. The World Bank is complicit in the impoverishment of the Third World. It legitimized the illegal transfer of sovereign debts from colonial powers to newly independent nations, and later it pressured poor countries to take on more debt, which many defaulted on after the US drove up interest rates four-fold in the early 1980s. The World Bank's own documents show the South was better financially managed than the North in the 1970s, but the South has had to pay for the mistakes of the North, once again. The South resists the North these days. The future balance is hard to predict.*

Poverty Rooted in Colonialism

To understand how we arrived at the present situation in Asia and Latin America, requires historical perspective. The year 1492 is the key date when Europeans began brutally to intervene in the history of the people of the

Americas. They destroyed the highly developed Incan and Aztec civilizations. From that moment forward, one may speak of globalization, because, over the course of the 16th century, all of the continents were connected with each other through European domination.

Normally, the harmful effects of European domination could take time. But in the Americas, the results were immediate. The Caribbean population was wiped out in a short time. The Inca and Aztec Empires lost perhaps three-fourths of their population. By contrast, it took a long time in Asia and Africa, where colonization did not begin in a serious way until the end of the 19th century.

It is interesting to consider that in the 15th and 16th centuries, Europe and the Americas were at the same level of development. China and India were more developed than Europe. Thus, one must explain how two or three centuries of domination by Europe caused a reversal.

By the end of the 19th century, a triad, composed of Western Europe, Japan, and North America began to dictate the rules of the game to the rest of the planet. They imposed a capitalist economic model, which involved transforming a series of elements of economic life into commodities. This process has not come to an end, because there are still societies in which water is held in common, which no one would think of selling. Land is also still held in common in some places. The last wave of capitalist globalization aims at transforming everything into a commodity.

Poverty is generated by a global system of private exchange that transforms human relationships into private goods. One social class controls the major means of production. They transform the rest of the population into salaried employees, sharecroppers, or underemployed informal workers in urban slums. Many people in the Third World have to work 10-14 hours per day, 6-7 days a week, even while the majority of people are unemployed. The threat of replacing a worker with someone who is unemployed enables managers to impose a 10-hour workday. Thus, poverty is not a condition. It is a system of exploitation.

After centuries of imperialism and colonialism, countries are, formally, politically independent. But they are imbedded in an institutional network of neocolonialism because the political options of the indebted countries of the South are largely dictated by the World Bank and the IMF in Washington or by the WTO in Geneva. Through an institutional mixture of rules, Latin America, the Caribbean, Africa, and a large part of Asia have been subdued by a new type of domination.

To keep these countries under control, external debt is a key instrument because it allows the creditor to manage the budget of the debtor and offer advice, in order to be reimbursed. The creditors are organized through the World Bank, the IMF, and the Club of Paris, an informal club of the Northern governments, where G-7 finance ministers meet informally once a month in Bercy. Then, there is the London Club, for the big international bankers.

Creditors impose on the countries of the South a set of disciplines called "conditionalities," which require them to privatize by selling their enterprises to the transnationals. They have to increase their consumption taxes, the most unjust form of taxation, since the people consume their income. In Kenya, 90-95% of the people consume 95% of their monthly income just to survive, and on that, they pay a VAT of around 18%. By contrast, a rich person spends only 5-10% of income per month, so the VAT is only 18% of 5 or 10% of income. If capitalists in the South receive no capital gains, then they pay almost no tax at all.

The World Bank and the IMF require an increase in the indirect taxes paid mostly by the poor. They also require the poor to pay school fees and fees for health care plus surcharges, imposed by the bank. As a result, in many African countries, when people arrive at a hospital in terrible shape, they are left in the waiting room if they cannot pay for the operating room. So, 25-35% of patients die without receiving care.

The World Bank and IMF also insist that countries create a land market. In countries where there is still a tradition of common land ownership, the World Bank devised a formula a few years ago for the creation of a land market. The World Bank required Mexico to change Article 26 of its constitution at the beginning of the 1990s to permit the private ownership and sale of what were common *(ejido)* lands. To escape the burden of their debt, peasants sold their land. The loss of their land was the basis of the *Zapatista* revolt on January 1, 1994, which signaled the beginning of a new international resistance. The resistance in Chiapas by peasants and Mayan population spread to Bolivia, where a similar struggle of indigenous people took place. It is extraordinary that oppressed people could form a movement that would formulate universal propositions for the emancipation of the world.

Historical Exploitation

The neoliberal thesis sees the wealth attained by Europeans under adverse conditions as proof that they are the elect, according to the Protestant religion. It proves that they adopted a better economic system than any other.

What no one says is that the Dutch were truly savage in the way they exploited their Asian colonies or that their commercial success came from products they imported from Asia. This enabled Amsterdam to become the financial capital of the world before it was transferred to London in the 18th century.

Financial centers determined the prices of raw materials from the South. Part of their power and wealth came from exploiting the South. Another part derived from exploiting their own people. This was notably true of the textile and ceramics industies, each of which the Dutch destroyed in Indonesia to construct their own. Dutch products were actually based on techniques copied in Indonesia, particularly Java. The Dutch industries exploited the Dutch people, who worked 12 to 14 hours a day.

The British followed the same pattern. At home, they deprived people of their land through the enclosure movement and then exploited them in urban factories. Abroad, they destroyed the Indian textile industry, which was clearly better than the British, and forbade the import of sheets and other manufactured products from the colonies. Then they copied Indian techniques, and exported cotton textiles to India and forced them upon the Indians. As Balzac wrote "Behind every great fortune lies a crime."* Genocide is the basis of the wealth of the businesses of the North. The wealth of the North, owes a debt to the South—historical, social, ecological, and cultural. The people of the South, as creditors of Northern wealth, are perfectly right to demand reparations. We should not speak of Northern generosity.

World Bank Mission: Not Fighting Poverty

Exploitation continues in the form of low export prices of raw materials from the South. Only 3% or 4% of the price of a cup of coffee in a supermarket goes to pay the producer.

Coffee produced in Kenya, Mexico, or Indonesia is sold to you by a chain of intermediaries. Even though the wealth is produced in the South, the profits are realized in the North, thereby perpetuating the domination of the North.

In my last book on the World Bank, *The World Bank, permanent coup d'etat,* and the hidden agenda of the Washington Consensus, I showed that the World Bank never had a mission to reduce poverty. Its mission has always been to open the economies of the South for the exports and investments of the economies of the North.

---

* "The secret of great wealth with no obvious source is some forgotten crime, forgotten because it was done neatly." (from Balzac's novel, *Le Père Goriot*)

I reveal in my book something you won't find anywhere else. A World Bank report reveals an "original sin" as follows: In total contradiction of international law, when Kenya and other African countries became independent, they inherited the debt the UK, France, and Belgium contracted in colonizing Africa. Since the Versailles Treaty, debts contracted by colonial powers in colonizing a country cannot be passed on to the colony upon independence.[†] The World Bank encouraged the new states to become more indebted, even though internal Bank documents revealed that the debt burden on the South was becoming unsustainable.

MacNamara became president of the World Bank in 1968, at the end of the Vietnam War. Putting a war leader in charge of an organization that is charged with fighting poverty is the wrong person for the job. He proposed to fight poverty within the World Bank ideology, but he also supported enormous energy projects that further increased the debt of the South, such as the Inga Dam on the lower Congo. He launched the Green Revolution, the development and use of new seed varieties, along with massive quantities of pesticides, herbicides, and fertilizers, which industrialized agriculture. That brought about the dependence of peasants on products that were then monopolized by Monsanto, such as herbicides and transgenic seeds. It seems to have been premeditated.

When the inevitable debt crisis in the Third World arrived in 1982, the World Bank was surprised, and said "Sorry, but you have to adjust your economies." Paul Volcker, head of the US Federal Reserve, had precipitated the debt crisis by raising interest rates by a factor of four. Many countries had variable interest rates, indexed to London and New York. When interest rates rose, they were strangled and defaulted on their loans. At the same time, in 1981, the price of raw materials (copper and nickel) and agricultural exports (coffee and tea) fell compared to the 1970s, along with petroleum prices, leaving the South more indebted.

The IMF and World Bank, which had created those conditions, began to impose "structural adjustments" on the economies of the Third World. As I show in my book, *The World Bank*, in its annual reports of 1979 to 1981, stated that the countries of the South managed their economies better than in the North, because in the North, there was an historic economic crisis.

---

† Ed.: Toussaint adds that the World Bank not only treated the illegal debt as legitimate, but also encouraged developing countries to take on more debt, to give up food security in order to concentrate on exports of a few tropical products, and to import grain from the North.

In 1983 and 1984, the World Bank changed its tune in its report and said, in effect, that the South had borrowed too much, that their economies were badly managed, and that they had to pay the price and make adjustments. Countries were first pushed into the debt trap, then the trap shut on them. People then began talking of globalization, which had a political dimension: the North aggresively seeking to retake control of the South.

In the 1960s and 1970s, there was progress in the South on many fronts. The nations of the South sought to create greater autonomy and greater solidarity and to implement a model of industrialization based on import substitution. Large industries were developed in Brazil, Argentina, and Asian countries. The UN created UNCTAD and adopted a resolution on the right of development. The nonaligned movement and socialist experiments (such as Cuba) brought about progress in education and health care. Many nations nationalized their resources.

Northern Domination, Southern Resistance

Nationalization was intolerable to the North, which is why structural adjustment in the 1980s forced privatization of petroleum enterprises, and put them in the hands of the majors. Fortunately, a few countries refused to privatize their oil companies. In others, such as Bolivia, governments are reclaiming control of their natural resources.

It seemed after twenty years of globalization that the World Bank, IMF, and WTO dominated everything. But a timid restoration of balance has begun. In some Latin American countries, they say they are going to break with the global system. On a planetary scale, we are in an extremely interesting period in which those who resist, including governments, are taking timid initiatives.

Those who dominate the world are once again reacting strongly to this, with bombardment, invasion, and subtle ways of issuing rules through bilateral treaties on investments via free trade agreements to codify rules that will imprison the South.[*] It is key to see in the years to come if the governments of the South will cave in or if, under pressure from their own people, they will reject as invalid prior treaties and agreements because they do not respect their national sovereignty. We can only hope they replace those rules with ones that are collaborative and favorable to the economic development of the South and the satisfaction of basic human needs.

---

[*] Ed.: Toussaint points out that the North has already begun to react militarily to changes, such as the US intervention in Afghanistan and Iraq.

Luciana Vanderlei and Husband *Recife, Brazil*

Luciana, her husband, and their children scrape by. The Bolsa Familia *(welfare) program allows them to survive with some dignity, but they still suffer from unemployment and low income.*

Luciana: My husband and I live here in *Brasilia Teimosa* [a *favela* along the water]. We used to leave our house between 4 or 5 in the morning to go fishing. We used to sell them, but few people bought them. Now my only money comes from the government's family grant, *Bolsa Familia.*[†] My husband has not had a regular job for five years. He sells bottles of mineral water for one *Real* each (US 50¢). With his earnings and *Bolsa Familia,* we buy things for our house, we pay for water and utilities, we go to the farmers market, and we buy medicine for the children. I sometimes ask my friends for a loan. They know I will pay them back from the 95 *Reais* (US$50) that I receive each month from *Bolsa Familia.* I go to the market to buy juice, cous-cous, bread, black beans, spaghetti, rice, and milk. Because they are important for my children. I also buy fruits, vegetables, and other things that in the past I could not afford. But now, thank God, I can afford the food for my children, and every day they have something to eat. Because of President Lula we are receiving this money. I also buy books because my children study.

Husband: I used to work delivering gas. But now I am unemployed. If we did not have help from *Bolsa Familia,* we would be living in total misery. I wake up around 5 or 6 in the morning and go to the market to buy bread and butter. At noon I leave my wife some money to buy beans, rice and meat. When we do not have meat, we have eggs. At night I leave her the money I saved during the day to buy coffee, bread, sugar and milk.

[†] Editor's note: At one point in the interivew, Luciana referred to an older program, called *Bolsa Escola,* or school stipend. She expressed confusion about the two programs, stating some other people she knew received money from the school stipend, but her family did not, even though she enrolled her eldest daughter in that program. The Brazilian interviewer offered advice about how to receive more benefits. The significant feature of this conversation was that program benefits are often subject to conflicting understandings among recipients.

Every day is like that.

Luciana: Since he has been unemployed, life has been very hard. We look forward to the time when we are not struggling to bring food home. If you have children, you have to fight to feed them. When they are hungry, they have to eat. With the *Bolsa Familia* [debit] card, I can buy clothes for my children for Christmas. I bought gas on a tab and I paid for it. I want to put my money together with his money and go to the market only once and buy everything for the children and also some clothes for him. We do not have lights. The utility department cut off our light three months ago. I had to choose between eating and paying the utility bill that sometimes is around 60 *Reais* (US$35). For someone who has nothing, that is an absurd amount.

In the past we did not live here. We lived by the beach, but because of a family accident, my little girl passed away at only 9 months. We had to beg for money to bury her body. With the money, we could bury her body and build half of our house, only one wall. But my brother was building his house and he helped us. Now I live here with my five children and my husband.

Adriana Veiga Aranha *Special Adviser on Fome Zero, Brazil's Official "End Hunger" Program*

The "End Hunger" program in Brazil began in 1989 as a proposal submitted by Lula to the then-President. Lula made the program the center of his campaign for president. There is now an integrated program in place, involving many departments of the federal government and local governments. It provides food and social assistance, supports family farming, and makes micro-credit available. These programs have been successful everywhere in Brazil except the rural northeast. In this region, hunger is due to lack of water. Also, Quilomobola (former slave) communities are difficult to reach. The program needs to expand to include agrarian reform and rural electrification. The UN Food and Agriculture Organization believes Brazil has a program that other developing countries can learn from.

History Of Fome Zero

There is enough food in Brazil to feed the whole population but there are people who either do not have money to buy food, or they do not have a piece of land to grow their own food. That is the situation that caused us to invest in a program to combat hunger and poverty.

In the past, several intellectual leaders raised this issue—José de Castro in the 1940s, and more recently Betinho de Souza, with the Committee to Fight Hunger. Now, the government is focusing on hunger and extreme poverty. This started in 1989, after President Lula lost the election. With public support, Lula's political party presented a national food security plan to the president, who created a national food security council. It was later shut down, but we have recreated it. In his last campaign, Lula made *Fome Zero* (literally, "zero hunger") his focus. As soon as he became president, he brought this issue up, despite concerns expressed by international specialists about the implications for the economy. He tried to calm poor people by guaranteeing them food at least three times a day. He then integrated the ministries and their programs in this direction.

Integrative Government Strategy

Fome Zero is a strategy of the federal government, but it integrates all levels of government to make access to food a right. This applies both to rural areas and to urban areas. It deals with food pricing, food quality, and sanitary food production. The law integrates twelve different ministries and forty federal programs. The largest is a family support program called *Bolsa Família*. In addition, there is a program to provide meals in public schools. In Brazil we have 37 million children who eat at school. We also subsidize food through popular restaurants, food banks, and urban agriculture, and we provide nutrition education.

A second element of *Fome Zero* is the strengthening of family farming under a program called PRONAF, which finances family farms. There are 1.65 million producers with access to federal financing, which was expanded from 2 billion to 9 billion *Reais*. The state buys directly from 200,000 family farms to supply its social programs. This helps both small farmers and the recipients of food.

A third element is income creation through micro-credit and other programs to support those who are self-employed.

A fourth component involves mobilization and control in these diverse programs. The national council works with civil society to create a food security policy. We are holding a third national conference with almost 2,000 people participating from every Brazilian state. We have 3,400 social assistance referral centers deal not only with hunger, but also access to information, alcoholism, domestic violence, or sexual exploitation of children.

Geography of Hunger in Brazil

If we could paint the face of hunger in Brazil, it would be a black girl's face. In Brazil, 80% of the population inhabits urban areas, but hunger in rural areas is even more serious because they lack the social webs found in cities (despite urban violence) Although we have reduced malnutrition nationally, our latest research shows we have had little effect on hunger in the dry areas in northeast Brazil. Hunger affects 12% of the children in this region, where a big problem is lack of water. We created a program in semi-arid regions to encourage the capture of rain water using cisterns, which hold enough water for at least a year for a family of four to five people, so they can bathe and cook. Today there 74,000 of them in the semi-arid regions

Quilombolas (communities of slave descendants) face hunger because of isolation and lack of legal title to the land they have been working for generations. We neglected them for 500 years, adding to their difficulties.

Agricultural reform camps in rural areas are another sad reality. Many are located by highways, far from urban areas and public schools, where the children could at least have one meal a day.

New Directions for Government Programs

We are trying to make up for past failures now. More than 90% of the people receiving family assistance are eating three times a day, and a greater variety of foods, with more meat, fruits, and vegetables, which are important in preventing degenerative diseases. We need to build more popular restaurants for the homeless population, particularly in the major cities. People on the street eat cheap food that is high in fat and carbohydrates. We need to expand the program of buying directly from family farmers. Finally, we need to generate employment with education and economic development. The biggest challenge is not only to diminish poverty, but to diminish social inequalities.

Agrarian reform is fundamental to promote access to land, but we also need to insure that small farmers have technical assistance, roads to transport their products to sell, and electricity (*"luz pra todos"* or "light for everyone" in rural areas). Agrarian reform is a comprehensive transformation of rural life, not just giving land. Progress in this area includes providing credit, infrastructure, and agricultural insurance, which helps producers recover in the event of a natural catastrophe until the next harvest.

What Brazil Can Teach the World

A study by the UN's Food and Agriculture Organization about Brazil's anti-hunger program describes the following lessons to be learned by others. First, there must be a political decision in order to make a program successful. Second, the volume of capital must correspond to the task. Third, there needs to be integration among social areas. Fourth, there need to be different programs targeted specifically to rural and urban areas. Finally, it is useful to create a profile of each family so that the best programs may be provided for them.

We have introduced into the international discussion the possibility of ending poverty. If a country produces enough food, there is no reason people should lack basic nourishment. *Fome Zero* brought that to international attention. We created Latin America Against Hunger. FAO has been working with Latin America and the Caribbean, and many countries are participating. Peru has engaged in revenue transfers. Mexico was already doing something before we did. We are beginning to rethink economic development so that it correlates with social development. I hope that we have learned a lesson from this and that we can keep improving these programs.

Antonio Vinidcativo and Edinaldo *Sugarcane Harvesters, Pernambuco State, Brazil*

Sugarcane harvesters in Brazil are forced to work long hours of grueling labor, and yet they do not make enough to provide even the minimum requirements for their families. They have to choose between eating enough to satisfy their own hunger and sending money home for their children. The company that hires them provides them with contaminated water, inadequate equipment, and procedures that cheat workers out of part of their pay. The workers are not happy, but they see little alternative to accepting these terrible working conditions.

Antonio Vindicativo: We are from Paraiba [a state in northeast Brazil]. We are working here as sugarcane harvesters, with a contract of five or six months. It all depends of the grinding. If the grinding lasts six months then we will work here that long. If it stops at five, we only work for five months. We have to pay the bills.

Before we got here, they promised we would have everything: bottles, boots, all set. When we got here, we did not find anything. We got some equipment, bit by bit: the hat, then the boots. When the gloves arrived, there was only enough for one hand. The same with the shin guard. Nothing comes right. Even now, there are some people working barefoot because they do not have all the equipment.

There are four burners for 80 people to cook on. We need to wake up at 1 a.m. to fix breakfast. Otherwise we do not have breakfast. The water for drinking, we need to get it from the well. Water in the sheds where we sleep is no good, even for bathing. If we want to bathe, we have to come at 2:30 or 3. We arrive from our sheds. Women have other days, not the same.

We leave for work around 4:30 a.m. and arrive in the fields around 5 a.m. The work schedule all depends on the person's willingness. If the person is willing to work more, he finishes later.

We bring our groceries from home. We bring it for the 2 weeks. We eat cornmeal, the meal of the poor, sometimes a cookie when we bring it, buy it, and beans, that we leave with the cook. Lots of them leave it with her, but I don't, but those you do, the food is ready when they get back. If we wait to cook the beans ourselves, or make rice or noodles, we eat when it is ready. We mostly eat noodles, rice and cornmeal.

We work for minimum wage. To get more than minimum wage for this work depends on how many *braças* (armloads or bundles) of sugar can a person can harvest. A bundle is about 18 kilograms (40 pounds).[*] Someone working at a fast pace can do 25 bundles.[†] We are paid every two weeks. The base pay is the minimum wage, but sometimes we can even make 200 to 250 *Reais* (about $100-$125), depending on your willingness, because they pay for the production.

We do this kind of work because we do not have any other means. That is all we know how to do. It is not a good job to do. I do not enjoy it. We do it because we do not have any other job opportunity. Some people do not have any education; they did not learn anything, so they do not have any other profession, only this one. We thank God to have this one. It would not be good otherwise. But I work here because there is no other job.

---

[*] Ed.: In a later discussion, one worker says a *braça* weighs about 12-14 kilogram. Another says it depends on how hard the cane is, and that the cane they were cutting at the time of the interview weighs 20 kilograms per *braça*.

[†] Ed.: This would add up to about 500 kilograms or 1,100 pounds.

I would like to work doing some other kind of farming, growing other kinds of crops. That could be better. Unfortunately there is no opportunity for that. I worked some in farming; but farming nowadays is only for those who have the means. Unless you have financial help, it is the same as cutting sugar cane. What you plant is just enough to feed yourself, fill your belly with a cassava, a potato, a yam, some beans. What you get is only for eating. But it is not enough for you to produce and live off it.

Interviewer: What do you think about these movements that help rural workers? Either non-governmental ones and governmental ones. Do you have any idea of what they do to improve your lives or to change it?

Antonio: If the government were going to help people in my situation, the main thing they could do would be to finance people to work. That kind of thing really helps people. But nowadays, many farmers are failing. I have a friend who used to work with twenty people on a farm, but now there are only four, and the owner is having difficulty paying them. This was due to the draught and the long summer. He lost everything as a farm-owner.

The people who get land can get a home. The poor who do not have a house to live in and needs to pay rent are the poor who beg. Nowadays the poor who have a house to live in, a room to live in, without paying rent, can be considered rich.

We make 12 *Reais* and 34 cents a day (about $6.50). To support a family, we have to make sacrifices. If I use all of my earnings for food, it will not work. I need to take some food to my family back at home. When I come to work again, I am broke.[‡] The groceries I bring from home are not enough. If I buy food at the shed, the shed is "rope around your throat." So, I have to go hungry sometimes.

When they pay us, they pay us by check. Since we travel a long distance, through very dangerous places, it is better to receive a check.[§] But it is not that much because they take out union fees. What union can receive fees

---

‡ Another cane harvester interjects: "We pay the Social Security tax, because that tax is on production." Note that the cane harvesters do not earn enough income to provide food for themselves and their families, but they must pay a social security tax on their meager wages.

§ Ed.: Another worker complains, however, about the cost of cashing a check: "Talking about money, you can only cash your check for free if you buy groceries in the market. If we simply want to cash a check, we lose half of the value, around 10 *Reais*. We could cash it at the bank, but no bank is open on the weekend when we might be able to go in.

twice a month? I don't know. We pay 12.80 *Reais* for union fees.*

Edinaldo: I have been working with this mill for four months, and they took my work permit, and they have not returned it to me yet. I have talked to all types of managers. They just keep deceiving me and do not return my card. They ask me to get another permit and to pay the cost of going to the mills I used to work for, to have them fill in the records on the permit.

I want to know when will they return my card. Even if I get the [name of document], it is not worth it, because it is outdated. They say I have to get a new card. For that I need to spend my own money. It will cost me at least 400 *Reais* [a month's wages] to update my card. He should pay for it. I told them if they do not solve this, I will go directly to the Department of Labor to solve this case. That shut them up. It has been fifteen days since I have seen these men.

I get here at 4 a.m. to work. Works starts at 4:30. When I leave for lunch it is already 12:30 or 1:00. Then I eat and continue my work until 5 p.m. That's to make a one and a half time minimum wage. We have to work like that, because there are days when we do not work and we do not get any pay. Just to get minimum daily wage, I have to cut 40 *braças* (bundles), or 32 if the cane is as hard as this one is. If I do not cut that much, I do not get paid.†

At noon, the weariness gets to us, so we look for some shade to be able to eat, the food we do not have. The food that the cook makes gives many of us a stomach ache, so it does not give us the strength to work. The water we bath in has rust. If we take a shower today, the next day we are sick. To avoid illness we go to the river to bathe. But they say that the river has lots of kinds of diseases in it. I cannot bear it. Where we live, the bathroom is not convenient; the water is not even good to cook with. The cooks have complained a lot, but the supervisor does not take any steps to change things. Talking to them is the same as talking to a wall.

They should supply water for us in the field, but they do not. They tell

---

* Ed: Another worker comments about union dues: "The union is inconvenient because we should only pay one wage at the end of the month. That is part of the law. But here we pay twice, since we get paid biweekly. Every two weeks, we get a cut of 12.80 *Reais*.

† Ed.: He later says he has to cut 3,000 kilograms per day, but that would amount to about 150 or more bundles, so it must not be true, based on what he says here and what Antonio has said.

us to bring water with us. By 9 or 10 a.m., our water bottles are dry. We are in bad shape.

For my future, I want to find a job better than this one, because this one does not provide enough pay. I have six children. What I get here, if I eat it all here, I go home with nothing. This way it is impossible to go on. I started cutting and planting cane when I was seventeen. Now I am thirty-one.

To plant the cane, we have to cut it, swing it, dig the juice, sanitize it, cover it, and add fertilizer. Then, during the dry season, we have to add water, or it won't sprout. And in the winter they all sprout.

The bosses here are decent to us generally. But if someone has an accident, there is no ambulance. It is their obligation to have a car here in case someone gets hurt. If the boss is around, he takes the injured person on his motorbike. He has done that. But we do not have an ambulance, which is important for us.

The Landless Worker's Movement, or MST, is very good. I do not know much about it, because I never was part of the MST. My life is just cutting sugar cane. What I think about this law, it's a very good law that was implanted in Brazil to help the poor like us. All those that get a piece of land, have the right to work on their land and produce what they wish. That way, nobody goes hungry or lives in despair as we do here to be able earn our daily bread. That is all done with the help of the government. That is what we need. Working like this is no way to make a living. That is why this world is infested with thieves and killing and unemployment.

At the time of weighing the cane, they cheat us. We call on the man to weigh the cane when it is still raw, right after we bring it in, but he waits until later to weigh it. By the afternoon, it is dry and it weighs less.

Every fifteen days, we take the company bus back to our villages. We go on a Friday and come back on Sunday. Then when we get back on Sunday, we work another 15 days. The bus is not that comfortable due to the ripped seats. We get there all sick from our trip. It is not a bus made to travel far. It would be better not to ride in it. An old bus has no security whatsoever.

They do not pay us well here. They rob us of half of what they owe us. That is not right. If we work four months, they only pay us 200 *Reais*. That is not enough. They even promised that after six months they would give us unemployment insurance. But I do not believe it. No company does that.

Grace Wambi *Tea Plucker, Kenya*

My name is Grace Wambi. I came from Nakuru in the Rift Valley District. I came here to search for a job. I am a tea plucker. My job is very good although sometimes there are some droughts. In January, there is so much sun, so the tea is dry. At that time you cannot even pick even 5 kilograms, which is how the children suffer. We earn only a little money. Our children go a long way to school, so we try to give them some food so that they can go through the day until evening.

Our job is good sometimes: when there is rain, we earn so much money that we can buy clothes and more food, and sometimes we can put a little money away, so when there is no tea we can use it. But in this area we get very little salary. I get about 100 [Kenyan] shillings per day [about $1.50] with my own hands. Some neighbors earn more than that. We work hard to give our children food, clothes, and some money to take to school. I have six children: three are boys and three are girls. So I am working hard so that they do not go to bed without food.

My husband went to search for a job but I still do not know where he went. I am working very hard. These friends of mine are hard workers. They are trying their best to have food and clothes. In our country, we have no permanent jobs. Sometimes we earn so much money, but sometimes we say God will help us when there is no rain. We find a little money that you cannot even divide. You can go to the shop and buy some flour [on credit] until the rain comes and you pay back the shopkeeper. We pay 50 shillings [75¢] for one kilo of flour. When there is no rain, there is not enough food. So you must go to the shopkeeper and borrow there until the rain comes. That is why we are so behind. When the rain comes, you must pay back that money fast, so that you can buy something to eat.

We eat only two times each day. We do not have lunch. So when you leave your house in the morning until this time [about 4 p.m.] you do not have food, but you will sometimes carry some small food, and if there is nothing you go until evening.

For breakfast, sometimes you have tea, sometimes you drink water, but when there is nothing, you go until evening. Our stomachs are very small, because we do not have food every day. So our stomachs are very small. At night we eat *ugali* [corn meal mush]. When there is no drought, we can also eat tomatos because they are very cheap. We eat meat or fish once a month or once every three months.

Michael J. Watts *Director, Institute of International Studies, Professor of Geography, University of California, Berkeley*

Poverty is now part of a world system that creates inequality. As a result of neoliberalism, poverty has taken on a new character. Privatization, unregulated markets, and loss of social services have driven formerly middle-class people into poverty in many countries. To get an accurate picture of poverty, both economic and social measures should be used. Much of the appeal of political Islam today in the developing world is that it seems to offer an alternative development model to neoliberalism and the impersonal forces of the market. The war in Iraq is  *less about control of oil than sending a message that the neoliberal order will be sustained through military force, if necessary. All of these events represent the process by which expansionary capitalism is sustained by looking for a combination of cheap labor, markets for goods, and strategic resources. Completely free markets have never existed. Markets can only operate in some institutional setting. What is at stake today is determining the rules by which markets will function.*

Poverty and the Rise of Neoliberalism

In the late 1970s to 1980s there was a break or watershed. Neoliberalism, laissez-faire economics, and free trade began to dominate development thinking. The counter-revolution called neoliberalism is based on the following ideas: 1) that markets, unregulated free markets, are always an unalloyed good, 2) that the state and the public sector have to be eviscerated or radically contracted, and 3) that development and the eradication of poverty are wrapped up with individual liberty and responsibility. This way of thinking represented the beginning of change in global poverty.

People are now exposed to new risks and insecurities tied to neoliberalism and the evisceration of public protection. In recent decades, most developing countries have undergone structural adjustment or stabilization programs of the World Bank or International Monetary Fund (IMF), which have whittled away social protections. There have been volatile changes in the economy. For example, the 1997 Asia financial crisis threw 40 million people in Indonesia into poverty. In Africa, average standards of living have declined to a level lower than 1960. Inequality has become more pronounced, between North and South and within many developing countries.

The Appeal of Islam in Developing Nations

Political Islam appeals to people across the Muslim world because it emerged from the failure of secular modern nationalism. That failure is tied to Cold War policies of bankrolling corrupt, authoritarian leaders in the Muslim world (among others). We passed over their human rights record and corruption because they were on our side. The Saud family was ferociously anti-communist, and they provided as much oil as we needed cheaply.

The model of secular national development they adopted was a massive failure in Egypt, Saudi Arabia, and Nigeria. Part of this failure comes from the neoliberal elements of the Cold War that tried to make the world safe for US corporate investments. The failure was not wholly due to the US, but to suggest, as Cheney and Rumsfeld have, that the rise of Wahhabism has nothing to do with US policy in Saudi Arabia is madness. The War on Terror and the rise of political Islam are wrapped up with the failure of development, which stems from the Cold War and geopolitics, not just the failure of political leadership in developing states and the austerity programs imposed by the IMF and the World Bank.

Political Islam does not provide a compelling and democratic model for alleviating poverty. But I understand why so many of my friends in Northern Nigeria, who were Marxists and secular nationalists when I first met them, are now Islamist. They rightly see modern development as being a sham. It is wrapped up in imperialism and the domestic failure of a political class. So Islamism holds enormous appeal. It offers a way of rethinking development in religious terms.

There are many Islams, just as there are many Judaisms. The religion of the dominant classes may ultimately be challenged from below. There are strains of social justice or equality within Islam. On the Web, there are ongoing Muslim debates about feminism, human rights, a religious theory of the economy, and Islamic banks. But the dominant strains of Islam are oriented to the centralization of power. Islam has never produced a church in the same way that Christianity did—an organization of political power within a religious community. What is partially at stake in Islam, particularly revolutionary Islam, is the question of authority. Who gets to issue a *fatwa?* Who defines the social and political structure of Islam?

US in Iraq: for Oil or Military Neoliberalism?

This particular moment is important because US policy towards Iraq represents an exercise of imperial power. The US has chosen to secure neoliberalism hegemonically. Normally, that means securing support or consent, but now, the US is shifting from a type of hegemony based on consent to one based on force.

Iraq represents for me not simply blood for oil. Of course, the [George W. Bush] White House has been captured by oil in an unprecedented way, and getting into Iraq was about liberating that oil. But that was not primarily what it was about. More than anything else, Iraq represents an instance of military neoliberalism—an attempt to push forward militarily the American neoliberal project, previously attempted to be secured through hegemonic consensual means. The US is using classic late 19th century gun-boat diplomacy to break down the doors of markets, to push forward its agenda. It is not, in any simple sense, about getting that black stuff. It is about using Iraq to achieve a particular neoconservative vision of exporting democracy through force. Iraq is supposed to serve as an exemplar that if you mess with the neoliberal project, we are prepared to do this. It is a military phase of neoliberalism. That is what is different. It is a continuation of the Cold War, even though there is no Cold War. It set a different stage for development.

Karl Polanyi and the Public Sphere

One of the greatest theorists of the market was a political economist called Karl Polanyi. In *The Great Transformation,* he said that the self-regulating market was always a disaster. It may be a very powerful way of mobilizing resources, but if everything can be and is bought and sold and constitutes a market, it will be at the expense of community, social solidarity, the very idea of civilization. Markets will destroy society, especially when "fictitious commodities" are bought and sold. Examples of fictitious commodities that should not be bought and sold are land, the environment, money, and labor. None of these things is produced to be a commodity, yet they end up in the marketplace. If they are bought and sold, you will have financial speculation, depression, and people buying and selling labor without any social protections.

Polanyi said that when free-market thinking flourishes, it will be captured by ideologues. He was incredibly prescient. He said the free-market ideologues will try to convince everyone that planning or state involvement is the antithesis of freedom. That is now the position of most development thinkers. So we have to reclaim the sense of the public, the sense of planning.

Polanyi felt that periods of neoliberalism would be followed by a return to protecting the environment, labor, and social welfare. When he wrote in 1947, he thought no one had to defend planning. In the last 25 years there has been a resurgence of free-market thinking. It is now difficult in the US to defend the social democratic position—public planning and social protection. We are dominated by a language of individual rights and responsibilities, the idea that the state should only provide an enabling environment for business. This is being contested in relation to development and poverty. We need to endorse and reanimate politics around public action. Social protections need to be in place, especially for the poor. Individual responsibility cannot deal with that.

The question is how public action, social protection, and the commons can be put back on the development agenda. Al Gore's movie, *An Inconvenient Truth*, is about things we share in common and that cannot be privatized. The market, left to its own devices, is not capable of dealing with this. It has to be managed as a commons. There are many kinds of commons: Social Security, land, the airwaves, genetic material. All are being privatized. Privatization is producing new and greater risks. We need a political project to share those risks and diminish them. We have to institutionalize various forms of protection with collective solidarity.

Primitive Accumulation as the Origin of Capitalism

The pre-conditions for capitalism are about what Marx called "Primitive Accumulation." You can only get someone to work in a factory if they do not have access to land. That is a dispossession. Something can only become a market if it is taken out of a non-market context. It can only be a strategic resource if you explore that resource. Primitive accumulation does not happen once. It happened under specific circumstances in Brazil in the 16th century. It is recursive. It happens time and time again under different sorts of conditions. In a way, Iraq is a type of primitive accumulation. It is an attempt to dispossess. History is a series of constant and recursive dispossessions. What is being dispossessed is the way these commons are being appropriated. The commons may be labor and land. The commons may be markets and strategic resources. We are now in the middle of what I call "military neoliberalism."

Diverse Combinations of the Elements of Capitalism

Start with the prerequisites of capitalism. First, capitalism cannot operate without free labor. Labor is a key cost of production. Expansionary capitalism will always be looking for those circumstances. Currently in the textile sector in Bangladesh and Mauritius, this means low-cost labor skilled in key areas and not encumbered by unions. Those conditions are central to profitability in a highly competitive sector, like textiles. Under some circumstances the combination of skill and locale is equally as important as labor costs. For example, the post-1978 expansion in China was about both labor costs and the skills and availability of female labor.

A second prerequisite for capitalism is markets. Opening markets means not only establishing new places to sell. It also means creating institutions for private ownership and dismantling state regulatory structures. The US concern about markets in Venezuela takes the form of applying pressure to return oil to private ownership.

Third, resources are a prerequisite of capitalism. Some have claimed that natural resources no longer matter in the new information economy. There is an enormous amount of hype around this but we are no less dependent on key strategic resources now than we were in 1890. And not just oil. A whole raft of minerals and resources are indispensable, some more than others. Oil is obviously one, but there are many others that are key. Expansionary capitalism is currently being reconstituted by powerful transnational corporations.

We have to somehow retain all of those things in play: that labor costs are key, that the question of markets and privatization is key, and key strategic resources are fundamental.

These stories combine in ways that give the development of capitalism an uneven quality, jumping all over the place. The textile industry is constantly refiguring those elements. At one point, it seems to be about cheap labor. Why else does Wal-Mart subcontract in Sri Lanka? But then, having skilled labor or being close to markets is paramount. After all, high fashion is a part of textiles in Los Angeles and the Lower East Side in New York. These recombinations show up in countries characterized by mass poverty. The indispensable parts of expanding capitalism show up in different constellations in different parts of the world.

Which Rules Should Govern the Market?

When we consider the rise of free market thinking, first it is important to emphasize that there are no free—i.e., wholly unregulated—markets. All markets presume some form of the rule of law and other institutions, even neoliberal markets. NAFTA is held up as an example of a free market system. But it is regulated. So the first issue is, are some rules better than others?

Second, what do these new rules, these new market dispensations, look like? The government of Nigeria used to regulate many agricultural markets by setting up a marketing board that set the prices farmers received. Those prices were typically ten to fifteen percent of the world market price. The government marketing board sold on the world market and pocketed the price difference. Ergo, farmers were taxed. In the name of economic reform, many of these marketing boards were abolished. Farmers could sell cotton through private means. To the extent that they received increased prices they benefited from the operations of the market. So why is this not better than being taxed by governments, many of whom were corrupt and did not return those taxes to the farmers and the community in the form of services.

The extent to which cotton farmers can expand their output and reach foreign markets depends entirely on two things. First, are markets open to their produce? A double standard operating today is that advanced capitalist states protect their markets even as they espouse free trade. This has been the source of debate within the WTO. The Doha Round of the WTO failed this summer because some powerful developing countries—Indonesia, India, and Brazil—were prepared to prevent any consensus until there was equal reduction of tariffs and protections in US agricultural markets as in developing countries. The WTO is now in ruins. Even the director of the WTO has said as much. That wreckage reveals the lack of an equal playing field.

Second, market prices subject small farmers to price fluctuations and to competition. As African governments were abolishing marketing boards in the late 1970s and early 1980s, the global markets hit an all-time low for virtually every primary agricultural commodity Africa produced. Prices were as depressed as any time since the Great Depression.

Third, free markets do not necessarily translate into benefits. State marketing boards not only determined prices. They also provided key inputs. Unless you have the assets and the endowments as a small farmer, then there is no automatic way in which you can respond to a "new market opportunity."

So put those three things together: first, the unlevel playing field; second, the inability of many farmers to respond; and third, volatile commodity markets. There is no automatic translation between free markets and the benefits they are purported to confer.

Colonial History and the World Market

Long before they became independent, developing countries had participated in the world economy, each in a different way. It would be entirely false to see Ecuador or Nigeria or Indonesia, when they became independent, as traditional, subsistence economies. They had already been transformed through exposure to the marketplace.

Equally important is the political legacy. It matters enormously what type of nationalist, anti-colonial project achieved independence. In Zimbabwe, a radical left-leaning party fought a 15-year guerrilla struggle in which it attempted to mobilize people in the countryside. That victory shaped the nature of future political rule. That is very different from the anti-colonialists in Kenya, who come to power not by a war of liberation or guerrilla struggle, but instead by negotiated solution. They were conservative nationalists, who positioned themselves quite well during the colonial period.

Look at South Korea. It is typically held up as a model or economic miracle because of its rapid growth from 1950 to 1980. This economic miracle was very much tied to the radical land reform pushed through by the US after the Korean War. The governing system set up at that time represented a developmental state in which a technocratic and military class with US backing was able to reshape the colonial legacy to promote rapid industrialization.

That is different from the experience of Nigeria, which became independent in 1960. In a highly segmented political economy, Nigeria was dominated after independence by three major ethnic groups whose powers had been vastly enhanced during the colonial period. Unlike South Korea, Nigeria lacked centralized political control of the state capable of directing and shaping development. The three powerful ethnic communities struggled for power. Typically, one ethnic group, primarily the north and Muslim, presided over the others. It used the state not in developmental terms to enhance the growth of the economy but rather to share the spoils of oil wealth. The state was able to capture those oil rents and correspondingly this fragmented, ethnically competitive economy fought internally and used the money that was at the center of the state, not to reinvest for productive purposes but to share out the spoils.

Eduardo Yssa *Bolivia, Aymaran*

Life is harsh in Bolivia for the indigenous people, the the Aymarans and Quechas. They suffer from discrimination and lack of education, which creates resentment. They receive nothing from the state, so they find work for each other. Colonialism left a scar on the Aymarans. They do not celebrate Christopher Columbus as a hero. The Spanish imposed their way of life and their religion on the people of Bolivia. The Aymarans have a distinctive culture, which they are trying to preserve and pass on to future generations. Previous governments have neglected the people of Bolivia and sold their resources without receiving proper compensation. That is beginning to change.

Early Experiences

I was born blind in 1954, but I was cured in Argentina. When I was seven years old, I lost my father and took my first trip to Argentina, to work cutting sugar-cane. After one year I came back to Bolivia. I worked two years for free, since I was the kid of a house-maid. I was sent to school for a couple of years. The mistreatment was terrible then. I returned to live with my mother and I worked in the cotton fields for four years, until I was 14. I farmed for awhile until a really bad "cold front" caused a major drought. There was no help for us. I left farming completely behind and ended up here in Cochabamba.

In Cochabamba, we arrived in the furthest valleys where the land was still available for purchase. However, these lands lacked basic services. We lacked proper instruction about how to live here. Now my job is to make sure that the generations to come are aware of the basic services that a person deserves, such as water, health, and education.

Working for Each Other

Since I was little, life was harsh and abusive. I definitely feel resentment because the authorities have never understood me. They have discriminated against us, the Aymarans and Quechas, because we are indigenous people. Therefore I have accepted the duty to do well for this community, by taking charge of an official post.

My work is to promote the kinds of work we can do for each other as neighbors. If we do not offer each other work in our neighborhood, nobody does. I did not know anything about construction, sales, plumbing, or electricity, but I had to learn, and since I never studied any profession, I had to push myself to learn this. Lately I have been working as a plumber. I also did construction, but I did not earn enough money to survive.

If this were a government job, then this would be a rentable job, but that is not the case. There are days when I work and days when I do not. Either in construction or as a plumber, there is no continuity. Roughly I earn 600 Bolivian *Pesos* ($85) per month. To live well, I would need more money.

If we get sick, we are on our own. Because we are immigrants from the countryside, we have always practiced the so called *aibi* in which we collaborate among ourselves. If we need or lack something, we help each other. That is what keeps us afloat.

Discrimination Against Indigenous People

To be of local origin, to have dark skin is still a sin here, a crime, not a good face, but now we are recuperating from that identity. Ever since I was a child I used to say that our identity, our originality, is the most important thing we have because we are Aymarans and Quechuas. For me that is Bolivia.

We are not hateful beings; we are sharing beings. If we were hateful, everyone would just look out for himself or herself. We do have a bit of resentment, that we are poorly educated but we are solving that. We are not liars, nor thieves, nor lazy; we are hard workers. We know how to survive, we even have our own medicines. We do not need pharmaceutical medicines because we have our own. On the ritual side we have always been very respectful of *Pachamama,* which means we respect mother earth.

It is sad that our children do not learn our language, Aymaran, anymore, because we are slowly losing our identity and our unity. That is our main enemy. We are recuperating today and showing the whole world that we are not resentful or violent, but caring.

Memories of Colonialism

To talk about colonialism is a bit painful. To remember this, it still hurts. I was never a student, but I like to research and read books and ask around. For some, the arrival of Christopher Columbus was a discovery, but for the Aymarans it was failure and a robbery of our culture. When Columbus arrived, they taught us to lie and kill. They killed us, took away our riches, and betrayed us. The arrival of Columbus was the worst thing in the world. It was not the discovery of America; it was the failure of America. They brought the cross, which made us forget our religion, which we loved. The looting of Bolivia began with that.

From that moment on we forgot our culture, our language and writings. The Aymarans were before the Incas, a very different culture, we had our own writing which was the *Kipus,* and that has been lost. It was stolen from us. For what purpose? To submit us to their whims, so we would become their servants. That is why they took away our culture and subjugated us to serve them.

Education has never been oriented to our social class or culture. It has always been conducted so that our minds do not develop too much. If education had been designed to help our class and culture, we would have been much better than them, maybe even be the greatest power in the world. With all of our wealth, what else could we be missing? We do not need to import gas or oil nor minerals or salt. We have it all.

Strength of Aymaran Culture

The Aymaran race is strong and resistant to any weather. It does not matter to us whether we are in the tropics or in the cold of the mountains. It is all the same. We can even live for months without eating chicken. We are strong and our bodies endure. I have tried to show the youngsters what we really are and what we are capable of. Many youngsters are recuperating their identity, and that is priceless.

We Bolivians are not poor or beggars. We just need a helping hand to emerge again. Because we are not selfish, we will help the rest of the world as needed. That is our goal: to rise and help because there are many who are in need in the world, and poverty has to end. Bolivians are not poor; we are rich. We are millionaires but we lack technology, due to colonialism. If the colonial power had given us all that we needed, today Bolivia would be a superpower. When Bolivia restores its culture and authenticity, we will be show that we are brothers to the world. The delay is due to the fact that we have had governments that were imported from other countries. They have subjugated us and looked out for their own interests, not ours. That is why we are far behind.

Our governments have not been administered according to the needs of Bolivian society. Because of policies fabricated in other countries, non-Bolivian governments have caused us to fail. They told themselves, "The people are not of our social class, so we will siphon off what we can to ensure the future of our own grandchildren." Our past presidents did that, and they sold our resources for very low prices, hurting the whole nation. But we still have non-renewable resources. Four years ago we did not know whether we still had natural gas. We still have oil and lately new gas and other natural resources have been found. That strengthens Bolivia. The failure of the past years is going to be reversed.

Afterword: Where Do We Go from Here?

There is an important reason *The End of Poverty?* refrains from offering a comprehensive set of solutions at the end. By showing the connection between poverty and a global economic order developed over centuries, the film reveals that the roots of poverty are far deeper than most people would have imagined. Short-term, superficial responses cannot succeed. What is needed is a general strategy for collective action based on a philosophy that can successfully challenge neoliberalism.

The beginning of wisdom for activists is the recognition that little can be accomplished by acting in isolation. That is a difficult lesson for North Americans, who believe that everything can be accomplished through individual initiative. But the harsh reality is that activism without organization is powerless.

Another important lesson from the film is the inability of conventional approaches to address the underlying causes that perpetuate poverty, century after century. Thus, before going any further, I will begin by explaining why certain conventional ideas are flawed.

Limits of Conventional Approaches

Foreign aid. Poverty cannot be eradicated with simple transfers. It may be desirable for wealthy countries to give more aid to poor countries, but not if aid is accompanied by strings and conditionalities as has been the case in the past. Aid is also worse than useless if it destroys local markets and causes unemployment in the receiving nation. Thus, what might seem to be a simple solution—a gift of mosquito nets, medicines, and other needed supplies—is fraught with difficulties. To make the foreign aid system more beneficial to recipients would require nations to act altruistically and to stop serving the personal and corporate interests of those who design national policy. The right answer then is not "more aid" but "different aid," and that difference will require fundamental changes in power and privilege.

Economic Development. Small-scale, locally-managed development programs have merit, but micro-level programs seldom have a cumulative impact on poverty. By contrast, large-scale development programs, financed by the World Bank or a similar institution, may raise average incomes in a country, but at the cost of widening the rich-poor gap. Often the poor are displaced by a development project, as the small-scale miners in Tanzania were when a large company took over. (See Arackha's interview). The fundamental problem with conventional forms of economic development is that they do not solve the "poverty paradox" that rising incomes are associated with growing poverty, because benefits are seldom shared among all members of society.* To resolve that paradox requires shifts in political and economic power not contemplated by conventional approaches to economic development.

Poverty without Politics. The dominant view of poverty in the North is that poverty results from purely technical characteristics and that it can remedied without changing the political and social patterns by which some people dominate others. According to this technician's view of poverty, a) foreign aid and unregulated trade are benign instruments of progress, b) aggregate growth will make everyone better off ("trickle down economics"), c) historical and cultural patterns of behavior can be ignored because development can be imposed from outside, d) the South is the source of corruption, and e) development is hindered primarily by "backward" institutions, such as traditional forms of property. There is no hint in this model that a) colonialism has enduring effects that did not disappear when political independence took place, b) the North has overthrown popular reform governments in dozens of countries and threatened even more with the same fate, thus preventing the conditions of true development, c) the governments of the G-8 largely serve the interests of banks and other corporations that hope to extract an economic surplus from developing countries by exploiting their labor, their resources, and their inability to prevent dumping of toxic materials, and d) the same forces that are creating a growing wedge between rich and poor in the North are also deepening poverty in the South. Because the dominant model of global poverty fails to consider the self-interested behavior of Northern institu-

---

* In the academic world, there is an unspoken division of labor between the "tough-minded" economists, who focus attention on increased production and national income, and the "soft minded" sociologists, who question the benefits of growth if it leads to a greater concentration of wealth. Few economists take distributional questions seriously. It is perhaps no accident that economics is a male-dominated discipline, whereas sociology has a greater degree of gender-balance.

tions (governments, banks, and other corporations), the roots of poverty remain hidden from view.

The failure of conventional approaches to poverty should serve as a warning that they are deeply flawed. The film and the interviews provide a number of clues about why that is the case.

Legacies of the Past

A central message of *The End of Poverty?* is the futility of acting in the present without understanding the past. Each of the key problem areas identified in the interviews—debt, trade, land ownership, privatization, loss of the commons, neocolonialism, and European, then US, hegemony—has a history. A solution to the poverty paradox can only be found by overcoming the systems of control put in place by colonialism and modernization.

Property Rights (Especially Land Tenure). A theme in many interviews is the change in property rights, particularly land rights. Until the past few centuries, most people in the world lived in villages in which land rights were held in trust by the village elders and allocated to households according to their ability to make use of it. Unused land was reallocated to another household. Since no one could hold more land than the household could use productively, this system provided a high degree of equality, and it ensured that productive land was not idle (unless it was being fallowed). It also effectively balanced common and private interests, a task at which both communism (collectivization) and capitalism (individual ownership regardless of use) have failed.

Many Africans would like to re-introduce elements of traditional land tenure. There are still traces of the old system that remain, because colonialism injected the concept of private ownership only a few generations ago. Thus, there may be a chance to reconstruct new forms of communal ownership and management in rural Africa, where other cultural elements have survived. It is not as obvious how this can be achieved in cities, where about half the population of Africa now lives. However, millions of Africans have migrated to cities—where they eke out a bare living—because they could not get access to rural land.

In Latin America, ancient traditions of allocating land based on use appear to be long forgotten. If those traditions were still alive, it seems likely that Eduardo Galeano would make reference to them in *Open Veins in Latin America* (an influential book in Latin America), but he does not. Instead, that continent is saddled with *latifundia* or "great estates," an aristocratic system of land tenure that goes back to ancient Rome. As a result, there are violent clashes over land rights in Brazil, with no end in sight. Land reform in Brazil has broad popular appeal, but the land being redistributed is almost always marginal, seldom the most productive. It seems that the *Bolsa Familia* (family grant) program is serving as a partial substitute for land reform by providing the poor in both rural and urban areas with a small monthly stipend. If that program were to be funded from payments made by the owners of land and natural resources, the circle could be completed, as it has been in Venezuela and Bolivia. In both of those latter countries, the value of natural resources is being used to fund social programs.

Trade. Logically, trade starts with an exchange between two individuals in which each is better off after the exchange. (Each side receives more value than is given, which is why trade adds value. It is not neutral.) Historically, however, trade started with non-mutual exchange—with piracy, plunder, and slavery. In some cases, it evolved into mutually beneficial exchange. (A classic example is the gradual shift in Viking behavior from plunder to mutual exchange around one thousand years ago.) The history of trade is full of this ambiguity. Achieving mutually beneficial exchange is an aspiration of trade, but one which is not always realized. At present, trade contains elements of both mutual exchange and plunder.

Politicians in Europe and North America talk about "free trade" as if the agreements that have been put in place under the control of the World Trade Organization have been neutral rules from which everyone benefits. None of the interviews in this book primarily dealt with trade issues. However, several addressed the hypocrisy of rich countries forcing poor countries to open their borders to accept cotton and other commodities produced in surplus or manufactured goods that wipe out efforts to establish new industries in the developing countries. Stiglitz cites a study showing that tariff barriers are four times higher against finished goods from poor countries than from rich countries—proving that there is a long-standing bias against development in the global South.

To modify trade so that it is not merely one more form of domination, the most useful insights in this book come from David Ellerman and Kipruto Arap Kirwa, Kenya's Minister of Agriculture. Ellerman refers to Jane Jacobs, who argued that trade is most likely to be mutually beneficial among nations on an equal level of technological development. Kirwa agrees with the value of trade among African nations, but he also explains that transportation costs within Africa are prohibitive. Presumably, that is another long-term effect of colonialism: the rail-lines are all designed to carry products from plantations in the interior to the coast. Cross-border trade within Africa was never encouraged by colonial governments. Would better railroads improve trade and raise productivity in Africa? Perhaps, but it is only one piece of a larger puzzle.

Debt. One issue raised in many interviews is the burden imposed by external debt. Collins notes that in Jamaica, 60% of the national budget is devoted to debt repayment. That would be an enormous burden in a wealthy country. (Interest on the federal debt in the US is about 8% of the budget, which some people consider alarming.) In a developing country, it is crippling. The debt has a direct impact on the poor, in terms of a) government services canceled, b) investments not made in roads and other infrastructure that could raise productivity and wages, and c) higher taxes on household commodities purchased for subsistence. As many interviewees note, the debt is also a political instrument by which foreign bankers and governments are able to control the actions of sovereign nations. As long as debt hangs over the head of government, taxing and spending policies that might transfer wealth from the rich to the poor are blocked by foreign agencies before they are even introduced.

Simple debt forgiveness is the solution desired by many interviewees, but there are numerous obstacles to that goal. The Jubilee networks (in the US, in the UK, and Jubilee South) are making slow progress, but the conditionalities for debt cancellation often disempower the countries supposedly being helped.

One way of applying pressure on the creditors in the North is through lawsuits that allege much of the debt to be "odious," acquired under dictatorial regimes that oppressed citizens rather than serving them. (The website **www.odiousdebts.org** has some information on these legal actions.) These sorts of legal actions are important not only in achieving debt relief in the present, but also in sending a powerful signal to future creditors not to finance dictatorial regimes. A handful of successful lawsuits could leverage a big change in the political and economic future of the relationship between rich and poor nations.

Taxes. The subject of taxation arises in interviews in different contexts. Perhaps the most obvious problem of taxation is the difficulty of levying them. As Guillet explains perceptively, the governments of poor nations are often limited in their ability to collect taxes, which is one reason they rely on foreign loans. Yet neoliberal ideologists seek to weaken the state, which will have the ironic effect of increasing their dependence on foreign assistance. Whereas the appropriateness of the size and power of the state in northern Europe is a topic on which reasonable people may disagree, the same logic does not apply to the weak states of the global South that were created by colonial powers and gained independence with the burden of colonial debts.

An important obstacle to collecting taxes is the lack of transparency in the accounts of the transnational corporations doing business in developing countries. Abugre describes the trivial amount of taxes paid by mining companies in Africa based on their declared profits, which are vastly understated as a result of transfer pricing. Christensen briefly discusses this issue, but he primarily focuses on the tax losses that resulted from trade liberalization—the reduction in tariffs on luxury goods for the rich and the rise in value added taxes, which are paid primarily by the poor. Tax evasion, with the aid of armies of lawyers and accountants, is another international conspiracy against the poor.

Another way taxes have an impact on the poor is through the effect on productivity and wages. Collins and Gaffney describe how a tax on the value of land has positive economic effects, particularly for the poor. It encourages more productive use of the most productive sites (both rural and urban) and draws labor away from marginal uses to more productive sites. In that roundabout way, it raises the general wage level and reduces unemployment. Since few people in Third World countries are employed in the formal sector, economic policy should aim at providing broad support for all workers. Tax incentives that increase the overall demand for labor by promoting the full use of and payment for natural resources are an essential part of any development program. The only people who lose from that sort of tax regime are the owners of plantations, mines, and underutilized urban locations—that is, the people who are responsible at present for stagnant wages.

The IFIs (International Financial Institutions). Judging from the interviews, the World Bank and the International Monetary Fund play a pervasive role in the economies of developing nations. Their role is problematic because they serve the interests of the rich G-8 nations, not the rest of the world. Regardless of their stated missions, they act on behalf of Wall Street and the Club of Paris.

The interviewees are divided over whether the IFIs are intended by banks and other corporations in the North to keep the South in a state of dependency and subservience. In fact, the conscious motives of Northern elites are less important than their behavior. Whatever the motives of their leaders might be, they act as if they want to prevent poor nations from directing their own destinies. They act as if they want developing nations to hand over public assets and resource concessions at "fire sale" prices and to act as if the colonial masters had never left. They act as if it were part of the natural order that the developing nations should ship raw materials to developed nations for processing, branding, and packaging and that the nations of the South should accept the handling and management of the toxic waste generated in the North.

The most emotionally satisfying response to the intrusive behavior of the IFIs would be to abolish them. However, they should be perceived as symptoms of a deeper problem—the continuation of colonialism by other means. As long as the North seeks to manage the governments of the South, new instruments for that purpose will be devised. (That is not to argue for keeping the present institutions that function that way, only to say that getting rid of them may do little to solve the problem.) The solution lies in circumventing the institutions created in the North by creating regional trade agreements among the nations of each continent. As Golinger points out, one of the reasons for the ongoing US efforts to overthrow Hugo Chavez in Venezuela is that he is supporting such a drive for regional autonomy in Latin America, in direct violation of the spirit of the Monroe Doctrine.

Privatization. Many interviewees discussed the issue of privatization. The IFIs have forced indebted countries, for ideological reasons, to sell state assets. The stated aim of the policy was to increase efficiency and reduce corruption. If it had achieved either of those aims, the people of the South would have forgiven the ideology. (As Jim Schultz says, poor people view ideology as a luxury they cannot afford. By necessity, they are pragmatists.) The ideological assumption behind the privatization policy is that private enterprises are inherently more efficient than government-managed ones. There are several glaring problems with that assumption.

While there are certainly many public enterprises that are inefficient, the question is whether they are more or less inefficient than comparable private enterprises. That is an empirical question, to be decided by fact, not theory. Several interviewees in Latin America and in Africa note that transferring assets to private companies did not improve efficiency.

Nothing in economic theory indicates that one should expect a private operation to be more efficient than a public one. Instead, theory suggests that competitive enterprises will, on average, be more efficient than enterprises in which customers have no choice. Private monopolies have no inherent advantage over public monopolies. In fact, the private monopoly is less accountable than the public one and therefore less likely to be responsive to consumer demand, which is ultimately the basis of the economic definition of efficiency.

Most privatization has not met the standard of an arms-length transaction. In practice, it has taken place through insider deals, in which assets have been sold at prices far below market value. In short, it has increased corruption, not decreased it. That is precisely what one would expect when the sale of a railroad, an airline, a power station, a water system, or a hospital is made under duress. Under ordinary circumstances, transfers of that sort take many years to find suitable buyers and to negotiate terms that are mutually satisfactory. When the IMF forces a sale as a condition of receiving a loan, the sale will almost certainly fail any meaningful test of public interest. Quite often, privatization is nothing short of theft of public assets by a few well-placed buyers—often family or friends of high-level politicians. If IFIs were truly concerned with the economic strength of poor nations, they would have warned against hasty sale of public assets.

A particularly painful aspect of the wave of privatization is that the governments of the South that carried it out were, on the whole, better managed financially than the countries of the North. As Eric Toussaint explains, the World Bank annual reports of the early 1980s recognized the superiority of the South, particularly after the Paul Volcker's monetary policies in the US drove the entire world into a depression in 1981 and created the Third World debt crisis. Logically, the IMF and World Bank should have been staffed by successful state managers from the South, advising governments in the North, not vice versa.

The War Against the South. Trade embargoes, blockades, sanctions, and other economic weapons are, at times, considered acts of war. Interference by a foreign power in the internal affairs of another nation can also be viewed as an act of war. Based on those considerations, the US and other rich nations of the North are in a continuous state of war against the nations of the South. Some might think it absurd to consider the constant interference in the economic affairs of other nations as acts of war. But whether an act is hostile or not should be judged by the aggrieved party, not by the person or nation that is acting. The testimony of nongovernmental organizations and civil society organizations in the South strongly suggests that they perceive the conditionalities imposed by the IMF as hostile gestures that impoverish their citizens and sabotage their economies. More generally, they view most trade agreements and most forms of development assistance as forms of interference in their sovereign rights.[*]

Most interviewees express hope that this situation might change, but this a rather vain hope. As Susan George notes, nations act in their self-interest, not out of altruism. It seems unlikely that the economic interest groups located in the North will voluntarily stop exploiting the South or will lose their connections to powerful people in government. Citizens in the North may protest against the policies by which elites control the lives of billions of people, but protests without countervailing power have limited political credibility.

The simple recognition that poverty is related to the global system of power would be a major step forward. In fact, the fundamental remedy for poverty is a permanent realignment of power in the world, both between nations and within nations. Alvaro Garcia Linera, Vice-president of Bolivia, envisions in his interview a post-capitalist world of cooperation. "The new humanity is not going to be the result of one leader or one country. The new humanity is going to be the result of a whole world. Either we are all emancipated or none of us is."

Conclusion

To those who see *The End of Poverty?* and want to take action, it should now be clear that action is needed in numerous areas: restoring the commons (against narrow forms of privatization), canceling debt (especially odious

---

[*] It is useful to review the specific grievances enumerated in the American Declaration of Independence, some of which bear an uncanny resemblance to the overbearing involvement of the IFIs and Northern strategic actors (such as the CIA and US military bases) in the affairs of Third World nations. Some of the grievances for which Thomas Jefferson and his colleagues were willing to fight against England were:

For Quartering large bodies of armed troops among us:

For protecting them, by a mock Trial, from punishment for any Murders which they should commit on the Inhabitants of these States:

For cutting off our Trade with all parts of the world:

For imposing Taxes on us without our Consent:

For taking away our Charters, abolishing our most valuable Laws, and altering fundamentally the Forms of our Governments:

For suspending our own Legislatures, and declaring themselves invested with power to legislate for us in all cases whatsoever.

debts), increasing tax justice (to reduce burdens on the poor), and reducing intervention in the South by the US and other powerful interests in the North.

For the individual, it is probably less important which of these (or other) issues you choose to become involved in. What is crucial is to become involved in a group and, through that group, to learn more. For students, one of the most powerful actions is to ask questions and make comments in class and to alert fellow students (and professors) about what is going on in the rest of the world. It is easy for those growing up in relative privilege in the North to forget that our comfort is tied in complex ways to the misery of people elsewhere. *The End of Poverty?* gives a face and a voice to a few of those people, so we also hope you will encourage your friends and colleagues to view the film and to talk about it.

— *Clifford Cobb*
September, 2009

Index

A

access to land, universal, in African tradition 296
Action Against Hunger 1
Africa
  little foreign investment in 269
  need to develop internal food supply 232
African trade, unfair pricing of 71
Africans, falsely assumed to be anti-women 286
African Union 301
agrarian reform, needed in Brazil 272
Agua de Tunari, Bolivian water company 168
AIDS. *See* HIV
Alaska, heritage fund in 211
Albright, Madeleine 92
Algeria, civil war in 207
Amazon, displaced peasants and deforestation 162
Anglo-European property law, counterproductive in Africa 301
Angola, resource curse in 165
Asian financial crisis, and privatization 185
assessments, need for frequent updates 210
automobile companies, and public transportation 90

B

"Brazilian Miracle" caused affordable housing crisis 329
Balzac, Honoré de 365
banking secrecy laws 71
Bechtel 17, 122, 302, 305, 320, 339
Blair, Tony, tax-free life of 217
Bolivarian Revolution 100, 135

Bolivia
  concentration of land ownership 97
  gas war 310
  land redistribution 97
  land reform in 178
  life harsh for ingigenous people 385
  new role of indigenous people in government 178
  resembled apartheid South Africa 179
  silver mines in 282
  Water War, casualties in 305
Brazil
  agricultural success has increased poverty 137
  coffee and slave labor 165
  demographic transition in 330
  land and slavery in 140
  land monopoly in 161
  law prohibiting hoarding of land not enforced 161
  micro-credit in 371
  National Forum for Urban Reform 330
  obesity in 159
  prosperity in south, associated with family farms 126
  reverse agrarian reform in 271
  segregated cities in 331
  slavery in 274
  squatters in 348
  sugarcane harvesters in 373
  urban migration in 329
  violence and inequality in 159
  workers' cooperatives in 273
Bretton Woods organizations. *See* IMF and World Bank
British
  appropriation of land in Kenya 297
  divide-and-rule strategy 230
  misconception that communal land tenure was no tenure 297

British jurisprudence, consistent with land seizures in Africa 298
British Petroleum 222
Brown, Lester 250
bubonic plague 116
bundle of rights 87
Bush, George W. 227, 342, 380

C

"corporatocracy" 314
    progressive leaders against this, not against US *per se* 318
campesinos, evictions of 196
capital flow liberalization 108
capitalism, origin of, related to Protestantism 247
Carson, Rachel 250
Castro, Fidel 136, 223
Castro, José de 370
chattel slaves, treated better than wage slaves 312
Chávez, Hugo 6, 93, 136, 191, 326, 347
    2002 propaganda campaign against him 193
    conspiracy against in 2001 135
    took control of oil industry 95
checks, high fees for cashing 375
China
    becoming world's most powerful country 225
    economic growth after 1977 338
Church Committee, and CIA oversight 226
Churchill, Winston, on land monopoly 123
CIA
    covert operations of 91
    not accountable 226
CITGO, Venezuelan oil company 326
    heating oil discounts in US 95
cities, conditions for success of 175
climate change, and poverty 243
Club of Paris 394

Club of Rome 250
Cochabamba 166, 260, 283, 301, 339, 386
Cold War, as a cover for imperialism 222
colonial governments, provided no support to Africans 299
colonialism
    inherently tied to capitalism 176
    legacy of artificial states 146
    may have financed industrial revolution 147
colonial powers, their debts inherited by newly-independent nations 366
colonies
    imposition of export crops in 148
    trade restrictions in 147
colonization
    and land appropriation 285
    religious and psychological 247
    safety valve for European poverty 120
coltan (columbite-tantalite) 313
Columbus, Christopher 136
    indigenous picture of 387
commodification 363
communal land rights, seldom recognized 131
communal land tenure
    in Africa 296
    in Africa, not entirely destroyed 247
    in East Africa 285
    in Honduras 196
    incompatible with neoliberalism 238
    starting to be taken seriously recently 298
concentration of land ownership
    in Bolivia 97
    increased by subsidies 163
Confessions of an Economic Hit-Man, by John Perkins 185, 312
consolidation of land ownership
    in England 117
Contras, in Nicaragua 191

corporations, rights of, in US 315
cotton subsidies, effect on African farmers 351
crime, correlates with unequal income distribution 160

D

de-privatization, of water service in Bolivia 307
debt, of colonial powers inherited by newly-independent nations 366
debt cancellation
  as partial solution 218
  in Leviticus 218
  must be unconditional 321
debt relief
  campaigns not successful 186
  in Tanzania 186
degrowth, requires pluralistic view of history 251
democracy, favorable to poverty elimination 339
demographic transition, in Brazil 330
Deng Xiao Ping 224
deregulation, requires a strong state 205
de Soto, Hernando 163, 198, 336
de Toledo, Francisco 283
development of agriculture, and beginning of poverty 115
Dickens, Charles 118
Doha Round, of WTO negotiations 383
Dominion Group 82
Drake, Sir Francis 283
Dumping, from North, cuts output in South 72

E

"economic theology" 341
East Africa
  declining literacy in 277
  pre-colonial land tenure 285

East Asia, development of, compared with Latin America 353
ecological footprint 250
economic rent, as social surplus 214
Economics of Welfare, The, by Arthur Pigou 253
Ehrenreich, Barbara 328
ejidos, destroyed by NAFTA 247
enclosure
  of common land in Britain 117
  effect on industrial workers 118
England
  consolidation of land ownership 117
  protectionism in 120
Enlightenment, and overemphasis on European ideas 242
environmental limits to growth, not yet reached 151
ethanol industry
  and pollution 273
  subsidized 273
ethnic diversity 130
Europe
  greatness of, created by colonial exploitation 142
  waves of poverty in 116
European Tribune 203
evictions
  becoming more and more frequent 236
  in Kenya 278
  in Mumbai 235
  more people displaced by, than by armed conflict 236
  political economy of 104
  protections against, in Brazil 239
Ewe tribe, in West Africa, split among four states 147
expansionary capitalism 378
export economy, emphasis on, raises local interest rates 183
externalities
  and Pigouvian taxes 253
  and pollution 206

Exxon, its profits, compared with Microsoft's 209

F

famines, as effective market solutions 208
Fannie Mae 143
 and affordable housing 144
Fanon, Frantz 241
farmers, traditional, left poor land by colonizers 325
favelas. See shantytowns
fictitious commodities 381
Fischer, Stanley 154
food security
 and lack of fertilizer 232
 and lack of infrastructure 230
food sovereignty 275
 goal, in Venezuela 191
Ford, Henry, on wages 188
foreign aid
 as "reverse Robin Hood" 171
 as investment in the future 265
 benefits landowners 201
 conditioned on privatization 113
 far less than worker remittances 184
 has not been efficient 264
 hinders agricultural development 153
 not altruistic 321
foreign debt
 African, after 1979 73
 and illegal drugs 186
 and immigration 186
 and the environment 186
Francis, St. of Assissi, and spiritual poverty 249
Friedman, Milton 17

G

Galeano, Eduardo 10, 391
Gas War
 children killed 310
 in Bolivia 310

GDP, focus on favors wealth concentration 203
George, Henry 2, 9, 116, 130, 200, 202, 221
George, Lloyd, on land monopoly 123
Ghana, diamond exports 71
globalization 179
 and deterritorialization 252
 began in 1492 363
 facilitates interaction and communication 179
 has good and bad aspects 156
 not a new phenomenon 246
Gomez, Juan Vincente 135
Gore, Al 381
government, role of in successful development 358
government debt, US, contributes to global instability 357
government spending, benefits landowners 216
Great Transformation, The, by Karl Polanyi 379
Green Revolution 366
 in Africa, can cause unforeseen damage 326
 worsened conditions for peasants 115
ground rent, vast unearned income 293
Guarani, enslavement of 97
Guatemala, biodiversity reserves in 132

H

hacienda, the vanguard of capitalism 242
heavily indebted countries, not powerless to improve conditions 237
Heavily Indebted Poor Country initiative (HIPC) 267
Helms, Richard 221
Henry VIII, massive land grab 215
historical understanding, need for 242
HIV and AIDS 247
 extent of, in Kenya 24
 in Honduras 196

Hodge, Helena Norberg 248
holding idle land, not allowed in Venezuela 361
Honduras, loss of connection with land 197
Housing and Land Rights Network 103
housing crisis, tied to land market 144
Huk Rebellion 219
human capital 120
human rights, and real estate markets 234
Hurricane Mitch 196
Hussein, Saddam 319

I

Illich, Ivan 252
IMF and World Bank 10, 16, 23, 112, 113, 146, 265, 275, 315, 341, 342, 350, 364, 394
 do not promote autonomy 152
 financing large foreign mining companies 291
 lack of accountability 150
 relationship with Wall Street 154
 role in mining company abuses 82
 take orders from US officials 154
 their real objective 275
imperial presidency, and decline of US empire 226
income taxation, paid back through rising land values 217
independence, results of, in Kenya 229
India
 land mafia 105
 repeal of urban land ceiling law 106
 tsunami in 2004 106
indigenous land tenure. See communal land tenure
indigenous people, and tourism 134
industrial policy 221
 and socialism 224
industrial revolution, based on colonialism 243

intellectual property, and biological information 197
Intelligence Oversight Board, dormancy of, in US 226
Inter-American Development Bank 302
internal markets, need for in Brazil 276
International Labor Organization 131
internet, power of, in popular movements 307, 343
irregular settlements. See shantytowns
Islam
 alternative development model to neoliberalism 378
 its appeal in developing nations 379
Islamists, formerly Marxists 380
Ivory Coast, foreign aid to 148

J

Jamaica 123
 foreign debt 125
Jefferson, Thomas 118
Jesuits, their role in subjugating indigenous people in Bolivia 96
Jubilee networks 393

K

Kebachia, Chege 287
Kenya
 challenges faced by agriculture 229
 colonial labor laws 287
 dam construction displaces people 83
 effect of trade barriers on agriculture 230
 extent of HIV in 24
 land and patronage 288
 land hoarding 257
 land policy in 256
 land reform promises not kept 279
 livestock industry 256
 pesticide pollution in 84
 result of independence in 229
 tea plantations 257
 tea pluckers in 377

Kenyatta, Jomo 24, 289
Kerala 338
Kiama kia Muingi, Kenyan peoples'
    organization 288
Konogo, Tabitha 287

L

lack of infrastructure, and food insecu-
    rity 230
Laffer, Arthur 112
Lake Kenyaboli, in Kenya, privatized
    84
Landless Workers' Movement 76, 139,
    345, 376
    seeks to enforce existing law in Brazil
        345
land mafia, in India 105
land monopoly
    in Brazil 161
    reduces production while increasing
        inequality 160
    worse than slavery 161
landowners
    as such, are not productive 293
land speculation 234
    and boom/bust cycle 202
    in India 103
land tenure, a controversial issue 267
land value taxation
    and interest rates 164
    and land prices 164
    benefits everyone 218
    benefits of 164, 174
    can replace regressive taxes 210
    considered in Latvia 210
    for Hunduras 195
    history of in Jamaica 123
    opposition to in Jamaica 124
    potential for in Russia 210
    redistributes land without violence 294
    successfully applied in Singapore and
        Hong Kong 175
    would remove windfalls for rich 219

Latin America
    development of, compared with East
        Asia 353
    historic movements in 244
    its poverty not explained by plunder
        of gold and silver 174
    neoliberalism in 245
    post-neoliberal alternatives 177
    transparency of government in 177
Latin America Against Hunger 372
Latvia, considering land value taxation
    210
Leviticus, and debt cancellation 218
Limits to Growth, The, by the Club of
    Rome 250
limits to growth. *See also* environmental
    limitis to growth
Locke, John 160
London, poverty in 216
Lula, Luiz Inácio Lula da Silva 11, 169,
    330
Luxemburg,Rosa 177

M

"Military Keynesianism" 225
Maasai 254
    displaced by national park 282
    displacement of 254
    livelihood endangered by national
        parks 255
Maathai, Wangari 289
MacNamara, Robert 366
Making Globalization Work, by Joseph
    Stiglitz 356

malnourishment, in Honduras, a new
    phenomenon 196
Manley, Michael 123
markets, are never completely unregu-
    lated 383
Mau Mau 228
McMansions 144
Mercado Común del Sur 244
mercury, used in silver mining 283

micro-credit
  in Brazil 371
  merely manages poverty 101
Microsoft, its profits, compared with
  Exxon's 209
middle class
  disappearing in US 145
  flight from center city 333
migration
  of poor people to cities 198
  primarily from small city to big city
  331
military industrial complex 222
Millennium Development Goals, on
  race and ethnicity 134
mining companies, deceptive practices
  of 81
monoculture, vs. diversification 79
monopoly, primary source of poverty
  324
Monopoly (game of) 88
  early history suppressed 89
Monroe Doctrine 244
  challenged by Chávez 191
Monsanto 366
Monterey Institute of Technology 157
Morales, Evo 16, 136, 178, 306, 312, 322
  success of his government 259
Mosaddeq, Mohammed 222, 319
Movimiento Sem Terra. See Landless
  Workers' Movement
Mugabe, Robert 25, 294, 299
Mumbai, evictions in 104, 235

N

National Endowment for Democracy
  and the CIA 192
  attempts to overthrow Chavez 190
National Institute for Agrarian Reform
  (INCRA) 138, 349
National Museum of the American
  Indian 133
national prosperity, building blocks of 151

neoliberalism 13, 379
  and Protestant tradition 365
  as continuation of colonialism 308
  as source of growing poverty 181
  ideology of 204
  incompatible with communal land
    rights 238
  its domination is ending 346
New Hampshire, successful reliance on
  property taxation 211
New Partnership for Africa's Development 266
New York City, affordable housing in
  143
Nicaraguan Contras, US support for 93
Nickel and Dimed, by Barbara Ehrenreich
  328
Niemeyer, Oscar 11
Nigeria
  education neglected 325
  resource curse in 165, 325
Nkrumah, Kwame 30, 93
Nyerere, Julius 29

O

odious debts
  legal concept of 187
  lawsuits over 391
Olivera, Oscar 343
Open Veins in Latin America, by Eduardo
  Galeano 10, 391
Organization of American States 132
overproduction, of export commodities 184

P

Pachamuma 17, 101, 305, 387
Pak, Simon J., research on transfer
  pricing 110
paternalism, and foreign aid 146
Patria Para Todos 362
Patrinos, Hank 133
Peace Corps 86

Perez, Carlos Andres 101, 191
Pernambuco, violence in 271
Philippines
  Huk Rebellion 220
  most farmers pushed to marginal
    lands 172
  unemployment in 220
Pigou, Arthur 253
Pigouvian taxes, and externalities 253
Pinochet, Augusto 17
pirates, stole silver mined in Bolivia 283
planet's resources, "overutilized" 241
Polanyi, Karl 381
poor people, considered dispensable
  237
Potosí 282
  once the largest city in the world 20
poverty
  absence of opportunity for a digni-
    fied life 88
  and climate change 243
  concept of, a modern, Western inven-
    tion 248
  condition that deprives people of
    dignity 270
  greatest in Sub-Saharan Africa 263
  has been reduced over human history
    334
  historic processes of 241
  in London 216
  in the Philippenes 219
  in the US 212
  its elimination requires action on
    many fronts 339
  limits of conventional approaches
    to 389
  monopoly is its primary source 324
  not a recent phenomenon 334
  not based on natural limits 200
  not exclusive to the South 122
press, failure of, in US 227
primitive accumulation, Marxist concept of 382

privatization
  and Asian financial crisis 185
  and protestantism 119
  benefits absentee owners 280
  of land, ideology of 216
  of water 75, 258
  promoted by aid agencies 304
privilege
  in Latin, "private law" 212
  rooted in government 213
Progress and Poverty, by Henry George
  2, 116
property taxes, reliance on in successful
  communities 174
Protestantism
  and privatization 119
  notion of radical individualism 120

Q

Qasim, Abd al-Karim 319

R

Raffles, Sir Thomas Stamford Bingley
  175
real estate
  and violence 236
  logic of 235
real estate market, and human rights
  234
Rebouças, André 127
Recife, Brazil 137, 169, 194, 349, 368
redistribution of land, in Bolivia 97
regulation, needed in energy and transport sectors 204
  needed to make markets work 205
remittances, from foreign workers far
  more than foreign aid 184
rent, higher in high-wage commuities
  328
reparations, due to people of the South
  365
resource curse 165, 176

resource policies, of the US, linked to terrorism 207
Robert Schalkenbach Foundation 200
Robin Hood 117
Russia, potential land value taxation in 210

S

Sachs, Jeffrey 5, 16, 146, 261
  blamed by Bolivians 21
  failed policies of 149
Sanchez de Lozada, Gonzalo 259, 310
São Paulo, wealth and poverty in 348
school fees 265
Sen, Amartya 358
Seven Sisters, transnational oil companies 94
shantytowns, legal status of, in Brazil 329, 331
Sierra Leone 1
silver, mined in South America did not benefit Spain or Portugal, but their creditors in England and Holland 20
Sinclair, Upton 327
Singh, Machan 287
slavery, in US, a "modern capitalistic phenomenon" 242
small farmers, education needed for 281
Smith, Adam 174
  on economies of scale 334
social sciences, complicity in life-destroying policies 242
South American Parliament 260
southern states, US, regressive taxation in 211
Souza, Betinho de 370
Spanish economy, failure to develop 174
Stang, Sister Dorothy 273
Stedile, Joao Pedro 130
Stiglitz, Joseph, on trade policy 392

structural adjustment 17, 148, 182, 265, 367
Sub-Saharan Africa, epicenter of poverty 262
subsidies
  for sugar and ethanol 77
  increase concentrationof land ownership 163
Sudan, land disputes in 300
sugarcane, ideological control of plantation owners 78
sugarcane workers 373
  daily lives of 76
  decreasing in stature 77
supply-side economics 112

T

Tanzania
  debt relief in 186
  intimidation of small-scale miners 291
Tanzanian Mine Workers Development Organization 79
tanzanite 29, 80, 290
Tax Justice Network 71
tea pluckers, in Kenya 377
terrorism, linked to US resource policies 207
Thailand, tsunami in 86
The End of Poverty, by Jeffrey Sachs 5, 261
tourism, and indigenous people 134
trade
  considered best among equals 155
  cross-border, not encouraged by colonial governments 391
trade agreements, and cultural issues 134
transfer pricing 95, 107, 261, 392
transgenic seeds 366
  rebellion against, in Brazil 347
trickle down economics 390
tsunami, in India, 2004 106

U

Uhuru 287
uncertain land tenure, benefits foreign investors 173
underproduction of public goods, as market failure 336
UN Development Program 133
unemployment, in the Philippenes 220
UN Food and Agriculture Organization 370
UNICEF 270
United Fruit Company 224
UN Millennium Project 261
urban land, most valuable natural resource 175
urban landless movement 329
urban renewal
  benefits landowners 202
  in Mumbai, modeled on Shanghai 104
US Agency for International Development, and the coup in Venezuela 192

V

value added tax (VAT), regressivity of 364
Venezuela
  export economy 99
  goal of food sovereignty 191
  improved medical care 100
  nationalization of oil 93
  oligarchs and dependency mentality 135
  public and private banks 102
  social history 99
Vesta Corporation, landholdings in Venezuela 173
vicious cycle, of land reform and debt 198
Volcker, Paul 366, 396

W

wages, on marginal land, sets standard for whole community 175
Wahhabism 379
war crimes, US benefits from double standard about 92
War on Terror 379
Washington, George, on the danger of standing armies 223
Washington Consensus 111, 342, 350
  and capital flow liberalization 108
  failure of in Argentina 353
Water War in Bolivia 166, 340
  origins of 305
Wealth of Nations, by Adam Smith 174
wealth transfers
  from Africa 70
  from the South to the North 347
wealthy people, gain power by restricting land use 173
Weaver, John 87
Weber, Max 247
Women's Development Bank 10, 99
World Bank
  and cultural diversity 133
  and ejidos in Mexico 364
  involvement in tsunami rehabilitation 106
  ordered water privatization in Bolivia 340
World Trade Organization 189
  Dispute Resolution Mechanism 189

Y

Yunus, Mohammed 10

The Robert Schalkenbach Foundation (RSF) was founded in 1925 to promote and develop the ideas of Henry George and to keep them in the public dialogue. George offered a response to the ideological polarization between collectivism and individualism, by presenting a social philosophy that reconciles the opposing features of capitalism and socialism.

RSF carries out its mission in several ways: 1) by publishing the works of Henry George and distributing the works of related authors, 2) by funding research to extend the ideas of Henry George in new contexts, and 3) by funding advocacy projects that apply his principles to specific situations.

RSF encourages those who are familiar with Henry George's ideas to approach the foundation through a one-page query letter about potential projects that might be of mutual interest. Please check our website for the most recent indication of the kinds of projects the foundation funds.

Robert Schalkenbach Foundation
90 John Street, Suite 501
New York NY 10016

Tel: 212-683-6424
Toll-free: 800-269-9555
Fax: 212-683-6454
www.schalkenbach.org